DATE DUE

OK 12-19-94			
JE 10 00			

DEMCO 38-296

THE
ORDER OF
LEARNING

THE
ORDER OF
LEARNING

Essays on the Contemporary University

EDWARD SHILS

Edited with an introduction by Philip G. Altbach

Transaction Publishers
New Brunswick (U.S.A.) and London (U.K.)

Copyright © 1997 by Transaction Publishers, New Brunswick, New Jersey 08903.

Bibliography of the Published Works of Edward Shils © Christine C. Schnusenberg and Gordon B. Neavill.

This book is printed on acid-free paper that meets the American National Standard for Permanence of Paper for Printed Library Materials.

Library of Congress Catalog Number: 96–47503
ISBN: 1–56000–298–0
Printed in the United States of America

Library of Congress Cataloging-in-Publication Data
Shils, Edward Albert, 1911–
    The order of learning : essays on the contemporary university /
  Edward Shils ; edited and with an introduction by Philip G. Altbach.
        p.   cm.
    Includes bibliographical references and index.
    ISBN 1-56000-298-0 (cloth)
    1. Education, Higher—Aims and objectives—United States. 2. Universities and colleges—United States—History. 3. Education, Higher—Social Aspects—United States. 4. Academic freedom—United States. I. Altbach, Philip G. II. Title.
LA227.4.S55   1997
378.73—dc21   96-47503
                                                                    CIP

Contents

Acknowledgements   vii
Introduction: Edward Shils and the American University
   Philip G. Altbach   ix

Part I: The Order of Learning

1. The Order of Learning in the United States from 1865 to 1920:
   The Ascendancy of the Universities   1
2. Universities Since 1900: A Historical Perspective   39

Part II: Perspectives

3. The Service of Society and the Advancement of Learning in
   the Twenty-First Century   71
4. The Academic Ethos under Strain   99
5. The American Private University   137
6. Governments and Universities   163
7. Dreams of Plenitude, Nightmares of Scarcity   189

Part III: Academic Freedom

8. Academic Freedom   217
9. Academic Freedom and Permanent Tenure   247
10. Limitations on the Freedom of Research and Teaching
    in the Social Sciences   261

Part IV: Policy

11. The Criteria of Academic Appointment   285
12. The Invitation to Caesar   299
13. The Confidentiality and Anonymity of Assessment   305

Part V: Reflection

14. The University: A Backward Glance   325

Bibliography of the Published Works of Professor Edward Shils   341
  Christine C. Schnusenberg and Gordon B. Neavill

Index   369

Acknowledgements

This book is dedicated to the memory of Edward Shils. I am indebted to the publishers who have permitted the use of previously published material here. I especially appreciate the cooperation of Peter deLiefde of Kluwer Academic Publishers in the Netherlands, current publisher of *Minerva*, for his assistance, and to *Minerva's* current editor, Michael Shattock. Both have supported this project from the beginning. Steven Grosby, a former student of Edward Shils, was both supportive and helpful. Joseph Epstein, Edward Shils's literary executor, provided his approval for project. Christine C. Schnusenberg and Gordon B. Neavill prepared a useful bibliography of Edward Shils's writing. Irving Louis Horowitz of Transaction Publishers, and a major sociological thinker in his own right, also provided support for this volume. Joyce McDonnell typed the manuscript. Eric Altbach, Jonathan Baker, and James JF Forest assisted with the proofreading. Patricia Murphy prepared the index.

The following permissions are gratefully acknowledged.

1. The Order of Learning in the United States from 1865 to 1920: The Ascendancy of the Universities. From *Minerva*, 16 (No. 2, 1978): 159–95. ©Reprinted by permission of Kluwer Academic Publishers and the Editors of *Minerva*.
2. Universities: Since 1900. From B. Clark and G. Neave, eds., *Encyclopedia of Higher Education* (Oxford: Pergamon, 1992): 1259–75. ©Reprinted by permission of Elsevier Science, Ltd.
3. Service to Society and the Advancement of Learning in the 21st Century. From *Minerva*, 30 (Summer, 1992): 242–68. ©Reprinted by permission of Kluwer Academic Publishers and the Editors of *Minerva*.
4. The Academic Ethos Under Strain. From *Minerva* 13 (Spring 1975): 1–37. ©Reprinted by permission of Kluwer Academic Publishers and the Editors of *Minerva*.
5. The American Private University. From *Minerva* 11, (January, 1973): 6–29. ©Reprinted by permission of Kluwer Academic Publishers and the Editors of *Minerva*.
6. Governments and Universities. From S. Hook, et al., eds. *The University and the State* (Buffalo, NY: Prometheus, 1978): 177–204. ©Reprinted by permission of the publisher, Prometheus Books.
7. Dreams of Plenitude, Nightmares of Scarcity. From S. M. Lipset and P. G. Altbach, eds., *Students in Revolt* (Boston: Houghton Mifflin, 1969): 1–33. ©Reprinted by permission of Houghton Mifflin Publishers.
8. Academic Freedom. From P. G. Altbach, ed., *International Higher Education: An*

Encyclopedia (New York: Garland Publishing, Inc., 1991): 1–22. ©Reprinted by permission of Garland Publishing, Inc.

9. Academic Freedom and Permanent Tenure. From *Minerva,* 33 (Spring, 1995): 5–17. ©Reprinted by permission of Kluwer Academic Publishers and the Editors of *Minerva.*

10. Limitations on the Freedom of Research and Teaching in the Social Sciences. From *The Annals of the American Academy of Political and Social Sciences* 200 (November, 1938): 144–64. ©Reprinted by permission of The American Academy of Arts and Sciences.

11. The Criteria of Academic Appointment. From *Minerva* 14 (Winter, 1976–77): 407–18. ©Reprinted by permission of Kluwer Academic Publishers and the Editors of *Minerva.*

12. The Invitation to Caesar. *Minerva* 10 (October 1972): 513–18. ©Reprinted by permission of Kluwer Academic Publishers and the Editors of *Minerva*

13. The Confidentiality and Anonymity of Assessment. From *Minerva,* 13 (Summer, 1975): 135–51. ©Reprinted by permission of Kluwer Academic Publishers and the Editors of *Minerva.*

14. The University: A Backward Glance. From *American Scholar,* (Spring, 1982): 163–79. ©The Editors and Phi Beta Kappa.

Introduction

Edward Shils and the American University

Philip G. Altbach

This book argues that the traditional research university performs a central role in modern society, that science and scholarship must be valued for their own sake, that governments should not interfere in the affairs of the universities, and that both students and faculty owe loyalty and commitment to their universities—and to the ideals of scientific inquiry. These are points that are frequently lost in this era of reengineering, downsizing, and university-industry collaboration. Edward Shils argues that we are losing the ethos of the modern university. The institution that emerged from von Humboldt's vision of a research university in Germany, devoted to the advancement of science, the teaching of advanced knowledge to students, and service to society provides Edward Shils with a powerful lodestone for his writings on higher education.

The defense of the traditional university, as well as the argument that academic institutions should be provided with the maximum possible autonomy to shape their own goals and organize their own affairs, is today not especially popular. For this reason, Edward Shils was, in recent years, not terribly influential in the corridors of academic power in the United States or Europe. Yet, his perspectives have consistency, and continue to be relevant in current debates. Indeed, we need more Shilsean voices—the traditional idea of the university needs powerful defenders because there is much to recommend the modern research university. The ideas and the scientific innovations that have been so powerful in the twentieth century emerged, in considerable part, from the research, both basic and applied, conducted in universities. Those professors involved in the research enterprise have played a central role in shaping modern science, and have trained generations of the top scientists and scholars who have literally shaped this century. Edward Shils reminds us that we are in danger of losing the ethos of this successful institution, so painstakingly built up in American and Europe over the past century.

Edward Shils, who died in January 1995, has a special place in the analysis of American higher education. He viewed the American university from a kind of mid-Atlantic perspective. Steeped in the traditions of European social science and holding simultaneous academic positions in Britain (first at the London School of Economics and then at Cambridge University) and in the United States (at the University of Chicago) throughout his academic career, he was convinced that the German research-oriented university constituted the gold standard of higher education worldwide. His commitment to academic freedom, to the concept of strict meritocracy, to the links between teaching and research, and to the traditional values of higher education informed his many writings on the American university over a long and distinguished career. Edward Shils' voice was a conservative one in the sense that he held rigidly to the traditional ideal of the research university and the accoutrements of this academic model.

II

Our purpose here is not to provide either a biography of Edward Shils or to assess his considerable impact in the several areas of his scholarship, but rather to place his views in the context of contemporary higher education, and to assess his views about the university.[1] It may, however, be useful to say something about Edward Shils' life and the range of his intellectual interests.[2] Born in Philadelphia in 1910, Shils studied at the University of Pennsylvania as an undergraduate. Although he never obtained a doctoral degree, he did graduate work in sociology at the University of Chicago, where he remained as a faculty member for more than six decades.

At Chicago, he was instrumental in designing several of the landmark general undergraduate courses in the social sciences. Later, he was a founder of the Committee on Social Thought, an interdisciplinary unit integrating several social science and humanities disciplines. His colleagues included Saul Bellow, Allan Bloom, and John U. Nef. In the 1960s, during the presidency of Edward H. Levi, Shils was a key adviser, and while he held no administrative position at the university, he had a significant role in shaping the institution's response to the turmoil of that period. The "two Edwards," as they were called, took a hard line with student and faculty activists. In many ways, the University of Chicago was the perfect institutional home for Edward Shils. It has traditionally upheld the highest intellectual standards, while providing the opportunity for innovative and interdisciplinary work. Especially during the presidency of

Robert M. Hutchins (who hired Shils and was supportive of him), Chicago was well known for its innovative approach to higher education. At the same time, Chicago remained very much a university in the German tradition. Founded in 1892 on the model of the German research university, the University of Chicago was an institution dominated by its senior faculty, and by the ideals of research and scholarship. Edward Shils was, in many ways, a quintessential Chicago professor—learned, committed to high standards of scholarship, interested in ideas about education as well as the disciplines—and deeply conservative on matters relating to education.

Britain was Shils' second academic and intellectual home. He was sent to England during the Second World War during his service in the Office of Strategic Services (OSS), the precursor to the CIA, with responsibility to interview German prisoners of war. This assignment utilized Shils' expert knowledge of the German language (he translated from German to English for publication the works of Karl Mannheim and Max Weber), as well as his sociological skills. Shils found that the willingness of German soldiers to fight against difficult odds was linked more to a sense of community and solidarity in the army than to Nazi ideology—an insight that helped to inform his later work. Shils liked England and remained there after the war. He was appointed to a teaching position at the London School of Economics, where he interacted not only with many of the key British social scientists of the day, but also came into contact with students from the British colonies. His long-standing interest in India and in the problems of socioeconomic development were kindled during this period. Shils later moved from the LSE to Cambridge University, where he held posts at King's College and later at Peterhouse, until the end of his life. From 1946 onwards, Shils had joint academic appointments in Britain and the United States, spending approximately half the year in Chicago and the other half in Cambridge.

Shils was, throughout his career, interested in the policy implications of academic work. Max Weber, whose work had a profound impact on Shils' thinking, had similar commitments.[3] His wartime work with German prisoners of war was in fact applied sociology. After the war, Shils worked with scientists at the University of Chicago on issues relating to the atomic bomb and was one of the founders of the influential *Bulletin of the Atomic Scientists,* serving on its editorial board for many years. He was close to the physicist Leo Szilard, who played a key role in trying to organize the scientific community to have an impact on government policy relating to nuclear weapons.[4] Shils' commitment to academic freedom, the autonomy of higher education institutions, and the civil society led him to write one of the most thoughtful books to emerge on McCarthyism, *The Torment of Secrecy.*[5] Toward the end of his life, Shils participated regularly in an annual seminar sponsored by Pope John Paul II at Castel Gandolfo. According to Joseph

Epstein, Shils and the pope held each other in mutual high esteem.[6]

In 1962, Shils founded *Minerva*, a quarterly journal devoted to science, policy, and higher education. He edited it uninterruptedly from its establishment to his death in 1995, certainly one of the longest periods of editorial service in academe. *Minerva* quickly established itself as one of the most serious publications in its area of concern. Again, it linked scholarship and policy, and reflected Shils' concern with the links between science, policy, and the university, and the interrelationship of these elements with government. *Minerva* also expressed Shils' internationalism, as it is one of the few journals that is self-consciously international in its coverage. Shils was an active editor, soliciting the best work in the field, and then heavily editing articles both for style and content. By the time an article appeared in print in *Minerva,* it bore the stamp not only of its author but of Edward Shils. Most of the chapters in this book are reprinted from *Minerva.*

Edward Shils was, first and foremost, a sociologist. He made significant contributions to the field through his original work, his translations, and his editing. He was a macrosociologist—as a scholar he dealt with large ideas and theories. While he did some research in the "Chicago school" tradition, his major contributions are probably more in the theoretical areas. He was strongly influenced by major European thinkers, and indeed Shils was a major bridge between European and American sociological thinking. He interpreted European ideas in the United States, and at the same time brought U.S. sociological thinking to Europe. He translated some of the works of Max Weber and Karl Mannheim into English, thereby bringing these major thinkers to the attention of readers in the United States and Britain. His work with Talcott Parsons in the 1960s provided a summary of sociological thinking at the time.[7] Along with Parsons and others, Shils helped to define the dominant sociological paradigms of the period.

Edward Shils was, as the *Times Higher Education Supplement* of London once pointed out, a "transatlantic polymath."[8] His breadth and depth of knowledge in a range of fields has been commented on by many. Those who experienced his seminars at Chicago or Cambridge can testify to his encyclopedic knowledge of history and sociology, and his immediate recall of information about many countries and historical periods. His interests ranged widely, and the three volumes of his collected essays reflect this range of knowledge.[9] One of his last essays was on "Reflections on Civil Society and Civility in the Chinese Intellectual Tradition," a detailed analysis of Chinese society reflective of Shils' scholarship and his comparative approach to knowledge.[10] He also wrote a perceptive book on Indian intellectuals.[11]

A recurring theme in Shils' work is his internationalism. At home in Europe and America, he was one of the few American social scientists of his generation with a genuine interest in and respect for European thought. In this way, he harks back to the generation of social scientists who studied in Germany at the end of the nineteenth century, and who brought the ideal of the German research university to the United States. Shils remained true to the ideal of the German research university, to the objectivity of science, and to the importance of research as a goal for the university. Shils was as much concerned with trends in European thinking in the social sciences as with transatlantic institutional patterns in higher education and science. He played a central role in introducing American sociological thinking in Britain, and later on the continent as well. Shils was also deeply concerned with developing countries, and indeed was one of the first American social scientists to seriously consider the problems of socioeconomic development and especially the emergence of a civil society in what he called the "new states."[12] He also wrote perceptively about the problems facing African intellectuals. India was of special interest to him, and he made several extended trips there in the 1950s and 1960s. He wrote extensively on Indian higher education, including an important article on the Indian academic profession.[13] *Minerva* published many articles on India, and reported extensively on university developments in South Asia. Shils was especially sympathetic to the plight of academics and intellectuals in societies in transition, pointing out the problems faced by them, and emphasizing their importance in the development of science and a civil society.

III

A concern with the societal importance of tradition was a recurring theme in Shils's work.[14] This underscores a deep conservative trend in his work. Shils feared social disruption whether from the right or the left, and felt that the basic center of society must be protected. Perhaps influenced by the rise of fascism in Europe in the 1930s, and exposed to social disorder as a social worker in Chicago during the Depression, Shils saw at first hand the dangers of societal disruption. He was sharply critical of the student radicals of the 1960s in several essays, including "Dreams of Plenitude, Nightmares of Scarcity," which is reprinted in this volume. He repeatedly stressed the importance of social cohesion, and emphasized the importance of intellectuals and of academic institutions in helping to shape the central ideas of society. He was quite critical of what he saw as the antinomian ideas of intellectuals, academics, students, and the university community generally, arguing that those with the power to shape the underlying ideas about society should respect the traditions of society, and build constructively on those traditions rather than constantly criticize social institutions and norms.

While not a traditional conservative, Shils's basic understanding of society led him to conservative stances on contemporary issues. His conviction that society is a fragile institution that requires nurturing led him to emphasize social cohesion and tradition. He examined the Confucian-based societies of Asia that have exhibited a strong sense of cohesion to see what lessons might be learned. Just as he was convinced that the individual needed to have a commitment to society, he also believed that society owed the individual freedom from undue restrictions on thought or action. Similarly, academic institutions were owed loyalty by members of the academic community, but at the same time had the responsibility to provide academic freedom as well as autonomy for the professoriate to govern the university.

IV

Higher education and science were among Shils's major concerns and preoccupations throughout his career. One of the essays included in this book, "Limitations on the Freedom of Research and Teaching in the Social Sciences," was published first in 1938, almost sixty years ago. It remains relevant today, and is an indication that Edward Shils's preoccupations remained consistent over a long academic career. Greatly influenced by Max Weber's classic essay, "Science as a Vocation," Shils stressed the value of objective research and the authority of science and research and their centrality in higher education.

The essays included in this book are, of course, situated in a particular time and space, and must be understood in this context. The following factors were among the most important developments shaping higher education in the postwar era that were important to Shils's concerns.

With one exception, these chapters were written during a rather unique period in the development of American higher education—the period of great expansion beginning in the 1950s and extending through the 1970s, and the following period of consolidation. This was a watershed period of American higher education, and Edward Shils provided a consistent perspective on the academic developments of the period. The period was marked by expansion in student numbers, the growth of public higher education (public institutions enrolled fewer than 50 percent of the student population at the beginning and 80 percent at the end), and a dramatic expansion and accompanying diversification of the academic profession. Student enrollments expanded from fewer than four million to more than twelve million during this period. The student population changed significantly as well, with students from racial and ethnic minorities enrolling in large numbers, and the proportion of women reaching half of the total.

The American university assumed world leadership in science and scholarship during this period. Research funds increased dramatically, with the federal government providing significant support for basic research. The top one hundred American universities became the major producers of science and scholarship. Scientific leadership passed from Europe, and especially Germany, to the United States. The culture of research came to dominate these top institutions as never before. English became the dominant language of world science, and more than half of the world's research and development expenditures took place in the United States.

By the middle of the 1970s, the academic boom was coming to an end, and a decade later American higher education was facing significant financial problems. Nonetheless, American academic leadership remained powerful, in part because of the size of the American academic system and the fact that American higher education faced the challenges of expansion, diversified populations, and integrating research, teaching, and service to society earlier than most others.

At the same time that the American academic system expanded, it faced a number of significant challenges—issues with which Edward Shils concerned himself, and that the pages of *Minerva* reflected during this period. Because government was providing an increasing proportion of money for higher education, in terms of research funds as well as grants, loans, and other programs to assist student access, there were increasing calls for accountability. Government regulation in many aspects of higher education grew dramatically. Edward Shils consistently argued that universities had to be autonomous to be successful. Shils was a strong voice arguing that governmental authority should support higher education and at the same time permit academe significant autonomy. He also argued that universities must be worthy of the autonomy granted by government. His was a minority position as academic leaders proved willing to accept considerable accountability in order to obtain funds. Perhaps influenced by the pre-Thatcher government British arrangement through which governmental funds were allocated by the University Grants Committee, which was a buffer between the universities and the government, Shils continued to argue for autonomy.

Edward Shils was a strong believer in academic meritocracy, and in judgment by peers. This increasingly placed him in opposition to affirmative action and other programs aimed at increasing access of specific population groups to higher education at all levels. As such programs became more entrenched in American higher education, he found himself increasingly isolated on the right.[15] He opposed affirmative action as inappropriate governmental interference in the business of academic institutions, and he felt that it interfered with the natural meritocracy of academe as well.

The Shils era was also the era of the Cold War. The struggle between the

United States and the Soviet Union, and their respective ideologies, played a significant role in Shils's thinking, and in his actions during this period. Shils was a strong supporter of the West in the ideological struggles of the period. He was involved with the Congress for Cultural Freedom, an organization of intellectuals that sponsored high-quality journals, conferences, and other programs. He was intimately involved with several of these journals, notably *Encounter*, which was edited by his colleague Melvin J. Lasky, serving as a member of the board of the Congress. This organization was one of the main groups involved in the ideological struggles of the period. Its main funding source for much of its history was the Central Intelligence Agency. The organization lost much of its strength after CIA involvement was exposed in the mid-1960s.[16]

The 1960s brought a period of unprecedented academic ferment. Again, Edward Shils had strong views and was involved on a number of levels. The student revolts of this period resulted in significant turmoil on campus. There were also movements for university reform in the United States and other countries, in many cases related to the demands of the students, and of some segments of the professoriate. Students demanded participation in academic governance, a voice in the shaping of the curriculum, and they wanted the universities to become directly involved in the social and political conflicts of the period. In the United States, this meant a strong opposition to the Vietnam War. One of the key slogans of the period was "participation"—the involvement of students in academic governance. In several European countries, including Sweden, France, and West Germany, students were given a significant voice in governance—one-third of the votes on many academic bodies. In France and many of the West German states, students had one-third of the votes in elections for university rector (president) as well as key academic officials.

Shils opposed student activism, as well as student participation in academic governance. He also felt that academic institutions should not as institutions take stands on political issues. This opposition was consistent with his support of the Humboldtian ideal of the university, with its professorial autonomy and domination of the structures of governance by the senior faculty. He saw student activists as politically antiestablishment, and felt that their influence in the university was a negative force. Shils was influential in the administration of the University of Chicago during the presidency of his friend and colleague, Edward H. Levi, at the height of the student revolts. Unlike many American universities at this time, the University of Chicago did not give in to student demands, and dealt firmly with protesters, expelling large numbers. Shils was equally critical of faculty members who supported student political activism.

Debates on higher education issues during the 1960s and early 1970s were heated. There was an unprecedented public interest in the affairs of the universities, and governments began at this time to exert increasing control over academe. A combination of forces contributed to this situation. Public interest was stimulated by widespread media attention to student political activism. Further, a larger proportion of the age cohort was participating in higher education, and developments in the universities affected a larger segment of the population. Student activism attracted media attention, and for a period constituted a major news story. For perhaps the first time in the United States, higher education issues such as reform, campus politics, and related university issues were covered in the national press.

In the aftermath of the turbulent period of the 1960s, there were few defenders of the traditional research university. Public confidence in higher education, which had been quite high prior to the period of unrest, plummeted. Many in the public felt that the academic community, including students and some faculty members, had acted irresponsibly. Others were unimpressed with how academic institutions themselves had reacted to activism and other disruptions. Many in government lost confidence in the ability of academic institutions to manage themselves effectively. This was combined with ever-growing demands by academic institutions for more funds to serve ever-increasing student enrollments and to support an expanding research infrastructure. Public reluctance to pay more taxes, negative public opinion concerning higher education, and pressing needs in other areas all contributed to unprecedented fiscal pressures on higher education. Few in government or in the media came to the defense of the higher education establishment.

Academe itself was dispirited and divided. The confident leadership of higher education which advocated for the universities and colleges became defensive, and had no clear vision for the future. Clark Kerr, who coined the term "multiversity," for example, grew increasingly pessimistic about the future of higher education, feeling that the negative trends of the 1980s and 1990s were long-term realities.[17] University leaders in the public sector were generally consumed with defending their budgets from increasing cuts. There were few spirited defenders of the traditional autonomy of the university. Most were willing to accept as inevitable ever-expanding governmental regulation of higher education, perhaps as a price for continued funding. While most in academe agreed on the configuration of the problem, and felt that the universities were facing a long period of difficuties, few provided an articulate analysis of higher education.

The past two decades have been "times of trouble" for higher education in America or Europe.[18] In the United States, financial problems and a lack of direction have characterized academe. Faculty morale has declined as the job market for professors has deteriorated. Media coverage of higher education continues to be largely unfavorable. Imaginative leadership in colleges and universities has been in short supply. The situation in Europe has been similarly difficult, and in some cases worse. In Britain especially, the policy changes implemented by the conservative Thatcher government had a devastating effect on the British universities. Institutional autonomy was destroyed by the abolition of the University Grants Committee. The morale of the academic profession was seriously damaged by the abolition of tenure and continuing downward pressure on salaries. Throughout Europe, student enrollments have continued to increase as the demand for access has continued unabated, but few resources have been added. This has led to deteriorating conditions for study, including larger classes, less access to faculty, and deteriorating libraries and laboratories.

V

Edward Shils held to his convictions during this difficult period. He wrote frequently about autonomy, academic freedom, accountability, the responsibility of faculty and students, the importance of research, and related topics. He continued to articulate a vision of the university that was true to von Humboldt and Weber. He held to traditional academic values, advocating autonomy for institutions, a sense of "calling" (as Weber would put it) for faculty, discipline and commitment from students, and public support for the academic institutions that form the basis of a modern postindustrial society. Despite his criticisms of the foibles of academic institutions and his dismay with the direction of public policy, Shils remained loyal to the traditional values of higher education.

Has Edward Shils been influential in the shaping of the modern American university, and has his vision been seriously considered by policymakers within and outside of the universities? His journal, *Minerva,* remains perhaps the best single source for thoughtful writing on issues of science and higher education policy, although its circulation is small and it is not widely considered in policy circles. Shils' own writings have brought a consistent perspective to the debate. His work has been taken seriously by scholars in the fields of higher education and science policy. It is, furthermore, internationally respected, and he has been involved in policy debates worldwide.

It is fair to say, however, that his perspectives are not shared these days by policymakers within academe or in government. The German-model research university that was so influential from the late nineteenth century until the latter part of the twentieth century is no longer the dominant institution. Events have overtaken academe, and Shils' ideas of institutional autonomy, of academic freedom, of the academic profession as a "calling" for high-minded scholars and scientists, and of a community of scholars seem quaintly anachronistic in this age of downsizing and accountability. More important, the idea that the university should be a home for basic science and research is no longer dominant.

Yet, Edward Shils brings an important message to academe. Now questioned, his perspective remains relevant. It might even be the case that the university of the twenty-first century needs to revive the ideas that Edward Shils so eloquently advocated throughout his life.

Notes

1. I studied with Edward Shils at the University of Chicago during the mid-1960s, participating in several of his seminars. He was especially helpful to me in shaping my doctoral dissertation on higher education in India, a topic that he had studied at first hand a decade earlier.
2. The journal that Edward Shils started and edited for three decades, *Minerva,* featured a special issue entitled "In Memory of Edward Shils." The issue included articles considering Shils' impact on sociology, the study of science, studies of higher education, and on his role as editor of *Minerva,* as well as several personal reminiscences. See *Minerva* XXXIV, 1 (Spring 1996): 1–129.
3. Edward Shils, ed., *Max Weber on Universities: The Power of the State and the Dignity of the Academic Calling in Imperial Germany* (Chicago: University of Chicago Press, 1974).
4. See William Lanouette, *Genius in the Shadows: A Biography of Leo Szilard* (New York: Scribners, 1992).
5. Edward A. Shils, *The Torment of Secrecy: The Background and Consequences of American Security Policies* (New York: The Free Press, 1956).
6. Joseph Epstein, "My Friend Edward," *The American Scholar,* LXIV (Summer 1995): 371–94.
7. Talcott Parsons, Edward Shils, et al., eds., *Theories of Society: Foundations of Modern Sociological Theory* (Glencoe, Ill.: Free Press, 1961).
8. Peter Hennessy, "Preserving the Faint Precipitate of a Humane Tradition," *Times Higher Education Supplement,* July 19, 1974, 6.
9. Edward Shils, *The Intellectuals and the Powers and Other Essays* (Chicago: University of Chicago Press, 1972); Edward Shils, *Center and Periphery: Essays in Macrosociology* (Chicago: University of Chicago Press, 1975); and Edward Shils, *The Calling of Sociology and Other Essays on the Pursuit of Learning* (Chicago: University of Chicago Press, 1980). See also Edward Shils, *Tradition* (Chicago: University of Chicago Press, 1981), and Edward Shils, *The Constitution of Society* (Chicago: University of Chicago Press, 1982). This latter volume appeared in The Heritage of Sociology series edited by Morris Janowitz.
10. Edward Shils, "Reflections on Civil Society and Civility in the Chinese Intellectual Tradition," in *Confucian Traditions in East Asian Modernity: Moral Education and Economic Culture in Japan and the Four Mini-Dragons,* ed. Wei-Ming Tu (Cambridge: Harvard University Press, 1996): 38–71.
11. Edward Shils, *The Intellectual Between Tradition and Modernity: The Indian Situation* (The Hague: Mouton, 1961).
12. See, for example, Edward Shils, *Political Development in the New States* (The Hague: Mouton, 1965) and Edward Shils, "The Military in the Political Develop-

ment of the New States," in *The Role of the Military in Underdeveloped Countries,* ed. John J. Johnson. (Princeton, N.J.: Princeton University Press, 1962): 7–67.

13. Edward Shils, "The Academic Profession in India," *Minerva* VII (Spring 1969): 345–72.
14. Shils, *Tradition.*
15. See Edward Shils, *The Academic Ethic: The Report of a Study Group of the International Council on the Future of the University* (Chicago: University of Chicago Press, 1983) for a comprehensive statement of Shils' views on the contemporary university.
16. Peter Coleman, *The Liberal Conspiracy: The Congress for Cultural Freedom and the Struggle for the Mind of Postwar Europe* (New York: Free Press, 1989).
17. Clark Kerr, *The Uses of the University* (Cambridge, Mass.: Harvard University Press, 1995). This classic volume, first published in 1963, charted a vision for the American research university. In prefaces in later editions, Kerr was increasingly pessimistic about the future of academe.
18. Clark Kerr, *Troubled Times for American Higher Education: The 1980s and Beyond* (Albany: State University of New York Press, 1994).

Part I
The Order of Learning

1

The Order of Learning in the United States from 1865 to 1920: The Ascendancy of the Universities

The history of the order of learning in the United States between the end of the Civil War and the end of the First World War may be seen largely as the history of a fundamental change in the institutional structure of learning; one particular class of institutions became dominant over other classes of learned institutions and particular institutions within that newly dominant class became especially dominant. The universities as seats of learning gained ascendancy over other institutional forms for the discovery and diffusion of knowledge. The ascendancy consisted in superiority in productivity—qualitative and quantitative—and in prestige. The prestige was equally prestige of institutions, prestige of works, prestige of individuals. The prestige was accorded both within the order of learning and by the wider public. The ascendancy of the academic order within the order of learning was accompanied by and in a certain measure furthered by the ascendancy of a small number of universities at the center of the academic order.

The Displacement of the Amateur

In one respect, the history of the period may be seen as one of the displacement of the amateur scholar and scientist. It may be seen as the history of the triumph of the scholar and scientist who devotes most of his waking hours and who gains a livelihood from study and teaching within an elaborate institution. It is also the history of the cultivation of learning through institutions where such an activity is the major obligation of its members. The productive scholars and the scientists of the United States became increasingly the members of academic institutions. Instead of working from his own financial resources, using his own books and his own instruments, and doing his work in his home or private libraries or those of private learned societies, the new type of scholar and scientist, by the end of our period, gained his livelihood primarily through employment by a college or university. He used mainly books and journals or the laboratory and equipment provided by his institution. This aspect of this major change has been depicted very graphically by Max Weber in *Wissenschaft als Beruf.* Weber did not, however, lay equal stress on the concomitant ascendancy of the university. Perhaps because in Germany a similar transition had already been completed he took the preponderance of the university in the order of learning for granted.

The scholar or scientist who had no obligation to concern himself as a member of an institution with the discovery and communication of truths to his peers and juniors through his learned papers, classes, and seminars became less common and less prominent. The scholar or scientist who lived from his own privately amassed or inherited fortune or who conducted his intellectual activities avocationally while his income was gained through employment as an administrative civil servant or diplomat, or through journalism or through private business enterprise or through the practice of a learned profession, sacred or secular, became rarer in the fifty-five years after the end of the Civil War. It is true that during this period the amateur scientist and scholar was also being displaced or absorbed by governmental research institutions such as agricultural experimental stations, the Geological Survey, including the Bureau of Ethnology, and towards the end of the period by such private research institutions as the Carnegie Institution in Washington, the Rockefeller Institute in New York, the research laboratories of the Bell Telephone Company and the General Electric Laboratory in Schenectady. Nonetheless, in the midst of this more pervasive incorporation of scholars and scientists into institutions, the growing dominance of the universities within the cosmos of American learning appears in retrospect to have been the most significant feature of the time.

At the beginning of the period, most of the serious and productive intellectual life of the country was still carried on outside the universities. Of the most famous scholars and scientists alive in the early part of the period, Henry Adams, J. L. Motley, George Bancroft, Joseph Henry and Henry C. Lea were not university teachers, although Adams and Bancroft both did hold posts briefly at Harvard. J. W. Powell taught for five years at Illinois Wesleyan University and at the Illinois Normal University. Charles Peirce taught at Johns Hopkins for five years.

There was a tradition of private and avocational learning in the United States; it had a long history. This tradition of amateur learning was unable nevertheless to maintain the dominance it had once enjoyed and it could not meet the growing demand for opportunities for scholarly and scientific research and training. Even had it had many more practitioners, it could not have met the demands which led to the institutionalization of learning in the universities. In the time of its greatest prominence in the United States, it lagged in scale and in achievement behind its European counterpart, particularly that of France and Great Britain. The striking difference between the United States on the one side and Great Britain and France on the other was that, in the United States, there was not that closely serried sequence of geniuses which made British and French science and scholarship of the eighteenth and much of the nineteenth centuries so great. The United States never quite generated the great achievement of amateur learning which in Great Britain was formed into a mighty mountain chain linking together peaks like William Harvey, Robert Boyle, Joseph Priestly, John Dalton, Humphrey Davy, Charles Darwin, Edward Gibbon, David Hume, T. B. Macaulay, George Grote, David Ricardo, and James and John Stuart Mill. Perhaps the original mental endowment was lacking, perhaps family traditions and the informal local, intellectual communities and the local academies were neither dense enough, intense enough, nor stringent enough in their demands in the United States to call forth the exertions and the accomplishments which emerged in Great Britain from the seventeenth to the nineteenth centuries.

American scholars and scientists were generally very conscious of their peripherality with respect to Europe and this probably held down their level of aspiration; American scholars and scientists seem not to have thought that it lay within their powers to produce works of the quality of their European contemporaries. There was not sufficient concentration of talents in a center; the intellectual community, such as it was, was too attenuated for the necessary self-confidence.

The long distances and the consequent sense of remoteness from each other stood in the way of the animating ties of intercourse which constitute an intellectual community. In addition, the reservoir of those persons sufficiently educated and sufficiently well off to devote themselves to learned pursuits was probably too small. Even in cities like Philadelphia, Boston, and New York, the persons with a high degree of concentration of purpose and energy were too few in number to embody and express in a sufficiently compelling way standards which were in competition with the absorbing immediately practical, professional, political, and commercial preoccupations of their devotees. The local and state academies did not have enough prestige to compel individuals without very strong intellectual character to live up to the highest standards. Perhaps there were just not enough geniuses who were sufficiently committed to scientific or scholarly studies to give an immediately apprehensible form to the mode of proceeding and the ethos needed for outstanding accomplishment. Undoubtedly, there was a circularity of effect. In any case, in no field except perhaps historical studies, did the United States have clusters of eminent amateur scholars and scientists of the quality attained at the higher reaches in Europe.

It is unlikely, however, that greater accomplishments would have saved the tradition of amateur scholarly and scientific research. It was bound to yield, just as a much more productive amateur practice had yielded in Europe to competing academic institutionalization, or—as Max Weber would have called it—academic bureaucratization. More young persons wanted to do research than were able to support themselves from their own private means, and the spread of knowledge of how this was rendered possible by the German universities increased the number of aspirants to careers in college and university teaching.

In the retreat of amateur research, the cognate institutions of amateur research, namely, the local scientific and scholarly academies, also went into attrition. What they offered was too slight in competition with the opportunities for intercourse and investigation offered by universities and especially university departments and laboratories as the most elementary institutions of the larger, translocal scientific and scholarly communities. The avidity of intellectual desire could not be satisfied by the occasional meetings of academies or by the limitations of private means. The local academies could not meet the desire for more specialized audiences; their resources were too scanty for them to become research institutions. Had they become primarily research institutions they still could not have competed successfully against the universities.

Defeated Rivals

The independent research institutions which appeared early in the twentieth century and which adopted the principle of specialization likewise were also not able to compete effectively with the universities, even in their own fields in which they did important work. Their accomplishments were not imposing enough for them to represent an alternative to the universities; they were dependent on and supplementary to the universities. The Carnegie Institution, the governors of which were determined not to make it into an adjunct to the universities for the support of academic research—as the Rockefeller and Guggenheim foundations were to do between the wars—did not pave the way for a superior or separate system.

The relationships between the universities and independent research institutions in this period are well exemplified by the development of the Marine Biological Laboratory at Wood's Hole. Beginning in 1888 with only seventeen members in attendance, it had several hundred by 1919, working in the fields of developmental biology, genetics, eugenics, and comparative physiology. As in the case of the universities, a German model was drawn upon. In this instance, the pattern was first sketched by Carl Vogt's summer classes in marine biology in 1844; it was then established in a more elaborate and stable form in the Stazione Zoologica in Naples which Anton Doehrn of the University of Jena created. Charles Otis Whitman, the first director of the Marine Biological Laboratory had taken a Ph.D. degree at Leipzig and had worked at the Stazione Zoologica; he had argued for the support of the American institution on the grounds that otherwise American work in the pertinent subjects would be permanently inferior to that done in Germany.

The Marine Biological Laboratory was not intended to be an autonomous institution with its own permanent staff of investigators and completely independent financial resources. The model from which it was drawn had grown out of a situation in which the academic order had become dominant and the institution in Naples was not intended to be more than an indispensable auxiliary in certain fields of science. The American institution was dependent on the universities from which came the investigators, young and old, to work there during the summer months. The leading American biologists of the period before the First World War worked at Wood's Hole—they included William Patten, Howard Ayers, A. C. Eylesheimer, D. S. Strong, and William M. Wheeler—but their sojourns were only interludes in academic careers.

The dependence of the Marine Biological Laboratory on the universities is illustrated by the career of Whitman. When he was young and not yet famous, he thought of the laboratory as a compensation for the deficiencies of research in the universities. After he became a famous professor at the University of Chicago he viewed it as ancillary or complementary to the work of the universities. It acquired a dual function which postulated the prior existence of the universities; it was something like a three-month-long meeting of a set of closely related professional scientific societies; and it was a laboratory where university teachers could work on special topics—difficult to work on elsewhere—while engaging in a continuous informal exchange of information and interpretation. It became an interuniversity institution, something like the consortia which developed after the Second World War around the accelerators at Brookhaven, Argonne, and Weston.

It became a special part of the academic order; it never became an independent research institution like the Carnegie Institution in Washington or the Rockefeller Institute in New York, neither of which could persist in its existing composite of activities without the prior and continuing existence of the universities. The situation of the Smithsonian Institution was little different. The New York Museum of Natural History, the Field Museum, and the National Geographical Society lived alongside the triumphant universities but they did not amount to a national system of the organization of learning. They sponsored important research and publications by members of their staff, who were also custodians of their collections. They maintained serial publications of scholarly monographs and developed their collections. Their work was, however, marginal and supplementary to the large volume of research of high quality carried out in their fields in the universities. For one thing, they covered only relatively narrow ranges of learning; they never reached the point of becoming parts of a national order of specialized institutions of learning which together covered the same ground as the universities. Thus, if they were rivals of the universities, they were rivals only in a relatively small number of fields. They never succeeded in acquiring the prestige of the leading universities as seats of learning as a whole, although in their respective fields, they were highly esteemed for the quality of their specialized research. Their dependence on the universities was inevitable since unless they were to be made up of learned amateurs—a category which had generally lost prestige—they had to recruit their staff from persons who had been trained in universities and who continued to look to universities as the centers of learned production. The main audience of the most important publications of the autonomous research institutes was in the universities also. For all these reasons, the autonomous research institutes, however distinguished their accomplishments in research, were compelled to function as somewhat peripheral parts of the order of learning.

The state agricultural experimental stations were no more able to attain a prominent position in the system of learning. It took them several decades to do more than meet the demands of their clientele for routine analyses, at a time when the universities were growing in accomplishments, pride, and prestige. The universities to which they were attached looked down on them as if they were no better than hewers of wood and drawers of water for farmers. They seldom worked on "fundamental" problems; the problems they worked on were specialized as well as practical. As a result, they too moved in the periphery of the academic order, which worked on the more fundamental problems and which had the whole range of learning in their jurisdiction.

Libraries, in a different way, were also confined to a peripheral position. University libraries were clearly, from the beginning, subsidiary. The great public and private libraries performed invaluable functions but mainly as adjuncts to the academic order. The world of learning could not exist without libraries but they themselves could not aspire to supplant universities; it is not in their nature to perform the functions of universities. Libraries ceased in our period to be collections which were assembled primarily for the sake of giving a permanent resting place to the results of human creativity; having ceased to be ends in themselves, they became instrumental to the desires of their users. Nonetheless, neither the Library of Congress nor the Library of the Surgeon-General, any more than the Bibliothèque Nationale, or the British Museum, or the Preussische Staatsbibliothek could become the centers of a national system of learning. The tasks of a library are curatorial and hence auxiliary to the use of the books, manuscripts, etc. for which it cares. A library does not teach; the training of librarians, archivists, paleographers, etc. in a library does not change the situation. The formation of a staff of research workers in a library, whether they are engaged full time in research or whether they do so supplementarily to their curatorial functions, does not alter the situation. The experience of the Newbury Library, the Athenaeum, and the New York Public Library showed that a great library could do more than collect, care for, and aid in the finding of publications and manuscripts: it could not, at best, do more than become a research institution. A scientific and technological library like the Surgeon-General's Library and the Crerar Library could not, as libraries, provide for research as could libraries in the social sciences and humanities. Libraries suffered the handicaps of concentration on limited functions and—usually—interests, in contrast with the combination of research and teaching over a range of subjects as wide as the whole horizon of learning.

Independent and specialized professional schools, particularly in the study of medicine, were also largely overpowered by the universities during the course of this half-century. Advanced technological institutions like the Massachusetts Institute of Technology and the California Institute of Technology were the only ones in their category which acquired some approximation to the eminence and centrality of the leading universities, and they did this by approximating universities in the fundamental nature of their interests. Independent engineering colleges like Rensselaer, despite their early beginnings, fell by the wayside. Once entry into the legal profession became conditional on systematic study, independent law schools, separate from universities, never emerged from a lowly obscurity; university law schools became preponderant in legal training. By the end of our period, only a few independent medical colleges survived without incorporation into universities. Again, it was the German model which showed the way. The more it became acknowledged that education for the learned professions required systematic and fundamental training in scientific subjects, the more imperative it became for professional schools to be parts of universities. The alternative was to wither.

Independent liberal arts colleges providing education for undergraduates were the only institutions which managed to withstand the tentacular dominance of the universities. They did this mainly by avoiding competition through concentration on instruction and by eschewing research. Their proponents fought a rearguard action for many years which was partly successful, partly unsuccessful. They became subsidiaries of the universities through sending many of their graduates into the universities for postgraduate and professional studies and by drawing some of their teachers from the universities. Those which grew into universities, as did Harvard, Princeton, Yale, and Columbia, were able to retain some of their identity, but they did so by resistance and concessions.

The question remains then: Why, in the period of institutionalization of science and scholarship did the universities succeed in establishing and maintaining dominance over the institutional system of learning? The main part of the answer is that the universities taught as well as did research. A type of institution which produced its own *Nachwuchs* and the personnel of other learned institutions assured itself of centrality in the system of learning. It aroused identifications and loyalties which later experience did not extinguish. It fostered parochial traditions which gave motives for institutional ambition for more widely acclaimed achievements. By teaching, the universities guided the future of their subjects; they infused their influence into the next generation while teaching it to go beyond what they taught and to do so in the tradition in which they themselves taught and discovered. The teachers were enlivened by their relations with their students. Teaching did not prevent specialization in research but it maintained identification with a wider discipline. The plurality of universities gave the impression of a mighty concourse, which was reinforced by the links between institutions. Young scholars and scientists trained in one institution frequently made their careers in others. A translocal identification was strengthened in the minds of those who had this plurality of connections. One consequence was that the participants felt themselves to be engaged in a vast, national and international movement of the spirit.

Despite the progress of specialization in research, the co-existence of the practitioners of disciplines within faculties and of faculties within universities created a density and radius of intellectual intercourse which supported the general conviction that the advancement of knowledge was an end of the highest value. In a society in which there was such great respect for "practicality" and for economic progress, the universities helped to provide the conditions in which the ethos of devotion to things which were not of immediate practical or economic importance could flourish. Disciplinary departments sustained the motivation which might often have relaxed under the conditions of isolation in which amateur scholars and scientists lived and worked.

The universities had another great advantage over all other types of arrangement of intellectual work in teaching and research—namely, their comprehensiveness. They taught and investigated over the entire range of learning. This not only attached to them a multitude of diverse, specialized interests but it also enabled them to receive the deference which had hitherto been given so generally to the churches. The simultaneity of their efforts to deal with all the objects of serious interest made them stand out from all other intellectual institutions with more specialized jurisdictions and fields of activity.

Another closely related reason for the dominance of the academic order is that the universities worked on fundamental problems; they were not circumscribed by practical necessities. They could explore, with all the respect of earnest seekers after fundamental truth in an age of faltering theological conviction but of unshaken earnestness. This not only enhanced their prestige in an ostensibly practical society but produced scientific and scholarly results which commanded respect. In the allegedly practical and "materialistic" American society of the period after the Civil War, there was still a deep piety which had ceased to be monopolized by the doctrines of ecclesiastical Christianity. The seriousness with which fundamental knowledge was pursued aroused the admiration of those possessed by this enduring piety. The universities were able, by their concern with fundamental learning, to be, in a sense, the heirs of the churches. More specialized, more practical institutions could not claim that vital inheritance, and the consequent support by private patrons and state legislatures.

In the age of specialization and practicality the university managed to accommodate specialization to breadth, and practicality to fundamental inquiry. The university was, moreover, self-reproductive and self-extending. The combination of research and teaching might have been adventitious. Once, however, the combination was found and put into practice, the outcome could not be surpassed. It was the ideal arrangement for discovery, diffusion, and influence.

Pervading all these contributory conditions was the all-decisive fact of the love of learning. Without it none of the favorable institutional conditions would have amounted to much. The same is true of the extra-academic conditions.

It is said, quite frequently, that the scientific side of the American order developed in response to the needs of industrial capitalism; in the United States, and particularly so in chemistry, this is not in fact the case. Whatever may be true of academic chemistry in Germany from the formation of the Reich and even earlier, this did not happen in the United States. Even as late as 1900 only 276 of the 9,000 qualified chemists in the United States were employed full time in the chemical industry. The United States Steel Company had no research establishment as late as the First World War. The General Electric Company which had a staff of 102 in its industrial laboratories working in street lighting, X-rays, metallurgy, radio, etc., was exceptional. In a period when firms with single owners and partnerships still prevailed, the units were too small to support research.

By the first decade of the century, there was much talk of the positive contribution of scientific research to industrial progress. Publicists and ceremonial orators repeatedly praised the practical powers of scientific knowledge. Academic scientists themselves began increasingly to legitimate their scientific research by reference to the practical benefits which would grow from it. Enthusiastic discussions about the introduction of "scientific methods" in management became common. Nonetheless, even in the large firms, Frederick Taylor's ideas were not taken to heart until after the First World War. Had industry been insistent on the utilization of the results of scientific research, the structure of the learned world might have turned out differently. Industrial laboratories, attached to particular firms and independent laboratories working on scientific problems on contractual terms would have been more common had industrial enterprisers been more interested in the promotion and application of scientific research. But this was not the case.

As it turned out, the motive force of scientific research lay within the university; it lay in the scientists themselves and in the willingness if not in the active desire of the strong university presidents to allow their academic staffs to fit research into their budget of academic activities. The situation was no different in the social sciences and the humanistic disciplines. The social sciences began quite early to thrive in the leading American universities because of intellectual curiosity. The desire for social improvement was a supplementary factor; it was not primary. The primary factor was an irrepressible desire to understand.

The ascendancy of the academic order came about also because universities had advantages over the alternative modes of provision for research which prevailed at the time. One of these advantages came from the pedagogical function of the universities. Their support came to them for the provision of instruction. Little money came to them explicitly and exclusively for research. Nonetheless, despite what might appear from the luxurious standards of the leading universities of the mid-twentieth century to have been an arduous round of teaching, those who wished to do research, especially those above the rank of instructor, could find time for it. They were paid their salaries to teach, but they also could do research in the "interstices" of teaching.

It was a time when the financial requirements for research were not large. There were few large-scale projects for which many assistants had to be used. Much research was conducted by single teachers, sometimes by a teacher and one of his pupils. The equipment, which was seldom very elaborate, did not cost much and a good part of it could be paid for from the costs of maintaining the laboratories needed for teaching.

As a result, research in the universities was almost unintentionally subsidized by the funds which were provided for teaching. This was the case in the state universities. In the leading private universities, there were sometimes benefactions intended to support the conduct of research; there too, however, a teacher in the higher ranks who did not have a special grant for research and who wished to do it could manage with the aid of his departmental funds and sometimes some of his personal financial resources.

The two decades between 1880 and 1900 were decades of praise for science. They were not, however, decades of readiness to spend much money on it, particularly on pure or fundamental research. Industrial enterprises moved very slowly into the establishment of laboratories; they still counted on purchasing inventions offered to them by individual inventors. Their owners did not regard the endowment of research in universities as a very pressing need although they did help universities in all sorts of ways. The federal and state governments recognized the value of research but they usually thought of it as survey, assay, testing, and routine analysis; the "users" in agriculture or mining wanted exactly such services. Here and there a great intellectual personality in the civil service like J. W. Powell managed to do more. The state and local academies of science, and the three national academies, had very little money for research; they aimed mainly to give honors to those who had done their research without their aid.

Thus the universities were in an advantageous position because they had relatively large staffs paid to devote themselves professionally to activities which were close to research, in places where libraries and laboratories existed. The universities were moreover increasingly committed to an ethos in which scientific and scholarly research as means of the advancement of knowledge had a very high position. Many of the members of their academic staffs and their presidents and deans had studied in Germany at a time when the universities were already making explicit provision in their budgets for the support of research. Their very notion of a university entailed the performance of research.

It may be surmised that much more money was spent on research in the universities than was spent on it in industry. In the universities, research was what later came to be called a "spin-off" from the provision for teaching. The sum might not have been as great as was desired by the academic scientists— although one does not encounter many complaints about its paucity—but because it was hidden in an "unvouched" or "unearmarked" budget, the emergent arrangements allowed the academic scientists to work on what lay in their own interests and what was prescribed by their own conviction as to what was scientifically important. Unlike the scientists in the agricultural experimental stations, they did not have a public of demanding "users," whose demand was for immediately practical but often scientifically uninteresting results. The tradition of "pure research" was taken over from the German universities, but the institutional condition for its cultivation was the structure of the universities which permitted it to be done.

They had furthermore no masters who prescribed practical or routine research for them. They were limited by their own capacities and imagination
and the demands of teaching which were not by any means always all-
consuming of their time and energy. In government and in industrial enterprises scientists could not choose their subjects of research nor were they
always free to publish their results. Again, those who did research in the
universities were at an advantage. Having a public consisting of other university teachers in their own fields, they could become famous in these fields
within the whole academic order. This was more difficult for those without
the advantage of a preestablished public and the means of communicating
with it.

All these features resulted in the increased visibility of academic research,
increased mutual awareness of members of the academic order, an increased
sense of community among academic scientists and scholars across institutional and disciplinary boundaries as well as within them. Universities became a massive presence among the objects which engaged public opinion.
They had already been visible to the educated and to some sections of the
governing classes. They were taken up by the organs of public opinion and
given more prominence as science gained in prestige. Science and the universities became almost identical to public opinion; scholarship in the humanistic and social science disciplines gained from the association. Then when the
"demand" for science increased as it did in the early decades of this century
and especially during the First World War, the universities were in the first
line to satisfy this demand. This increased the ascendancy of the universities.

The American path from 1865 to 1915 was not the only one which the
course of learning could have followed. The outcome would have been otherwise had the federal government chosen to promote science in the same way
as the French government had done in the seventeenth century through the
honors granted and the resources and provision allotted by the Académie des
sciences de Paris, or as the Soviet government had deliberately done in elevating the Academy of Sciences above the universities and by giving it
control over all research except that carried on by the various ministries. The
government of the United States, despite the widespread confidence in progress
through the "arts and sciences," was not at all inclined to do so. It had no
comprehensive program because it was believed that the "arts and sciences,"
like economic life, would develop from the initiative of private persons. Its
scientific interests were limited to very specific things such as the Coast
Survey, the Geological Survey, the Permanent Commission of the Naval
Department. The Smithsonian Institution was given to it and could have been
used for the furtherance of scientific research but the government never attempted to build it up. This is the reason why the National Academy of
Sciences, until the end of the period, scarcely had more than honorific func-

tions. Since it had no resources for the support of research, it could do little to promote it in general, or in particular directions.

In a sense, the abstention of the federal government from promoting the National Academy of Sciences into a position in which it could exercise influence by its accomplishments, example, and prestige left the way open for the academic order to come into a position of dominance. The National Academy could not even function as a meeting place as the Royal Society of London or the various German academies had done because of the large distances which separated its seat from its members. Until the creation of the National Research Council it did not even perform the advisory function to the government for which it had been expressly founded.

The Decisive Step: The Establishment of Postgraduate Studies

When the great state universities of the Middle West were created, the conduct of research was not prominent among the responsibilities which were assigned to them by legislators and public opinion. They were thought of as being primarily agents for the spread of an improving knowledge. The idea of improvement was vague and comprehensive. The improvement was not just improvement of a practical sort; it was improvement of the spirit. The universities were thought of as distributors of the best of inherited knowledge, and only very secondarily as creators of new knowledge. The creation of new knowledge was supplementary; it had to be done in the "interstices," The interest in practical improvement was not identical with an interest in research. The colleges of agriculture and mechanical arts were to be like the German mining, agricultural, animal husbandry, and medical academies, that is, technical colleges, but—unlike Germany—one of them, at least in each state with a state university, was to be attached to a university. The central part of the university was devoted to less practical knowledge. The Scottish universities were the models, as they were indeed in matters of curriculum, for the independent liberal arts colleges and the undergraduate colleges of the leading private universities of the eastern seaboard.

After the Civil War, as the reflux of young men from the German universities began in earnest, complaints were heard among them. There were complaints that the universities did not conduct research, that it was not sufficiently demanded of teachers that they should conduct research, and that consideration of accomplishments, past and prospective, in research should be given cognition and reward in appointment and promotion.

It was, however, only with the foundation of Johns Hopkins University in 1876, of Clark University in 1887 and the University of Chicago in 1892 that a very pronounced turn occurred. The foundation of Johns Hopkins University was perhaps the most decisive single event in the history of learning in the Western hemisphere. It was under the impact of competition from Johns Hopkins University and the embarrassment of comparison with Johns Hopkins that university presidents began to respond to the demands of some of their teachers to make provision in various ways for them to do research. Harvard was already astir before Johns Hopkins appeared, but the stirring did not affect President Eliot very much until Johns Hopkins threatened the reputation of Harvard. President Eliot was not opposed to research; he did say in 1869 that "the strongest and most devoted professors will contribute something to the patrimony of knowledge," but he did not move to make that easier. He simply noted that except for its observatory, "the university does not hold a single fund primarily intended to secure to men of learning the leisure and means to prosecute original researches."[1]

President Gilman, although definitely intending that Johns Hopkins should be a university like the German universities in which scientific and scholarly research was to be accorded ample opportunity, did not expect that teaching would be given a secondary position. "The university is a place for the advanced and special education of youth who have been prepared for its freedom by the discipline of a lower school." The university must have the "freedom" to do research; it has the "obligation" to teach.[2] Nonetheless, despite these qualifications, Johns Hopkins University, practically from its beginning, placed the research of its teachers in a position of unprecedented prominence. By 1890, Harvard University established a Graduate School of Arts and Sciences, meaning thereby to train young persons to do research in all fields and to have teachers who did research themselves responsible for training the graduate students. The existence of Johns Hopkins and Clark made it easier for the University of Chicago to launch itself upon its career as a university where research was the *sine qua non* of appointment and promotion and where much of the teaching was intended to be connected with research, both as training and in content.

The American universities during the half century of our concern did not divest themselves of their obligations to teach. They simply, in the second half of our period, were determined to honor accomplishment in research more than had been done hitherto and to proclaim it as a major part of their program. They generated an atmosphere of expectation that everyone in the university should do research.

They did not succeed. Not everyone did research. Then as now, there were some who did a great deal, many who did a little and some who did none. There were also some who protested plaintively or vehemently against the growing appreciation of research. Their criticisms were sometimes intertwined with the resentment of scholars in the humanities against the natural sciences, which seemed to be the epitome of all that was most detrimental to the maintenance of the traditional culture of the educated man.

In some respects a compromise was attained through division of labor. There was in the first instance a division of labor between the universities which did both research and teaching with a marked insistence on the former, and the liberal arts colleges which concentrated mainly on teaching and in which research was neither much practiced nor provided for. Within the universities, there began to emerge a division of labor between the younger teachers who taught the more elementary courses and the older teachers who taught the more advanced courses in the subject, courses which had more to do with research. (This had been observed by Max Weber when he traveled in the United States in 1904.) The younger teachers had little time for research, the older teachers had less teaching to do and their teaching was more congenial to their research. The younger teachers too were expected to do research, especially in the Middle Western state universities and in the new private universities. At universities like Harvard, Columbia, Princeton, and Yale, there were large blocks of teachers who regarded the teaching of undergraduates as the primary obligation, and who viewed uneasily the precedence which their colleagues who were more productive in research were receiving in fame and salary.

Nonetheless, the universities were not unfaithful to the obligatory function which permitted their ascendancy in the first place and which enabled the academic order to attain and maintain its dominance within the order of learning. Except for the compromise of the division of labor between liberal arts colleges on the one side and the universities on the other, the balance between teaching and research was never free from stress. It was a delicately poised equilibrium in which each part appeared to be ready to fly off centrifugally. Yet the disassociation never occurred. The equilibrium, delicate and distressing though it often was, was held within the institutional vise of the university as an institution. It was also held together by the ideal of what a university ought to be. The ideal was contained in the Germanic tradition which had been carried across the ocean by the many hundreds of young men who had studied in Germany in the last third of the eighteenth century.

The Provision of Qualified Audiences

The increase in the number of scientists and scholars and the increased prominence of their national scientific and scholarly associations and journals were marked features of the development of American learning from the 1880s to the end of the First World War, running alongside the increase in the number of scientists and scholars. The two things went hand in hand. The activities of the American Association for the Advancement of Science before the Civil War and the two decades immediately following it, like the earlier established Gesellschaft deutscher Naturforscher und Ärtzte and the British Association for the Advancement of Science had been to a large extent efforts to gain the attention, esteem and support of the larger public throughout their respective countries. They had also been intended to provide occasions for intellectual intercourse. Contact with each other within the boundaries of their loosely defined disciplines had been much desired and that is why the special sections of these societies multiplied. They had not been sufficient.

From about 1880 to 1900, the holders of doctorates from American universities and those who had studied in German universities—in increasing numbers, they were identical—became aware of the distinctiveness which they had in common as practitioners of particular disciplines. The disciplinary learned societies in economics, history, etc., which were formed in the last quarter of the century, were the expressions of a desire for a more regular and more intense intellectual intercourse which could undo the distances which had separated men of learning dispersed over a large national territory.

Scholars and scientists had become more aware that there were many other persons far off who were interested in the same phenomena, who were devoted to similar ideals of learning and of the influence of learning in public life. They increasingly desired to be in contact with each other. It was a desire which for many had been quickened by their intense intellectual experiences in the small German university towns or in university quarters of larger towns where they had found themselves in the company of a few other young men equally passionately devoted to the enhancement of their understanding and the increase in their knowledge, and where the "professor" appeared to be the very embodiment of learning in its most exalted form. This ideal appeared to be densely settled in Germany at particular places and visible too as a national presence through the existence and activities of national scientific and scholarly associations such as the Verein für Sozialpolitik. They had never had such an intense experience of intellectual activity at home in the United States. This experience left an indelible mark on their memories.

Returning to the United States for these young men had been like entering into life where, despite exciting events, the intellectual air was very thin. Those who found employment in most colleges and universities felt themselves to be nearly alone. Not many of the older generation knew the kinds of things they knew. Departments which first emerged as administrative conveniences attendant on the system of "electives" were small at most colleges and universities; there were no or few like-minded colleagues. Serious students, as serious as they themselves had been in the pursuit of learning, were very few. The "Germany-returned" Americans—to use a term parallel to the "England-returned" which became current in India—had a sense of being cut off from the source of a vital intellectual substance; but unlike the "England-returned" Indians, they were in a more invigorating environment. They felt a need not only to teach and to do research in their chosen fields but also to enjoy the experience of intellectual community. They did not repine or lose themselves in day-dreams or feelings of impotence. They set about making good their lack by their own scholarly and scientific labors and by the creation of institutions such as societies and journals which helped to fill up the empty, isolating space around them.

The organization of scientific and scholarly societies and journals from the 1880s onwards was more than an effort to confer legitimacy on and to elevate the status of the new academic professions and to increase their public influence. They were intended at least as much to sustain the intellectual morale of the young generation of academics who were not wholly at ease in the sparsely settled intellectual domain of their own country. They provided the conditions of intellectual community; they gave them a sense of the strength for scientific and scholarly progress which lay in their own numbers and powers. The journals which they founded were of course a means of communication; they were also means of reassuring themselves that there were many like themselves, carrying on sturdily and courageously. These institutions, learned societies and journals helped to sustain their faith in the value of their undertaking by bringing more impressively into their consciousness the similar interests and activities of others.

They were fortunate in living at a time when the larger movements of events before and in their own time were favorable to their projects. At the very foundation of their good fortune was the current state of Christian belief; their own seriousness about moral and intellectual things depended on it. They were still living in a time of firm Christian belief and their own falling away from acceptance of its basic theological and historical tenets in literal form did not dissolve the more general bearing and active force of character which such belief engendered. They believed in the value of exertion for the high ends of seeking an ultimate truth and of transfiguring the earth in accordance with it—in whatever sphere—and they believed that exertion brought commensurate reward. They were determined, where they had ceased to believe in the Christian interpretation of the universe and of human existence, to repair that loss by replacing it or shoring it up by scientific and scholarly knowledge, which if it did not disclose God's design, at least showed the lawfulness of the workings of nature and society.

They were fortunate too in returning to the United States at a time when the authorities in universities and colleges were beginning to look favorably on "modern subjects," at least to the extent of willingness to employ young scholars who had studied them. The departmental pattern of organization gave these young scholars, as soon as they found time for research, the opportunity to settle into the specialized investigations which their training in Germany had taught them was one of the decisive requirements of intellectual progress. The departmental organization of universities had not been designed to create local intellectual communities but it made their formation easier by bringing together in circumscribed spaces persons of overlapping and sympathetic interests.

They were fortunate too because their investigations were not costly. The amount of equipment and material needed for research was relatively slight at a time when there was little financial provision explicitly made for the support of research. With small grants or even none at all they could launch into research. Being engaged in research enabled them to keep their heads up and to consolidate their identification as scientists working in particular disciplines. It is true that they did not have the leisure and freedom of the German *Privatdozent*; they had to teach elementary courses and they had to teach more hours weekly but they also had the advantage of being paid. However unsteadily poised on the lowest rungs of the academic ladder, they were at the beginning of an academic career. The increased number of posts in a department and the gradation of ranks offered the promise—not certain but at least possible—of advancement. A young scholar or scientist was no longer a school teacher, an assistant master serving at the pleasure of the head master or president. The college or university teacher was no longer a person of no consequence, a "hand," taken on at short notice and dismissible at equally short notice. He was beginning to become a "college teacher" or a "university teacher." There was a new dignity in this status, a new conception of the self, of its powers, privileges, and obligations. "Practical men" might have spoken disparagingly of them but they themselves often felt that they had embarked on a lofty calling.

These things would not have been possible if there had not been another closely allied change. Presidents of colleges had been imperious and autocratic before the Civil War; they were the chief agents of their governing bodies; all their teachers were their "assistants." Powerful though the presidents were in their colleges and universities, they had not been powerful on behalf of learning; they had regarded themselves as being in charge of schools where the moral character of selected youths was to be formed. It is exactly at this point that from about 1870 onwards a major change occurred. College and university presidents remained powerful but now some began to exercise their power on behalf of learning. There were only a few. Daniel Coit Gilman was the first and foremost; Andrew White was another; G. Stanley Hall and William Rainey Harper were two more under their influence. Charles Eliot moved in the same direction. Like their juniors they had become persuaded that the life of learning had become one of the highest vocations of man.

Just as the young teacher could feel himself at the beginning of an academic career, full of potentialities, so the president too acquired a similar sense of his own potentialities. This was the time of the great magnates of industry and commerce who appeared to educated opinion to represent, despite the roughness of their methods, the forward surge of the country towards greatness. University and college presidents imbibed some of this sense of moving with the powerful wave of moral progress and national greatness. The presidents shared the confidence of leading businessmen, politicians, and publicists in the grandeur of the collective national undertaking. Their particular jurisdiction was the world of learning and they benefited from the grave approbation which was accorded to it by many of the leading figures of American society. There were various "anti-intellectual" tendencies in the United States—fundamentalist Christians, rough and vulgar politicians, Gradgrind-like businessmen, cultural philistines, and the ebbing reservoir of the genteel tradition—but they did not dominate the newly forming and reforming universities. The forthcomingness of state legislatures in the Middle and Far West and the philanthropic largesse of great businessmen assured the university presidents that the currents were running in their direction. Despite the bruises of occasional altercations with politicians, businessmen, and presidents, university teachers did not think that they were confronted by immovable obstacles.

The "Germany-returned" young American scientists and scholars had not returned to a barren waste. Even the hindrances to their progress were in flux and they took heart from their awareness of like mind and situation. They knew that there were others, facing similar problems and possessing a similar resolve to prove themselves in the world of learning and to bring that learning to bear on the shortcomings of their society. They gravitated towards the universities which had such presidents and which had already attracted a few scholars and scientists a little senior to them. They saw the lamps of the German tradition burning in them, dimly in some, more brightly in others.

The Formation of a Hierarchy of Universities

Within the ascendancy of the universities over the rest of the system of learning, a few universities began to attain ascendancy within the national academic order. The activities of the new generation were not evenly distributed in space. Scientific papers and learned dissertations did not grow equally in all parts of the academic order; they were not equally addressed to all parts or areas. The audience was as unevenly distributed as those who addressed them. There were certain points of greater concentration of scientific and scholarly activity, certain points from which communications emanated and at which they were received. Certain places came to stand out in the cognitive map. These were either the new universities like Johns Hopkins, Clark, Chicago, and Stanford, the slowly self-transforming older universities of the Eastern seaboard or the state universities of the Middle West and California. These were the centers, the influence of which helped to create the intellectual consensus about problems and procedures in each field. The consensus in a given field about what was true and important emanated from the center. Those fields which did not possess a dominant center tended to be more nondescript. The development of a discipline depended on its having one or more centers where outstanding individuals worked as teachers of outstanding students and as investigators whose work was carefully studied and creatively emulated.

The emergence of a central constellation made up of a small number of centers helped to make the academic order into a community. This was a necessary condition of the ascendancy of the academic order in the order of learning. There was practically never a complete concentration of intellectual production and of eminence based on it in some particular subject in a single university. One university might have been ahead of the others in the number of its eminent teachers and investigators and in the number of Ph.D.s granted in a particular field but it never could have a monopoly. Even when the University of Chicago awarded 24 percent of its Ph.D.s in mathematics, there were still many eminent mathematicians at other universities and three-fourths of the doctorates in mathematics were awarded by universities other than the University of Chicago. There was then not a single institutional center but rather a constellation of centers which were in competition with each other and which were also at the same time infusing their viewpoint into the peripheral universities.

Peregrination from university to university was a common pattern in the United States, even though the American academic order never adopted the German custom of the *Wanderjahre*. A student who went on for graduate studies seldom stayed for his postgraduate studies at the institution where he had taken his first degree. Sometimes a graduate student took the master's degree at one university and the doctorate at another. Then if he succeeded in entering the academic profession, he relatively rarely did so at the university where he had taken his advanced degree. As he moved ahead in his career, he also moved from one university to another. American universities did not have the degree of "inbreeding" which was characteristic of the ancient British universities; the greater egalitarianism of the American ethos permitted a young man from the center to settle more easily into an institution a little removed from it than appears to have been the case in Britain at that time. Of course the movement of individuals among universities once they entered their careers was easier in the United States because there were more universities than there were in Great Britain or Germany, and because the student bodies and the numbers of teaching posts available were growing more rapidly in the United States than elsewhere.

These movements within the central constellation and between the centers and the concentric peripheral circles consolidated the collective self-image of the academic order and the position of the central constellation within it. It led many of its members to conceive of themselves as parts of a mighty regiment, somewhat distinct from the rest of American society, contributing to it, criticizing it, supported by it, and harassed by it. It also induced in academies an image of themselves as separated from the other intellectual institutions of the learned and the literary worlds—from industrial laboratories and governmental scientific services with whom academics had only irregular and uneven contacts, and from the world of artists and literary men with whom they had very little contact, even in New York and Chicago.

The formation of a sense of collective identity was nurtured by intra-academic movements which gave those who participated in them a wider experience of the academic order and of their own scientific and scholarly communities. The result was a common universe of discourse. At least as important in the maintenance of the common universe of discourse within the scientific and scholarly disciplinary communities was the preponderance of the production coming from the central constellation. Separated by fields and specialization within fields, as they were coming to be by the end of the century, they were also bound together across institutional boundaries by their reading of common bodies of scientific and scholarly literature. The multiplication of journals did not work against this. In every field some journals were more prized and more read than others and, in any case, the numbers of journals in our period did not so greatly exceed the reading capacity of individual scholars and scientists as they have since done.

The elevation of a department to a central position was frequently the result of the towering accomplishments of one person. The simultaneous elevation of four or five departments within a major branch of learning or eight or ten in a university as a whole made that university into a center to which particular attention was paid. Graduate students came and appointments were sought and accepted. Yet, even though the outcome was the eminence of the institution as a whole—vaguely perceived—it was at bottom the work of outstanding individuals.

Columbia University was one such center. In anthropology, for example, it took the lead because the figure of Franz Boas towered above all others. From the department of anthropology at Columbia University there issued a steady stream of learned publications and distinguished research students. Boas' own work was not only an enduring contribution to knowledge; it was also a model for other workers in the field. Anthropology had existed in the United States before Boas but the coming into existence of a department which trained future anthropologists and formed men like Kroeber, Lowie, and Sapir, each of whom in his turn became a point of crystallization of anthropological study, transformed the loose "consciousness of kind" into the sense of being part of a discipline of universal validity. H. L. Moore and Seligman in economics, Burgess in political science, Dewey in philosophy, Morgan in genetics, Charles Beard and James Harvey Robinson in history, were a few of those who made their departments and Columbia University as a whole into a center.

Chicago was another such center. Moore in mathematics, Michelson and Millihan in physics, Loeb in physiology, Manley in English, Thomas and Park in sociology, Freund and Merriam in political science, Shorey in classics, were the individuals whose light was diffused over the rest of their institution. Harvard, Johns Hopkins, the University of California at Berkeley were other such centers. Slightly peripheral were Wisconsin, Illinois, Michigan, Yale, Princeton and Pennsylvania, at varying distances from the center.

Sociology at Chicago illustrates the role of a center of research and training. Sociology was a "movement" of the mind before it became a discipline with a substantive body of literature, which as it grew academically, consolidated the subject and strengthened the sense of identity of its practitioners. The department of sociology of the University of Chicago under W. I. Thomas and Robert Park was crucial in the process. It was in its field, what the department of anthropology at Columbia University was in anthropology. Nonetheless, "Chicago sociology" like "Columbia anthropology" never monopolized all the activity in its field. What it did was to draw out and give emphasis to certain themes and techniques; it focused attention and supplied a common conception through the works which its members produced.

Johns Hopkins University and Harvard University in historical studies, Johns Hopkins, Harvard, Chicago, Columbia, and Wisconsin in economics, performed similar roles for their subjects. In the social sciences as in other subjects, the development of academic departments turned heterogeneous and somewhat inchoate bodies of intellectual activities and beliefs into disciplines.

Centers did not always remain centers, and within the constellation at the center particular institutions waxed and waned. Subsidiary status did not always persist; some of the lesser institutions became independent centers in their own right, each sharing and reinforcing the common culture of their subject and developing its own distinctive features.

Academic Loyalties: Center and Periphery

Beneath the publicly visible arguments for the legitimacy of their disciplines as bodies of knowledge of universal validity and the ultimate benefits each would confer on their society and humanity more generally, there was a sensitive institutional parochialism among American academics. Like all loyalties to a collectivity which are not equally felt, it was very unevenly present among academics. Young teachers recently recruited could not be expected to have the same loyalty to their university as those who had been there for a longer time. Those who remained year after year and who rose to prominence by office, seniority, and accomplishment in "their" universities and colleges, were more possessed by it. Just as an emulative pride and sensitivity about the reputation and good name of their college or university had existed even before the "cognitive revolution" which spread and deepened after the Civil War, sentiments of loyalty in the president and the professors were touched by the standing of their university as a center of scientific and scholarly endeavor. When William Rainey Harper was founding and presiding over the University of Chicago, he clearly aimed to have an institution which, while specifically "American" would be in the same class as the German universities which were his standard. Daniel Coit Gilman had wished to do the same. They wanted their universities to be "the best." The presidents of the universities bore the responsibility for making their universities as "great" as they could be; the professors wished to make their departments as "great" as they could be. For the former, "greatness" was not only greatness in intellectual accomplishment, it was also greatness in public reputation and in the financial benefits of such a reputation. Among the professors, aspiration for the greatness of their departments might have been intertwined with personal vanity and corporate pride, but they believed that the aspiration could be gratified only by intellectual achievement. This meant addressing themselves to other scientists and scholars in the United States and abroad. These were by now mainly in universities. The self-awareness of the academic stratum of the intellectual world was thus made more acute, as well as the awareness of the hierarchy of center and periphery.

Eminence in the larger academic order could be attained only by the achievements of departments, which for individual teachers meant their own departments and for the president and some teachers the achievements of many departments within the university. Funds for research supplied mainly by patrons outside the universities were scarcer before the First World War than they became after it; they had to come usually from the internal budget of the university. As university presidents became sensitive to the extent to which scientific distinction aided them in their efforts to "build" their universities, this in turn induced willingness to support distinguished appointments. Many appointments of scholars and scientists who were less than eminent had to be made to provide for the routine teaching of the elements of the various subjects, but at the level of professorships, the more ambitious and successful departments were enabled by their proud and aspiring presidents to attract the best available scholars or scientists, given the resources at their disposal. Departments and universities which were content to do no more than "fill the slots" allotted to them sank in the hierarchy. Some institutions with more limited resources or those in which emulative institutional patriotism was weak did so content themselves. Such institutions "contracted out" of the race; they accepted their peripherality, although even in such universities there were sometimes outstanding departments.

Only a small number of universities were determined to be at the forefront and thus to live up to the German standard. They were determined to be so, not only for the benefit of their students, who would gain by being instructed, supervised, and inspired by the most outstanding workers in their respective subjects, and not only for the stimulus which the individual members would receive from their outstanding colleagues, but also because their personal pride demanded the distinction of association with a "great" department and a "great" university.

The effort to be among the best, as institutions taken as wholes, or as departments, was spurred by the growing prominence of research. As long as universities and colleges confined themselves to teaching, to the formation of character and the "molding of men," they were visible only locally and to those who had direct experience of them. There were few easily and widely discernible marks of accomplishment resulting from such pedagogical activities. Achievements in research were publicly discernible, not so much by the larger public but by the public constituted by other workers in the same or nearby fields. The existence of national scientific and scholarly communities and the organizations and organs in which they were given form aided this comparison and assessment. Through publication of the results of research, individuals and their works were placed on a stage which enhanced their visibility. Assessments of particular works and their authors were consolidated into the assessments of departments and whole institutions. Their colleagues at other universities were more effectively present in the minds of those academics who did research than was the case of those whose affections were given in the first place to teaching. The audience of the latter was the student body, locally circumscribed; the audience of the former was national and international. The translocal scholarly and scientific communities, loose and indistinct in outline though they were, were more palpable than were the ties of those in colleges and universities which confined themselves to teaching.

The generation of central and peripheral universities was conditional on the existence of the translocal academic communities. The stratification of works, individuals, departments, and institutions was a result of the emphasis on research. Some individuals withdrew from the competition and some never entered it. Others, at or nearer to the center, were sensitive to their reputation and were close enough to distinction to believe in the value of such prominence. This belief was especially effective when appointments were to be made, and there was an opportunity to raise the prestige of one's university by attracting to it a distinguished scientist or scholar. The assortment of the universities into the ranks of a national hierarchy was affected by the policies of university presidents and professors who deliberately intended to maintain or raise the position of the peripheral institutions. Self-conscious efforts were made to get ahead of others through decisions to bring about the appointment of persons of eminence.

The American university teachers and administrators developed in this period the policy of "going after" a man, of making a deliberate effort to bring to their universities the present or prospectively best scholars and scientists in their respective fields. The practice of *Berufung* had already been in long-standing use in Germany when it was taken up in the United States. The new universities tried to win to their service the best of the newer men of the older universities. It was relatively easy for Johns Hopkins, Chicago, and Stanford to leap to the forefront when the other universities of the country were slumbering, and outstandingly ambitious and talented younger persons were suffering from the restraints imposed upon them by their more traditional universities. The older universities rallied; they made efforts to satisfy those who wished to do research, and to bring back the best of those they had lost. They became alarmed about the competition of the newer universities like Johns Hopkins, Chicago, and Stanford with the once securely preeminent like Harvard and Columbia.

The role of American university presidents energetically determined to enhance the reputation and hence to build the fortunes, intellectual and material, of their universities, stood in contrast with the practice of the older English universities which were so confident of their superiority that they did not have to exercise themselves to attract the leading scientists and scholars.

In Great Britain the pattern of an academic career from the 1870s to the First World War was relatively simple: to graduate from Oxford, Cambridge, or London, then to go to one of the provincial universities like Manchester or Liverpool for a time and then, for those who reached the highest eminence, to return as professors to Oxford, Cambridge, or London. The provincial universities could compete only for scholars or scientists who had not yet come to the peak of accomplishment; once they did so all the advantages lay with the three universities in the south. There was no such predetermined path and no such unchanging hierarchy in the United States and competition for the best men was therefore more intense. The vice-chancellors of the modern British universities either did not have or did not exercise the powers of the American university presidents. In this matter, the American academic order was more like that which prevailed in Germany. Friedrich Althoff in Prussia was much like an American university president in his solicitous intrusiveness. In some of the German states, the initiative was borne by a few senior professors who were determined to attract to their university the best men available anywhere in Germany. They were also the beneficiaries of a tradition inherited from the time of the princely states when princes vied with each other for the greater glory of an eminent university. There was nothing like the American or the German system in France where the Sorbonne so far outdistanced the universities of the provinces that they reconciled themselves to their inferior status. Only the University of Toulouse once sought to break out of that condition, largely on the initiative of Paul Sabatier, but in the end the effort was not successful. In consequence of this, and despite the fact that the national university system was a legal reality—unlike the other major Western countries of the period—the stimulus of institutional emulation was absent. The preponderance of the *grandes écoles*, the Collège de France and the École pratique des hautes études prevented the universities from attaining the ascendancy in France which they obtained in the United States and Germany and to a lesser extent in the United Kingdom.

None of the emulative actions of the American universities would have occurred without this passionate attachment to their universities and departments on the part of presidents and professors and a jealous concern for their reputations. It was a parochiality which was perfectly compatible with intellectual attachment to scientific and scholarly communities running far beyond the boundaries of the individual universities.

Ancillary Institutions

The centers were strengthened in their ascendancy by their university presses. The Johns Hopkins University Press, the University of Chicago Press, Cornell University Press, Columbia University Press, Harvard University Press, and the University of California Press were at first the organs for the publication of the works of the teachers of these universities and of the learned series and journals which they edited. From the last years of the nineteenth century, the universities at the center of the university system were able to focus the attention of the American world of learning on their publications. The university presses did not cause the centrality of these institutions but they gave them additional prominence and authority. The various series, such as the Johns Hopkins Studies in History and Political Science, the Columbia University Studies in Public Law and Political Science, the Harvard Oriental Series, and so on, offered opportunities for the newer members of the various

disciplines to show their results to the world; they also underscored the identification of these younger scholars with the institutions where they were
trained and where some of them held appointments. These publications coupled
the scholarly and scientific eminence of the institutions and departments with
the names of particular scholars. They thickened the lines which defined the
centers and which ran from them to the periphery.

The transactions and proceedings of these academies which managed to
survive the general displacement of academies as learned institutions could not
compete with the specialized learned journals emanating from the universities
and published by university presses, scientific and scholarly societies, and
sometimes by commercial enterprises under academic editorship. The increasingly intense flow of learned communications drew little which originated
under the auspices of the academies; amateur scientists and scholars formed a
diminished proportion of their audience. Industrial research in so far as it
became established in this period likewise contributed little to the flow of
learned communication. In the particular fields in which they specialized,
independent museums such as the Field Museum and the American Museum of
Natural History produced works which were attended to and respected. Some
parts of the governmental scientific services such as the Bureau of Ethnology
published reports which became part of the standard literature of their subjects.
Taken as a whole, the network of scientific and scholarly communications was
filled with publications arising in the universities. The institutions which made
up the nodal points of the network were often owned by universities or by
scientific and scholarly societies which were made up largely of persons
following academic careers. In short, the universities were filling up much of
the space of the world of learning and they were also expanding the space.

The earliest learned societies, in contrast with the academies, formed around
specialized disciplines; they were relatively independent of universities. They
represented an effort by amateurs and scientific and scholarly organizers to
break out of the boundaries set by locality and to reach across space into
national communities. Increasingly they were taken over by academics, in
consonance with the ascendancy of universities as centers of science and
scholarship. They were not as closely bound to particular universities as the
university presses were but they served a similar function. They became the
periodic gathering places of academics from the various universities. They
too became organs of academic communication.

Specialization

The triumph of the university over the amateur was made possible by the
greater resources in wealth and numbers of the university and by their combi-

nation with teaching. It was also made possible by the emergence of specialization as a requirement of scientific and scholarly achievement. Systematic, especially postgraduate, training in the universities was more conducive to specialization than was the self-education of the amateur. The specialized academic had other specialized colleagues to speak to; his colleagues expected the detailed mastery of numerous minute details and of a large number of publications dealing with very small subjects. He had large collections of scientific periodicals near his laboratory and scholarly periodicals in his library. He would be regarded as slothful if he did not show mastery of all this matter. The amateur following some other occupation and proceeding at a more leisurely pace could not cover the same ground at the same speed. Specialization required speed of work which was not in the tradition of the amateur man of learning. Speed was being rendered necessary as the numbers of persons working on a limited range of closely linked or similar problems within a relatively narrow range of specialization increased. If one wished to receive acknowledgment of a scientific discovery one could not allow one's results to lie in drawers. The need for a feeling of achievement, the desire for recognition, loyalty to one's department and university, personal ambition, the scientific ethos all pressed for publication as speedily as possible. The humanistic disciplines were less hurried.

The new academic science and scholarship, even with the distractions of teaching and administration, were more productive in quantitative terms than the leisurely mode of proceeding of the amateur. The more productive specialists became, the more imperative specialization became, for otherwise they would not have been able to master the narrowing and multiplying sector of the body of scientific literature. The existence of new journals and of extended numbers of contributors which the creation of new journals brought with it enlarged the body of literature on particular topics; the enlargement of the holdings of university libraries likewise made the task of "keeping up with the literature" more demanding. This could be done only at the cost of general reading.

Specialization had its lights and shadows. Its lights were the lights of seriousness of purpose, of the intention to make a contribution, that is, to be acknowledged by others qualified to judge whether a given piece of work added to the body of significant knowledge in the field and whether it made further progress possible. The growing conviction that "truth always lies in the details" meant that the details had to be explored with increasing thoroughness. The model of German *Fachmenschentum* lay ready to hand; to be a serious scientist or scholar required that one be a *Fachmann*. The word dilettante became a term of scorn. There was a stern moral overtone to specialization. It meant no trifling, no self-indulgence, getting on with the job. It was uncongenial to false pride and all-knowingness. Specialization was quite consistent with the secularized Protestant Puritanism of the quarter of a century which preceded the First World War.

It should not be overlooked that many of the scholars and scientists of the generation which came into American academic life in the 1880s and 1890s were extremely widely read in philosophy and literature. Despite the current praise of the specialist which was heard everywhere in Germany, the breadth of reading of the German professors appeared to the young Americans to be overpowering. William James' description of Dilthey in one of his letters home in 1867 spoke for the thousands who came after him. Many of the young Americans themselves had already read with omnivorous zeal before they went to Germany; they had already studied modern literature and classics as well as scientific subjects. In Germany they sometimes became intoxicated with reading, not just in their own subjects but over a very wide range. The aftermath of religious doubt deepened their philosophical interests. In later years many of those who had studied in Germany retained their knowledge of German; this too kept them from narrowness since the ideal of *Bildung* had not been wholly vanquished by the idea of *Fachmenschentum*. Nonetheless, specialization was making its way, under the shadow of a narrowing range of attention. The departmental system aided the progress of specialization by permitting a measure of specialization in teaching, but teaching was never as pronounced as the degree of specialization in research. All teachers had to teach undergraduates and such teaching could never be as narrow or as intense as the focus of attention demanded by research.

Specialization in research went hand in hand with the extension of the radius of interest beyond the boundaries of one's own university or college. Research, in contrast to teaching, even when it was less specialized than it later turned out to be, would have enforced more attention to colleagues in other universities in one's own and other countries, wherever, in fact, similar research was being done. The individual investigator who wished to follow closely the most recent literature on his problem was forced into a national and international community—or subcommunity—and the hierarchy of eminence which that entailed. The names of institutions were never completely severed from the names of individuals and the deference accorded to individuals for their respective achievements was diffused onto their institutions. In this way specialization in research supported the translocal elements of the scientific and scholarly community and its stratification. The specialization of research which required an outward direction of attention led more easily to the definition of the centers of the order to which attention was directed and from which models of topics to be investigated, observations and interpretations and standards of achievement were drawn, applied and built upon.

The images in which centers were defined were compounded from achievements in many different fields of research. From many specialized fields, a reputation of the institution as a whole was generalized. Specialists did not form their own image of the center only from its eminence in their own specialized field of research. Specialization did not result in the fragmentation of the academic order, although it did reduce the magnitude of a culture common to most academics. In some respects it consolidated the academic order and it reinforced its hegemony over amateurs and intellectual institutions outside the universities.

The Formation of a National System

Until the formation of the Johns Hopkins University, the learned world in the United States was rather inchoate. It had no center, it had no hierarchy. It was differentiated enough. There were governmental scientific bureaus and the bare beginnings of research in a few industrial enterprises; there were very few learned societies or associations, few scientific or scholarly journals; there was one national quasi-governmental academy and a number of academies of local jurisdiction, two old academies which purported to be national; there were museums and a few large libraries and there were many universities and colleges. It was all an amorphous agglomeration of institutions and activities. They were not only scant in number and widely dispersed territorially but the connections between them were infrequent and of marginal importance.

There were a number of outstanding individual organizers, such as Asa Gray, Louis Agassiz, Joseph Henry, and Simon Newcomb. There were a few outstanding individuals in science and scholarship. No single institution or institutional order predominated; in so far as the organizers thought that there should be predominance they assigned that role to the National Academy of Sciences or to the Smithsonian Institution. They thought it should recognize and honor past achievements and give advice to government on matters which involved science and scientific technology; they also thought it should guide and encourage scientists towards certain fields and problems by its rewards and declarations. They did not plan for or foresee the ascendancy of the academic order.

The appearance on the scene of Johns Hopkins, Clark, and Chicago universities changed the scene in an unpremeditated way. Governmental scientific institutions receded from their previous relative prominence into the performance of mainly practical services and surveys. Governmental scientific institutions were not put forth as rivals to universities once the universities struck out on their new paths. They became uncompetitive institutions doing things which universities did not do or they became ancillary to the universities, offering employment to their graduates and facilities for publication of their research. Their work lost the prominence which it had enjoyed when it was exceeded in volume and at least equaled or surpassed in quality by the products of academic research in the fields in which they both worked. There were, moreover, very many fields from which governmental scientific institutions abstained, and in which therefore universities had a free field.

At the turn of the century, the establishment of the Carnegie Institution in Washington seemed to present the opportunity for an alternative type of dominant order, namely one that centered on independent research institutions. The aspiration could not be fulfilled. The new institution had nothing from which to grow, it had practically no similar institutions for alliance and the growth of a sense of community, and it was not part of an intellectually self-sustaining order in the way in which universities were. There were just too few of them to provide effective competition to the academic order. The subsequent establishment of the Rockefeller Institute for Medical Research added a very productive new center, but the two together were not enough to serve as a point of crystallization. Independent research institutions as constituents of an autonomous and dominant order within the whole order of learning had no precedent. The Kaiser-Wilhelm Gesellschaft was still to be established when the Carnegie Institution was founded. The Physikalisch-technische Reichsanstalt was largely governmental as was the National Physical Laboratory. The Royal Institution, distinguished though some of its associates were, never presented a pattern which was recognized by public opinion as an example of how scientific research and teaching should be organized.

The universities could be self-sustaining by re-incorporating into themselves their best qualified graduates. There were already many universities and their very existence challenged and supported those who would reform them. The universities had to be reformed before they could ascend to preponderance but their prior existence in considerable numbers gave substance to the belief that they were endowed with the power of endurance. In other countries universities had been reformed; in the United Kingdom, royal commissions were helping along the internally generated processes of improvement; in Germany, there were the accomplishments of Humboldt. Some awareness of the benefits of these reforms encouraged Americans to think that existing universities did not have to remain as they had been or that the new ones should be what the older ones had been.

The universities had another advantage over the independent research institutions. Although each section of the university was specialized in its interests and activities, the university taken as a whole covered the entire range of learning. There was therefore always an opportunity for a specialist whose interest impinged on an adjacent or occasionally remote field to seek guidance from a colleague in that field. Research institutions, private and governmental, were designed to cover a narrower range of topics than the universities and they were therefore less attractive to the best products of the universities. Their specialization also diminished their status; the prestige of specialization was great but not unequivocally. With all respect for specialization as a form of moral self-discipline and as a more efficient way of doing research, the older ideal of breadth of perspective was still very vital. The standing of specialized research institutions suffered accordingly.

The industrial research laboratories were even less well qualified to compete with the universities. They were very few in number, relatively small in size; they were specialized within a narrow range of specialization; they did not accord freedom of publication to their scientists; and they were for the most part concentrated in applied or practical research. They were regarded as serving the standard of profitability rather than an ideal of the selfless pursuit of truth. They were regarded in public opinion as less worthy of deference than the universities.

The Dependence of the Nonacademic Periphery on the Academic Center

In agriculture, where governmental science reached its highest point, agricultural experimental stations which in the course of time did distinguished work, had to await the ascendancy of the universities before they could become effective. The first agricultural experimental stations more or less coincided with the foundation of the Johns Hopkins University. The first land-grant colleges preceded it by about a decade. Both the land-grant colleges and the agricultural experimental stations were in some measure the result of the same ideals as had inspired those who created the new type of university. These ideals had been seen—or were thought to be seen—in real embodiment in German practices. Even before the Civil War, these ideals were being argued for—with direct reference to the German universities—by persons like Evan Pugh and Samuel Johnson; they believed that scientific results such as had been achieved in the German universities could contribute to the improvement of the quality of agriculture in the United States. Yet until the new type of university was well underway, these two new types of institutions—agricultural colleges and agricultural experimental stations—scarcely advanced. Until the Hatch Act of 1887 was passed, there was little opportunity for research in the few existing agricultural experimental stations. In the agricultural schools of the land-grant colleges and the state universities, teaching was the main thing and there was little time for research. Neither their first staff members nor their public "believed" in science with the ardent conviction which led to its application. The farmers who wanted their services really knew nothing about what fundamental scientific research could contribute to their farming activity. They wanted information about the quality of the seeds they purchased and about the fertility of their soil. They did not seek scientific research: they sought only testing by specific and reliable methods. They thought that agricultural colleges should provide practical training in farming.

The administrative enterprisers like Eugene Davenport, William A. Henry, and Eugene W. Hilgard, spent much time trying to develop interest in and appreciation of the agricultural experimental stations among farmers and particularly among the leaders of farmers' organizations. They were trying to create the demand for the results of science which they were not yet in a position to deliver, partly because they did not have the scientists, who were in short supply, and did not have the money to employ them and to give them the resources which they needed for research.

When, after 1887, money became more plentiful, they turned to the universities for the scientists. The scientists whom they brought in were affected by the new ethos of the American universities; they were offended by the expectation that they should do tests and analyses, or manage model farms. They shared the ideals of the pious pioneers, Pugh and Johnson. They wanted to do scientific research and to be regarded as scientists; they were offended by the contemptuous attitude towards them of the teachers in the humanities and sciences in the state universities to which they were members, just as they were offended by the layman's belief that they were simply analysts. The ideal of the university as a place of fundamental learning gripped them and they wanted to conform to its implicit demands.

The entry of the United States Department of Agriculture into the promotion of agricultural research and the bonds which were established among the younger scientists on the staffs of the agricultural experimental stations—through the formation of sections of the American Association for the Advancement of Science and of specialized scientific societies and through the creation of journals—reinforced the pressure of this ideal. This made them more sensible of their being scientists. Their conception of themselves as scientists was strengthened by their attendance at conferences and by the reading of scientific journals, and this fortified their attachment to their scientific ideals. It may be mentioned in this connection that Alfred C. True, the head of the Office of Experimental Stations in the United States Department of Agriculture, had been a classical scholar at Wesleyan before he became an administrator vigorously promoting scientific research in agriculture. His predecessor was Wilbur Atwater, a chemist trained in the German universities.

The forward movement of basic scientific research, indicated by the Adams Act (1906)—originally drafted by True—whereby the federal government allocated to each state $30,000 for "original" scientific research, bore witness to the ascendancy of the standards of the university over the scientific activities of extra-academic institutions. Adams himself, before he became a congressman, had been a student at the University of Wisconsin, where he had imbibed the belief in the indispensability of science to the progress of mankind. It was "the influence of the institutional values of the scientific disciplines which sanctioned and shaped the ambitions of the American scientists and administrators involved in promoting the Adams Act."[3]

The Department of Agriculture provided a center for these scientists who felt themselves cut off from the academic center. It gave them the experience of solidarity and consensus with like-minded persons; it embodied the ideal to which they were devoted. But they could not have been what they were without the presence of the university. They could not, for one thing, have had a wholly separate system of science from that cultivated in the universities. They were trained in universities, some of them had taught in universities, the basic sciences on which they drew were produced in universities, and the universities represented to them the realization of the scientific ideal. They wanted the approbation of their colleagues within their own scientific disciplines. Their chief scientific achievements in genetics and plant pathology were offshoots of the science of the universities:

> The leading experiment station figures never doubted that ultimate progress, expressed either in terms of farm practice or absolute knowledge, could come only through a willing adherence to the standards accepted by the academic scientists of France and Germany.[4]

Countercurrents to Academic Ascendancy

The story of the ascension of the academic order is not one of even and unimpeded progress along a single front. There were contrary movements in public opinion and within the learned world against the dominance of the universities, and against the major universities which were the most visible parts of the academic dominance. The universities were criticized by radicals for being too subservient to the earthly powers and by conservatives for being too critical of them; they were criticized by "practical" men for being too remote in their interests from the ordinary business of daily life and by men of letters for being too close to it. Members of more rustic universities criticized the universities of the Eastern seaboard. Specialization and narrowness, "utilitarianism," triviality and the "ivory tower," the reactionary support of capitalism and irresponsible radicalism, excessive secularism and excessive piety, were among the charges made against the universities. The criticisms which have been made in recent years have nothing original in them; they have repeated, with greater acerbity, criticisms which were asserted seventy-five years ago.

There was a kernel of truth in all these accusations. There were features of the American universities to which, expressed less pejoratively, these criticisms applied. The American universities were sometimes subservient to external powers who thought that university teachers taught doctrines subversive of existing institutions and arrangements. The cases of Edward Ross at Stanford, Scott Nearing at Pennsylvania, Louis Levine at Montana, and Charles Beard and McKeen Cattell at Columbia show that these criticisms were not baseless. At the same time, the universities also gave their hospitality to stringent critics of the existing order such as Thorstein Veblen, John Dewey, Richard Ely, Simon Patten, and their numerous intellectual progeny whose ideas contributed markedly to the collectivist transformation of American society in the half century which followed ours. Those businessmen and publicists who thought that "the universities" were preaching "socialism" exaggerated but they were not wholly off the mark. The American universities also performed all sorts of trivial activities from semicommercial football spectacles and numerous practical programs with little respectable intellectual content, to worthy but distracting activities in extramural teaching and service. Yet, in the half century between the Civil War and the end of the First World War, these criticisms and diversions did not deflect the universities from the course on which they had been launched by the zeal for learning of the "Germany-returned" generation and the attendant circumstances in learning and society to which it adapted itself. They withstood critics, opponents and rivals, and developed, among other things in the years before the First World War, economic theory, Oriental studies, sociology, genetics, theoretical physics and the most recondite branches of mathematics.

Successful as the universities were in outdistancing all and gaining intellectual dominion over the alternative modes of organization for the cultivation—both in discovery and transmission—of learning, they were less successful in their relation with alternative modes of thought and expression. Whereas their organizational rivals fell into the places "to which they had been called by God," their intellectual rivals did not take the ascent of the universities so well. Academies, amateurs, librarians, officials of learned societies, directors of independent research institutions, governmentally employed scientists took the ascendancy of the universities with good grace. Priests and clergy, bohemians, socialists, literary men and artists, mystics and devotees of the occult were not so reconciled. The opposition was never unified, even within each of its constituent currents. The Christian rivals were not unified against the universities since there were so many Christians within; the populists were not wholly unified since there were so many populists within the universities. There were even a few novelists and poets in the universities, although their tasks were to do research and to teach from the general body of learning. There were mystics and pantheists in the university, but they had to do science and scholarship. Artistic expression and communion with the deity did not fall within the terms of reference of the university; those who practiced them had to do so avocationally. The university had no place for their kinds of activity on its agenda. The radicals and the bohemians were excluded. Both were held at arm's length and prevented from entering the universities or were in this period extruded from them if they did succeed in gaining entrance.

The profession of letters would have been in more severe conflict with the universities but for a spontaneously achieved division of labor. The universities studied literature historically and philologically in a scholarly way; men of letters wrote of contemporary literature and contemporary authors. The universities studied philology, they edited texts, they wrote historical works about genres, traditions, epochs, and individual authors of the past; the men of letters were generally less interested in these things. For a time there was a truce or an alliance when the men of letters, such as Ellery Sedgwick and Paul Elmer More, were still predominantly devoted to the genteel tradition. Novelists very seldom treated universities or the subjects dealt with by universities. The break took place first in the outer areas of the republic of letters. But as the period ended the members of university departments of English and modern languages and literature began to deal with contemporary works. Men of letters, particularly H. L. Mencken, became aggressively scornful of universities and of university teachers. A conflict broke out. The academics were generally against "modern" literature, the men of letters were generally for it. Students of literature within the universities, although much criticized from outside, were themselves critical of important features of the universities. Some of them bitterly criticized the scientific and scholarly side of university activity. They were against graduate research and for undergraduate teaching. They thought that scientific methods were "dehumanizing" in their effects.

In literature, unlike religion, the external critics of the university were ultimately triumphant—but not in our period. Scholarship triumphed over the genteel tradition and then, after the Second World War, scholarship itself was shaken by "modernism" which ended by bringing the bohemian outlook into the universities. But this belongs to a later chapter.

Irving Babbitt was a scholar who belonged to the ascendant academic order, but he was hostile towards the scientism and utilitarianism which he saw in the universities. He was anti-utilitarian. This he had in common with the exponents of the genteel tradition who really did not like the research activities of the graduate schools and who were committed to the undergraduate schools. The survivors of the genteel tradition became the defenders of "the humanities" within the universities, and they continued their defensiveness against the sciences, technology, and the social sciences.

Agents and Beneficiaries of Cognitive Expansion

The severity of their critics, internal and external, did not move the universities from the path into which they had moved with the foundation of Johns Hopkins University, Clark University, and the University of Chicago. Columbia University and Harvard regrouped their forces and moved in the same direction. Yale did the same. They were joined by Leland Stanford University, the University of Michigan, and the University of California; the Universities of Illinois, Wisconsin and Indiana were scarcely behind their sister-universities in the Middle and Far West. Only Clark University fell out of the forward movement but that was not because its beliefs were in disaccord with those of the ascendant academic order.

There was a great force of opinion behind this movement. This drift of opinion was towards the appreciation of knowledge, particularly knowledge of a scientific character. There was general agreement that knowledge could be accepted as knowledge only if it rested on empirical evidence, rigorously criticized and rationally analyzed; this was the kind of knowledge which was worthy of all the effort and resources required to attain it. Great businessmen and leading state politicians as well as a few major national politicians and important publicists and, in a vague way, much of the electorate, joined in the appreciation of this kind of knowledge and the university as its proper organ. The universities were supported because they performed the dual function of infusing knowledge into the young who would apply it in their professions and whose lives would be illuminated by its possession, and of contributing to the improvement of the stock of knowledge, penetrating further and further into the nature of reality. The knowledge which was appreciated was secular knowledge which continued the mission of sacred knowledge, complemented it, led to it, or replaced it; fundamental, systematically acquired knowledge was thought in some way to be a step towards redemption. This kind of knowledge held out the prospect of the transfiguration of life by improving man's control over the resources of nature and over the powers which weaken his body; it offered the prospect of a better understanding of society which it was thought would lead to the improvement of society. It was thought that the progress of mankind entailed the improvement of the understanding, simply as a state of being and not solely as an instrument of action. The honor and the glory of a country which promoted the acquisition of such knowledge was assured; its power and influence would grow proportionately and deservedly.

This was the movement of belief which carried forward the universities. The leading academics and the leading university administrators believed approximately the same things. There were of course disagreements on this point and that, on the emphasis to be given to theoretical and fundamental knowledge in comparison with the emphasis to be laid on practically useful discovery, or on the value of immediate intervention into practical affairs as against the postponement or avoidance of intervention until knowledge was sufficiently reliable. Certain studies were sometimes more favored than others because it was thought they might attract more financial support or at least not discourage it. There were other disagreements too, and not all institutions and subjects moved with equal speed in the same direction. Nonetheless the movement went on, the centers spreading their influence over the peripheries, the centers competing with each other and sometimes changing places. The universities at the center moved into new spiritual terrain, drawing the rest of the intellectual order with them.

The universities were vouchsafed this vocation because they appeared to be the best imaginable instruments for the performance of this dual cognitive function. No other arrangement of intellectual activities could come near to the universities in this regard. The universities could produce more knowledge more reliably and more continuously and they could transmit it, thus making provision for the persistence of that progress. Universities moreover moved forward over the whole of the legitimate cognitive front. They worked in a way which drew most fruitfully on the cooperation of numerous individuals and institutions in many countries. Libraries became their instruments, industrial and governmental laboratories their executants. Within the ascendancy of the academic order of the universities, order was maintained and kept in movement by the ascendancy of a number of other universities over most of the others.

This was the situation at the end of the First World War. Traditions of thought and loyalty had been founded and reinforced in the preceding half century. In the ensuing half century, these traditions and loyalties were to bear their fruit and they were also to be subjected to unprecedented strains precisely because they had been so successful.

Notes

1. Eliot, Charles William, "Inaugural Addresses as President of Harvard College," *Education at Reform: Essays and Addresses* (New York: The Century Company, 1898), p. 27.
2. Gilman, Daniel Coit, "The Johns Hopkins University in Its Beginnings," in *University Problems in the United States* (New York: The Century Company, 1898), p.13.
3. Rosenberg, Charles, *No Other Gods* (Baltimore, Md.: Johns Hopkins University Press, 1976), p. 174.
4. Ibid., p. 179.

2

Universities Since 1900:
A Historical Perspective

Universities before the First World War

The Situation in 1900

The main universities of the world at the beginning of the twentieth century bore the imprint of the idea of the university as it had been promulgated by German thinkers about a century earlier and as it had been embodied in German universities of the nineteenth century. The German universities were at the height of their greatness in their intellectual achievement and in their reputation in Germany and the world. Oxford and Cambridge were by then fully awakened from the torpor of several centuries. All over the continent of Europe, universities were in bloom. France finally reached the point where it had real universities as legally recognized corporate academic entities, which replaced local unconnected faculties and a centralized ministerial administration, misleadingly called the Université de France. In Canada, Australia, and New Zealand, the universities were beginning to produce scholars who would later, mostly as professors at British universities and, then only a good bit later at their own universities, become famous for their works and their pupils. In Russia a handful of universities, in Austria the University of Vienna, and in Austrian Poland the ancient University of Cracow, were the homes of scientists and scholars of international renown and young persons of great promise. In India a few government and missionary colleges were beginning to offer courses of undergraduate study comparable in standing to their parental university in the United Kingdom; in Calcutta, the great vice-chancellor Asutosh Mukherjee, was on the verge of launching a campaign to establish postgraduate studies leading to advanced degrees on the basis of research. In Peking, the National University had been established in 1898 with the intention of laying, before the best of the younger generation of Chinese, courses of study concerning all of Western learning and Chinese as well. Japan was already well under way in its deliberate program of creating imperial universities which would teach all of modern—Western—knowledge to young Japanese.

In the United States, with all its wealth, moral seriousness, national and denominational piety, pride and ambition, the universities and colleges were flourishing. The older universities on the East Coast were still institutions aiming to transform youths of upper- and upper-middle-class origin into Christian gentlemen and leaders of society, but they were also moving toward the advancement of scholarly and scientific knowledge. In the Middle West, several state universities such as the Universities of Wisconsin, Illinois, Iowa, and Michigan were bright with optimism on the good grounds afforded by their learned and civic achievements over the past quarter of a century. At the forefront of all stood the new private universities; the University of Chicago and the Johns Hopkins University in Baltimore, which bore the deep impress of the German model, were together already leading the country in training the new generation of scientists and scholars. In the West, the University of California at Berkeley was already an institution of achievements and good prospects.

The idea of the modern university was a creation of the end of the eighteenth and the beginning of the nineteenth centuries. By the beginning of the twentieth century, that idea had approached fulfillment.

The University as a World Apart: The Inwardness of Universities

Internally, the universities of the first two decades of the twentieth century had not departed markedly from the point which they had reached a half century before in their progress toward the idea of the university.

Irreducible links and separateness. Externally, during this period, universities had rather clearly demarcated boundaries separating them from the rest of the societies in which they lived. They had vaguely defined but distinctive purposes which were to a large extent accepted by society, both its lower and its upper strata. They provided advanced education to a sector of the population, which was distinctive in its age and in its social origins; they offered their teaching to young persons—mainly male—between the ages of eighteen and twenty-two and coming mainly from families of the upper and middle classes. Their teachers conducted research.

Some of the kinds of knowledge which the universities taught was regarded as a necessary prerequisite for the study and practice of particular professions, most notably the medical, legal, and clerical professions. The higher civil service was likewise a profession for which the universities offered the educational prerequisites. Engineering was also a professional destination for which universities in a few countries offered preparatory training. The universities in certain countries—probably those of the United States more than any others—offered courses of study which were intended to prepare their graduates for careers in private commerce and industry. In many countries, university education served to qualify young persons to become teachers in advanced secondary schools.

Teaching and inward focus. The universities provided teaching in subjects which were intended to meet the intellectual requirements for the performance of certain practical professions. In addition to these, universities had to offer training for teaching and doing research to persons who regarded such knowledge as an intrinsically valuable good. They were, in close connection with this, to improve and transmit an understanding and appreciation of the world and of the society and the works of human beings. The universities became in varying degrees communities of scholars and scientists, teachers and students, unified by their common devotion to learning, which comprised what was already known and what could be discerned by "original research," whatever the subsequent use or application of that knowledge. This community was the heart and internal center of the university, even though it was not identical with the entire university.

The size of universities in that period also helped to make the university relatively self-contained, that is, as self-contained as an institution can be when it operates with traditions claiming universal validity—as does scientific work—or of interest to a whole society or civilization—as do the social sciences and humanities.

Research was relatively inexpensive and research projects were carried out on a small scale; this was an important factor in the maintenance of the boundaries between universities and their respective national societies. Governments, even in countries where the universities were state universities, provided little special financial support for academic research apart from the general allocation to the universities for their several purposes.

The self-containment of the universities in most Western countries at the beginning of the twentieth century was helped by the fact that university teaching had become a full-time occupation which excluded the necessity of income-earning activities outside the university. University teaching also became a lifelong career, and not just a way station on the road to another career in the law and church—as it had been for many fellows of the colleges at Oxford and Cambridge in the preceding century.

Autonomy and the outward focus. The external aspect was the autonomy of the university. The universities had extended and consolidated their autonomy in this period which ran up to the First World War. The gradual withdrawal of the churches from the co-responsibility for the government of the universities in Western and Northern Europe and North America enhanced the autonomy of the universities. In actual fact autonomy prevailed in the universities of other parts of the world as well.

There were points, however, where the lines between the university and society were breached. One of these had to do with financial support; there, the breach was in the nature of the universities as institutions which could not or which did not attempt to support themselves by the sale of their services.

The Interior of the University: The Distribution of Authority

Concentration of internal authority. The autonomy of the university entailed the absence of intrusions into the university from the outside. The center of decisions lay within the boundaries of the university; this did not mean an equal distribution of authority within the university. In the German universities, which had a considerable measure of academic self-administration, authority was very unequally distributed; the full professors had the decisive power within each faculty or major division of the university. In the United Kingdom, in the modern universities, the members in lower ranks in the teaching staff had a small representation in the university senate, of which all professors were members ex officio. In the United States, universities, public as well as private, were in a similar situation. They had a large measure of autonomy but in internal matters, the "faculty"—even the full professors—had no powers as a corporate entity. Presidents, sometimes in consultation with heads or chairmen of departments or with deans, exercised authority within the university under the final authority of the board of trustees. Junior members of the teaching staff and frequently full professors could have no influence on strong-willed presidents.

The strength of the central authority of the American university helped to underscore the boundaries around it. The president "stood for" the university to the outside world. Dominating the university, watching over the activities of the teaching staff, he wanted to guarantee that they would do nothing to "bring the university into disrepute" or to "damage its reputation." This is why some of the teachers were roughly treated by presidents when they engaged in radical political activities outside the universities.

At the beginning of the twentieth century, the power of the president of a university was limited from above by the board of trustees and from below by deans and departmental chairmen. Since the latter were appointed by the president, there was usually harmony between them. This orderly pyramid of authority made the university appear to its members as a coherent entity, perhaps more coherent than it really was since specialization of fields of interest within the sciences and among the various professional schools made for internal barriers.

In the ancient universities of the United Kingdom in 1900, the colleges were reduced in their power in the universities from what had been the case fifty years earlier. The aristocratic democracy of the senior members of the colleges, therefore, meant that there was not such a concentration of authority in the two ancient universities in the United Kingdom as existed in the United States.

The Interior of the University: Department and Discipline

It was impossible to avoid the subdivision of knowledge and the corresponding subdivision of the university. Although philosophers and theologians sought to find a single unifying principle underlying all the varieties of ordered knowledge, it was evident that such unity, if ever found, could not overcome the diversity of natural phenomena and of human activities. The earliest European universities began with the scheme of four faculties of philosophy, law, medicine, and theology. Not all of them had all four faculties, but a full university had to have four, distinguished from each other by their substance or subject matter. By the end of the nineteenth century, it was regarded as inevitable as well as practically necessary to divide universities into divisions, departments, and chairs. No professor could be thought capable of mastering all knowledge and the students who had only a limited time in universities could certainly never do so. There was a marked diversification and multiplication of the subjects taught in universities, accompanied by the creation of new chairs and new departments.

Many academic subjects which had been largely the domain of amateurs the universities now took into themselves. The universities altered these subjects when they took them into their jurisdiction. They introduced more rigor into the techniques of research. They made research more a matter of the use of standardized procedures rather than a series of improvisations and ingenious inference. Archaeology, the study of folklore, anthropology, and others became objects of university study; they were made more methodical. Each of these extensions, differentiations, incorporations, and new emergences required new courses and often new teachers, sometimes new departments, and new professorships.

Within the universities, the various subjects were fairly strictly demarcated from each other by departments and by chairs. In the continental universities, the disciplines were defined by professorships. There was usually one professor for each subject—in some subjects, there might not be a professorship at all if the ministry thought it not important enough or if it were not studied by enough students.

Of course, the "disciplines" overlapped with each other although many academics, particularly in Germany and the United States, sought to lay out the boundaries of each discipline in a way which reduced the extent of the overlap, but such efforts were never intellectually conclusive. Nevertheless, boundaries were certainly essential to the administrative structure of the university. Persons who went beyond those boundaries were regarded as dilettanti. Sometimes, these intrusions were resented by those into whose terrain they encroached. The elective system which was permitted for students in some countries—for example, the United States and in a different way, Germany— was not regarded as proper for professors.

Although the disciplines or at least the idea of disciplines was accepted, it was impossible for the universities to maintain the existing pattern of disciplines without modification. The prime movers in the creation of new disciplines were the university teachers, who, beginning a new line of research which drew on the knowledge and techniques used in several other disciplines, found enough response among other scientists for the development of a new field.

By the end of the First World War, specialization and disciplinary boundaries within a university called forth doubts and criticisms. This was more pronounced in the United States than in Europe.

The Interior of the University: The Moral Intention

Even before the First World War, the increased numbers of students in the universities and the consequent increase in the numbers of teachers meant that where research was expected of university teachers, as was coming to be almost universal in the natural sciences, there was a consequent marked increase in the number of scholarly publications. This increase was a powerful force in the increase of the detailed knowledge of a particular subject matter and in restricting the range of knowledge and interest of academics in the larger fields of their research.

The production of knowledge had become, with training young persons for the production of knowledge and with training for the practice of the intellectual-practical professions, the preferred function of universities.

Universities, as Wilhelm von Humboldt conceived them, were intended to form character, to mold an outlook on life through the experience of research. That was one important part of the idea of the university which the universities of the nineteenth and twentieth centuries did not succeed in realizing. Nevertheless, one part of the ideal of the formation of character by academic research did survive—that was the ideal of scientific integrity or the ethos of science.

In this particular respect, the universities of Europe and North America did succeed in inculcating into their students one valuable element of a moral attitude, namely, the obligation of honesty in scientific and scholarly research. This required readiness to acknowledge the value of achievements of other workers in the same field. The critical attitude towards the observations and theories current in any field, including one's own observations and theories, presupposed an affirmation of the value of truth. Objectivity was a cognate value; although it was adduced sometimes to justify the refusal or even the rejection of the rendering of moral judgments and even to deny the validity of moral judgments, it was nonetheless a moral appreciation of truth. In this way, the ethos of science become a part of the academic ethic, which asserted the value of the university as an institution. It served thereby to strengthen the image of academic life as different from the life of the market place and the political platform, and with a claim to dignity at least equal to the claims of the other spheres of life. This may be regarded as the moral achievement of the universities by the opening decades of the twentieth century.

The Universities in the Order of Learning

Within each national society, universities were in contact with each other. They shared in a common tradition of learning in each of the disciplines and in their conception of their calling as universities. Sharing a common intellectual culture and a common conception of themselves as distinctive institutions uniquely concentrated on learning or ordered knowledge, they were also stratified in a hierarchy of deference. In each national society, a minority of universities stood out from the others and embodied patterns which other universities wished to emulate.

There was also an international order of learning, in which universities, especially those most eminent in their own national societies, were linked with each other. The links were through certain scientific and scholarly publications, personal friendships, visiting professorships and traveling fellowships, foreign studies, international scientific and scholarly associations, and with meetings and conferences.

The internationality of universities is a necessary or constitutive limitation on the institutional self-containedness of universities. Just as there are inherent limitations on the self-containedness of universities given by their dependence on external individuals, governments, and private corporate bodies for their financial support, and by their obligation to train young persons for the intellectual-practical professions, so the nature of learning also places a limit on the self-containedness of universities. The growth of learning is a collective activity, and thanks to print and other physical forms of communication, the territorial scale of the collective action of the advancement of learning is greatly extended beyond the boundaries of any single university.

In the first two decades of the twentieth century, the German language was still the dominant medium of scientific publication. Such was the respect for the work done in German universities that it was thought that the desire to follow a career of science or scholarship required the mastery of the German language at least up to the point of reading it fluently. French and English were obligatory but not as imperative as German. The First World War shook this supremacy of the German language as the linguistic basis of the international bond between the universities of the various national societies.

This testified to an irresistible internationality of those branches of knowledge which are of universal validity, interest, and persuasiveness. Publications in the natural sciences must be known to any scientist who wishes to acquire the most advanced knowledge and who also wishes, in research, not to pursue demonstratedly false problems or to discover solutions which were in fact discovered previously elsewhere.

The self-containedness which is the counterpart of autonomy of individual universities—which is partial at best—is an autonomy with respect to external nonacademic demands and standards—not with respect to external academic ones. The national and the international orders of learning are limitations on the self-containedness of each individual university, but they are necessary for the functioning of any single university.

Universities within the World: Commerce and Industry

Universities were slow in bridging the gap between themselves on the one side and industry and commerce on the other. In Germany, they made deliberate efforts to remain apart from commerce. In France, commercial subjects were clearly outside both the *grandes écoles* and the universities; technological subjects, except where they were the object of interest to the *grandes écoles*, were shunned by the universities. At the other extreme, were a number of American universities in which by 1900 there were well-established schools of business studies within universities—as well as schools of engineering. Many of the graduates of the schools did enter business; but many other graduates also did so without a specialized training in business subjects.

Chemistry was the first academic science where industry and academic departments met in close cooperation; similar contacts obtained in engineering. The rest of the university usually remained aloof from "trade"; avoiding it, rather than embracing it.

The state universities in the United States often had as part of themselves the state colleges of agriculture. (In some states, the state universities did not include the "agricultural and mechanical colleges" which were established as separate institutions of higher education.) There was often a close and frequently fruitful cooperation between agricultural scientists and farmers who made use of the results of the research conducted in the university.

In modern universities of the United Kingdom located in industrial areas, the situation was somewhat different. There, local industrialists occasionally endowed professorial chairs in scientific subjects bearing on industrial problems.

In France, there was a definite gap between industry and the universities. The University of Toulouse in the early part of the twentieth century did initiate such relationships, thanks to the efforts of the academic scientists and local industrialists, but these efforts were few and short-lived.

Paths to the World: Social Investigations and Politics

The discovery of society by methodical empirical investigation was not at first a work of the universities. When the universities began such investigations, they, like their amateur predecessors, focused on society in its most distressing aspects such as the contrasts between wealth and poverty, or criminality and vice.

Academic social science as it developed in the latter part of the nineteenth century in Germany and the United States became willy-nilly a part of public opinion. University teachers in a number of countries became participants in efforts to influence public and political opinion through the publication of the results of their investigations into the conditions of the poor—the working class and the *Lumpenproletariat*—and the associated conditions of disrupted families, petty criminality, alcoholism, vagrancy, and other deviations from what was regarded as the normal life of society. A great deal of empirical academic—as well as nonacademic—sociology was focused on these subjects. Many authors proposed remedies for these unsatisfactory conditions; others studied them because these conditions interested them intellectually and because it had become the tradition of sociology and political science, academic and nonacademic, to do so.

In the last part of the nineteenth century, some university teachers, students, and graduates attempted to bring superior education to the mass of the population which did not and could not attend universities. Adult education, workers' education, extension lectures and courses, and "settlement houses," were among the institutional provision for extending the benefits of university education beyond the boundaries of the university.

Another closely related breach in the line separating the university from its environing society occurred through the heightened political interest of academics. This was already very well advanced in the nineteenth century. Some academics sought to make parliamentary careers while others contributed to political publications; still others became active in public contentions regarding intellectual and academic matters, like the theory of evolution, the "higher criticism" of the Bible, the freedom of scientific research, or of academic freedom in general. The numbers, however, were not large; only a small minority of academics took part in politics and public contention by delivering speeches from public platforms or by their candidacies for public office; they also became occasional political publicists; the rest, whatever their sympathies, did not participate in political activities.

The universities were never ivory towers as some of their critics have charged. That would have been impossible. However, they were also far from "service" institutions, delivering knowledge and skill on demand. Populist critics held this against them but not very effectively.

The Expansion of the University Model

One of the most important developments of the nineteenth century was the expansion of the German university model to the United States, and the influence of the German model on the reform of higher learning in France and the United Kingdom. By the turn of the century, the tide of expansion directly from Germany had ebbed. The American universities ceased to emulate the German model; American students went only in much diminished numbers to study at the German universities, and the American entry into the First World War stopped the movement altogether. Russia too was influenced by the German model.

The model of the American college was evident in China and Japan; many new colleges and universities, much aided by Christian missionaries, were founded in those two countries. In India, unitary universities influenced by the model of the provincial British universities, were founded to take a place alongside the federated universities which had been formed on the model of the University of London in the middle of the nineteenth century.

Thus the new type of university, originating in Germany, became a worldwide model.

Universities between the Two World Wars

The Impact of the War: The Task of Restoration

The First World War and the years which followed it brought abrupt changes to the universities. Students and younger teachers went into the armed services. Older teachers, scientists particularly, shifted their focus onto topics which could be useful to the military efforts of their respective countries. The strength of metals, explosives, chemical warfare and defense, aeronautics, and medicine and surgery, took up the attention of academic scientists, some in uniform, many of them still working in their universities. Historians, linguists, classical scholars, economists, worked on cryptography and crypto-analysis, problems of international law, food supply, transportation, administration, and the production of armaments and aircraft.

When the war was over, the organization to prosecute the war was dismantled and the universities tried to resume where they had left off. The organizational patterns of universities remained as they had been. The patterns of patronage changed significantly.

The years that succeeded the end of the First World War were to some extent recuperative. It took some time for universities to get back into their stride. They did not succeed everywhere. The deformations of hypernationalism on the continent took several years to be undone; the boycott of the German universities by the universities of the victorious countries lasted through much of the first half of the 1920s. The normal internationality of science and scholarship revived only slowly. The great private philanthropic foundations of the United States were very active in the restoration of normality.

The restoration was nevertheless largely successful. The European and American universities came back, at least for a time, to the condition in which they had been in the decade and a half before the outbreak of the First World War. The universities again became "mistresses in their own houses."

There were two absent members in this process of restoration. The Russian universities, which had before the war come increasingly to be parts of the European scientific and scholarly communities, suffered the physical ravages of famine and civil war after the end of the Great War itself. As a result of the disorders and deliberate policies of the communist regime, the Russian universities were in certain fields effectively dismantled. The slow establishment of the Soviet regime led to the exile of many leading professors and the harassment and derogation of those who remained; then the rise of Stalinism and the beginning of the "trials" and the "purges" kept the universities from recovering.

The establishment of the fascists in Italy had an effect on universities almost as disastrous as the communist regime in Russia.

The National Socialist regime in Germany undid the restoration of the German universities to some of the eminence which they had achieved before the First World War. The restoration had been only partial, but in certain fields like physics, mathematics, chemistry, classics, and ancient Middle Eastern studies, they had succeeded in restoring their earlier prominence. The National Socialist regime, almost immediately on its access to power dismissed from their academic posts all Jews or persons of Jewish ancestry—with very few exceptions. Teachers who were liberals or socialists were also dismissed or allowed to retire or resign. Those dismissed and otherwise removed constituted about one-third of the German academic profession; the exceptions were dismissed about five years later. These dismissals were a very disfiguring blow to the German universities.

Thus, the universities of Europe in the two decades between the two world wars were disrupted by the destruction of the *Nachwuchs*—the academic succession—by the death in combat of many young and promising scholars and scientists during the First World War; they suffered next from political agitation and the civil wars, from the distractions and the political intrusions of jealous dictatorships. They suffered from the surge of fanatical nationalism which made honest and sober research and teaching very difficult. The Second World War and the extremes of nationalism which preceded it on the Continent also broke once more the international community of academic learning. The closure of universities on the continent of Europe by the Nazis did immense harm. The Soviet Union was scarcely better in Poland. After the war, Eastern European universities suffered great harm from the communists, both Russian and domestic.

Governmental Financial Support

In the countries which were able to maintain more or less liberal-democratic constitutions, the universities were successful in returning to what was regarded before the First World War as the normal state. The major innovations of the period were innovations in the models of financial support for universities and for scientific research. In Germany, one major innovation was the Notgemeinschaft der Deutschen Wissenschaft which was introduced soon after the end of the war. Much later France followed on the same pattern by the creation of the Conseil national de la recherche scientifique. The University Grants Committee in the United Kingdom was also a successful innovation.

The University Grants Committee simply did in the two decades between the two world wars for the British universities what the continental support by government had done for a long time. The University Grants Committee was unique in that it was not an arm of a ministry but was rather an independent institution which received its funds from the government. The British universities were still not in the position of the German universities of almost complete dependence on government financial support. By the outbreak of the Second World War, most universities in the United Kingdom except for Oxford and Cambridge, had moved well into the path of the continental universities in their financial dependence on government.

Those universities of the United States and Canada which were state or provincial universities continued to receive their support almost exclusively from the vote of the state or provincial legislature; most of them had only small endowments and they received little of their income from the low fees which students paid. Some of them began to receive grants from private philanthropic foundations for specific purposes. In the United States, the private universities received nothing from the central or state governments; most of their budget was provided for by income from endowments and fees paid by students, supplemented with gifts from private individuals and private philanthropic foundations. The tuition and other fees made up a significant part of the total revenues of the private universities.

There were other signs of the times, signs that universities were being encircled in ways which endangered their relative self-containment, their insulation from "distraction," which von Humboldt called *Einsamkeit*. Shortly before the First World War, the British government created the Medical Research Council and allocated funds to it for the support of scientific research to be done within the research institutions created by the council or to be done in independent institutions such as universities, medical schools, and hospitals. The Council for Scientific and Industrial Research followed in 1916; it had the same kinds of responsibilities as the Medical Research Council except that it supported research on industrial problems; scientists in universities received financial support from it when they worked on problems of interest to industrial firms. In Germany, the Notgemeinschaft der deutschen Wissenschaft, in France, the Conseil nationale de la recherche scientifique made grants to individuals, mainly in universities.

The upshot of this was that scientists and scholars in the 1920s were beginning to look beyond the boundaries of their own universities in order to obtain the wherewithal needed for their research.

The Role of the Private Philanthropic Foundation

At about the same time, private philanthropic foundations were beginning to become active. In the United States, the Carnegie Foundation for the Advancement of Teaching and the (Rockefeller) General Education Board had come into operation before the First World War. They both interested themselves in universities. The former established a scheme for providing pensions for university teachers. The latter made large block grants to universities. The Carnegie Foundation had also commissioned a survey of medical education which was very influential in the improvement of American medical schools.

Before 1929, the several Rockefeller foundations supported universities or particular parts of universities; after 1929 they directly supported individual teachers. The change of policy also presaged a turn from the self-containment or autonomy of the universities which had been characteristic of the decades before the First World War.

By the end of the interwar period, officers of the foundations were taking the responsibility for initiating substantive programs, rather than allowing the universities or individuals within universities to make those decisions. It is true that they left individual academics free to work on the foundation's project or not as they wished. Nevertheless, the individual academic scientists did not promulgate the problem. Thus, the center of gravity was moving slightly to the outside of the universities, lessening the autonomy of the universities as largely self-contained institutions.

The Interior of the University: Incipient Dispersion of the Center of Gravity

This slight outward displacement of the center of gravity of the universities was concurrent with an incipient dispersion of the center within the American university. Very gradually, the overpowering president began to yield some of his powers. It was more by a tacitly accepted convention rather than by changes in the university statutes and by-laws that individual professors who held no administrative offices began to have a little more weight in the decisions taken in their universities. The movement between the wars was, however, still relatively slight.

The interwar period was also a time when research institutes and research committees began to be formed within American universities. Research institutes in the German universities were less of an innovation; they had in the past usually been attached to the professorial chair: they were part of the structure of the university and were not phases or parts of an outward displacement of the center of the university.

The Expansion of the University Model

Except for the United Kingdom, none of the European countries created a university in their colonial territories during the period between the two wars. Meanwhile, the propagation of models of the European and the American universities, derived earlier from the models of European universities, was not as profuse or intense as it had been before and as it became later; the implantations ran along the lines earlier laid down.

Meanwhile, the movements of ideas and persons continued. The British and other Europeans still continued to be teachers in Indian government colleges and those founded and run by European missionaries. Americans, some British, and sometimes continentals taught in the Chinese colleges founded and supported by American missionary organizations. The Yenching University was an academically valuable instance of such expansion and implantation. The University of Peking, founded entirely on Chinese initiative, had implantation as its specific objective. It contributed greatly to the movement of ideas; one if its most daring actions was to bring John Dewey to China.

In Japan, the major universities were imperial universities and they were staffed entirely by indigenous scholars and scientists, many of whom were doing research in the style received from Europe and some of whom were doing it at a very high level. There, too, universities and colleges were formed on European and American models by missionary societies.

In the Middle East, universities and colleges followed the European patterns—French, British, and German. The American model in the 1920s and 1930s was implanted only in colleges of American inspiration and financial support. The American University of Cairo was founded in 1920; the American University of Beirut was founded in the same year, but it was the successor of much older missionary colleges. The state universities of Middle Eastern countries were perforce formed on European models. The traditional Arab University of Al Azhar provided no model for the universities of the region; on the contrary, it underwent reforms in the direction of the European models.

The University in the Widening Order of Learning

Another sign of the incipient outward movement of the cultivation of the order of knowledge from the universities, at least in the United States, was the founding of the Institute of Advanced Study at Princeton, New Jersey in 1929. It was intended to be an institution devoted entirely to research in the humanistic disciplines and those scientific subjects which did not require expensive equipment. Although there was a velleity in the beginning towards graduate students, the idea of an institute devoted entirely to research was triumphant. The Institute of Advanced Study was an effort to offer *Freiheit und Einsamkeit* to a handful of distinguished scientists and scholars; it was thought by its founder that American universities could not offer such advantages to the life of the mind at the highest level.

The Bell Telephone Laboratories in New York City and the General Electric Laboratory in Schenectady, New York, were among the first of the great laboratories attached to industrial firms which did scientific research at the level of the best academic scientists. Outside the chemical and the electrical industries, there was relatively little collaboration in the postwar period between industrial firms and academic scientists. The pharmaceutical industry, linked with chemistry, was one of the harbingers of the new relationship between applicable scientific research and industrial production.

Agriculture was the one long-established branch of economic life in which there were close contacts between production and scientific research. The actions of the federal government in the United States in encouraging the establishment of state agriculture and mechanical colleges, the state agricultural experiment stations which were closely connected with the colleges, and the actions of the county agents as intermediaries between research and practical farming combined to be exceptionally effective in inducing academic scientists to contribute to practical affairs.

The Universities in and after the Second World War

New Demands on Universities

The coming of the war of 1939 to 1945 changed much in the world; it had its effects on universities, too. The prosecution of the war eroded the boundaries of the university as an institution, the guiding principle of which had been so insistently enunciated by von Humboldt.

In the war itself, the universities, university teachers, and students were drawn into practical affairs on a scale never known before. The conscription of students and young teachers into the armed services was like that of the First World War, only of longer duration and more thoroughgoing. Much more impressive in the United Kingdom and the United States were the great research teams made up mainly of academic scientists who produced the atomic bomb and radar, who improved military medicine and surgery, and who administered vast economic programs. The great projects of crypto-analysis in which academics—mainly mathematicians and humanists—played such an important part were, with the more conventionally technological achievements, evidence that academic training and experience had a very great deal to contribute to practical projects in peace as well as in war. The academic scientists of Germany made no comparable contribution to German military action.

The result of these experiences of academics in the United Kingdom and the United States, and the appreciation of their achievements, was a profound change in the role of universities in society. The expectations directed towards universities became much higher, more comprehensive, and more insistent. From admiring esteem as beneficially disciplined seekers after truth, as contributors to the dignity of the human race by contributing to its understanding of the world, and as appreciators and interpreters of its past achievements, the image and status of universities and their teachers changed pronouncedly. Esteem was replaced by expectations of practical benefits. The beliefs of academics about universities also changed in the same direction. Indeed, academics encouraged the higher expectations by their own confidence in their capacities in practical affairs.

In all those countries and states where governments had taken on themselves the responsibility of supporting universities for all sorts of reasons— for training civil servants, lawyers, physicians, teachers, clergymen, men of learning and, in a few countries, for training engineers and businessmen and for working quietly to improve agriculture and health—governments made much larger sums available to universities.

Universities seemed to be the institutional instruments for enriching societies, for preventing and curing their diseases, for feeding them better, and for elevating them in the opinion of the world. Countries which had little industry became ambitious to increase their industrial production; universities were held to be efficient instruments for this purpose. They could train planners and technologists; this was regarded as a responsibility of universities in rich countries and poor countries alike.

There was another factor which helped to move universities more into the center of the public and political field of vision. Universities came to be looked upon as instruments for the fulfillment of the ideal of social equality, or at least for the fulfillment of the ambition to rise from the lower to the middle classes. For many decades it had been known that universities were frequented mainly by students from economically more prosperous families, from the more esteemed strata; they were not generally regarded as accessible to offspring of the lower classes or even of the lower-middle classes. (The American state universities were partial exceptions to this situation.) Although there was public awareness of this situation, it seemed to be one of the facts of life about which little was to be done. Before the Second World War, the universities did not trouble themselves about it, nor did governments.

The Second World War changed all this. There was a surge of egalitarian sentiment after that war; it first manifested itself in "demobilization grants," in the "GI Bill of Rights," and similar measures to allow young persons who had served in the armed forces to attend universities. This permitted many who otherwise never would have attended universities to do so. These were additional to the young persons who would have attended universities had the war not intervened and had they not been taken into military service for several years—in numerous cases in Europe, for as long as six years. Both of these groups now supplied university students in large numbers.

Governmental policies in all countries were determined to increase the fraction of the age groups between eighteen and twenty-four years of age. They did so by making more provisions for attendance at secondary schools, by providing studentships, scholarships, and grants for maintenance.

One result of these many demands and motives was the crowding of universities. Classes and seminars became much larger. There had been a lull in building during the war; in some of the European countries, university buildings had been much damaged or destroyed. Another closely related result was that students, especially in their early years at university, received less attention from their teachers.

Increased Financial Support by Governments

All of these factors together—the demands directed towards universities to perform, by their research in peacetime, deeds of discovery and invention like those which they had performed for their countries in wartime, the surge of egalitarianism, the insufficiency of the physical premises and equipment for meeting those demands, and the increased size of teaching staffs and student bodies—led to a tremendous increase in governmental expenditure for universities. Private individuals and foundations—especially in the United States, but also in the United Kingdom and the Federal Republic of Germany, added substantial sums to the much larger ones being supplied by governments.

In every country, the number of universities increased. The great period of new university foundations—the Reformation and the Counter-Reformation and the nineteenth century—had seen nothing like it. In the United States, universities multiplied by fission. In some states, the state university divided itself many times over through the creation of branches in numerous parts of the particular state; in other states, lesser higher educational institutions—agricultural and mechanical colleges and teacher-training colleges—were elevated to university status, either as branches of the state university or as separate universities. Colleges became universities by offering postgraduate training. In the United Kingdom, there was a simple multiplication of the number of universities, many wholly new, and some through the elevation of university colleges and local technological colleges to the status of universities. Comparable increases in the numbers of universities and of students occurred in Germany, Austria, Italy, the Netherlands, Denmark, Norway, and Finland. Throughout sub-Saharan Africa, where there had been one university college before the Second World War—the Fourah Bay College in Sierre Leone—scores of new universities were founded. India, which had less than a score of universities before the war, increased the number of its universities more than sixfold. Japan, which had two major imperial universities and a number of municipal and private universities before the war, increased on a similar scale. Canada, New Zealand and Australia, and South Africa, likewise multiplied the number of their universities and increased the size of existing ones.

Generous though many governments were in the first few decades after the Second World War in their financial provision for universities, the sums allocated were never large enough to satisfy the existing demand for places for students or for the salaries for teachers and auxiliary and administrative services. At the same time, the costs of research increased, as did the cost of books and the staff required to keep laboratories and libraries in good working order. These have been common features of universities everywhere, and where a university could not pay sufficiently high salaries and meet the cost of equipping and maintaining laboratories and libraries, it fell behind in the now worldwide competition of universities. However, whatever its fortunes or misfortunes in the latter respects, the numbers of students continued, in most years, to increase over the previous year.

The Increased Presence of Government and Increased Busyness within Universities

With the increased financial support which they provided, governments increased their interest in university affairs. They demanded more than just a proper accounting of how these much larger sums were spent and assurance that there had been no peculation or negligence. They required larger "intakes" of students. They have determined the composition of governing bodies of the universities. In the United States, they have intruded into appointments. They have above all increased the fraction of "mission-oriented research" in universities. Such intrusions are not all equally present in all countries. Nonetheless, the presence of government in universities became much more substantial than in the past.

As a result, the amount of administration within the university has grown, and with it there has been a marked multiplication of the amount of bureaucracy. More forms have to be filled out to apply for funds and to account for how they have been spent. Governments have become inquisitive about how professors spend their time. "Management," such as used to be found in very large business firms, has now been introduced into universities. Universities have become much busier places than they had been. The sheer number of teachers and students, the enlarged size of individual universities and of departments, the increase in the numbers of courses, lectures, seminars, the increased size of auxiliary staffs, secretaries, administrators, technicians, and so on, have made the university scenes of complication, bustle, and hurry.

The days of the university teacher are fuller. There are more students who have to be met with, not just in class but in direct consultation. The increased number of graduate or research students means that more time must be spent with them in discussion about their research and in reading and annotating drafts of their dissertations. More testimonials must be written about students seeking appointments; more testimonials must be written about colleagues and former students seeking fellowships, grants from foundations, and appointments at other universities. The devolution of authority within departments means that there are more meetings of departments and, with the increased size of departments, more reading of the works of candidates for appointments and promotions.

The increase in volume and scale of research with the collaboration of colleagues and assistants means that more time must be spent in the administration of research, apart from the research itself. Numerous academics engage in several research projects simultaneously, and since these projects are staffed by assistants and since the grants which support the research are for defined periods in which the research must be completed, the academic who takes the responsibility for the project must adapt to the sequence of the phases of the investigation. Since research requires not simply the collection of freshly made observations but also a mastery of the literature, the papers in journals and monographs must be read or at least scrutinized. There are more journals and more publications of the larger number of workers in each field. The larger number of journals and the larger number of papers call for more assessment of the papers by referees who take their academic duties seriously. This too is another call on the time of the academic.

All these things taken together are a far cry from the "absence of distraction" which von Humboldt thought was necessary for a university teacher.

The University and the Outer World: The Economy

Economists, whether as academics, publicists, or as civil servants, have attempted since early in the nineteenth century to influence governmental economic policies by their writings, by their representations before governmental commissions, and by occasional participation in administration.

It is not uncommon for a chief economic adviser to the government or a minister of finance to be an academic economist. The list from Hugh Dalton, John Maynard Keynes, Hugh Gaitskell, Ludwig Erhard, and Raymond Barre to Martin Feldstein is a long one. It is certainly usual for the monetary policy of the government to be influenced by the ideas of academic economists. Academic economists have also engaged themselves in "development economics," particularly in the efforts of governments of the new states of Asia and Africa and in the older states of Latin America.

It is, however, in scientific research that the intimacy between universities and the economy has been most tangible. Ever since the development of molecular biology there has been considerable coming together of academic science and profit-seeking industrial firms in the application of biotechnology.

The insufficiency of the financial support of government has driven academic scientists to seek the financial support by private business firms in return for their close collaboration in research. It is not only the desire of academic scientists for more financial resources for their research that has led to this narrowing of the gap. Industry too has changed, and this had led industrial firms to come closer to the universities.

Technology in certain fields has become much more scientific in the sense that the scientific component has become more prominent. As a result, there is a more active interest, on the part of business firms using this kind of technology and in the scientific research done by or susceptible to being done by university scientists. There is a much more immediate relationship between scientific discoveries and their use in industry; the time between discovery and application has been much reduced. There is a much more active and effective demand on the part of industrial firms for the results of scientific research. There is, in consequence, a much greater interest on the part of industrial firms in having research done which will be of practical value to them.

In consequence of these changes in the scientific component of technology, universities concerned to increase their revenues and individual scientists interested in increasing their income, have contrived a variety of forms of close collaboration between universities and industrial firms. These range from the licensing of patents taken out by universities on discoveries made by their scientists in university laboratories, the establishment by universities of companies to exploit these patents commercially, and the formation of private commercial enterprises by individual scientists to exploit their discoveries for their own private profit, to the creation of institutes jointly owned and managed by a university and a private business firm.

Industrial firms in the fields of microbiology, electronics, and computers have established themselves in the vicinity of universities; Silicon Valley in California and "Route 128" near the Massachusetts Institute of Technology and Harvard University are prototypical of this relationship. Another variant of this close collaboration is the "science park"; a number of universities in the United States and the United Kingdom have leased land and buildings in the vicinity of the university to private business firms which have a strong commercial interest in the application of scientific discoveries made in the university.

These developments have been attractive to administrators of both state and private universities desirous of increasing their revenues. They have also attracted many scientists in the universities by the prospects they afford to seeing their discoveries more speedily employed. At the same time, they have aroused the opposition from some academics who are apprehensive of the encroachments on academic autonomy and even on academic freedom. There are worries lest these arrangements will interfere with one of the cardinal points of academic freedom, namely, the freedom of publication. They fear that publication will be delayed, not only by the time required for obtaining a patent but also by the interest of the business firm in question in gaining an advantage over possible competitors by withholding crucial knowledge from them. There can be no doubt that the traditional location within the university itself of decisions as to what research should be done, and how it is to be done, and when and where it is to be published, is affected by the narrowing of the distance in time between a scientific discovery and its industrial, profit-seeking application.

These problems are not often encountered in the universities of the European continent because the universities there have kept themselves more aloof from industry in most fields.

The Universities and the Outer World: Society

When universities took the social sciences into themselves, they accepted a breach in the wall. As long as universities studied things remote in time and space, or timeless and spaceless things, they could maintain their freedom from the distraction of the contemporary and the near at hand. However, when they accepted as a legitimate academic subject the empirical description of the contemporary society, a close cognitive and moral interest in affairs outside the university was a breach in the separation of the university from its environing society.

"The poor" were dramatically rediscovered by public and political opinion in the United States and the United Kingdom in the 1960s; they were rediscovered by academic social scientists at the same time. This rediscovery coincided with the upsurge of uncritical confidence in "science" among politicians and publicists. There was confluence of governmental and academic interest in illuminating in a scientific way the magnitude and composition of the phenomenon of the poor. This precipitated programs of "mission-oriented research" for which money was made available on application. This was also true of the private philanthropic foundations. The upshot of this was that much academic empirical social research came largely to be commissioned research.

Contemporary empirical social research has become costly because the sample survey conducted within a short time over an extended area requires a large staff of interviewers, and the efforts to use exact and reliable techniques requires coders and programmers in fairly large numbers. The chief but not the only source of funds for such research is to be found in agencies of government. To obtain funds for their research, academic social research workers must turn to governments or to private foundations which have similar interests. This means that the decision as to what is to be studied lies, to an increased extent, outside the universities.

The situation in this regard is very much like that of the natural sciences, although social research does not require such expensive equipment as radiotelescopes, electronic microscopes, and accelerators. "Scientific" social research is no longer a single-person affair, requiring as it does a rather numerous staff; it, therefore, requires relatively large sums of money. For this reason, it makes research dependent on the objectives of the patron. It contributes to the outward displacement of the center of gravity of the university.

The Universities and the Outer World: Politics

At the beginning of the twentieth century there was no very widespread and acute interest in political matters in universities. Heads of universities were always officially loyal to their regimes and to incumbent governments. Except in Italy and France, there were few socialists among university teachers. Political science and *Staatswissenschaften* insofar as they were taught at all, did not deal with contemporary politics. They dealt with the history of political thought, with constitutional law, and administration. Perhaps the closest approximation to an interest in contemporary politics was to be found in France and there mainly among the teachers of the *École normale supérieure* and of the Sorbonne.

Despite notorious exceptions, most academics, apart from the disfiguring fervor of wartime patriotism, were very moderate in their political views and not active in public. The students were more vigorous politically and more outspoken; they more often took up extreme positions—nationalistic in most continental countries and pacifistic in the United Kingdom. In the United States, academics became more interested in politics in response to the Great Depression in 1929 and the "New Deal" of President Roosevelt. Except for the countries where totalitarian regimes prevailed or which were on the verge of totalitarianism, the working of the universities was relatively unaffected by political contention. Teaching, research, and appointment in the universities of the liberal-democratic countries were, by and large, untouched by the political convictions of their teachers and students during the period between the two world wars.

Those academics who participated in political activities outside the universities or who had strong extra-academic political sympathies observed, as well as it could be done, a separation between their political beliefs on the one hand, and their teaching and research on the other. They did not usually attempt to recruit students to their political beliefs or affiliations; they did not contrive the appointment to their universities of persons who shared their political beliefs. They tended in the main to accept that the university was a self-contained and bounded corporate body to which they owed obligations which were compatible with their external political convictions and aspirations. They were, regardless of their substantive political convictions, liberals in that they believed in the rightness of the separation of the spheres.

Perhaps this statement needs to be qualified with respect to those who sympathized with communism but the qualification is a minor one. Quite apart from the Marxist theory of the impossibility of separating science and scholarship from class struggle, many of the adherents and sympathizers of Marxist political parties or sects usually respected the boundaries; at least they did so in the countries where a communist party did not dominate. This may be contrasted with the adherents of National Socialism who derided bourgeois learning and its aspiration to the attainment of objectivity. The same is true of academics in leading positions in universities under communist regimes.

The relations between universities, university teachers, and political activities in the liberal-democratic countries changed in the late 1960s. At first, the new attitude towards politics and learning became visible in the students who began a long series of disruptions against universities. The disruptions ran for nearly a decade. Although nominally the revolting students were protesting the policies of the governments of their countries, they tended to confine their demonstrations and disruptive activities to university grounds and buildings. Although they proclaimed themselves to be enemies of the entire bourgeois liberal-democratic order, their actions were concentrated mainly in and on their universities. In the United States, France, Germany, Italy and to more limited but still significant extent, the United Kingdom, they occupied and defaced buildings, boycotted classes, occasionally damaged or destroyed equipment, and, in general made their universities filthy and unsightly, sometimes preventing them from operating. They were extremely aggressive against their teachers and the administrators of their universities whom they denounced as accomplices and pawns of the government and of capitalists. Most teachers were horrified by the behavior of these students, but many of those who were horrified also declared that the students were in principle justified in their abhorrence of bourgeois society and the universities. There were teachers, mainly among the younger ones but also in the older generation, who actively encouraged the students.

By the mid-1970s, the disruptions came to a halt, with rather few disciplinary actions being taken against students who had turned their universities into a pandemonium. The universities became more quiet and orderly, and in the course of time, they were cleaned up. The succeeding cohorts of students were not so aggressive; in fact, they manifested no sympathy with their revolting predecessors.

Nevertheless, the disruptions had an effective afterlife. In Germany, the Netherlands, France, and other continental countries, new university laws were enacted, granting power to the students to share in the government of their universities, reducing the powers of the professors, and increasing the powers of the lower ranks of the teaching staffs. In Germany, these new laws were markedly influenced by the unprecedented intervention of the federal government: the enactment of the *Rahmengesetz* ("frame-law"), determined the pattern for state legislation on university affairs. Previously the states were not constrained by the central government in their enactment of university laws. The West German "frame-law" and ultimately the West German constitutional court of Karlsruhe confirmed the pattern of the *Gruppenuniversität*.

The *Gruppenuniversität* is fundamentally destructive of the Humboldtian idea of the university. The principal of the *Gruppenuniversität* conceives of the university as a site of conflict of fundamentally divergent interests. Von Humboldt postulated a consensus in the university regarding the value of truth and the value of discovering and promulgating important new truths. The fact is that in Germany the university has been defined by the federal legislature and the constitutional court as a political institution, the task of which is to compromise the conflicting interests of students, of the different strata of teachers, of administrators, and of secretarial and custodial employees of the university. This is a sign of how far the revolting students have been successful in eroding the boundaries of the universities.

The politicization of the universities is paradoxical. It is political while at the same time its focus is largely within the universities. It has no procedure for transforming society; its objective is the dissolution of civil society by the discrediting of the cultural tradition which the politicizing humanists claim is an instrument of bourgeois and plutocratic domination. Their political activities are part of what the late Helmut Schelsky called "the long march through the institutions." The objective of this long march is the destruction of liberal-democratic society; the way to that remote end is through the dismantling of the university from within. The more immediate means are the control over the syllabus and appointments. So far the departments of modern literature and languages have been affected, although that is not equally the case in all universities or in all countries. The American universities are in the forefront of this movement; the theory comes from Western European universities, mainly in France and Germany.

The Universities and the Order of Learning: Learned Societies

Quite apart from congeniality, few university teachers can find among their own colleagues those whose knowledge and understanding are most fruitfully complementary to their own. They will try to reach outside their respective universities to find the persons whom they need and who need them to give them what they want intellectually.

There are many instances of the insufficiency of the universities to contain the intellectual interests of their teaching-cum-research staff. A feature of modern scientific and scholarly communities, national and international, is the frequency of conferences, seminars, workshops, and so on. In the mid-nineteenth century there were very few such conferences, but after 1945, there was a great leap ahead in the number of conferences and of the societies which sponsored them. The conferences no longer covered only whole disciplines and groups of disciplines. Meetings have become common which embrace not entire disciplines or subdisciplinary specialties but rather only particular topics or very special problems. What is true for national scientific communities and subcommunities is also true for the international ramifications of learning. International learned societies and international conferences, workshops and seminars, which were infrequent before 1939 and almost very rare before 1900, are very commonplace. In addition, life in universities has become hectic and distracting to their members.

These are among the reasons for the proliferation of the phenomenon of the "institute of advanced study." Universities used to be institutions of advanced study; that was the heart of the university. It is necessary to place the heart of the university outside the body of the university in order to sustain it.

Universities in the second half of the twentieth century no longer have the distinctive role in scientific and scholarly research which they enjoyed between about 1870 and 1939. After having gained the upper hand over their amateur rivals, universities came under the competition of the independent research institutes.

Research institutes had been unknown through most of human history. The first modern research institute was the Physikalisch-technische Reichsanstalt in Berlin; it was founded in 1878 when German universities were at the height of their greatness. One of the justifications for the creation of the Institut was that the universities were unable to perform all of the research needed in German society. The Reichsanstalt was followed by other similar institutions in other countries; The National Physics Laboratory at Teddington (United Kingdom) was founded in 1902; the National Bureau of Standards in Washington, D.C., was founded at the same time as was the Carnegie Institution in Washington, D.C. These institutions were manifestations of a lack of confidence in the capacity of universities in the performance of research or of a belief that there were kinds of research that could not or should not be done in universities. Since that time, there has been a great increase in the number of research institutes independent of universities.

The Heart of the University: Conditions and Prospects

The power and multiplicity of the centrifugal forces working on the universities, from within and from outside, have become very great since the 1950s. Under these circumstances it may be asked: what is left to the university as an autonomous center of discovery and transmission of the most advanced fundamental knowledge about important things?

Bureacratization within the university has gone on apace; politicization within the university has also gone on apace. External bureaucratic and political influence over the interior life of the university, that is, the life of the pursuit and acquisition of serious knowledge, has also increased. Universities out of financial necessity, out of the desire to be of service to their societies and out of the aspirations—intellectual, political, and pecuniary—of their teachers have been invited to accept many responsibilities outside the universities while performing their traditional academic functions.

The modes of exercise of the external power of the state, in the support of universities, the exigencies and rewards of closer collaboration with business firms, the need for additional revenues to supplement what government and private patrons offer, and the greater opportunities for influence and rewards by public and political action outside the universities, have all had a disaggregative effect on the university as a community of learning.

Specialization, which is more integral to the process of discovery than the other factors, has worked in the same direction. It has made the specialized individuals less solidary with their colleagues who specialize on neighboring subjects within the same university and more solidary with colleagues in other universities who work on the same special subjects as they themselves do. The awarding of grants to individuals by external patrons has a similar effect; the individuals' ties with their universities have become more attenuated.

The tribulations of the university are the measure of its success. Had it not done so well what it set out to do in the nineteenth century and through so much of the twentieth century, not so much would have been expected of it and the support and appreciation which it has received would not have been so great. It has achieved so much through the industriousness, the intelligence, and the imagination of its best members. These are qualities of individuals. These qualities would never have been called into continuous and intensive animation had there not been within those individuals a powerful desire to discover the truth about the subjects they studied, investigated, and taught.

The powerful desire for truth and the energy to pursue it have not been produced by tradition. Where the potentialities existed within individuals, the traditions and the internal intellectual atmosphere of the institution within which the individuals were placed, played a very important part. Tradition sustained and guided the realization of the intellectual potentialities of individuals.

The universities of the nineteenth century had been constituted in part by the intellectual tradition which they received from the prior conditions of universities. These traditions were embodied and made visible in the conduct of the best senior and junior members—from the most eminent professors to the most assiduous and most learned students. Such individuals were fortunate to find their way to the traditions of their subjects and their universities. They in turn embodied the tradition of learning and helped to focus the minds of their colleagues. This imaginative appreciation of the intellectual standards manifest in the actions of others is generalized into a consciousness of the university as a corporate entity with an ethos and a complex of orientations towards the intensive pursuit of knowledge. We may, therefore, speak of the collective self-consciousness of a university in which its individual members share. That is an important condition of intellectual achievement. James Garfield was wrong when he said that the proper education was provided with Mark Hopkins at one end of a log and a boy at the other. An institution which condenses and infuses intellectual traditions is of fundamental importance. The university is such an institution, par excellence. Without universities, scientific and scholarly knowledge would not have grown as it did in fact grow during the nineteenth and twentieth centuries.

The effectiveness of universities has been partly a function of their collective self-consciousness, of their perception of themselves as single coherent entities which impose norms and rules and set a standard to conformity with which their individual members were forced to exert themselves.

The universities of the nineteenth and twentieth centuries included within themselves a community of teachers with each other, of teachers and students with each other, and of students with each other. The communities were patchworks; not everyone at a university participated equally in them; some, while being administratively and functionally within the university, did not share in that collective self-consciousness to the same extent as did others. To what extent has the university, which embraces this community, survived the tremendous changes which the increased importance of the university has brought about?

No unambiguous answers can be given to this question. The humanistic side of the universities, and not just in the American universities, has been badly damaged. At one time, the humanistic disciplines, the "arts and sciences" or the "philosophical faculty" were the center of the university. There were, of course, great scientists and scholars in the other parts of the university but the humanistic departments or faculty represented to their colleagues what a university ought to be.

There are in the late twentieth century some very distinguished scholars in the humanities, but they are just not in the ascendancy; they are living on the defensive, surrounded by very alien spirits. These alien spirits are at present in a self-indulgent delirium of destructiveness. They have broken with the traditions from which they have come and what they have to put in its place are things of only very small value. They are not in the majority, but they have their own way, disproportionate to their numbers. There are many who do not share their views but they lack self-confidence in the face of the aggressive certainty of the ascendant minority.

The social sciences are mixed. The solid part of sociology continues on its way, uninterested in the rest of the university or in anything other than its own research and its own graduate students. Thanks to its efforts to be scientific and the esteem which its surveys have come to have in the wider public, it has been ranked relatively highly in the hierarchy of academic subjects. At the same time, throughout Europe and America, what is called "sociological theory" is riddled by the intellectual detritus of the radicalism of the 1960s and 1970s; this is widespread and is not confined to any single country. The economists are in a better position. They have a very exigent subject in which they have full confidence and which enjoys high esteem generally. They are much in demand outside the university because of the importance of their subject matter but their subject has become very technical and most of them too are little interested in the rest of the university.

Historical studies also have many distinguished achievements and receive much attention. They continue in a steady productivity. They, too, however, are afflicted by some of the fashionable hostility to the belief that historical research aims to discover the truth about its diverse subject matters. Nevertheless, they are thoroughly trained in exacting methods of scholarship and it is to historical studies that the university must look for recovery of the lost ground of humanistic studies. Oriental studies too stand on relatively firm intellectual ground in the universities of many countries. It is there that the idea of the university still resides, if it resides anywhere in the university. They are still resistant to the degradation of the humanistic studies. Yet because they are remote from practical activities and have relatively few pupils, they are in danger of being further reduced in resources.

Anthropology has become infested with relativism and agnosticism and it is often under attack from within its own ranks for having been an instrument of imperialism and of being at present a part of a "neocolonialist" ambition of the main Western societies vis-à-vis the "Third World."

The intellectually least disordered part of any university is the natural scientific side. The natural scientists have genuine, widely acknowledged achievements to their credit; they are heeded in governmental counsels and are often called upon for advice. Even those who disparage science and regard it as a part of a corrupt bourgeois society still want more scientific research to be done, and they want more governmental support for it. Scientists disagree among themselves on scientific questions as well as politically, but their disagreements do not weaken their intellectual zeal and their confidence of the importance of what they are doing. They do not, moreover, allow their political convictions to affect their own scientific work or generally, their assessment of the scientific work of those with whom they are in political disagreement. The general derogation of science in some intellectual circles does not have much impact on them. They care for their departments and their students. They complain about the insufficiency of governmental support but this does not reduce their passion for their subjects. Again, they do not take great interest in the university as a whole.

The medical schools and faculties are in a similar position. They too know that the world looks to them for the improvement of its bodily health and they have made so much progress since the beginning of the nineteenth century that they are confident that their science and their students will go on as they have done. The terribly difficult moral problems raised by improvements of medical treatment and the extremely complicated economic and administrative problems of the provision of the care of health, do not cause them to repine.

The intellectual life of the scientific side of the universities has so many triumphs, so many glories, that the difficult problems of the various subjects in themselves and in their unsolved repercussions do not dismay them. However, they too, in consequence of specialization and busyness, tend to neglect their universities as coherent entities and sometimes neglect their students and their junior staff with injurious results for their assimilation of the ethos of science. It is not likely that their work will run into a dead-end because of this. Nevertheless, the university as a whole loses by the concentration and specialization of their attention and their busyness.

Thus, as universities approach the completion of a voyage which has covered nearly two hundred years of intellectual achievements and which has changed our knowledge of nature and in many respects improved our knowledge of society, the university as an institution is navigating in dangerous waters. The universities, or at least some of their members, have tried to be all things to all men, more pleasing and accommodating to the external world, or more preoccupied with changing or abolishing the condition of the external society.

The university has become a way station, performing services for others and not concerned enough to maintain itself as a central institution of society with the major task of improving the stock of ordered knowledge and rational judgment. The maintenance of the university for the performance of just that function is a precondition for its performance of services of so many different sorts for the rest of society.

To do this successfully a university must be to a certain extent inward-looking. It must look to its maintenance as a corporate body entrusted with the responsibility for maintaining, extending, and deepening learning at an advanced level.

Of course, it should not and cannot be wholly self-contained. Neither the objects of its knowledge, nor the condition, economic and political, of its economic provision, nor its sense of responsibility towards society or the infusion of ordered knowledge and rational judgment into society would ever permit it to be wholly self-contained. Its invaluable tradition of autonomy, received from its medieval forebears, never required utter isolation from its society and in its greatest periods of the nineteenth and twentieth centuries, it was never separated in practice or in theory. The university has never been an ivory tower. The danger which it runs in the coming decades is in fact just the opposite of being an ivory tower. There is a danger that it will cease to be a tower at all. If this happens, then it will cease to be a vantage point for understanding and assessing the world. If it ceases to be that, it will also cease to be able to perform the many functions which are demanded of it.

In the early 1990s the external world benefits from the spiritual capital, from the traditions which universities accumulated in the nineteenth and the beginning of the twentieth centuries. This stock of capital and traditions had to be in a continuous process of maintenance, addition, and revision. These were both intellectual and social or institutional processes. If they were not used, reinterpreted and added to, they would have lost their vitality and become fruitless. This is the danger in which universities are being placed in the midst of this centrifugal outrush. More centripetality is required to permit the traditions to be enriched so that the beneficial outflow can continue.

References

Ashby, E., Anderson, M., 1966, *Universities: British, Indian, African: A Study in the Ecology of Higher Education.* Harvard University Press, Cambridge, Massachusetts.

Bartholomew, J.R., 1989, *The Formation of Science in Japan: Building a Research Tradition.* Yale University Press, New Haven.

Ben-David, J., 1968, *Fundamental Research and the Universities.* Organization for Economic Cooperation and Development, Paris.

Ben-David, J., 1977, *Centers of Learning: Britain, France, Germany, United States.* McGraw-Hill, New York.

Ben-David, J., 1984, *The Scientist's Role in Society: A Comparative Study,* rev. edn. University of Chicago Press, Chicago, Illinois.

Berdahl, R.O., 1959, *British Universities and the State.* University of California Press, Berkeley, California.

Beyerchen, A., 1977, *Scientists under Hitler: Politics and the Physics Community in the Third Reich.* Yale University Press, New Haven, Connecticut.

Busch, A., 1959, *Die Geschichte des Privatdozenten: Eine soziologische Studie zur grossbetrieblichen Entwicklung der deutschen Universitäten.* Enke, Stuttgart.

Clark, B.R., 1977, *Academic Power in Italy: Bureaucracy and Oligarchy in National University Systems.* University of Chicago Press, Chicago, Illinois.

Committee on Higher Education, 1963, *Report* [Robbins Report]. Cmnd 2154, HMSO, London.

Craig, J.E., 1984, *Scholarship and Nation Building: The University of Strasbourg and Alsatian Society, 1870–1939.* University of Chicago Press, Chicago, Illinois.

Cummings, W.K., Amamo, I., Kitamura, K., (eds.) 1979, *Changes in the Japanese University: A Comparative Perspective.* Praeger, New York.

Daalder, H., Shils, E., (eds.) 1982, *Universities, Politicians, Bureaucrats: Europe and the United States.* Cambridge University Press, Cambridge.

Geiger, R.L., 1986, *To Advance Knowledge: The Growth of American Research Universities, 1900–1940.* Oxford University Press, New York.

Government-University-Industry Research Roundtable 1990, *The Academic Research Enterprise within the Industrialized Nations: Comparative Perspectives*. National Academy Press, Washington, DC.

Halsey, A.H., Trow, M.A., 1971, *The British Academics*. Faber and Faber, London.

Jarausch, K.H., (ed.), 1983, *The Transformation of Higher Learning, 1860–1930: Expansion, Diversification, Social Opening, and Professionalization in England, Germany, Russia and the United States*. University of Chicago Press, Chicago, Illinois.

Nagai, M. (ed.), 1971, *Higher Education in Japan: Its Take-off and Crash*. University of Tokyo Press, Tokyo.

Oleson, A., Voss, J., 1979, *The Organization of Knowledge in Modern America, 1860–1920*. Johns Hopkins University Press, Baltimore, Maryland.

Paul, H.W., 1985, *From Knowledge to Power: The Rise of the Science Empire in France, 1860–1939*. Cambridge University Press, Cambridge.

Ringer, F.K., 1969, *The Decline of the German Mandarins: The German Academic Community, 1890–1933*, Harvard University Press, Cambridge, Massachusetts.

Schelsky, H., 1971, *Abschied von der Hochschulpolitik oder die Universität im Fadenkreuz des Versagens*. Bertelsmann, Gütersloh.

Schelsky, H., 1969, *Einsamkeit und Freiheit: Idee und Gestalt der deutschen Universität und ihrer Reformen*. Bertelsmann, Düsseldorf.

Shils, E.A., (ed. and tr.), 1973, *Max Weber on Universities: The Power of the State and the Dignity of the Academic Calling in Imperial Germany*. University of Chicago Press, Chicago, Illinois.

Trow, M.A., 1973, *Problems in the Transition from Elite to Mass Higher Education*. Carnegie Commission on Higher Education, Berkeley, California.

Veysey, L.R., 1965, *The Emergence of the American University*. University of Chicago Press, Chicago, Illinois.

Vucinich, A., 1984, *Empire of Knowledge: The Academy of Sciences of the USSR 1917–1970*. University of California Press, Berkeley, California.

Weisz, G., 1983, *The Emergence of Modern Universities in France, 1863–1914*. Princeton University Press, Princeton, New Jersey.

Wittrock, B., Elzinga, A., (eds.), 1985, *The University Research System: The Public Policies of the Home of Scientists*. Almqvist and Wiksell, Stockholm.

Part II
Perspectives

3

The Service of Society and the Advancement
of Learning in the Twenty-First Century

My remarks are about the prospects in the twenty-first century of universities
of the type which gradually emerged in modern times in Europe and then,
since the third quarter of the nineteenth century, in the United States. I do not
have in mind all institutions which are called universities. I think primarily of
those which have traditions of the advancement of learning. By the advancement of learning, I mean the successful effort to discover fundamental truths
over the whole range of important subjects through scientific and scholarly
research, to educate outstandingly able young persons towards deeper understanding and appreciation, and to train them for the intellectual-practical professions. I do not think that those kinds of universities are the only ones
which will exist or should exist. The leading universities even in the best of
times have never had a monopoly of higher education and research in Europe
or North America. Indeed higher education, in Great Britain, Germany, the
United States, Italy, the Scandinavian countries, has always been polymor-
phous. There have been specialized colleges of particular sciences, engineering colleges, commercial colleges, mining academies, colleges of chemistry,
teacher training colleges, and many others. These institutions have offered
professional and advanced occupational training and certification. Sometimes,
they have been called universities, sometimes they have been called colleges,
normal schools, institutes, and so on. Even where they are called universities,
it is well understood that they are different from universities given to the
advancement of learning.

It is in the nature of modern societies—perhaps of all societies in which
there are universities—that there should be a division of labor in the education of young persons in the later years of their second decade and the first
part of their third decade. Each of the organs of this division of labor has an

important and distinctive part to play in the life of society and mankind as a whole. But it is primarily universities as centers of higher learning in teaching and research that I will discuss here.

Among universities, in the more restricted sense, those at the higher levels of the hierarchy, ranked in the order of their prestige, are the kind on which I shall concentrate here. These differences in prestige have not just been a function of the social status of their students, although in the case of the ancient English universities and the American Ivy League colleges and universities, this has been an important ingredient in their prestige. Much of their prestige has, however been a function of the quality of their intellectual achievement in teaching and research. It is difficult to assess the quality of achievements precisely, although it is very evident that universities vary in this respect.

Latterly, some of these leading universities have been called "research universities," a designation which I do not like because it seems to exempt them from their responsibilities in teaching. But even for those who like to use the term, the dividing line between the "research university" and the other universities is shadowy or permeable. There is no easily drawn dividing line. There are gradations in activities as well as in accomplishments.

Those universities which are outstanding in the advancement of learning have usually enjoyed a considerable amount of at least de facto autonomy, a relatively high degree of academic freedom and some measure of internal unity of spirit, sometimes called esprit de corps and which I will call collective self-consciousness. These three institutional features have become the very conditions of the advancement of learning.

Increased Connections with the Outer World

Universities have always trained young persons for the learned—the intellectual-practical—professions. The existence and the very names of the faculties of law, medicine and theology testify to this. Technological studies came into the universities slowly and relatively late and unequally. (Provision was frequently made for higher technological education in specialized institutions.) It was only in the United States and in the modern British universities that technological teaching and research in preparation for the engineering profession became well established by the beginning of the present century. Training in professional careers as scientific and scholarly research workers-cum-university teachers began in Germany in the first quarter of the nineteenth century and spread to other Western countries over the course of the next century. The demand for careers as professional scientific research workers—separate from university teaching—is a demand which universities have been meeting for nearly two centuries in Germany and for about a century in other countries. That indeed has been one of their main services to society; the intensified demand of recent years is novel only in its magnitude. It is a demand which, of all recent demands, is the most consistent with the capacities of universities. The novelty lies in its scale and, like scientific research itself, its increasing costliness. The devotion of so much energy and time by university teachers gives the lie to the silly charge, frequently made, that universities have been "ivory towers," cut off entirely from the practical affairs of society. The universities have always been intimately linked with their societies. In the coming decades, university teachers—although they are not only teachers—in most fields of the natural and social sciences, and even in the humanistic subjects, will turn their attention outwardly towards their own societies and towards other societies, more than they did before the First World War.

This more pronounced turning outwards will be in part a consequence of a reduction in the economic self-sufficiency of universities in the next century. Universities will be forced increasingly to depend on revenues from sources other than the tuition fees of students and the interest or dividends from endowments. The greater costs of research, resulting from the growing sophistication of scientific research and the increase in the size of academic departments, in the salaries of academics and administrators, and the costs of services needed for the health, well-being, and security of their staffs and students, as well as the increased costs of libraries, and of costs imposed by government welfare legislation—all these will make universities even more dependent on the financial support of patrons outside themselves.

The outward turning of universities will also be a consequence of the growth in demands made on them by the societies in which they exist. These will include the following: demands for the improvement of health through medical research, and in international and regional economic competitiveness through technology; for better communications and better transportation by land and air, for improved production and transmission of energy, for the prevention of pollution of the environment, for advances in calculation and record-keeping, for the improvement of animal health and breeding, and so on. These are all demands for scientific research which can be applied with beneficial practical results.

Some but not all of this research will also be fundamental research requiring the kinds of talents and skills to be found in universities. Some of it will be done in governmental laboratories or private business firms or other private institutions. To a greater extent than in the previous century, academic scientists will be constrained to be in very close contact with nonacademic scientists. Furthermore, most of the research on these "practical" problems will have to be supported financially by external patrons, governments, private firms, and private foundations. Thus, the sources of the demand for the results of the research, the sources of financial support and the dispersed locations of research, will all contribute to focusing the attention of the academic scientist beyond the boundaries of the academic world.

The research done by physical scientists and by biomedical scientists usually aims to discover a solution to a specific practical question, such as a cure for a particular ailment or the provision of a less costly way of producing a particular product. Sometimes large projects are undertaken with a rather wide or general objective—for example, the "war on cancer"—but these general objectives are broken down into numerous, more narrowly focused parts with a particular objective and a particular applicable result in mind. Research in the social sciences includes certain kinds of sociological and economic research which are thought to be desirable by government, private business firms, and civic and political organizations. Though not immediately applicable in practical action, they are thought to provide reliable information about existing situations in which practical decisions must be taken. Whether the summary of the reports of these particular investigations are read and considered by those who participate in the making of decisions is uncertain; the investigations are in any case commissioned with that intention. An increasing portion of sociological and economic research is supported by governmental bodies.

Social scientists have almost always focused on their societies, which made up most of their subject matter, but the new "outwardness" is somewhat different. Empirical social scientists have often hoped that their research would have some influence, sooner or later, on public opinion and legislation. Now they are brought closer to their respective societies, by the commissioning and support of their research by governmental and private bodies which assert that they wish to "make use" of its results in their own practical activities. The research of social scientists becomes more "policy oriented" because that is what their patrons want.

The results of research in the physical and biological sciences have turned out to be more applicable, and much more immediately so, than used to be the case. Those who would use them are more insistent on having these results sooner rather than later. The exigencies of economic competition and the urgency of social problems render unavoidable these demands for speedily applicable results.

The prospect of applicable results produces in patrons a stronger disposition to specify in advance the research which might lead to the practical results desired. More research will thus be prescribed by patrons. Even if the maxim of "he who pays the piper calls the tune" is not fully realized, there will be a pronounced tendency to listen to the piper. Research projects will be conceived with an eye on the interests of prospective patrons.

It should not be thought that in their response to these demands from government, private business firms, politicians, publicists and civic agitators, university administrators, and teachers are merely passive recipients of stimuli from the outside. Quite the contrary. They are in fact frequently eager collaborators. Their interests, their ideals, and, in some cases, the traditions of their professions, make them genuine partners in the effort to supply the knowledge needed, or thought to be needed for the practical purposes of the world outside the university.

Natural scientists can no longer be supported from the universities' own regular budgets; their income from tuition fees paid by students in the natural sciences, and from endowment and gifts "earmarked" for research in the natural sciences, is insufficient. Without external patronage, research in the physical sciences in particular but also in the biomedical sciences would have to come to a halt. This is also true in the social sciences where the older pattern of research by one teacher or of one teacher and an assistant-cum-graduate student is no longer feasible, except in marginal cases. Both in the natural and social sciences, external patronage is necessary to meet the expenses of graduate students who work on the research projects of the "principal investigator."

"Economic necessity" thus compels academic scientists and social scientists to look outside the university for the wherewithal to meet the costs of their research. Furthermore, many of the research projects for which external patrons are willing to pay are initiated by academic scientists, not merely because funds for the particular projects are available, but because the academics themselves share the ideals and practical ends of their patrons. Academics have always lived in a world which was not confined within the boundaries of their universities. Now and in the future, less of their life and attention is and will be confined within these boundaries.

It is not only in finding patrons for the financial support of their research and in the choice of problems for research that universities will have to look outwards. In their policies of admission to student bodies and in the appointment of teachers, criteria are being voluntarily used by administrators and teachers, or are being imposed on them by governments, to look beyond academic and intellectual qualifications and make decisions on the basis of criteria of social justice or plain political influence and threat—in the case of appointments, not only by those criteria but also by the criterion of ability to procure funds from external bodies.

Universities in the past have not always been free from some control by governments over their policies of admission of students. When governments stated that young persons who had successfully completed certain courses of study in secondary school were automatically entitled to be admitted as students in state universities, that was a form of control over admissions. It was, however, one resting on the application of criteria of intellectual achievement and inferred intellectual capacity. In the last decades of this century, governments have extended their interest in admissions. Criteria of race, sex, and social status, all different from the criterion of the aspirants' intellectual achievements and capacities, have been introduced from outside the university.

There has been an increased demand for higher education among young persons and their parents. Many young persons now accept that going to college or university is a normal stage of life. Among politicians, educational publicists, and academic administrators, there is a steady insistence that educational opportunities on grounds of social justice and economic efficiency must be extended, and that the possibility of fulfillment of individual ambitions for rising in society through educational qualifications be offered to social strata or ethnic groups which previously did not demand or receive such education. This has increased the size of student bodies and has widened the range of variation and diversity of intellectual ability within the university. A further result of the pressure of public opinion reinforced by government is enlarged teaching staffs to deal with increased numbers of students. This increased number of teachers has rendered more difficult the process of assimilating young teachers into the academic ethic.

Less pressing but insistent nonetheless is the demand by educational publicists and by bureaucrats, academic and governmental, that the universities accommodate "continuing" and "permanent" education, that is, the provision of education for the older generation. Much of the demand—at least, the demand predicted and demanded by the publicists of higher education— seems to be for specialized technological training. This is likely to fall, to a considerable extent, on advanced and specialized institutions outside the universities. Where such persons attend universities, they are not likely to do so as ordinary undergraduates; they will rather participate in advanced seminars and in research projects. They will not add greatly to the numbers in any single department, and they might contribute substantially by their superior experience in modern technology.

In recent decades there has been an increase in the universities in the numbers of persons older than the ordinary undergraduates of the past century and a half, but these still make up a very small part of the total number of students. The probable progress of "open universities" is likely to forestall any strain which might arise from older undergraduates. Older students, or "mature students" as they are called in Great Britain, have thus far not been a burdensome problem for universities; nor are "returning scholars" in the American university a source of distraction. The older students themselves face difficulties of adjustment to a mode of life which they have outgrown, but they do not raise a severe problem for the universities. Most of these students in "continuing education" will already have completed their undergraduate studies, so they will find themselves mainly among graduate students. Since graduate students are often in their thirties, the difference between them and the "returning" students will not be great enough to cause any problems out of the ordinary. On the contrary, they might even have a sobering effect on their younger classmates.

Although "recurrent education" or "permanent education" is frequently invoked by the educational experts of UNESCO and the Organization for Economic Cooperation and Development and parallel national associations as an instance of what awaits the universities of the twenty-first century, and as an argument for the renunciation of the "traditionalist" and "elitist" ways, I doubt whether this will raise much of an obstacle to the advancement of learning.

Perhaps more serious for the advancement of learning will be the disproportionate increase in the number of students who wish to prepare themselves to earn their livelihood on the basis of what they have studied and the certificates, diplomas, or degrees they have received. They will add to the large fraction of students who are not very interested in the intellectual offerings of the university. But such students have never been absent. Their increased fraction will encroach on the intellectual or strictly scientific and scholarly parts of the university. There seems to be no way out of this. The demands of parents and young persons, the insistence of government and the desire of administrators to increase the number of students and the income from tuition and other fees, render an increased representation of intellectually relatively uninterested students highly probable.

It should not, however, be thought that this expansion in size of the student body and the broadened range of recruitment are simply results of the pressure of external demands and of the desire for increased revenue from tuition fees. The expansion is quite in accord with the political and social ideals of university teachers themselves, as well as with their interest in increasing the size of the teaching staffs of their departments.

Whereas the demands for many types of research, for trained scientists, technologists and administrators and for the realization of various practical ideas come primarily from outside the university with willing collaboration from within, there is another drive towards closer connections between society and the academic profession. Academics in many fields, in the social sciences and in the more theoretical natural sciences and in recent decades in the humanities, have become much more political. They have become more actively partisan in the political contentions of the day. They have become more actively partisan in the political contentions outside the universities, and they have also thought it permissible and proper to express their partisanship in their teaching; this is especially the case in the social sciences and the humanities, where the boundaries between teaching about political and social life and asserting partisan attitudes cannot be so clearly delineated as in the natural sciences. They sometimes justify this by asserting that objectivity in scientific and scholarly research is impossible and that university teaching and research are inevitably partisan. This attitude is freely conjoined with radical collectivistic and emancipationist political attitudes.

The increased prominence of expression of political partisanship has gone hand-in-hand with a greater attention to contemporary works and activities in courses of study in the humanities and the social sciences. Contemporaneity of subject matter does not make partisanship inevitable but makes it more likely. This is definitely one of the injurious consequences for the universities of their closer connections with the "world."

Now none of these connection with the "world," that is, with practical activity outside the universities, is entirely new. The real divergence from the past, and particularly since the nineteenth century, lies in their quantitative expansion. It is not so much that new activities are required, but rather the new scale of those desired activities and their distribution among the various subjects or disciplines cultivated in universities. This, and the increased size of the student bodies of universities seems to me, once realistically assessed, to be within the compass of the capacities of universities to do more or less what is sought of them.

Many of the scientific or technological services which are demanded are already on some considerable scale being provided by the universities within the limits of their intellectual or scientific capacities. Some of the services sought are perhaps beyond human powers—at least as far as the foreseeable future is concerned. Some of the services demanded of the universities are probably unrealistically assessed, both by those who assert them and by those who are apprehensive of them. The impediment which some of them would present to the advancement of learning is not likely to be realized.

I think in particular of "universal access to higher education." It is probably a mistake to think that all the young persons in any generation desire to attend universities, whether for advancing their careers, or for learning about and understanding the world. They are not moved by the prospect of aspiring to a higher social status; they will not exert or deprive themselves for an extended period in order to attain a much higher level of income. They do not want to engage in activities which entail ends or responsibilities which run even a year or two into the future. They do not want to have to worry about tasks which take months or years to carry out. Hence, universities, as they are or as they are desired to be in order to accommodate themselves to "universal access," will have no fascination for such persons. Universities will bore or repel them.

Even in the relatively "elitist," "mass higher education" in the United States which serves as a yardstick to measure the achievements and the deficiencies of "access" in other countries, the "drop-out rate" is about 50 percent. Furthermore, a large fraction of the student body in higher education in the United States is enrolled in community colleges. In those colleges, only a rather small fraction is inscribed in the two-year programs which permit those who complete them to transfer to a "four-year college" or to a university. Again, only a very small fraction of those who complete these programs ever go on to further study. It should also be remembered that much of what is taught in those programs would be taught in secondary schools in Western Europe. In short, the scale of "mass higher education" in the United States is much inflated.

Even if we disregard the fictions of "mass higher education" in the United States, the number of persons attending university is still very far from the entire cohort of young persons of the appropriate age. The era of "universal access" is still very remote from realization, even in the United States. There is no reason to believe that it will ever include the entire cohort. Of course, this does not mean that student bodies will not become larger and that there will not be the pressure of increasing large classes, heavier teaching obligations and an increase in the size of teaching staffs. The task of teaching will be multiplied and the problems of teaching the unqualified and uninterested will be aggravated.

Resources: Financial, Social, Intellectual, and Moral

Financial and Social

L. T. Hobhouse, when asked in a seminar at the London School of Economics what was the ideal standard of living, answered, "Ten percent more than you have." That is the way it is with universities. They never have enough. The map of knowledge is unlimited in its surface and its depth. The appetites of professors, once they have tasted the funds of their financial quarries, are never satiable. University administrators in recent years always find new uses for money; they never have enough. Quite apart from the appetite for money, the costs of research, of salaries, of equipment for laboratories, of books for libraries, seem to rise without cease. The "sophistication factor" in scientific research will probably go on increasing as instrumentation becomes more powerful.

With all these extreme demands on universities, it is obvious that they will need both external support and inner strength. The external support is partly financial, partly moral. The financial support must come from governmental sources, from private philanthropic institutions, from individual philanthropists, from private business firms, from parents willing to pay the fees for tuition, maintenance, etc., and, in some cases, from the students themselves who "work their way through college."

Governments for their part assert that they want the universities to accommodate more students, but they are rarely willing to provide for the numbers which they allege that they desire. They are willing to pay for research; they are less willing to pay for education, although they do in fact provide vary large sums for it.

It is unlikely that universities can cover any large part of their budgets from earnings on patents or from the commercialization of their scientific discoveries. Professors might add to their incomes by consultation, but those gains do not flow to the universities. Gifts and grants and contracts for their performance of research must make up a large part of the current operating budget of a university.

Universities need the financial support of governments to enable them to try to meet the demands which governments and societies direct towards them. Governments have come forth eagerly and generously but, in recent years, they have become somewhat more reluctant to do so. The demands on governments are greater and no less demanding than the demands on universities by governments and societies.

Governmental financial support depends on political and public opinion. At one time, the standing of universities was not an issue for the universities; they could take their own good standing for granted. Only a small part of the population was clearly aware of universities. Journalists had relatively little interest in them as compared with the present. Legislatures in the American states where there were outstanding state universities, as in the Middle West and Far West, valued them benevolently.

The degree of open-handedness of any government depends on the convictions of legislators, cabinet members and their staffs in the executive branch, and civil servants, and on their assessment of the political support which alternatives of policy have in the opinion of the electorate. There have been societies in which the public and its politically active component were relatively ignorant of and indifferent towards universities. This is scarcely so any longer. Universities receive much attention nowadays. They have become newsworthy—their internal affairs have now become sources and objects of news. The state of public opinion about the universities, and the state of mind of those who write or broadcast about them, create the medium in which legislators have to decide how much money should be spent on universities. Philanthropists are likewise alert to what "the public" wants partly because they do not wish to be out of step with prevailing currents of political and public opinion, and because they do not have enough ideas of their own. A part of the public consists of the parents of university students, who have an additional interest because they pay or have paid so much to have their offspring attend university.

It is clear that universities must now take into account what others think of them. The esteem or disesteem in which they are held in their societies can affect them in many ways, not least financially. Hence in thinking about the universities of the next century, it is certainly relevant to speculate about their standing in the public mind; it is relevant because the munificence of governments depends in part on public opinion.

At present, universities are both esteemed and disesteemed. Let me begin by discussing first the disesteem of universities.

There are many persons in the wider society even today who have no appreciation of universities. Universities do nothing to please their taste. Universities until recently were not for those romantics who believed that nothing inherited by tradition and formalized and learned by study has any value. They were few in number. The heirs of this romanticism have now firm places in the universities, but they remain inimical to them. They are no longer few. For persons who believe that universities should do what churches once did—and which they still do although much less than in the past—in providing an incontestable, absolutely compelling belief in the ultimate meaning of life, as they now exist and are likely to be in the next century, universities are of little value. Then there are many persons "who couldn't care less," who are not only "religiously unmusical," but also spiritually and intellectually unmusical, who have no care for the transfiguring potentialities—real or putative—of universities. There are very many persons who are insensate to the sphere of the transcendental, who do not puzzle about the world, who are interested only in the moment, in momentary pleasures and immediate tasks. The things about which the universities teach and do research leave them cold. There are probably numerous persons in positions in political life who are like that, but they do not wish to appear to be that way. It is part of the cant of politics to praise universities, and only uncouth brutes disregard the necessity of saying that universities are very important.

Universities are no longer so remarkable to ordinary persons. They are not so remote from them. They do not stand on such a lofty promontory as they once did when few persons attended them and when it was thought to be a distinguishing privilege to do so. Over much of the past two centuries and even longer, it was thought that being associated with a university conferred a status almost on the level of that of the upper classes. So many persons have university degrees nowadays, that a degree from a university no longer confers a high distinction.

Universities certainly seem to have lost some of the aura which once surrounded them. This is true of state universities in Europe and the United States as well as of American private universities. Furthermore, some persons are still angry at the universities for having allowed themselves to be intimidated by the *soi-disant* revolutionary students a quarter of a century ago; others are still displeased with them for having resisted. In the European state universities, many states have enacted legislation which has treated the universities as not fit to be trusted with their own affairs. The powers of professors in their universities have been restricted, those of students increased in certain respects but, above all, the powers of civil servants over universities have been increased. Even British universities, which seemed to be safe from these types of legislation in the 1960s and 1970s, were very roughly treated by their government through the 1980s. In the United States, universities have come in for severe censure.

Both from outside and from within, universities are castigated. Professor Allan Bloom's *The Closing of the American Mind: How Higher Education Has Failed Democracy and Impoverished the Souls of Today's Students*[1] is an eloquent and vehement denunciation of American universities and university teachers. It was an unprecedented "bestseller"; more than a million copies of the book have been sold. No other book on universities has ever sold in such great numbers in any country. Although it is an eloquent book and is generally on the right side, it is not well argued and is full of irrelevant and insufficiently informed statements. But it denounces American universities very relentlessly. Scarcely a good word is said in their favor. I think that its immense sale is a result of the desire of a public discontented with the universities to seek an explanation for their deficiencies. Mr. Charles Sykes's *ProfScam: Professors and the Demise of American Higher Education*[2] is not so eloquent, not so concerned with fundamental principles, and it has not sold in such large numbers as Professor Bloom's book. The author does not write from inside the universities as does Professor Bloom. Nevertheless, he has compiled a large dossier of academic malpractices and has attracted much attention. Mr. Roger Kimball's *Tenured Radicals: How Politics Has Corrupted Our Higher Education*[3] is a very solid piece of work and at the same time a *chronique scandaleuse* about the teaching of the "humanities" in American colleges and universities. His book too has been purchased in large numbers. The widespread interest in these books, all of which place American universities in a very unfavorable light, seems to me to indicate that the public thinks something is amiss.

Latterly, in the United States, certain quite widely read periodicals have begun to write about the prevalence of the practice of "political correctness" in appointments to universities. The introduction into academic appointments of criteria of "political correctness" has been repeatedly exposed to the general public. Editors and journalists who are not zealots report on these activities; the result cannot be anything but prejudicial to the standing of universities.

All this evidence of dissatisfaction notwithstanding, the standing of the universities in liberal-democratic societies is fundamentally very high. Why else do governments turn to them for the scientific and technological and even social and economic knowledge which they think is necessary for conducting their affairs? Why else do journalists turn to them for their ostensibly authoritative opinions on all sorts of topics? Why else do so many young persons take it for granted that they must attend universities? Why else should young persons be urged to attend them? Why else should some older persons, who did not attend them when young, wish to make up for their lost youth and for opportunities passed over? Why else should it be asserted that those who have been to them should return recurrently in order to bring themselves "up to date"?

Why are young and middle-aged persons urged to attend university? Why is it intimated that their lives will be blighted if they do not "go to college"? This paradox of censure of universities and repeated emphasis on their indispensability could be dissolved if one could reasonably assert that the whole campaign for higher education is an insincere hoax. It is perhaps "in the interest" of the administrators of colleges and universities, college and university presidents, professors of education, educational publicists who are in the forefront of those who encourage this campaign. After all, the more students the more revenue, the greater the enhancement of their own importance; they all stand to gain from an increased number of students. The professors and publicists of education have nothing material to gain but they too join in the chorus of a song which is easy to sing. No, it is not a hoax. The belief that participation in the learning of a university improves the lives of those who pass through it is very deep. The clichés of presidents, deans, et al., are repugnant, but they are so because they are merely lifeless reiterations of something very serious.

Courageous is the person who would say to them: "Halt; this far and no further. It is simply not true that you will benefit from attending a college or university more than you would by spending those years in some other useful and honorable way—such as working in a bank or a factory or an office." He would not be thought courageous; he would be regarded as foolish, flippant and reactionary.

"More is better" is the governing maxim. Better for whom? Better for everyone! Better, for one thing, for the persons who attend university. The theory of human capital claims that the life-time earnings of persons who have more "schooling"—"schooling" includes attendance at university—are greater than those of persons with less schooling. It is furthermore better for society. A large part of the increase in the productivity of workers in industry and commerce is attributed by economists to the increased "investment" in education.

There is something more than mere increase in "life-time earnings" which underlies the urge to attend universities. Universities are the way to a superior mode of life. What was once a feature of the American image of the right ordering of society, namely a society in which members of the lower classes could enter the middle classes or even the upper classes, has now come to Great Britain and is making its mark on the Continent. The percentage of offspring of the working classes—"*Arbeiterkinder*"—at university was thought and is still thought to be a measure of the goodness of society. In the United States, the low percentage of "minorities" in universities is regarded by the spokesmen for associations intended to advance their cause, by university administrators and by publicists and teachers of radical disposition, as evidence of the extent to which the universities are failing to do their duty by the ambitious and hitherto deprived. This too is evidence that universities are regarded as indispensable to raising the lowly.

It is thought that the universities must become avenues, and more than avenues, to higher positions and a better life; they must be the vehicles which carry their passengers on the avenues which lead them upwards. Those who urge this do not like to hear it said that they wish to turn the lower-class beneficiaries of university education into members of the middle classes. But that is what they want. They studiously avoid such language; the idiom of "social mobility" is more agreeable to them, but where will this mobility lead? They do not like to name the destination, but the fact remains that the destination is the "middle class." (I recall the late Professor David Glass of the London School of Economics reviling contemporary capitalistic society because there were so few offspring of the working classes among university students, while, in almost the same breath, he denounced the universities for preparing their students for middle-class careers.)

Of course, many of those who demand this opening of "life chances" do not care much about what many of us regard as the real business of universities. They seem interested primarily in the certifying capacity of the university. Having the certificate will enable its holders to obtain a "better," more highly remunerated position, with higher social status. These zealots of social mobility are uninterested in the intellectual activities which go on in universities. They want to admit everyone to the point of "universal access" and to certify them with degrees. Despite the evaporation of that aura which used to be attached to university degrees, there has never been a time when so many individuals have sought to acquire them and in which the possession of a university degree is regarded as an indispensable or minimal qualification for appointment to numerous relatively elevated positions in society.

This does not sound like evidence that universities are regarded seriously in our contemporary Western societies. I think, however, that regarding the advantages of higher income and higher social status which result from attendance at a university does not tell the whole story; it really hides a deeper respect for what universities are and can offer to their pupils. Persons who do not have a university degree feel, at least partly, deprived of something ineffably precious. I have from time to time been told by taxi drivers and waiters that the regret of their lives was not having "gone to college." Jude the Obscure wanted to become a student at Christ Church because he thought, ignorantly and vaguely, that his life would be translated into a higher spiritual sphere if he were admitted to Christ Church. It might well be that the passionate and often ignorant urging of young persons to attend college or university, and the strong desire of many of them to do so, are both fundamental manifestations of a belief that the university is a charismatic institution, that it knows sacred things, that it participates in the life of "the idea." For this reason, which cannot nowadays be expressed in such a "spiritualistic" idiom, young persons aspire and their elders wish them to be students at university.

What all these aspirants seek and yearn for is the university, as it is or has been, or as it should be. The majority of the great number of seekers for admission do not know anything about the kind of university which is foreseen by those who would reform universities into institutions such as they are not at present. They know, dimly and ignorantly, about the universities as they exist, unreconstructed or traditional universities. They wish to be at a university where as a simple person, a doorman, once said to me, "boys and girls study." These "boys and girls," their parents and their teachers, do not know anything about "the university of the future"—they do not know about "lifelong education," "recurrent education," "education by satellite," "interdisciplinary education," "multi-media education"; they do not know about all those things which universities are urged to become or do. Of course, neither do they know about fundamental research, the transmission of the best intellectual traditions of Western civilization or any of the other merits, which the critics of universities as they are at present, denounce. Nevertheless, what little these relatively uninformed persons do know about universities is formed out of vague notions of universities as they exist at present or in the recent past and which the reformers wish to obliterate—and not of universities of the future, which the reformers wish to bring into being.

All these observations seem to me to establish the contention that, at least in contemporary liberal-democratic societies, universities have a very high standing indeed. More young persons seek to enter universities than seek to enter the armed forces, or the churches, or even to seek careers as professional football, basketball, or baseball players. It might be that they are wrong—many of them do not knowingly or explicitly wish to attend university in order to participate in an elevated stratum of spiritual or intellectual existence (which is not quite the same as a higher social status!).

Universities are much criticized nowadays by governments, civil servants, professors of education, journalists, et al. There are numerous reasons for these denunciations—some are good reasons, many are poor. The universities do cost immense sums of money, their achievements cannot be measured in any clear and reliable way, many persons fail in them, and they certainly do not accomplish the solution of economic and social problems which some persons expect of them. Nevertheless, these societies cling to them. The universities do not survive simply because professors have a vested interest in their survival, since their livelihood and their conception of their calling depend on the continued existence of the universities. That would never be enough. These societies cling to them because, in the last analysis, they are their last best hope for a transfigured existence.

Kingsley Amis, nearly thirty years ago, when the Robbins report appeared, said "More will mean worse." He has not found many who have followed in his footsteps. Rather his apothegm is often cited as an epitome of a reactionary view which no one in his right mind would espouse.

The plain fact of the matter is that our modern Western societies (and increasingly the more advanced societies outside the West, such as Japan and India), have become intertwined in so many ways with the universities that they cannot get along without them. Too many persons, too many activities, too many ambitions, too many undertakings have been launched and too many important functions are performed by them for societies ever to say: "We have had enough trouble with universities. They cost too much; they do not serve us well; they are contrary to our ideals of equality and social justice; they have not removed our budgetary deficit domestically or the negative balance in our international accounts; they have not found ways of diminishing juvenile delinquency or adult crime; they had not found cures for cancer or AIDS; they have, through their discoveries and inventions, polluted the atmosphere and befouled the landscape. Let them go! Let us hear no more of them!"

There is not a chance that such notions would ever be uttered aloud by anyone who is in any position of authority. There would be an outcry of public denunciation from all the *bien pensants* who make a livelihood from casting stones at the universities, an outcry from parents who are so dissatisfied with them that they purchase a million copies of Professor Bloom's book, demonstrations, obscenities, graffiti from mobs of ragged students complaining that insensate professors are destroying their opportunities to ascend into the reviled middle classes, or to realize their aspiration for success in a society which they denounce for its worship of success.

I have sketched this fantasy to make clear that it has no chance of coming about. The universities are here to stay. Much of the criticism of the self-indulgence of the universities is an act of hypocrisy by their beneficiaries. They mean it and they do not mean it. They are like the radical students of a quarter of a century ago who delighted in abusing the universities and formed "critical universities" of their own, but as soon as they were threatened with expulsion or suspension from those allegedly hateful institutions, they fought like tigers to avoid it. As a student newspaper of the University of Chicago of that time—a proponent of the abuse and degradation of the universities—cried out when about forty of the "occupiers" were expelled and about eighty suspended for as long as two years: "Think of their careers!"

It is too late—too late by about seven centuries for Western societies—to decide whether modern societies can get along without universities. For good reasons and bad, they must have them—much as they have been.

A project to abolish the universities or condemn them to pay their own way using income from tuition fees, from the sale of their services in the market and from gifts from private patrons, would soon be abandoned. Governments will continue to support them because society depends upon universities and wants to have them much as they are now.

Intellectual and Moral Resources

It seems to me to be clear that governments—and private patrons—are going to continue to support universities, because both governments and societies believe that life would be worse without them. Both governments and societies know that they cannot exist without them. It is also likely that the financial support which the universities desire, and which they think they need, will be insufficient for all the activities and arrangements which they will want.

The question then arises: even if they have more money than they are likely to have, can the universities satisfy the numerous demands which are laid upon them? I doubt whether they will be able to do this. None of these demands can be successfully met solely by scientific technological, sociological, and economic knowledge. Perhaps some of them cannot be met at all. Nevertheless, in so far as scientific knowledge can contribute to some extent to improvements in dealing with the numerous problems put before the universities, the universities can do at least a little of what is sought from them.

In one respect, universities can do what no other institutions can do, namely train scientists and scientific technologists and physicians and produce fundamental scientific and biomedical knowledge. The universities certainly have the intellectual capacity to teach and to train and to do research. No other institutions can perform these three closely interdependent activities so well. Other institutions, for example, research institutions, might do research very well, in some cases better than the universities, but they cannot teach. If they do, they become like universities and, for many reasons, they will not be able to do it as well. In the provision of fundamental scientific and scientific technological knowledge and in the training of persons to devote their lives to the pursuit of such knowledge, the universities are irreplaceable. There is no substitute for their intellectual achievements and capacities. If universities do not do these things, they will not be done.

At a time when there are persistent, oblique demands for the suspension or relaxation of standards in the assessment of students and in the appointment of teachers, the natural sciences seem to be holding the line unwaveringly. When it comes to supervising those who are learning to do research, there are some indications that not all is as it should be. Some senior scientists— "principal investigators"—who undertake to conduct more projects with larger staffs and groups of graduate students, do not guide and supervise their charges adequately. This is perhaps the source of some of the unseemly events in the recent history of biomedical research in distinguished universities in the United States.

These occurrences would seem to indicate, not deficient intellectual capacities but rather insufficient deference to the scientific and academic ethic. For several decades, there have been complaints about senior teachers avoiding the teaching of undergraduates, and sloughing off the responsibility for teaching onto inexperienced graduate students, called "teaching assistants." When confronted with these charges, the reply has often referred to the fact that supervising the research of graduate students is also teaching. Cases of malpractice by younger scientists seem to indicate that the supervision of research and the inculcation of the scientific ethic in the training of graduate students has been neglected in teaching at that level too.

Nevertheless, given the vast size of the profession of science, cases of malpractice are relatively few—as far as is known. In the large majority of cases, responsibilities are probably taken very seriously and the scientific ethic is effectively instilled in the oncoming generation of scientists. In this respect, the future seems to be assured. The tradition of science in the universities will be maintained.

The same cannot be said with equal confidence regarding the other parts of the university. Although it may be assumed with reasonable assurance that the intellectual quality of young persons entering the physical sciences and mathematics, etc., will remain high, despite the deteriorated condition of secondary education, this is less certain for the "human sciences" ranging from biology to the humanities, particularly the study of modern literature. These are the fields which have shown most responsiveness to the demands for social justice in their policies of admission, promotion and appointment.

The University as a Moral Entity in the Twenty-First Century

A university is not simply a center of instruction and investigation. It is a center of the advancement of learning. There is an ideal inherent in the idea of the advancement of learning. It is an ideal of a life illuminated by understanding. The understanding in question is not just the understanding of physical and organic nature. It includes the understanding of man and of his powers and capacities, not only in relation to physical and biological nature but in relation to fellow human beings and the ends of life. There has long been a division of labor in the universities. The tasks of dealing with the latter have fallen to the social sciences and the humanistic disciplines.

It seems most probable that the physical sciences and mathematics will be up to the demands for scientific and scientific technological knowledge, and for dealing at least with the cognitive component of the problems with which governments and societies are concerned. I am more doubtful about the other subjects and the problems with which they deal. For one thing, the problems of justice and the government of society are not only or even primarily cognitive problems. But I doubt whether the social sciences—except for economics—have a great deal to offer on the cognitive side in their present and prospective situations. Certain aspects of the descriptive capacities of sociology have improved markedly but not their analytical achievements; I do not think they are likely to improve in the proximate future because they are on the wrong track and are obdurately unaware of that. These disciplines have become technical without becoming scientific. In so far as they have not become technical and relatively rigorously descriptive, they have become political and wrongheadedly so.

This raises fundamental issues regarding the university of the twenty-first century, as a center of the advancement of learning.

Questions have been raised about whether the universities could survive as centers of the advancement of learning under the conditions which life in the twenty-first century will impose on them. Demands for all sorts of practical purposes will be imposed on them, and their funds for doing what has to be done in the way of teaching and research will be short. It is my view that, thanks to the division of labor among institutions of higher education, the universities will be able to accommodate themselves to the demands of the time without losing their souls. At least they will not lose their souls just because of the demands of their societies. Nor will they necessarily lose their souls because they are straitened financially. Of course, both the demands of society and the insufficient funds made available by society will make life for universities as centers of learning more difficult. Survival will not be easy. Universities which attempt to conduct themselves under present and prospective conditions along the lines laid out by Wilhelm von Humboldt will have a hard time of it. Scientific research is extraordinarily expensive research. The social sciences, which were scarcely known in Humboldt's time, have become both widely practiced and very expensive, although not in comparison with the costliness of research in the natural sciences. Even humanistic research, which was long the work of individual scholars working without machinery and teams of assistants, has become more expensive than it used to be, partly as a result of a rise in expectations about amenities and conveniences.

Universities are bound to be straitened financially. Against the competition of the demands for health and welfare, universities will not be able to raise the funds to meet their ideal budgets. Universities have limitlessly expanding "needs" for additional funds, regardless of how much they already have. Policies for welfare and health also have indeterminate objectives and can never obtain enough support. The demand for health services increases with their provision. Whatever the scale of support of the welfare services, it is never enough. It is a journey without end. Every failure is a challenge to spend more from the public treasury.

When universities began to receive the funds which permitted so much equipment, building and books as well as amenities, they did not have this competition. Funds from governments are, even for the great state universities, bound to be curtailed by the condition of the economy as well as because of the demands of other users. Private foundations are not nowadays likely to concentrate much of their revenue on private universities, and to support subjects which are costly and show very few monetarily calculated benefits. Private philanthropic foundations do not wish to have it thought that they are "elitist." Insufficient revenues are likely to change the balance of universities from what it was under conditions of greater affluence.

It will probably be necessary for universities to narrow the range of the subjects they teach and in which they conduct research because they will find it more difficult to raise funds for various fields commensurately with their envisaged necessities. The subjects which are left short of funds are likely to be humanistic subjects because certain of them attract relatively few students, and the cost per student of maintaining an adequate library and enough teachers to cover the subject well is rather higher than in more populous fields, especially those without the need for expensive equipment like radiotelescopes. Such relatively costly subjects are likely to be sacrificed to the god of "cost-effectiveness."

Of course, universities have not always taught every subject. There were, from the beginning, universities which did not have all four faculties. In modern times there have been distinguished universities without schools of engineering or architecture. There have been outstanding universities without medical schools and without schools of divinity.

Nevertheless, the general pattern of the university has been to teach all established subjects over their whole range and to teach the more recondite subjects as long as they are intellectually established. Tibetan religion is thought to be a proper university subject, but not astrology. Under present circumstances, some of the small number universities teaching Tibetan and Tibetan religion are likely to think it necessary to discontinue those subjects because the number of students studying them is too small and the number of teachers needed for the subject is too large, given the smaller income available from tuition fees and grants and interest from endowments and gifts.

Let us say that a university discontinues the study of Tibetan and Assyrology, perhaps also Egyptology. This would be a heavy blow against the humanistic disciplines at a time when they are especially important to a university, particularly in the present situation. I do not refer here to intellectual importance, but rather to the importance of the teaching of such subjects in the spiritual economy of the university.

It is often said that a university is more than its separate departments and its administration. It is thought that it is a whole; at least some of its members think that it should be a whole. It is difficult to say what they mean; many of those who say this are hard put to tell just what it means to say that a university should be a "whole." Nevertheless, it is not just a figment of the imagination. By "whole" they mean that all the parts or most of the parts of the university are thought by their members to belong together in the sense that they have common values. A university is a whole when the individual members define themselves by their membership in it because they see themselves as all adhering to certain common values. The chief of these is the common value of fundamental truths and the means of seeking them. Not all the members of a university seek these fundamental truths, even under the best conditions. They do not participate equally in this collective self-consciousness. Some are more prominent than others as representative of the idea of the university as whole.

In the past two centuries, some of the more prominent bearers of these values, and of their universities which embodied those values, were humanistic scholars. It has been in the humanistic subjects within a university, especially in the recondite ones, that the care for the university as a whole was often found. Perhaps this is a precipitate of the period when classical studies and Biblical studies, including the study of the ancient Near East, were at the heart of a university, and when the teachers of these subjects were convinced of their centrality in the whole world of learning. They thought themselves to be not only the teachers and investigators of their subjects but the heart of the university. The teachers of other subjects, for example, political science or genetics, might have regarded themselves as peripheral, but not those in classics or Biblical subjects. When humanistic studies came in the present century to include modern English and European literature, these new subjects never acquired the dignity of classics or Biblical subjects, including ancient Near Eastern studies. In American universities, the study of English literature, inheriting the tradition of the study of Middle English and of Shakespeare, had a comparable prestige at a time when American universities and American genteel culture were more Anglophile or Anglocentric than they are now.

These subjects together were regarded by their practitioners as the central subjects of the university. Scholars in these subjects were and are still specialized, just as natural scientists are, but the scholars of the ancient humanities bore themselves with the air of being men of universal culture. The empirical natural scientists did not think of themselves in that way.

All this has changed. The physical sciences, mathematics and astrophysics and to a smaller extent the biological sciences, especially genetics, molecular biology and evolutionary biology, have come to the fore in the universities. They have done so in a period of intellectual and financial prosperity for their subjects and of the unrelenting forward movement of specialization. Most scientists in these fields have tended not to interest themselves in the university as a whole. For them the university has become an administrative convenience, a faculty club which is a place for departmental lunches. The central administration is a burden, a taker of excessive overhead charges on grants which the individual scientist has acquired through his own exertions outside the university.

It is necessary to separate the intellectual merits of Oriental and ancient classical studies from the importance of their teachers in the university. There are numerous academic citizens outstanding in their concern for the university who do not come from these fields. Furthermore, classical scholars, scholars of the ancient Middle East, of China, Japan, and India are nowadays as specialized in their work and interests as any physicist, biologist or economist. Nevertheless, I have an impression, formed over many years, that these humanistic scholars have been among the chief carriers of the academic ethos. It is their subjects, and hence their presence in universities, that are likely to be affected by the necessity for the central administration of any university to save money by eliminating subjects with very small numbers of students. This does not mean that these subjects will be erased from academic life. It does mean that important universities will have to renounce something which has played a vital role within the life of the whole institution.

The performance of this vital role cannot be expected to be provided by the modern Western humanistic studies. At present, these subjects are a danger to the idea of the university. They aim to destroy it, as part of the revolution which they hope to bring about in society and in the world. They wish to destroy the intellectual traditions which they were appointed to transmit, investigate, and interpret; they wish to destroy the society in which they live. Of course, their ideal is a childish phantasm; they will not succeed in doing that. They like the idiom of a revolution which will bring Western civilization to an end. Their only following is in universities where they have established their ascendancy over the administrators. They are not utterly without influence; they have come into domination over certain learned societies and they can make themselves heard occasionally before governmental bodies and legislators. Above all, they dominate decisions regarding appointments in their departments. They act in concert and are very persistent. They hate the university and wish to use their secure and well-remunerated positions in it to abolish it as a place for the advancement of learning.

The sense of and solicitude for the university as a whole are essential ingredients of the academic ethic. The scientific ethic is no less important to the proper conduct of academic life. The scientific ethic overlaps with the academic ethic. Openness to sound evidence, adherence to strict rules in the assessment of evidence—one's own as well as that of others—honesty in the recording of observations, scrupulousness in the interpretation of evidence, distinguishing between varying degrees of certainty in the interpretation of evidence, fairness to the arguments of others, etc., are absolutely fundamental in science. They are the objects of obligations to the idea of science and to other scientists who participate in the idea of science, regardless of their location.

The academic ethic affirms all these obligations but it adds the obligations to institutions, to the university, to the department, the academic profession within one's own university, and to the academic profession wherever it is. This means that in deciding what is true and in the assessment of the work of present and prospective colleagues, loyalties of friendship and the sympathies of political, ethnic, national, sexual or religious attachments, must count as nothing. The criteria of academic, that is, intellectual, scientific or scholarly achievement must prevail above all others. The academic ethic condemns the introduction of political criteria into appointment. In the recently communist countries and in countries where the Communist party has been large and influential, political criteria have been given primacy in academic appointments.

The invocation of political, ethnic, and religious criteria has never been entirely absent from even the better universities in other countries. For example, in Germany before 1918, the appointment of a social democrat to a university professorship was rare and difficult. Nevertheless, this type of political exclusion has not been a prominent feature of the life of universities in liberal-democratic societies in the present century. It is, however, in these countries that departures from the academic ethic have made a prominent appearance since the Second World War. It is not a factor of any consequence in the natural sciences, but in the social sciences and particularly in the humanities, it is a danger to be noticed and guarded against.

Unlike the strict requirement of the application of political criteria in academic appointments in totalitarian countries, which was externally imposed, in liberal-democratic countries the application of political criteria in appointments is imposed from the inside by influential groups of teachers. It is an important divergence from the academic ethic.

The departments of English and American and comparative literature are rather large departments, particularly the former. Decisions to reduce the number of departments which are not cost-effective will not fall on the department of English; they are unlikely to fall on the department of comparative literature. They are much more likely to fall on ancient Middle Eastern studies, Indology, Sinology, and similar subjects.

If departments of English were the only ones to have been infected by this antinomian attitude, this would be bad enough. In fact, however, history, anthropology, sociology and other departments of social science are being touched by the same outlook. "Gay studies," "gender studies," "African-American studies" (which were recently "black studies") have been promoted. It remains to be seen whether these subjects will be placed under the scrutiny of the experts of "cost-effectiveness." Deans, provosts, presidents will have to be stronger than they are to lay a diminishing hand on them. They will be resisted by their teachers, fervently and abusively, and students, undergraduate and graduate, will be recruited to help.

Although the antinomians in the modern humanities departments and their allies in the departments of social sciences and in the various "studies" are a small bloc in academic staffs, they are fairly sophisticated in their mastery of academic politics. It is possible that they have inherited their techniques from the fellow-traveling partisans of the Communist party cells at a few colleges and universities in the 1930s and 1940s. The line of inheritance seems clear. In any case, they organize and, in academic politics, a stable small group with dominantly political standards and objectives can make a considerable difference in a body of university teachers who are interested in their own research and their own graduate students within the university and in their own discipline outside it. The majority of teachers in most academic subjects have no strong political passions. Yet, outside the schools of business, the medical schools and to some extent the law schools, the political views of most university teachers are collectivistic liberal, so they are not entirely without tolerance and even sympathy towards the camarilla antinomians.

The Prospect

I have little doubt that universities of the sort which I have in mind will continue to be effective over a fairly broad range of their activities. There is too much demand for the things they can do, and they have shown in the course of their respective histories sufficient adaptability to render it very likely that they can satisfy enough of the demands on them to continue to receive much of the financial support which they will need.

Despite a few instances to the contrary, the scientific ethic is strong and is likely to continue to be so. The scientific parts of the universities seem to me to be reasonably secure.

It is often said by critics of the universities that they are dispensable. All the research that needs to be done can be done in research institutes and in governmental and industrial and commercial laboratories; the residual colleges and universities can then concentrate on teaching. It is proclaimed by such connoisseurs that the days of the "Humboldt university" are over. Many of them are generally ignorant of what Wilhelm von Humboldt thought and wrote; but they know about "elitism" and are against it, and his name gives off an aroma of elitism. Hence they are against the "Humboldt university" and they want to see it extinguished.

One of the chief features of the idea of the university as conceived by Wilhelm von Humboldt was the unity of teaching and research. In the words of Clark Kerr, the university as conceived by Humboldt was the "research university" but the "university" was as important as the research. Humboldt had various reasons for wishing to keep them together against proposals, which had been in the air in Germany—mainly in Prussia—for several decades, that they be separated. One reason, which seemed too obvious to mention, was that there would be no scientific *Nachwuchs*, no succeeding generation of scientists, if there were no education and training of scientists. Another was that teaching of scientific subjects by teachers who did no research in the fields in which they taught would be incapable of stirring scientific imagination and curiosity. (This seems to me to be well demonstrated by the Indian "presidency colleges" in Calcutta, Bombay and Madras, where teaching is excellent, but it does not stimulate the ambition to do research because the teachers do not regard this as falling within their jurisdiction.)

Whatever else may be said about the interdependence of research and teaching, it seems clear that if potential scientists are to be aroused to become scientists, they must be taught in universities by persons who are already scientists, which means not just teachers of science but scientists who are doing research. In short, the future production of new scientific knowledge on the scale on which it is demanded nowadays, and is likely to be demanded in the near future, will depend on whether the producers of that scientific knowledge have been taught by practicing scientists. The future production of scientific knowledge, and derivatively the future supply of productive scientists, depends on the continued existence of universities which embody the Humboldtian idea of the university. If the university dies, they will die too. If the university withers, they will wither too.

The question remains, can universities—that is, the major universities, the research universities—survive under the conditions of the twenty-first century?

The external conditions—social and financial—will not be indulgent, but they are not severely threatening either. The survival of the major universities in the twenty-first century will depend on the internal conditions of the universities and on the state of the scientific ethic and the academic ethic.

The former—the scientific ethic—is at present in quite good condition. It is not without its problems. Some of the external problems are financial, such as finding proper appointments for the most promising young scientists; some are moral, such as the capacity of the professors to resist the temptation to act as the "principal investigators" of so many projects that they cannot supervise and guide their juniors adequately. Their failure to do so will endanger the persistence of the scientific ethic.

The academic ethic does not appear to be equally strong. The specialization and intellectual narrowness of so many scientists have reduced its presence in the universities. The social scientists are so interested in the society outside the university, as a result of their political partisanship, the fascination of their subjects—almost invariably, their own contemporary society—and the necessity of looking outside the university to find money to support their research, that they have little interest in what goes on in the rest of the university. They are ignorant of it and unconcerned about it.

The members of the humanistic departments, especially those teaching mainly undergraduates, once had a tradition of concern for the whole institution. Indeed, they sometimes thought they were the institution. The tradition dated from a time when they were in fact the dominant power in the universities, and when their own subjects were less specialized and when not so much research was done in them. The present situation is much different. The tradition has become very faint. The small departments which are linked to an older kind of scholarship are in danger of further shrinking or abolition in order to save money. The larger departments are in the possession of an evil spirit. A combination of rude aggressiveness of a minority and of supine complaisance of the majority has delivered these departments to a spirit which is the very antithesis of the academic ethic.

It is difficult to believe that anything as silly as the outlook on scholarly matters which is making the running in the larger departments of modern humanistic studies can survive. Yet, in the present state of attrition of the academic ethic in most universities and the timidity, cowardice or indifference of most academic administrators on the matters at issue, the present rage is not likely to be checked by decisions which are made outside the departments in question but from within the university. In the present state of emancipationism which is regarded as a mark of liberalism, there is not likely to be any very articulate and insistent effort to dissuade the emancipationists, multiculturalists and deconstructionists from their injurious follies.

Whether the follies will die away of their own intellectual inanition is very uncertain. They belong to a tradition the long existence of which is evidence that its survival is not just a "survival," a vestige, with no life of its own. It is an heir of Western Marxism, of the bohemian hatred of bourgeois society, and so on. It has had many forms but it has a constant theme: the hatred of civil society and Western civilization from which that society has grown. In the past, this attitude had a small but audible following, with some very distinguished intelligences and talents among them, but they practically never held appointments in universities. They did not seek them. The present disorder is part of the wider process of the bohemianization of American society and the attendant spread of the belief that human beings must be emancipated from all traditions and norms, from all crippling belief in rationality and objectivity.

The outright and acknowledged failure of communist societies is not a severe check for any except those who had committed themselves to the particular type of planned economy and tyranny. It is not a defeat for the bohemian, emancipationist attitude towards life in general and towards one's own society.

It is comfortable to be in a university. It provides the freedom of bohemia with a good salary and permanent tenure. How much better that is than living from hand to mouth, not knowing where one's next meal is coming from. I see no reason why academic bohemia should renounce the comforts of the university, and I do not think there will be any shortages of recruits for the antinomianism which enjoys the benefits of institutions and the freedom and self-indulgence of bohemia. It is also much better paid and much easier than the philistine life of an office-worker in a large firm.

I do not foresee the emergence of a generation of courageous and intelligent university presidents, provosts, and deans who can render discriminating judgments when they have to approve or disapprove of appointments proposed by departments. Nor do I foresee the growth in other parts of the university of care for the entire institution which would be sufficiently attentive to recoil in repugnance from the disregard for intellectual standards being practiced in the modern humanities.

Perhaps that will make no difference. Much of the literary scholarship—for example, biographies, 1,000 pages in length, of minor writers—which came from departments of English was not very good; that strand of the modern tradition can be dispensed with. The great works of literature will still exist and will continue to be appreciated by human beings outside the universities and by some within them, as they have been throughout much of the history of civilization.

It was a mistake to allow so much of our literary life and of the assessment of literary works to settle in universities. As long as the barrier between bohemia, Grub Street, and the universities remains as ineffective as it has become, it will be impossible—and not entirely desirable—to expunge from the universities the preoccupation with contemporary things.

Of course, there might emerge a new generation of presidents, provosts and deans who will say "So far, and no further," and stick to it in the face of protests about racism, infringements of academic freedom, neocolonialism, sexism, etc. I do not foresee this. Even presidents who are strong in speech and obstinate and aggressive in temperament have not shown themselves to be concerned about such developments in the modern humanities.

The question come down, therefore, to whether the university will be able to withstand its own internal enemies. It might well be able to do so. Some parts will probably remain very strong, while others will be very weak and infectious. After all, the École polytechnique is a great institution and it lacks the humanities.

Perhaps Napoleon will replace Wilhelm von Humboldt as the guiding star of our academic intellectual life.

Notes

1. Bloom, Allan, *The Closing of the American Mind: How Higher Education Has Failed Democracy and Impoverished the Souls of Today's Students* (New York: Simon and Schuster, 1987).
2. Sykes, Charles, *ProfScam: Professors and the Demise of American Higher Education* (Washington, D.C.: Regnery Gateway, 1988).
3. Kimball, Roger, *Tenured Radicals: How Politics Has Corrupted Our Higher Education* (New York : Harper & Row, 1990).

4

The Academic Ethos under Strain

The decade before the outbreak of the Second World War had been a very hard time for universities. The worldwide economic depression affected universities as it affected all other institutions. In Great Britain, which was perhaps least injured, the chances of employment of university graduates did not decline markedly, but the universities did not recruit many young members to their teaching staffs. The already established university teachers were not loosened from their moorings. A small number became communists or supporters of communism, but this did not interfere with their performance of the tasks of teaching and research to which they had committed themselves.[1] They did not attempt to impel their universities towards their own political objectives.

Under the dominion of an ungenerous ministerial bureaucracy, French universities carried on in a humdrum way. Their graduates were finding it difficult to obtain employment, their teachers were becoming somewhat more radical politically. Nonetheless, French academics retained their traditional views that teaching was a chore, that the supervision of dissertations was a little better, and that to do scientific or scholarly research was best of all.

In the United States, the universities were more sorely affected. Salaries were reduced; there were few new appointments, and in the middle of the depression the student body even contracted slightly. But those who persisted or who came to the surface in the depression had no novel conceptions of the academic calling: it was as in the past a life to be spent among books or in scientific laboratories and with young students. The radicalism of a few younger teachers in New York, Wisconsin, and California did not attenuate devotion to learning in the sense which that idea had acquired in the course of moving from the study of the Bible to the study of history and nature.

In Germany, the universities were struck by a catastrophe. A large proportion of the teaching staff was dismissed on ethnic grounds; the student body declined from 124,500 in 1931 to 85,000 in 1935. New appointments were made in the light of political and ethnic criteria and many teachers, already established or newly habilitated, trumpeted Nazi phrases which were the very antithesis of scholarship but which flattered the prejudices of their politicized students. Those who were not expelled, who did not feel morally obliged to resign and who did not become Nazis carried on silently in an atmosphere very different from the gravity—often oppressively grim—of the old German university. Despite the flattery with which many professors greeted the Nazi regime, the Nazi leaders did not conceal their animosity towards the universities.

In Italy, where the universities had already been afflicted by the requirement of the oath of loyalty to the Fascist regime at the end of the 1920s, the depression and the racial laws of 1938 had effects resembling those in Germany; distinguished scholars, both young ones and those already established, had to leave their posts to go into exile. Time-servers were appointed, and others just carried on. Yet in Rome in the 1920s and until 1938, physics had an extraordinarily fruitful existence. The Spanish universities had been lagging far behind the universities of Great Britain, Germany, and France for some time. The Civil War set them still further back, disrupting studies, driving many teachers into exile, and further depressing the mood of those who survived. Spain became even more of an academic backwater, and the morale of its academics declined accordingly.

The war years accentuated the trend of the depression. In all the combatant countries, the conscription of young men who had already come up to university, or who would have done so had the war not intervened, reduced student bodies drastically. Teaching staffs, already attenuated by the financial stringency of the 1930s, were now depleted by the demands of military and civilian governmental service. Buildings deteriorated; in Germany, and to a lesser extent in Great Britain, many were destroyed by enemy military action.

Nonetheless, despite economic depression, and then the loss of students and staff in the war, powerful academic traditions in Great Britain and the United States showed great hardiness. The universities remained productive centers of scientific and scholarly knowledge during the years of the war, just as they had during the depression. The best academics believed in what they were doing, and the combination of tradition, intellectual power, and conviction produced impressive results. The natural sciences had flourished even during the depression years of the 1930s. Since the physical equipment which they needed for their great advances was still relatively inexpensive, their straitened financial situation during the depression had not restricted them greatly. The new arrangements for financial support, which came into exist-

ence or which expanded after the First World War, were a great encouragement. The United States had already advanced to become an important center
in the natural and social sciences in the 1920s; the increment of displaced
Germans and Italians as a result of oppressive laws of ethnic discrimination,
together with the active part played by the private philanthropic foundations,
led to a further access of creative power which brought the United States into
the front rank of these sciences by the time the country entered the war. The
Second World War, although it deprived scientists of their students, gave
them an unprecedented material prosperity and increased their confidence in
the profession to which they were committed. The sciences prospered intellectually, although for a time in secrecy.

In the humanistic and social science subjects, traditions of the humanistic
erudition of the nineteenth century still prevailed. Research was largely conducted in the style of a handicraft and it could continue under conditions of
relative adversity, as long as there was a will to do it. It was done by scholars
who had been appointed as university teachers, and the additional sums needed
for such research were not large. Expenses had often been met by scholars
from their own pockets, and from meager grants which had been made by
academies, foundations, individual patrons, and by the universities themselves from small funds especially designated for the support of research. To
the extent that humanistic scholars were not drawn into the service of the
war, and although they, too, lost their students, they continued nonetheless to
work in a number of countries. In the occupied countries, material hardship
and Nazi oppression placed a great strain on scholarship—some great scholars were killed in concentration camps or were executed by German soldiers,
or they were arrested—but it was not extinguished. In the Axis countries, the
brutal repressiveness of the regimes joined the material hardship of life in
rendering scholarship more difficult. There, too, it flickered on faintly and it
proved harder to revive in more favorable times.

Valuable work was done in sociology, political science, economics, and
anthropology in the United States and Great Britain during the depression.
Historiography flourished in these countries, and also in France and the Netherlands. The war gave much encouragement to the social scientists of the
United States and Great Britain. Many were enabled to do research of a sort
which would have been out of the question in the immediately preceding
decade, and ideas which flourished in the open after the war germinated in
governmental and military service. The exhilaration of discovery was undi-
minished.

In both depression and wartime in the United States and Great Britain, and
in the smaller democratic countries of Western Europe, universities were
generally esteemed. They were considered to be among the important institutions of their respective societies, like the church, the army, the higher civil

service, the judiciary, and private business enterprise. They were not regarded as inherently more important than these institutions but as being approximately of the same order of merit.

By and large, the respect which universities received was accorded on the grounds of their dispassionate concern for truth, and of the contribution which they made to national well-being, by training young persons for the practice of important learned professions, by their scientific and scholarly accomplishments, and by serving their respective national societies in war and in peace. Even before the war they were regarded in all Western countries as the source of the kind of knowledge which improves the life of man, by protecting his health and by improving his standard of living through the increase of the productivity of industry and, above all, of agriculture. In war-time their capacity to contribute to military technology brought them even more appreciation. This was especially the case in the United States, where the state universities and engineering schools had traditionally been expected to concern themselves with matters of fairly immediate practical importance.

In the United States, there was an approximate consensus between the expectations of the more serious parts of the lay public—state legislators interested in higher education, members of the classes whence came the private patrons of higher education, and more serious publicists—and the beliefs of academics about what academic life should be about. The situation was little different in Great Britain, although there was less concern on both sides with the immediate services which universities could provide for industry and government. Even the experiences of the Second World War did not fundamentally change these attitudes in the laity or in the academic profession.

In France in the quarter century which followed the end of the First World War, the universities were viewed grudgingly by civil servants and legislators. Little seems to have been expected of them except that they should qualify young persons for the professions and for the middle ranks of the civil service. Many academics had a correspondingly dreary conception of their role. The intellectual traditions of the Collège de France, the École normale, of the École practique des hautes études, and of the Sorbonne carried with them a sense of obligation to live up to the highest standards in research and in advanced teaching. Generally in the Western countries, except in the colleges of the ancient universities of Great Britain and in certain small liberal arts colleges in the United States where the teaching of undergraduates was regarded as the primary object of the academic calling, the tasks of teaching were taken as an inevitable and unquestionable part of the profession of learning. Especial attention was, however, given to the training of postgraduate students and those in certain professional schools, particularly the medical schools and, in the United States, the law schools as well.

In Germany, the twelve years of Nazi rule shook the self-esteem of the universities very badly. The Nazi government, unlike previous German governments, did not take the universities seriously. Although many German university teachers had welcomed the Nazis after hating the republican regime, the Nazis did not reward them. They appointed unworthy men of no scholarly or scientific accomplishments to leading positions. The decent Germans who had remained in the German universities were humiliated by their own acquiescence and by the indignities imposed by Nazi appointees and policies. These good men in a wicked state did not lose their love of learning, but felt ashamed of themselves as Germans and as once proud professors. They had no sense of affinity with their students who were by and large permeated by the antiintellectual outlook of National Socialism. They saw no *Nachwuchs* in sight.

In most Western countries, except for those under totalitarian or authoritarian rule—German, Italy, Spain, and Portugal—it was generally thought that the high status of the members of universities entitled them to freedom to pursue the truth in accordance with the rules and traditions of their various disciplines and institutions; indeed, it was thought that this freedom was integral to the effective performance of their calling. It was also thought that they should enjoy the same freedom of political action which was the right of citizens in a liberal and democratic society; it was generally believed in most Western countries that even the radical political views of a university teacher, as long as they did not intrude into his teaching, should be ignored in his appointment or promotion.

Academics were jealous of their rights but were seldom courageous in defending the rights of academic freedom of colleagues who had been deprived of them. The academic profession in Great Britain was probably not only the freest from external intrusion, it was probably also the freest from internal restrictions in the application of strictly intellectual and academic criteria in appointments. In Germany, where the literature on academic freedom was greatest in quantity and elaboration and where there was great insistence by members of the academic profession that once habilitated or appointed they must be free from external intervention, they were also not very zealous in defending the rights of those whose freedom was in fact infringed upon.[2]

In Germany, before 1918—unlike Great Britain, Sweden, France, and Italy—it was very rare for socialists to obtain university appointments. Within this restriction those who were appointed enjoyed, and were aware that they enjoyed, the prerogative of *Lehrfreiheit*. Despite some striking infringements on academic freedom, as in the Gumbel case in Heidelberg,[3] the Lessing case in Hanover,[4] and a number of others[5] in which the academic profession and not government were at fault, there was a general observance of the standard during the time of the Weimar Republic. The affronts against academic freedom in the Weimar period arose mainly when teaching staffs gave preeminence to political and ethnic criteria of assessment on these and other occasions. Even the reactionary professors who mourned for the Wilhelmian Reich and who hated the liberal, democratic republic, were staunch in their devotion to the older idea of the professorially ruled university. Indeed, one of their charges—unjustly made—against the republic was that the new regime was destroying the old university and degrading its dignity. Nonetheless, the academic ethos was weakened by the partisan political and ethnic drift of many German scholars and scientists. As soon as the National Socialists acceded to power, the traditional standard was replaced by one which was practically its diametrical opposite, and the replacement was, moreover, appreciated widely in the German academic community, at least, at first.

In Italy, the Fascist government, as in Germany, replaced a regime which showed a very high degree of respect for academic freedom by one which, as the years passed, approximated closer and closer to the practices of National Socialist Germany. Even before the alliance with Nazi Germany, Carlo and Nello Roselli were persecuted—they were later murdered. Gaetano Solvemini and Giuseppi Borgese were forced to retire from Italian academic life. An oath of allegiance to Fascism was required to which many yielded unwillingly and many others eagerly.

In the United States, academic freedom, particularly in the major private universities, was generally very far-reaching and respected in the 1930s and during the war. Nonetheless, in the state universities, even in some of the most distinguished, the principle of freedom of university teachers in their civil role was, on various occasions, under assault from state legislatures and from civic bodies, as well as from influential—especially wealthy—individuals. Within the universities, which were from time to time afflicted, there was no doubt that these political intrusions were wrong and contrary to the right ordering of academic life. There was much resentment against these intrusions. On the whole, however, during the period of the depression and even during the war, academic freedom and the freedom of the university teacher as a citizen outside the academic sphere increased. Some of this improvement may be attributed to the complex combination of an enhancement of public esteem for the academic profession and a correspondingly heightened self-esteem, which was engendered by its considerable accomplishments since the beginning of the century.

In Switzerland, and in the Scandinavian and the Low Countries, academic freedom was very seldom infringed. University teachers were respected, they were enabled to go about their business with practically negligible external interference within the framework of their own charters, or of charters which—although laid down for them by the state—recognized the autonomy of the university in governing itself and the academic freedom of its members to teach and do research according to their best lights. The high status of the university teacher was acknowledged by the lay public and taken for granted by the academics. In France, too, despite the high degree of centralization of governmental control over the budget and courses of study of the universities, the academic and civil freedom of university teachers was firmly established and immune from questioning. Scholars and scientists were respected by the wider public.

In all the Western countries, excluding the totalitarian and authoritarian countries, despite the hard times through which they passed, there was never any doubt within the universities about the definition of their fundamental and permanent tasks and the obligations of academics. It was to teach the best that was known as a result of dispassionate and zealous study and to pursue new truths in the most scrupulous manner. In doing so, university teachers believed that they had a vital role in national life. This view was shared by influential parts of the larger public; it was recognized that universities enriched the national culture, contributed to national prestige, supplied trained young persons to the professions and provided knowledge which improved health and wealth. To teach in a university or college was thought by those who did it to be an honorable and esteemed career. To attend a university was thought by many of the students to be a privilege—accepted out of diverse motives—for relatively small groups of young men and even smaller groups of young women. The elevated position of the universities in the life of their societies made it easier for academics to believe that the standards to which they adhered were the right standards.

In the period before the war the universities were not at the center of intense and frequent public attention. An important discovery by a university scientist or a rare incident of political commotion might gain attention in the press of any of the Western countries; in the United States, cases of infringement of academic freedom or campaigns against subversion might from time to time bring universities into the public press. Athletic contests in the United States—much less frequently in Great Britain and practically never in the rest of Europe—called the attention of the wider public to the existence of universities. Otherwise, the universities were left largely to themselves to get on with their academic tasks of teaching, training, and research. This is, on the whole, what they did.

There were, of course, many exceptions. There were failures who bored their students and taught them little; there were those—the majority—who did little research of any consequence. There were those who "played politics" within the university. There were some whose interests were largely external—gardening, the stock market, earthly pleasures, or social reform. Despite these exceptions, the standard was generally clear and unchallenged.[6]

Expansion after the Second World War

There were many changes after the Second World War. First of all there was the enormous swelling of the size of the student body once the young men were released from military service. The accumulated "deficit" of the war was being made up, and much more. The provision of grants to demobilized soldiers not only aided those who would have gone to university in any case, had they not been called up; they also made it possible for young men to attend university who would not otherwise have been able to do so because they did not have the financial resources. The new access of university students who were making up the "deficit" of the years of the war was strongly reinforced by drafts of young persons from classes which before the war had not sent their offspring to universities.

The teaching staffs of the universities also expanded markedly, with the expansion being greatest in the lower levels of the hierarchy. After the fall in the rate of recruitment during the years of depression and the practical cessation of recruitment to teaching staffs during the war, there had to be a rapid expansion to meet the requirements of teaching. The continental universities responded more slowly than the Anglo-American universities.

In Germany candidates for recruitment were just not available, and teaching staffs were further shrunken by the exclusion of those who had been the most arrant Nazis. Very few of the refugee scholars and scientists returned. Some very old men who had retired early in the Nazi period were recalled to service. The system of large audiences of lectures by the professor permitted the old system to continue simply by increasing the numbers of those who attended the professorial lectures. Seminars became extremely large. Still, the universities on the continent moved very slowly to expand their *Mittelbau*. This expansion was much disliked by many older academics who thought it was disastrous to the old pattern of the university. Habilitation in Germany and *agrégation* in France restricted recruitment. But there, too, the staffs had to expand. The new recruits were usually appointed from the generation which had been trained in the overcrowded and undertaught generation of the period when the professorial lectures had become a travesty of higher education.

The British and American universities moved more swiftly, with the larger American universities resorting also to the creation or enlargement of a stratum of "teaching assistants." The greatest expansion in Great Britain occurred only in the 1960s with the realization of the proposals of the Committee on Higher Education under the chairmanship of Lord Robbins. British universities were thus able to draw on the products of the more moderate expansion which began in 1945, but there, too, they began to press against the outer limits of the well qualified and deeply devoted.

One of the consequences of the expansion at whatever stage in the quarter of a century in which it occurred was the encroachment on the teaching staffs of secondary schools. Not only were persons who otherwise might have become sound secondary school teachers drawn into university teaching, but there were also transfers of already practicing secondary school teachers. This little noticed and insufficiently documented phenomenon, which had been going on in the United States for a much longer period, has not only lowered the quality of secondary education in most countries, but has also had a serious effect on the conception of the tasks of universities. The more poorly prepared the secondary school leavers who came up to universities, the more the tasks of the universities diverged from the traditional ones. Latterly in the United States, where "open admission" has been instituted, a certain amount of the required teaching has been not only elementary, it has had to be "remedial" as well. This has meant the recruitment of teachers to do this kind of teaching, onerous but alien to academic traditions. It has also meant that the intellectual seriousness of the academic staff has been affected.

Higher education was ceasing to be regarded as a privilege: it was beginning to be regarded as a right of which all young persons should seek to avail themselves. Governments in most Western countries which desired or accepted this expansion of numbers now became much more munificent towards higher education than ever before. They began, in varying degrees, to provide funds to construct buildings, to found new universities, and to establish new libraries and new teaching posts.

Great Expectations: The Idea of a Society Based on Science

Governments, impressed by the accomplishments of research in the various fields on which emphasis had been laid during the war, turned their attention to policies which would maintain a high standard and large volume of civil and military research. They became concerned lest there might be insufficient "scientific manpower" to meet the diverse needs of societies aiming to promote their own military strength and prestige and the health and economic welfare of their people. This naturally meant support for the study and teaching of scientific subjects in the universities—at least in countries with a tradition of viewing the universities as the center of gravity of scientific research. This was one of the main sources of the series of decisions whereby higher education in the United States came to depend increasingly on the federal government for financial support. The same thing happened somewhat differently in the United Kingdom, since the universities had earlier come to depend on the central government for the support of their teaching and training activities as well; in the modern universities this arrangement was already dominant in the period before the Second World War. It also happened in West Germany and Canada—where, like the United States, the federal system had previously denied the central government a dominant position in higher education—until the pattern of central government support of science spread throughout the world. The training of scientists and technologists was not the only objective of the policy of this mode of support for higher education, but its effect was to involve the universities much more closely with the central governments than had been the case previously.

Governments also began to spend much more money directly on research. They did it through a great increase in their own departmental research activities and through the support of independent research institutions, for example, the institutions maintained through the Max-Planck-Gesellschaft, the Conseil national de recherche scientifique, the Medical Research Council, and so on. They did it through contracts with private bodies such as business firms and research institutes; this was especially common in the United States. They also did so through grants to and contracts with universities. All these activities increased the demand for research workers and thereby enabled the universities to train more graduate students and also to employ more persons to do research. Every grant for research to a university, by providing income to pay the salaries of collaborators, also permitted more graduate students to be trained for careers as scientists by employing them as assistants or as fellows on the research projects supported by the government. As a result, the scientific faculties of universities thrived as never before. One of the consequences was that scientists in universities became less centered on their universities. A university became a convenience which housed their research projects, administered the funds which they had obtained on their own initiative, and which provided certain conveniences. The university as a community, already weakened by specialization and by the growth and the size of its constituent departments, lost in coherence.

This development in governmental policies for the promotion of science was part of a movement of ideas which included the idea of "science-based industry." This ripened into the idea of a "science-based society." The university naturally appeared to be the device by which such a society would be created and maintained. The idea of a "science-based society" rested in part on the expectation that great numbers of occupations which in the past had been carried on on a strictly empirical basis and which were therefore to be learned by experience and apprenticeship rather than by academic study, did in fact, or would in the near future, require academic qualifications. Although this view had been canvassed by various visionary writers of the present century, such as H. G. Wells, Thorstein Veblen, and J. D. Bernal,[7] it gained wide acceptance first in the United States after 1945. From the United States it returned to Europe where it had been born. In a very modest way it was espoused in the United Kingdom, reaching a high point of public enthusiasm in Harold Wilson's Labour Government of 1964 with C. P. Snow as its prophet. It came later to France and West Germany. In this, as in other respects, the Organization for Economic Cooperation and Development served as an amplifier for the scientistic outlook and for the adaptation of the universities to its exigencies. It did so through a large number of publications and conferences and particularly through the conferences of ministers of education and science of the states which were members.

If the traditional manual occupations were in fact about to disappear—the proportion of the gainfully occupied in the primary and secondary occupations had been declining steadily while their output was increasing no less steadily[8]—then the future of society appeared to depend on higher education for the administrative services and professional and quasi-professional occupations. Since industry, transportation, and commerce were increasingly dependent on research, they would necessarily be dependent on institutions which did such research and which trained young persons to do it. Research within and outside the universities and the training of research workers both required that universities be supported in order to increase the study of science at universities. Only in this way could "highly qualified manpower" be obtained to meet the needs of society for more productive technology.

There has always been a tendency towards this kind of scientism in the United States where many "newer professions," such as social work, town planning, library administration, etc., with only a slight scientific or scholarly content, have sought to increase their standing through the prescription of courses of study under the auspices of universities.[9] Abraham Flexner had already noted this feature of American universities at the end of the 1920s. The trend of opinion which was so marked in the United States in the late 1940s was only an extension of the older view of the desirability of a marked practical intention in university education. University administrators, especially in the United States, took like ducks to water to this appreciation of universities and to the endless horizons of opportunity which it seemed to offer.

A new branch of journalism, to which many university teachers contributed, arose; it was concerned with science policy and higher educational policy. Journals like the *Times Higher Education Supplement,* the *Chronicle of Higher Education, Change,* the *New Scientist, Atomes* (later *Recherche*), were replete with articles about the "new challenges" to higher education. Newspapers like *le Monde,* the *New York Times,* the *Guardian* (once the *Manchester Guardian,* of lamented memory), *Die Zeit,* etc., added their powerful voices to the promulgation of the new tasks of the universities. The officials of foundations, the officials of professional associations, particularly those concerned with educational administration, and the practitioners of the new journalistic specialization all proclaimed the new tasks of the university. In doing so, they produced a chorus of criticism of the universities as they had been.

There had, ever since the nineteenth century and above all in the United States, been a demand that the universities should cease to be "ivory towers" and should contribute directly to the well-being of their societies. After the Second World War, this demand was taken up in Europe. It coincided with the expansion of the student bodies. It was clear that not all of the students were to become university teachers or pure scientists or teachers in *lycées* or *Gymnasia* or grammar schools, or lawyers or physicians or higher civil servants, nor would they enter into business firms owned by their relatives. They would have to enter occupations for which a university education qualified them, and these occupations could not be those for which universities had educated and trained their students in the earlier decades of the century. Furthermore, many of these students did not have strong intellectual interests in the traditional sense. The traditional education in the sciences, mathematics, classics, modern languages, history, and economics was not for them. In the light of all these considerations, the conclusion was drawn that universities must be more "practical," less "idealistic," less "remote" from the realities of contemporary life.

Great Expectations: Equality through Higher Education

The transition from "elite" to "mass" higher education was, of course, as far as numbers alone were concerned, a step towards the realization of the democratic ideal and the ideal of equality of opportunity. Its occurrence aroused populistic sentiments which had been strong in America ever since the Jacksonian revolution but which had been rare in Europe. Nonetheless, populism began to appear in intellectual and political circles in Europe too.

The upsurge of "anti-elitism" in the latter 1960s naturally found the traditional university with its intellectual demands and "archaic" conventions a fitting object for its critical attitude. Politicians who in most countries had not taken much interest in universities responded sympathetically to these programs for making the universities useful to "the people." Resurgent populism in the United States and a more newly born populism in Europe helped greatly in heightening the demand that the universities adapt themselves to the practical requirements of the new "science-based," "post-industrial" society.[10]

The "cognitive expansion" of the postwar period—long in gestation—has resulted in cognitive idolatry. The juggernaut of cognitive expansion will, in this view, go on steadily rendering obsolete old beliefs, old practices, old institutions. Human beings will become obsolete if they do not move apace with the cognitive expansion. The solution to this particular problem has been discovered in "recurrent education" or "life-long education." Human beings have recurrently to "retool" themselves, discarding old knowledge and replacing it with new knowledge. The universities are not merely to provide training for many new occupations or professions, but they must go on re-training, and retraining still further, those they have already trained. Thus still another responsibility has been laid upon the universities.

As the "propaganda of the degree" replaced the "cult of success" in the United States and in Europe and pushed aside the inarticulated traditional principle of "each in his own stratum," it began to become apparent to the reformers of universities—as it had long been apparent to sociologists in Europe and to common sense in the United States—that the acquisition of a university degree by a person who came from a family in which no one had ever been at a university constitutes ascent in the social hierarchy of status and income. But neither in the United States nor in Europe did this insight lead to demands to change the substance of what was taught in universities nor in the intellectual qualifications for admission. The "transition to mass higher education" and the attendant—perhaps consequent—"anti-elitism" have led to a demand that the universities go further in offering opportunities for substantial social ascent. The new demand has been that the universities should promote substantive social equality. Failure to do so would leave them condemned as "elitist." Although European universities have not been subjected to this demand to the same extent as those in the United States—and even there it is the demand only of the most extreme reformers—similar views have now begun to be voiced in Europe, too.

Universities had never been concerned with equality except as an object of study in genetics and in social philosophy and the social sciences. They had never before been regarded as devices for the establishment of equality of status. Even in countries like the United States with the most open access to universities, an approximation to equality of opportunity to make entrance into universities available to larger numbers of young persons than was the case in Europe was all that was sought. It was only equality of opportunity, not equality of status, which was demanded by the critics of inequality in modern Western societies. It was never thought, however, that there could be anything like "universal higher education," or the substantive equality of status which would flow from it. The university's task in this regard was to educate and train those who came to it for education and training, and to discover new truths. If it had anything to do with changing society, this was thought to be only through the knowledge it offered. There was no idea, furthermore, that as a result of university education the degree of substantive equality in society would be increased, since only a small proportion of the relevant age-groups could ever receive higher education. At most, equality of opportunity could cause rewards to be more justly distributed, that is, to be distributed proportionately to natural endowment and exertion in the exercise of that endowment.

It could not have been otherwise while the opportunities to enter university seemed inevitably to be very narrowly restricted. It would have been deemed preposterous before the Second World War to believe in the possibility of universal higher education. After the war, the idea made steady progress, even though the reality—less in the United States, however, than in Europe— lagged far behind. The notion that everyone in the appropriate age-group should go to university has slowly taken hold as one of the criteria for assessing the adequacy of the higher educational system of a country. Although there is in fact little chance that universal higher education will be realized in the present century—if ever—the standard or ideal of universal higher education has become one additional platform of the argument against the universities as they have been heretofore.

There is no evidence that this particular argument is widely shared, least of all among disappointed aspirants for admission to higher educational institutions or among their parents. But it is heard among disgruntled radicals on the staffs of universities and among some of the "higher educational publicists"; in a more amorphous form it penetrates to the minds of those who are already ill at ease about the "elitist" character of universities.

Great Expectations: The Perfection of Society and the Individual through the Universities

Universities, especially in the United States, have become, in the minds of some persons, the vehicles of a new utopianism of which equality of status is only one part. It is not a revolutionary utopianism; it is a progressivistic, rationalistic, scientistic utopianism in which the ideal of a problemless, fully gratified society is conceived of as possible, as a result of the application of scientific knowledge. Although the shining prospect of this ideal society has been tarnished by the recent flurry of apprehension of fuel shortages and environmental pollution, the demand that the universities supply not just the manpower, but the solutions to all the problems and difficulties which human beings encounter, has scarcely diminished. Despite the setback, there are still persons who think everything possible and who believe that the ideal can be realized if only enough higher education is provided. Recently one American university president, attempting to overcome the pessimism of university administrators about the future demand for higher education, said: "The [political and educational] leaders must decide what kind of society we want and how much higher education will be needed to build that society."[11]

One current of this utopianism—which is not just to be found in an energetically asserted public opinion outside the universities but within them also—believes that it is not a universally solvent knowledge alone which the universities should provide, but other kinds of gratification as well. The older tradition that the higher educational system should form character—through games and clubs, as the Anglo-American ideal had it, or through the experience of research, according to the ideal of Wilhelm von Humboldt—has been transformed into the demand that university education should make its beneficiaries creative. This has two subsidiary aspects. One is that the universities should become places where training in the arts—plastic, literary, and representational—should be given. The universities must have schools of drama, painting, sculpture, writing of novels and poems, and musical composition and performance. The universities are thus urged to replace bohemia and to incorporate or reproduce the schools of *beaux arts* and music which grew up in Europe from the seventeenth century. The universities of the United States began to take in writers-in-residence, musicians-in-residence, painters-in-residence, composers-in-residence, after the end of the Second World War. Even in the 1950s it was possible to obtain a Ph.D. at a prominent American university by the submission of a novel. The teaching of "creative writing" became common in departments of English—alongside the teaching of elementary composition. Once such "creativity" had obtained a foothold, thanks to the zeal of university authorities to be all things to all men, the demand was extended.

"Creativity" was not confined to works; it was also to be seen in persons, regardless of whether they produced works or not. This demand for universal creativity continues and extends the traditional progressive educational program. It requires that the universities modify their aims and methods of instruction so every student should be able to realize the potential originality which is believed to reside in all human beings. It has come to be taken for granted that an objective of undergraduate education should be the student's discovery of himself, of his "true self," of his "identity."

It became fashionable in the 1950s in the United States to speak about an "identity crisis" among young persons. This postulated that there was an essential core in every human being, which was suppressed or disordered by the pressure of institutions; it became therefore a task of undergraduate education to enable the student to discover and bring to expression this essence of his being. "Doing your own thing" was a colloquial way of formulating the end-state of this process of uncovering the suppressed self and giving it expression. The syllabus and methods of instruction, it was said, should contribute to the growth of the student's personality. The exercise of the intellect was made secondary to the expansion of personality. "Experimental colleges," student-designed courses, courses taught by students and examined by students, have found a place in certain parts of the American higher educational system. The power of tradition and the resistance of governmental bureaucracy have prevented such manifestations in Great Britain and on the continent. Nonetheless, there too, are a few unheeded critics of universities who demand something similar. In a more radical form, the demand for a "critical university," which flourished in the second half of the 1960s in Europe and America, was a variant of this demand for courses of study in which students could "realize themselves," instead of being suppressed by the discipline of study.

The demand for "relevance" is an amalgam of many of the conflicting demands which are directed towards the universities. The demand for practical service, the demand for training for numerous "minor professions," the demand for contemporaneity of subject matter, the demand for exciting, gratifying, and developing the personality—each of these is a demand for relevance to the interests of the demanders; these demands are very different from each other and some of them are incompatible with each other. Each of these types of relevances has it supporters. Of course they have not had their own way, either in the universities or in public opinion. But they do have an effect. They do have some effect on opinion in the universities. It seems so self-evident that every activity should be "relevant" to something. The obligation to educate the mind, to interpret, revise, and transmit the great accomplishments of the human mind, to train young persons for intellectually demanding professions and to discover important things which were not known before, are not often justified as "relevant." Yet, "relevance" is a word which commands deference even from those who are committed to academic lines which do not receive its benediction.

In addition to all this, there has been another fashionable demand made on the universities—although it seems to have abated somewhat recently. This is the demand that universities become centers of criticism. It is not just the old demand that students be taught to think independently, to scrutinize discriminatingly the tradition which they inherit, to seek evidence rather than to accept dogmatically asserted propositions from their teachers or their textbooks. What is demanded now is much more. The ideas of "thinking independently" and "thinking critically" came for a time to mean thinking hostilely about contemporary society. The "status quo" having become morally abhorrent, it is asserted that the task of teachers and students and of the university as a corporate whole is to set its face against present-day society and to criticize it relentlessly, without let or surcease. In West Germany and in France, this point of view is now well established in certain universities, especially in the social sciences. Even in Great Britain it has its followers, naturally mainly in social science departments. This is a radical extension and application of the more general belief that the universities should be at least "abreast of the times," and even better, should meet the "needs" of the society of the future, for the definition of which the reformers take responsibility.

To succeed in the attainment of these grand ends, the universities must change. They must innovate, innovate, and innovate again. To become innovators they must outgrow their attachment to old tasks, to old learning, to old beliefs, and to old ways of doing things. They must reorganize themselves internally so that the confining boundaries of disciplines are transcended. They must become interdisciplinary. In some circles, within as well as outside the universities, it is thought that the failures of the universities to solve the problems of society and to bring their students into the creativity which lies dormant in them arise from the inherited constriction of departmental boundaries. The resolution of "ecological" problems, problems of transportation, drug addiction, criminality, unhappiness and mental disorder, conflict, poverty, divorce, boredom, etc. rests on the utopian belief that a synthesis of the knowledge contained in a plurality of at present separated disciplines can "solve" the problems of contemporary society. Hence, new "problem-oriented" courses of study must be devised. New syllabi and new methods of teaching must be devised. New conceptions of the learning needed for the resolution of problems are demanded for this titanic undertaking.

The university must, to accomplish these ends, "go beyond its ivy-covered walls." It must go into the streets, into workshops, and into offices. It must bring the streets and workshops into itself. It must bring together "work and study." It must recognize that learning is not to be got solely or even primarily in libraries and in laboratories, in lecture halls and in seminars; "learning and living" must, according to these, be seen as one. Students must therefore be given "credit" for "off-campus experience." The "walls between earning and learning" must be brought down.

One current of this movement to obliterate the boundaries of the university is that which demands the "comprehensive university," the *Gesamthochschule*. The American state universities and the "multiversity" have already reached this goal. The universities of California and Michigan are *Gesamthochschulen*. In Germany it is still being striven for. In Great Britain, the criticism of the "binary system" represents a similar tendency. The examples of Berkeley and Ann Arbor show that the aspiration is not necessarily injurious to the higher intellectual functions of a university. Still, the movement in its most recent form, like the terminological reduction of university education to "tertiary education" or "postsecondary education," shows an animus against the distinctive features of the university as a place for the training, refinement, and disciplining of the intellectual powers of young persons and for their exercise of those powers in the discovery of new truths.

The upshot of all these demands is that the universities must recognize that they have many "constituencies" and they must serve them all at the same time and in the same place. These various programmatic utopian demands appear in many shades and variants. The entire program is rarely put forward in all its elaborations. Bits and parts are variously demanded by various reformers, but they all fit into a single and consistent pattern. Some variants are more progressive; others, closely akin to them, are more radical or revolutionary. The radicals and revolutionaries, much as they dislike the existing society, are as insistent as the moderate progressivists that the universities must serve society immediately and directly. It is not society as it is now constituted, or the institutions which are the centers of this society, which they must serve. From these they must isolate themselves—except of course that they will continue to receive financial support from the condemned society. They must associate themselves with "people" who are the bearers and harbingers of a new and better society and they must serve their interests. The natural sciences must become "people-sciences," the social sciences must cease to be the instruments of an internal and external "colonialism"; they must forswear their "spying" on the poor at the behest of their paymasters. They must become a "true learning community" where students and teachers abolish arbitrary differences and boundaries between themselves in order to bring into being "participatory democracy," which will be a prototype of the future of the entire society. This is a theme which is common to the new radicalism and no West country has a monopoly. The publications of Suhrkamp[12] in Germany and the Penguin Education[13] series in Great Britain keep those countries abreast of the United States and France. The radical criticism is not an affair of "outsiders." A great deal of it originates from within the teaching staffs of the universities.

The clearly visible successes of this campaign of radical reform are relatively few; yet that is not a measure of its influence. Much of it appears in convocation-day addresses, speeches before professional associations, and the popular literature of university reform. It has never taken a palpable hold in the daily life of any worthwhile American university, although there are places where some of the demands have been granted an officially acknowledged realization.[14] It does, however, form an element in the atmosphere in which universities have been living in the United States. Like torn newspapers on a windy day, bits may be found in many gardens. Naturally such reforms have not made much progress in British universities, although in these, too, there is a handful of vigorous spokesmen. In France, although it is more the stock-in-trade of radical students and the teachers who make common cause with them, real advances have been made. Universities there have been made into spurious "communities" by the system of tripartite governments in which the various "constituencies" are given a role as well as a voice. In German universities tripartite government has become a reality, to their great loss as institutions of teaching, training, and research. They are less "communities" than they ever were, even in the time of the now hated

"*Ordinarienuniversität.*" In Denmark and Holland similar things have happened. But the effect of all these demands is not to be looked for in substantial institutional modifications. Their more serious effect is to be found in the disordering of the academic ethos, in the conception of what a university ought to be and what its members owe to it and hence to each other.

Ambivalent Expectations

The universities have never been the objects of so many and such diverse demands and aspirations; never has so much been demanded of them, and never have they been under such scrutiny and publicity. It could scarcely be otherwise when such unprecedentedly large sums of public money are given to them, when so many persons aspire to—and do in fact, for the most part—enter them as students, and when there is so much sensitivity to and discussion of the problems and "needs" of contemporary society, and so much animosity against the existing society and its authorities.

Contemporary culture inherits a powerful and triumphant tradition of "cognitive expansion." Curiosity about the world has never been greater; it has been sustained by its long record, several centuries old, of one great success after another. The idiom of the "breakthrough"—the idiom of tank warfare—in the cognitive sphere has become an essential part of the contemporary vocabulary. Scientific progress has supported and drawn support from a scientistic outlook which has placed systematic empirical knowledge of the universe, the earth, and all its inhabitants from viruses to man, at the forefront of the objects it prizes. The rationalistic, hedonistic, individualistic progressivism which has been expanding since the seventeenth century has risen to a crescendo in the period since the Second World War. The close association between science and the universities had made the universities into the bearers and agents of these grandiose hopes.

Little is now expected of churches—certainly not of the ecclesiastical hierarchies themselves. Armies are no longer the glory of the nation. More and more is demanded of governments at a time when popular disenchantment with authority in general, and distrust of political leaders and bureaucrats, are greater than ever. The family has been shorn of its responsibilities. Trade unions never carried the hopes of any but a few syndicalists that they would become harbingers of a new social order of which they would be the center. Business firms are likewise in the shadows, powerful though they are. The old pride of businessmen in the firms they built through their own exertions has yielded to an eagerness for wealth and an indifference to the moral dignity of the institutions through which they gain that wealth. Where else then can a beleaguered and demanding humanity turn for its redemption, except to education? Of the entire educational system, the universities are the pinnacle which alone holds out the promise of the redemption which mankind, and especially the irrepressibly idealistic American part of it, seeks in an inchoate, inarticulate way. Even eminent literary men, the heirs of a long tradition of independence, now demand that the universities shelter and provide for them.

There is public ambivalence about the universities. They are on the whole greatly esteemed. They are esteemed for what is believed to be their practical value which is widely acknowledged and cultivated. They are also esteemed, in part, as places where there is disinterested submission to a transcendent ideal. There is a real respect for truth in society and for those who devote themselves to it dispassionately. Not all parts of society are equally respectful, and such respect as there is, is often overlaid by practical considerations and by the idiom of practical value.

Before universities attracted the expectant hopes of human beings as excitingly as they have done since the Second World War, they flourished in Germany, Great Britain, in the Netherlands, in the Scandinavian countries, and the United States; they managed to survive and even do distinguished work in France, despite a dominating central bureaucracy which wanted only a few services from them and neglected them in favor of other institutions of learning like the *grandes écoles*. The reverence for learning still exists in all these societies and it is effectively supported by approbation of the performance of the universities in training for the professions and in conducting research which is often beneficial to health and wealth. Yet, in the utilitarian mode of thought which is dominant, university teachers find it difficult to justify this reverence for disinterested learning and are not inclined to think that it exists in the broader public.

The universities are the objects of all sorts of contradictory sentiments. They are nowadays disliked for being "elitist," although they are supported because they are, in fact, "elitist," training as they do young persons who become well-paid and influential lawyers, civil servants, journalists, business managers, and even politicians, as well as physicians and engineers who are also well paid and sometimes influential. Although university education is widely recommended and urged upon young persons by arguments which cite the higher incomes received by graduates compared with those who are not graduates, they are, nonetheless, criticized for producing an "elite." They meet with disapproval because many of their students, at least over the past ten years, have behaved atrociously and have not been censured or punished for doing so; they are also disapproved of because there is some sympathy with the criticisms which the radical students have directed against the universities.

Opinion about the universities outside the universities is complicated and heterogeneous. It is ambivalent. In the present and recent situation, those who from the outside press upon the universities to reform themselves or to be reformed, stress their practical value if they are sympathetic and express traditional animosities if they are unsympathetic. Within the universities, where every increment to revenue is welcomed, it seems most feasible to address the utilitarian, practical, and nationalistic interest in the universities. It is difficult for modern intellectuals, even those who are far from radical and who do not hate their own society, to believe that their fellow countrymen, and especially the powerful who dispose over great wealth—their own or the taxpayers'—can have reverence for the disinterested pursuit of knowledge. This very much affects the university teacher's conception of his obligations. Devotion to the academic ethos is rendered insecure by the complex situation in public opinion.

All this attention and criticism is new in the history of universities in most West countries during the past 100 years—except, of course, for their mal-treatment at the hands of Nazis and fascists. University teachers believed themselves to be part of the center of their societies even in the United States. This was not denied on the outside. There were conflicts within universities about courses of study, about the relative dignity of various subjects, about the creation of new chairs and the filling of old ones, but there was no challenge to the idea that universities, at least as far as teaching was con-cerned, existed for the cultivation and advancement of the higher learning. All else flowed from that. Training for the professions, and even practical service, derived equally from the character of universities as institutions de-voted to the disinterested and disciplined pursuit of understanding. This was taken for granted and not much discussed. When reformers wished to change universities, they did so in the belief that their reforms would bring them closer to this ideal.

All the more recent attention, when it has been favorable, has made for unthinking pride and ambition. When it has been negative it has made for a shaking of self-confidence and a weakened fidelity.

The Costs of Being Important

Those who take upon themselves the task of conducting the affairs of the universities—teaching, research, administration, the procurement of funds, the admission and examination of students, the maintenance of buildings and all sorts of equipment, the acquisition and care of books and manuscripts, and much else—have to face in many directions simultaneously. They must at-tend to the expectations which are directed towards them from the outside by their various "constituencies" in order to assure the continued flow of finan-cial resources which they need, to do their duty to society, and to maintain the dispositions and opinions which affirm their value and encourage their support. They must look also to their own maintenance and improvement. They must recruit new members at all levels and they must assimilate them into the culture of the university in general and into that of the particular university of which they are members. They must educate and train a wide variety of students, differing in their tastes and ambitions. They must make decisions regarding whom to admit, appoint, promote, dismiss. They must allocate their resources to satisfy the many conflicting demands within the university for new appointments, for additional funds, for more space and equipment, for new fields of study as well as for old ones. They must, if they are to perform well their fundamental functions of teaching, training, and research, keep this ravenous leviathan in a state of coherence. They must strive against dispersive forces in order to maintain the corporate integrity of the institution. They must govern themselves in a way which permits needed decisions to be made, which does justice and gives consideration to the diversity of interests of the various sectors and strata of the university's membership. They must also maintain and extend the favor of their patrons and please them by their readiness to serve interests which are not necessarily the interests of the university.

All these tasks have become much more difficult in these times. The greatly increased size of the student body, even if all else had remained constant, has necessitated larger teaching staffs. The larger the numbers, the greater the danger that some things will be overlooked; the larger the numbers, the greater the diversity of interests, concerns, and tastes which must be gratified, reconciled, contained, and assimilated into the traditions of the university. The increased numbers of students have brought into the universities types of students who have differed markedly from their predecessors. They come from strata of society with cultural outlooks different from those of earlier generations.

In the generalized expectation that a university education is what young persons must have before beginning life in a profession and a career, many students have been carried along by a wave of unthinking assumptions. Many, hence, have found themselves at university without having thought much about why they should be there: many have been disappointed, perplexed, recalcitrant, and dissatisfied. The university has turned out for many to be not what they wanted, even though they had had no clear notion previously of what they would want from a university. Reluctance, the dragging of feet, being ill at ease, have all been symptoms commonly observed within the university community. Types of students and groups which would have been small in a university of 5,000 or 10,000 students, are larger, more noticeable, more self-reinforcing, and more demanding of attention and influence in a university which is twice as large. They have been much more difficult to assimilate.

Growth in numbers would alone have necessitated an increase in the size of the administration of universities. But the number of things to be done by administration has also increased. Standards of amenity have risen and more provision must now be made for student health and psychiatric and counseling services. The great increase in the number and proportion of students who do not pay their fees from their parental income or their own earnings means that more studentships must be provided, more contacts with external bodies which support students must be maintained, more facilities for the borrowing of money by students must be created. In the United States, the recent insistence on increasing the proportion of "minority" students—blacks, "Spanish-surnamed Americans," American Indians, etc.—who attend universities, has resulted in a draft of students whose culture markedly differs from that of students who formerly came to universities: many of them were even more ill-educated in secondary school than the majority of students and they require "remedial instruction." All these things require more staff, which in turn requires more money, more accommodation, and more paperwork within the university. Each sector of this auxiliary staff acquires a momentum of its own; each develops its own "professional culture," as sociologists would say. Each thinks it needs more colleagues to do the same things; each needs a secretary to type letters, to file them, to handle the ever multiplying forest of forms which governments and specialized administrators require.

Teaching staffs have increased. They require more space. They are more actively engaged in more connections with the outside world: they apply for more research grants and for more research fellowships then their predecessors of forty years ago, because in accordance with the increased importance attributed to universities there have been more opportunities for these and more pressure to do research. Staff members attend more conferences, do more research and write more monographs and papers. Research and publication have become means of self-legitimation of teachers; even in colleges which traditionally concentrated on the teaching of undergraduates, more research has been done and more publications have been produced. There is more contact with colleagues in other universities, within their own countries and abroad. More secretaries are needed for these purposes, and proportionately more space is needed for the secretaries. The universities of the United States and Great Britain have gone furthest to meet these needs, France and Italy have done least.

Research has become more expensive, in whatever country it is carried on. In the natural sciences, the scale of equipment has become much greater and more assistants, graduate and post-doctoral fellows and technicians have been needed to use and maintain it—as well as to manufacture some of it. In the social sciences, research projects have become more numerous and more expensive, especially since sample surveys and computers are now so widely

employed. Large grants from governmental and private bodies have consequently become necessary. The National Science Foundation, the National
Institute of Mental Health in the United States, the Social Science Research
Council in Great Britain, the Conseil national de recherche scientifique in
France, and numerous private foundations have attempted to respond to these
demands. Individual scientists have become a little more independent of the
rest of the university and more concerned about their projects and their research assistants. As a result, they have become less attached by sentiment to
the university as a whole and have less sense of responsibility for it. They
have also tended to become more distant from the administration of the
university and to look upon it as an antagonist.

In the humanistic subjects, where previously, as in the social sciences,
research was a "one-man affair," or the affair of a teacher and graduate
students paid for by a very small grant of a few hundred dollars from an
internal university research fund or an academy, grants have been sought
from private foundations or from governmental institutions such as the American National Endowment for the Humanities. All these grants have had to be
administered and scrupulously accounted for to the donors. The amount of
administration in the offices of deans and of vice-presidents has accordingly
increased many-fold. Paperwork has increased proportionately. Parkinson's
law operates here as well as in the Admiralty.

Custodial staffs have become larger since there is more to clean, and more
to watch. The amount of wastepaper to be collected from the offices, libraries, staff, and laboratories has increased, and more workers are needed to
collect it. More university guards or "campus police" have been required
because there has been more depredation, especially in the larger universities
and in those in large cities. Security departments have had to be enlarged to
supplement the regular police. This has been especially true of the American
urban universities. More money is required to pay the wages of the custodial
staff and more administrators are required to administer them, their wages,
and their "fringe-benefits."

The larger budgets needed to cover all this required larger staffs to assemble all the necessary money and to administer its allocation and expenditure. In American universities, "development offices" have become large-
scale enterprises with their own culture and momentum. Even in Europe,
where governments provide most of the funds for higher education and where
private foundations and individual patrons have been less forthcoming, the
financial administrations of universities have grown. The belief that a stronger and larger administrative hand is needed has been growing in the European universities. The recent decision of the University of London to have a
permanent vice-chancellor, the decision of Oxford in the past decade to have
the vice-chancellor serve a four-year, rather than a two-year term, and deci-

sions in the same direction in France and West Germany, are evidence of the increase in administrative tasks.

Where university administration is prominent and strong, there is a tendency for the academic staff to become alienated from it. The distinction between "we" and "they" has become more pronounced. In consequence of all these developments, universities have become less unitary. Even within departments, the increase in size of staffs has led to a situation where older teachers scarcely know their younger colleagues.

The academic staffs of American universities, by and large, have been very serious about their work. They have certainly been very conscientious and scrupulously devoted to their research. They have taken the teaching and supervision of graduate students and training students for the professions with the utmost seriousness. They have also, despite what has been said, usually been painstaking in the teaching of undergraduates, especially in smaller colleges where traditionally there have been no graduate students and relatively little concern with intensive research. In British universities, teachers have been even more painstaking in the teaching of undergraduates, as graduate students have been thought to be more capable of looking after themselves intellectually. The tradition of concern by teachers for students has been weaker in Italian and French universities. The Germanic universities were in between. The principle of *in loco parentis* did not obtain on the continent, but in seminars and in institutes where students worked under the professor they received much attention. Both the expansion of numbers and the radical politicization of students in certain faculties have weakened this relationship.

In the United States, on the whole and thanks to competition from governmental, quasi-governmental, and private research organizations, and from private business, university teachers are paid relatively munificently. In impoverished small colleges this is not so, but in major private universities, in the municipal college systems of large cities, and in the state universities of the prosperous states, they have been paid salaries equivalent to those of moderately successful businessmen. The situation has not been very different in Europe. This has been a marked change from the situation which prevailed before the Second World War.

In the great period of expansion in the quarter century which followed the war, departments and faculties went on growing in all Western countries. Each member could lecture on whatever subject interested him most, he could pick and choose among the research students whom he would supervise. If an American university teacher wanted an interesting colleague from another university, and if he could persuade his departmental colleagues to agree, that colleague could be appointed. The grants for research from government and from the private foundations helped greatly in this. Each member of a department could do pretty much as he pleased. In Great Britain, France and West Germany, the older tradition of one professor for each major subject has given way to something like the American pattern of several professors in those fields in which there are many students. In these countries, too, departments have become larger, more diverse in their interests, and less solidary and submissive to the authority of the head of the department.

Generally speaking, in most of the period after the Second World War, the prestige of university teachers and especially of professors was high, and their confidence in themselves, their intellectual powers, and their subjects was great. The pride of the continental professor was legendary. Modesty of aspiration was not a universally practiced or admired virtue among American academics during that period. This was one of the sources of great accomplishment, but it is also one of the sources of their discontents at present.

There is still a great deal of money available for research in the United States and Great Britain, in France and West Germany, but there is a sense of constriction. Graduate fellowships are in shorter supply than they were in a number of fields, and the dramatic gestures of the United States government, such as the abolition of the post of Presidential Scientific Advisor, as well as the repeated insistence that research should be "related to national needs," the "crash" program in cancer research with its implied criticism of the National Institutes of Health, as well as the Mansfield amendment which prohibited expenditures by the Department of Defense on research not clearly related to military problems, have caused many American academic scientists to feel they are now living in a hostile society. British scientists too feel that they are more straitened now than before.

Actually, the difference is not great when compared with the period of expansion, and the contrast with the condition of austerity which used to prevail before the Second World War is very great. Still, it is not seen that way: most contemporary scientists and other academics do not remember that earlier period and have only the universal affluence which obtained until relatively few years ago as a standard of what scientists may regard as their proper due. Their sense of buoyancy is somewhat deflated. Less melodramatically, the same thing has been happening in Great Britain where the displacement of the Dainton report by the Rothschild report represented a similar development. In West Germany, professors are a beleaguered class, not because of the niggardliness of governments but because the university laws have greatly restricted their powers. In France, the situation is very similar, even though teachers are not given such a hard time by their radical students as are their German colleagues in a number of universities.

The Loss of the Sense of Buoyancy

Not all this collapse of buoyancy can be attributed to difficulties in obtaining funds for research. Many scientists have become aware that after the savage attacks on American scientists for their connection with the government which was conducting the war in Vietnam—even though not very many scientists were directly connected with the conduct of the war—and for their vaguely conceived connection with the technology of automobiles, strip-mining, and industrial effluvia and liquid and solid waste—again, very few scientists have been connected with these particular activities—they do not have the world at their feet as they had it only a decade earlier. In Great Britain as well as in the United States, scientists also feel the atmosphere of constriction which affects the universities beyond the scientific departments. They are aware, too, that the graduate students whom they trained for the doctorate have not been able to find appointments at the same high level of opportunity and remuneration which was expected in the immediately anterior generation. All this has made for a certain despondency of spirit. It has made some scientists who feel less appreciated, also feel more skeptical about the value of what they are doing.

The same sense of constriction affects the social science and humanistic departments, although they, too, have not suffered from a severe diminution of research funds; the humanistic departments in American universities are indeed rather better off since the establishment of the National Endowment for the Humanities, and the situation is not too different in most Western countries. The social scientists in nearly all these countries have felt the sting of the students' rebellion and the rancorous and irrational criticism of the social sciences by radical sociologists, political scientists, and anthropologists. It was in social science departments that the student disorders had—and in some cases still do have—their greatest success. There is very little substance intellectually in the criticisms which the radical students make of their social science teachers, but social scientists—except for economists—have felt them nonetheless. The currency of the critique of disinterested research, and the denial of the worth and even possibility of objectivity among members of the social science professions, have made social scientists who do not share those beliefs more uncertain of the value of their intellectual activity.

The culmination in the United States of two great bursts of productivity in the study of political development and in the construction of general sociological theory coincided with the outcrop of radical vituperation. Perhaps in these fields the social scientists who are the most progressivist liberals feel sufficient affinity with some of the radical aspirations to take their criticisms more to heart than their intellectual insubstantiality merits. Perhaps it is the mere fact of being so startlingly and abusively criticized and frustrated at the annual meetings of their professional societies which has discomposed many American social scientists. But justifiably or not, many social scientists have fallen into a state of dismay and diminished self-confidence about their own powers and that of their subjects, about which they were so overwhelmingly optimistic only some ten years ago. The sense of buoyancy has receded there, too.

What I have said refers mainly to senior members of faculties and to those appointed on permanent tenure. It applies rather differently to junior members of academic staffs. For one thing, their economic position was not as favorable as that of their elders. However, in the younger generation, two factors have coincided to give some foundation of justification for a considerable degree of unease. For one thing, in the period of expansion many quite young men were made full professors. This meant that faculties and departments acquired a disproportionate number of persons on permanent tenure, at rather high salaries and with a long period of service ahead of them. The United States, Great Britain, Canada, and France are all suffering from this situation. In West Germany, university teaching staffs have continued to expand, so this particular problem is not yet acutely felt. The expansion could not have continued at the rate at which it went from the early 1950s until nearly the end of the 1960s, and the recruitment of new members of departments was bound to have slowed down. Still, the young persons who were at university in those expansive years anticipated that they, too, would benefit from an unceasing expansion of opportunities. Now, however, because some universities in the United States and Great Britain are even reducing their staffs by not replacing retiring and deceased senior members, the chances for advancement and permanent appointment of the younger group have been pushed back.

In addition to this, the drive in the United States for "equal opportunity" for blacks and women has made a difference. Departments for a time leaned over backwards to appoint blacks, even though their quality was not up to the standard of the department; still, many appointments were made and this caused the preponderantly white graduate student body—whatever they thought about the justice of the procedure—to see a further restriction of their opportunities. After a time the movement to appoint blacks lost its momentum. This afforded no respite. The "women's liberation" movement, far more persistent, energetic, and resourceful than that of the blacks—and perhaps with better grounds, as far as quality of achievement and capacity for future achievement are concerned—came next onto the horizon and darkened the air around the young men with recently received doctorates. This affects all fields.[15]

The disaffection of some of the younger members of the academic profession in the universities of most West countries is of course not a monopoly of this generation, nor is it expressed only in a loss of buoyancy. It is also expressed in a disparagement of academic work and in ideological radical-ism. American academics in all fields outside business studies, medicine, law, engineering and economics have long tended to be progressivistic in the special American way. The radicalism which was interwoven with the stu-dent agitation of the second half of the 1960s was an abrupt extension of this progressivistic outlook. The younger generation of teachers—teaching assis-tants ("TAs") and teaching fellows, as they are variously called, and instruc-tors and assistant professors—were close to the agitating students in age and in cultural outlook and they were also sympathetic with their demands for equality in the exercise of authority in the university. Many of them shared the "Vietnik" culture; they were sensitive to the actuality of the war in South-east Asia and they had little sympathy with the centers of American society.

Disparagement of the Academic Ethos

For all these reasons, the younger generation of academics, including many of the blacks and women whose appointments have cut into the prospects of the young white male academics, have a sense of bitterness and even resent-ment against universities as they are and against their own branch of the academic profession. Many of them deny its validity. In so far as they are victims of the recent campaign—which many of them join—against the stan-dard of objectivity in science and in scholarship, they feel that they have been launched on a vain enterprise, which, quite apart from its personal frustra-tions and practical disadvantages, is itself very problematic. If they are radi-cals then they are actively aggressive, although this tendency has gone down pronouncedly in the past few years. In some universities, they are in favor of the formation of trade unions of university teachers; in others, they form part of the radical block who support radical student initiatives and join camarillas against "the administration." Where they gain permanent tenure, they seek to further the appointment and promotion of those who share their political outlook. In general they are the carriers of the politicization of the university; they regard the academic ethos as having nothing to do with them.

The situation is little different in the European universities. In West Ger-many, the denial of objectivity, the conviction that politics is the "be-all and end-all" of academic life, has gone much further than it has in the United States. There, the "assistants" are far more radical than the professors, and are in fact often, in alliance with radical students, at war with the professors. This is especially so in the popular social science subjects, but it is also prominent in the humanistic disciplines. Objectivity as a guiding standard in the assess-ment of scientific and scholarly beliefs is denied. In appointments, thanks to their cooperation with radical student representatives, they are much more active in bringing onto the teaching staff politically sympathetic persons with little regard to their qualifications. In fact, in some German universities the deterioration has gone so far that scarcely any academic ethos remains into which new appointees can be assimilated. The groups of radical students are more entrenched and they supply a powerful reinforcement for their radical teachers.

In France, the assistants, who are in a terribly difficult situation in which they have little hope for promotion, are very disaffected.[16] Italy seems to be in the same situation.

Great Britain is the least afflicted by the alienation of the younger generation from the academic ethos, but there, too, there are pockets of radicalism among teaching staffs. Very few, however, go as far as their fellow-believers on the continent, in cooperating with or in encouraging their radical students. A more sedate radicalism has a longer tradition in British universities; when the situation in the universities is calm, radical staff members usually behave in a conventional academic manner—at least in comparison with the conduct of academic radicals in West Germany and the United States. In Britain, too, the disaffection is most pronounced in the social sciences, and especially in sociology.

Except for several West German universities, the radical teachers in practically all universities form a quite small minority. But they sometimes wield an influence which outruns their numbers because of the many dissatisfactions among those who do not share their ideology. In this period, when so many spirits are in the slough of despond, bits of their radical ideology often find occasional resonances, even if not a large and continuous following. The radicalism of students and teachers in West universities is not confined to a radical antagonism against the existing society. It is directed as much against the universities. They share the view, which prevailed in the great period of expansion, that the universities are integral to the operation and growth of their societies; the radicals hate society, they therefore hate the universities which serve society. Their more or less Marxist ideology furnishes them with an elaborate criticism of the entire cognitive enterprise of modern culture, and it renders them alien to the academic ethos which postulates the appreciation of the disinterested cultivation and pursuit of knowledge.

Radical disturbances have affected the mood and the quality of performance of the universities. For one large cohort of students, there were several years when classes were frequently suspended or boycotted and minds were more generally unsettled. The students of that generation can look back on the exhilarating experiences of the occupation of buildings and much time wasted. The enthusiasm of those years has largely gone from student bodies. However, some professors in the more affected West German universities declare that it is still impossible to teach effectively under the conditions which prevail,[17] although this probably does not apply equally in all faculties or disciplines, even in the more troubled universities. In the French universities, the reorganization which followed the enactment of the *loi d'orientation* has still not been completed, and at least some professors have quietly withdrawn from teaching in the first two cycles, confining themselves to work with the more advanced and earnest students in the third cycle. Students in the Italian universities seem still to be in a state of turbulence. In the United States, although the angry enthusiasm has gone, its recession has left considerable stains on certain departments, even in outstanding universities. The coherence of academic staffs, already damaged by the increase in size, the self-centeredness of many individual members, the attraction of external interests and possibilities, has been further impaired by the memory of the conflicts of the time of the student disturbances.

Even more important is the change in the conception of what education in a university might be. Whereas long years of immobility have left Italian university teachers cynical about change, short of the change brought about by revolution, change beckons to American university teachers as an ever present possibility. "Innovation" had permeated the atmosphere before the disturbances; the disturbances made some of the innovations come about. There are in the United States many colleges where students initiate and conduct courses of study, set and mark their own examinations. Even in Great Britain there have been innovations in examination procedures, which have little to recommend them except that they were vigorously proposed by some students and supported by others. Examination assessment is said to have become less scrupulous in many Western countries; it is also said that political considerations enter into the assessment. There is certainly more preoccupation with the political views of colleagues and more political factionalism in universities.

Whereas the radical and excited students of the generation of the period of disturbance have left the universities and have presumably developed somewhat more civil attitudes, their teachers who took sides in the conflict remain members of the universities. Cleavages within whole faculties and particular departments still persist and find new issues on which to be sustained. Those who sympathized with the radical students are still bitter against their colleagues who opposed them. The wavering of university administrative officers left both radicals and moderates discontented. These discontents persist and are even aggravated by the ending of the period of expansion which places administrations in the position of refusing to continue certain activities, or to continue certain posts which have become vacant, and to make other "hard decisions" which departments do not wish to make or cannot make.

The ethos of academic life had already been under strain before the students ran amok. Universities had become too dispersed in their activities and in the objects of their attention; they were so eager to satisfy the many demands made on them and to seize all the opportunities which where offered to them. They tried to do too many peripheral things and they forgot some of the central things. They forgot, above all, that even though universities are not their own justification, their existence as coherent institutions is requisite to their doing the teaching, training, and research which justify the existence of universities.

The Task Before Us

Against this background of great expectations on the outside, great and conflicting demands and some uncertainty on the inside, it is appropriate to ask what the universities should do in these times which seem unprecedentedly difficult for them. There is no doubt that genuine difficulties exist and that they are not difficulties arising simply from the inflation which raises all costs and causes hardships and necessitates renunciations. The internal coherence of the universities has already been damaged by the availability of large sums of money for research projects for which the university is little more than the physical site, and it has been even more damaged by the divisiveness precipitated and aggravated by student agitation. The strain on the younger members is helping to maintain the divisions.

The simplest fact is that the universities, above all in the United States but elsewhere too, allowed themselves to be seduced by affluence in the first two decades following the Second World War. There was little that they could do to resist the expansion of numbers, and they should not have done so, even if they had been able to do so. But they should have insisted that they be given the means and the time to develop the conditions needed to provide for the expanding numbers. They should have insisted that they be allowed to obtain the kinds of teachers they needed rather than be forced to take whatever they could find. This would not have been easy because politicians would not have been sympathetic. It was impossible to expand the staff with sufficient rapidity and to bring it sufficiently into the state of mind in which it would take seriously the tasks of the university. This occurred not only at the lower levels of the staff but also at the higher levels where many persons who were not of high intellectual quality were appointed to permanent posts. The universities were in some measure responsible for the rapid expansion; they welcomed it partly for the morally good reason that it represented an extension of the equality of opportunity, partly for the much poorer reason that it flattered their vanity and brought an affluence such as they had never had before. Teachers and administrators were both swept along by the belief in education as a universal solvent. Most teachers and administrators, went along, in differing degrees of activity and passivity, with the idea of a "science-based society" in some of its most extreme forms.

There are certain things which cannot be changed. The numbers attending universities will never go back to what they were. Nonetheless, it is likely that, quite apart from some fluctuations in applications for admission in consequence of fluctuations in birth rates twenty or so years earlier, there will be a little less eagerness to attend university. The wide experience of universities might make it appear as less of a right to be fulfilled; young persons might decide, to a greater extent, not to seek admission, having heard of what the privilege demands. This is especially likely to be the case as the student's responsibility for bearing some of the cost of preparing for an occupation which brings a superior income is enlarged. The availability of other paths in life and of university education at a later stage in life might also help to reduce the pressure of numbers.

It is also likely that governments will continue to expect the universities to do certain kinds of research and to train young persons for careers in research to a far greater extent than was the case before the Second World War; this will provide an assurance to the universities that they will not be forced into attrition. At the same time, university teachers must set their faces against accepting proposals from governments and foundations which have some merit and which will for a time give them additional financial resources, but which will after five years leave them to support these schemes from other sources of funds. Such arrangements cause excessively rapid expansion in certain fields, and when they are concluded, many persons who have been recruited to teach in them, or who have been trained and have specialized in order to work in them, are left without equally remunerative employment. This counsel is especially relevant in the United States where "bright ideas" and "crash" programs are favored. In the United States, "innovations" are much esteemed: bodies external to the universities will often support "innovations" but they will not support them past that point. Now some of these "innovations" are worth adopting, when there is a substantial body of sound scholarly or scientific knowledge on which to build. Often, however, the knowledge needed to enable the desired practical or technological goal to be attained does not exist. As a result, the universities have added staff and institutional arrangements which only increase their financial and administrative burdens and are alien to their primary tasks.

It is difficult to resist these temptations. The projects are often attractive, the funds and staff which they would bring appear desirable. They also appear to contribute to the public good, enabling the universities to do their public duty and causing them to be esteemed for having done so.

The issue of innovation is one of the most serious of all those with which universities must deal. I have no doubt that great mischief is done in the name of innovation, as in the past great harm has been done by the invocation of the sacredness of tradition. Universities exist for the purpose of promoting important discoveries in science and scholarship and in teaching and training students in the substance and spirit of the best of the newest and older discoveries. In that sense universities are "about" innovation. But innovation nowadays has come to be very indiscriminately used, and it is very indiscriminately sought. Just as being "innovative" is one of the most laudatory adjectives in the vocabulary of the publicists of university affairs, so anything new, however trivial and however superficial its novelty, is welcomed. Universities should be on their guard against this. They must be on guard against their own *faiblesse* for "innovation" which combines transient publicity with short-lived support.

There are certainly some innovations which universities ought to make in their courses of study. New "majors" or "special subjects" should be available to students as soon as they can be taught and supervised at a high standard; sometimes such innovations may require the establishment of a new department or a new committee, and universities should not fight against such an innovation as long as there are good intellectual or professional arguments for it and able scholars or scientists who will take administrative responsibility for it. But to rush into a new "interdisciplinary" arrangement just because there is money to pay for it brings trouble in its train. There is much clamor for this from many who do not know what is involved, either on the scientific side, in the organization of instruction, or in the technological or practical application of what is taught. "Interdisciplinary innovation" appeals to those who cling to the idea that the university can solve any problem as long as the necessary money is supplied.

The duty of the universities, in the United States at least, is to rid themselves of some of the institutional encumbrances acquired during the period of expansion. Indeed, one of the benefits of more limited resources is that universities might be forced to discontinue certain activities which they should not be carrying on. The universities must find a means of declaring that they cannot do all the things which society needs to have done.

The myth of the university as redeemer will die hard. It is painful for human beings in their existing state of mind to believe that some problems are not wholly soluble and might be forever, that we do not know how to solve them and that their solution might not rest on scientific knowledge about the factors at work in them. It seems inhumane to tell this to those who suffer from these problems; it seems unduly defeatist to say in advance that a problem cannot be solved, when in the past some problems which were thought to be insoluble turned out to be ameliorated by improved knowledge and improved administrative procedures, as well as by more enlightened and generous political attitudes. It is least easy to do so when governmental bodies and foundations are ready to grant financial support for those who will undertake to work on such problems.

This does not mean that the universities should turn away from the society outside themselves and disregard it. This would be wrong in itself and imprudent as well.

It is also terribly difficult to decide in advance whether or not a problem is soluble. It is certainly important that the universities render unto Caesar what is Caesar's, not only because Caesar is powerful and wealthy but also because they owe something to him and to the society of which they are equally members. But it also is necessary not to promise all things to Caesar and his society because in the end they will become disillusioned and distrustful. Once it becomes fixed in public opinion that academics will promise anything if money is provided for it, and are then unable to deliver the promised solution, the universities will reap a crop of resentment—and deservedly so.

The position of the universities in public opinion is one of their greatest problems. The good opinion of the public and of politicians about the universities cannot be neglected, but it must not become a preponderant concern of universities. The universities will fare better in public and political opinion if they do what is right, rather than allow themselves to be blown about by every breeze of policy and opinion.

The universities must be jealous of their reputation for honesty and disinterestedness. These are in danger. Intemperate and unreasoned partisanship on the part of individual scientists and scholars, and the corporate declaration of partisan attitudes by universities, can harm the public image of the universities and the individual academic person's conception of the true calling of the university. It alienates those who have an equal and opposite partisanship and it discredits academics and universities among those who are not partisans. This, too, is extremely difficult when our Western societies have become so politicized and when it is generally believed that there is little that governments, if they are so minded, cannot accomplish. It is especially difficult when the social sciences are so much looked to, and when social scientists quite justly are so concerned with public issues, and are so often involved as advisers of various levels of government and as beneficiaries of their financial bounty.

Disengagement from political partisanship is difficult for those who are partisan and to whom it would seem to make life more rewarding. Radical partisanship is often stimulating and it sometimes is accompanied by an intellectual *élan* which generates interesting ideas and worthwhile research. Subservient partisanship also seems to be rewarding. It was one of the vices of the German universities in their greatest age, and it was covered up by great intellectual accomplishments; but it brought a bitter harvest, especially in the lean times when the German universities seemed to lose their creative intellectual powers. It is one of the reasons for the revenge taken in recent years by politicians against the universities in West Germany. Partisanship is a danger to universities, both externally and not least internally. The universities must become more centripetal. I do not mean by this, as I have said before, that they must cut themselves off from society and disregard their obligations to it. Nevertheless, one of their main obligations is that each university should be a university. I mean by this that the university must not be simply an assemblage of diverse and separate activities of research and teaching. It must be an institution in which such activities are carried on; the fact that they are carried on in the same institution makes a tremendous difference to each of these activities, however separate they seem to be from each other. Thus a university teacher must not only perform his obligations of teaching, training, and research, he must also perform obligations to his university and to the idea of the university. This is what I mean when I say that the observance of the academic ethos is a necessary condition for the fulfillment by the universities of their obligations.

The disaggregation of universities and the decomposition of the academic ethos are a menace to universities as they become more specialized, as their members come to regard them only as administrative conveniences for their own particular interests, and as they become larger, richer, and more differentiated. The academic ethos is weakened by other factors, too, such as administrative high-handedness and arbitrariness and the individual's parochial and self-interested conception of his tasks.

The academic ethos and academic citizenship, focused on the university as a corporate cultivation of important truths in the various disciplines and among them, and in the long-term service of society and civilization, are the decisive factors in determining the fate of the universities. All those strains and distractions of "busyness," of the desire to please one's patrons by flattering subservience and large promises, of self-advancement and radical partisanship, and of all the burdens of large numbers and insufficient resources, are significant because they weaken the academic ethos. The same is true of student radicalism and public dissatisfaction with scientific technology. They becloud the minds of academics and weaken their adherence to the ethos of academic life. This weakening spreads its injurious effects in many directions.

Lord Ashby a few years ago wrote a moving paper on "A Hippocratic Oath for the Academic Profession."[18] It was a courageous start on a momentous undertaking. The academic ethos is hard to grasp and resistant to systematic formulation. But we all have some traces of it in our consciences which have been formed and nurtured by our own training in universities, our long experience in them, and the academic traditions which we inherit. It is that element which we must affirm and strengthen.

Notes

1. I was once told that Rutherford, on an occasion when a junior teaching post became available in Cambridge, said: "I won't have Bernal in my department; if he were appointed he would then try to have other communists appointed." On the whole, there seems to be no evidence that being a communist or fellow-traveler made its converts any less meticulous in the execution of their academic duties.
2. See Weber, Max, *On Universities: The Power of the State and the Dignity of the Academic Calling in Imperial Germany* (Chicago: University of Chicago Press, 1974) reprinted from *Minerva*, XI, 4 (October 1973), pp. 571–632.
3. E. J. Gumbel was a statistician who published several important works on political violence; as a result he was persecuted by nationalistic colleagues and students and censured by the philosophical faculty of his university. He was later dismissed.
4. Theodore Lessing was teacher of philosophy at the Technical College of Hanover. He wrote disparagingly of Field Marshal Hindenburg and was transferred to a research post in consequence of the protests of nationalist students.
5. These included the censure by the academic senate of George Frierich Nicolas, a pacifist who was assistant professor of medicine in Berlin, and of Hermann Kantorowicz, an eminent teacher of law in Freiburg who criticized the tradition of Bismarck.
6. A book like Upton Sinclair's *The Goose Step*, which challenged the legitimacy of the universities and of the academic profession, was a rare phenomenon. It was written by an "outsider" who had no contact with universities. Thorstein Veblen's *The Higher Learning in America*, scathing though it was, did not depart from the widely accepted standard of what a university should be, namely, an institution of science and scholarship. There was, indeed, some criticism of universities, but most of it was intended to bring them closer to the traditional ideal.
7. Wells' ideas of a "scientized" society may be seen in *Anticipations: Of the Reaction of Mechanical and Scientific Progress upon Human Life and Thought*, eighth ed. (London: Chapman and Hall, 1902). Veblen's notions are pervasive throughout his writings. I mention here only *The Engineers and the Price System* (New York: B. W. Huebsch, 1919), *The Theory of Business Enterprise* (New York: Scribner, 1904), and *The Place of Science in Modern Civilization and other Essays* (New York: B. W. Huebsch, 1919). J. D. Bernal's views are to be found in *The World, the Flesh and the Devil: An Enquiry into the Future of the Three Enemies of the Rational Soul* (London: Jonathan Cape, 1970, new ed., original ed. 1929), and *The Social Function of Science* (London: George Routledge, 1939). The history of the idea goes back to Francis Bacon. See especially *The New Atlantis* (1626).
8. These trends had been observed by German writers as early as the first decade of the century; they were again taken up in the 1920s by various German writers on the "white collar worker." Just before the Second World War, Colin Clark's great book, *The Conditions of Economic Progress*, gave it the authority of a daringly imaginative economist. Since that time many writers have rung changes in the tune. The numerous names, "postindustrial society," "information society," "techtronic society," "science-based society," "automated society," etc., all testify with varying degrees of learning and sophistication to the common belief that the future belongs to science and technology. These ideas go back at least as far as St. Simon in some respects and to Francis Bacon's phantasy of the House of Solomon.

In the postwar period they were put forward in the Steelman report in the United States and in the Barlow report in Great Britain, both of which stressed the urgent need for the production of scientific manpower by the universities. These reports did not go as far as the later prophets of "high-level manpower" but they were steps in that direction. All these prophetic writings were eagerly welcomed by the spokesmen for economic growth and the reshaping of universities to the "needs" of the "science-based society"—which is as yet still awaiting its birth—although it is being announced by so many self-appointed midwives.

9. See Glazer, Nathan, "Schools of the Minor Professions," *Minerva*, XII, 3 (July 1974), pp. 346–64.

10. It is now called "the information society" in Japan, which refuses to be behind hand in these matters.

11. Report of a talk by President Howard Bowen, Claremont University Center, in *Chronicle of Higher Education*, VIII, 32 (13 May, 1974), p. 4.

12. See, for example, Leibfried, Stephan, *Die angepasste Universität: Zur Situation der Hochschulen in der Bundesrepublik und den USA* (Frankfurt am Main: Suhrkamp Verlag, 1969); Hoffman, Werner, *Universität, Ideologie, Gesellschaft: Beiträge zur Wissenschaftssoziologie* (Frankfurt am Main: Suhrkamp Verlag, 1968).

13. See Arblaster, Anthony, *Academic Freedom* (Harmondsworth: Penguin Books, 1974), and Pateman, Trevor (ed.), *Counter-Course: A Handbook for Course Criticism* (Harmondsworth: Penguin Books, 1972).

14. See Riesman, David, "Evangelism, Egalitarianism and Educational Reform," *Minerva*, XI, 3 (July 1973), pp. 296–317.

15. In the United States, these demands have been given force by the Office of Equal Opportunity of the Department of Health, Education and Welfare. This body demands huge amounts of statistical documentation which the universities under attack have not had readily available. To supply the information demanded by their governmental tormentors, they have had to employ considerable staffs. One major university has had to devote the equivalent in salary of more than twenty full-time teachers to assemble the desired information. Approximately similar cases are not rare. This aggravates the financial straits of the universities.

16. See Gaussen, F., "Academics without Careers," *Minerva*, XI, 3 (July 1973), pp. 372–86.

17. See, for example, "The Resignation of Professor G. N. Knauer from the Free University of Berlin," *Minerva*, XII, 4 (October 1974), pp. 510–14.

18. *Minerva*, VII, 1–2 (Autumn-Winter 1968–69), pp. 64–66.

5

The American Private University

The ten or so most eminent American private universities of the present century are very unusual in the world of contemporary higher education. Their uniqueness resides in their private character and in the distinction of their intellectual accomplishment. No other national higher educational system possesses anything like them. There are some private universities in a few other countries, but none occupies the position of eminence in their respective national system such as is possessed by those of the United States. There are also great universities outside the United States and within it which are more or less in the same class as the leading American private universities but they are public or state universities. The continent of Europe has or has had a few private universities. The Université libre de Bruxelles was a private university, so is the Bocconi University in Milan. In Japan and the Philippines there are numerous private universities, but none has the place in its own national system or in the larger world of learning which is occupied by the leading American ones. There are numerous private colleges in India, but they are parts of public universities and, in any case, none of them, even the best, is on the level of intellectual distinction of the leading American private universities.

Recent discussions in the United States have expressed doubts about the future of these private universities. The costs of maintaining them are so high that in the past few years a large proportion of them has been operating with budgetary deficits.

The salaries of academic, administrative, secretarial, maintenance, and custodial staff all increase steadily under the pressure of inflation; the two latter groups are organized into trade unions which strengthens their bargaining power. The cost of books for the huge libraries which are indispensable for the quality of research continues to rise; the demand for costly scientific equipment is insatiable. Services for students, counseling, medical, and psychiatric and even child care, on a scale unknown in European universities, continue to expand. The increased numbers of graduate students who are married, and so require special housing provision, add to the cost. The effort to bring into higher education a larger number of black students who must be provided with studentships is a further addition to costs. Of the leading private universities, at least four—Columbia, Chicago, Harvard and Yale—are in large cities and their immediate physical and social environment has deteriorated so that large expenditures, previously not needed, are required for security services auxiliary to those provided by the municipal police; these universities are also pressed by their slum-dwelling neighbors, civic groups, and their own student bodies to provide housing amenities and health services for the neighboring poor and this is a further call on their resources.

The anticipated rise in costs and predictions about the return on investments combine to place the private universities in a perilous financial position. The policies of the major private philanthropic foundations which have contributed so much to them in the past have begun to change in a direction which is unfavorable to their continued existence.

In this situation, public and political opinion has begun to turn against the private universities. Many assert that the need for them will disappear. The difficulties which the leading private universities experience in attempting to gain financial support from private persons and bodies and the increased proportion of their income which now, as compared with forty years ago, comes from the federal government, seem to show their unviability; the great accomplishments of the leading state universities of California, Michigan, and Wisconsin demonstrate their superfluity. At one time in American history, when governmental support was meager, the private sector of the higher educational system added many more places for students to work for first, advanced, and professional degrees and did a large amount of needed and useful research. As state-supported research and instruction have increased to the point where the leading private universities provide only a small and, for some time to come, diminishing proportion, this function has thus become less urgent. So it is said.

There is another wind in the heavy weather now surrounding the leading private universities. They are charged with being "elitist" and to be elitist nowadays is a bad thing, particularly in a country as endemically populistic as the United States. Politicians have been populistic for a long time; intellectuals and higher civil servants are now populistic; so are students and many of the academics. Even the rich and the snobbish have become populistic. It is an old thing in the United States but it has become more pronounced recently. It affects the attitudes of the federal government in all its branches and it affects the attitudes of the class of persons who are wealthy enough to contribute substantially to the private universities.

The Position of the Private Universities in
the Higher Educational Hierarchy

It is pertinent in view of these developments to examine the position of these leading private universities in the American academic system, to consider their function in the total system and to pass a judgment on the proposition that the functions which they have performed can readily be borne by the state systems of higher education.

Regarding the past there can be no doubt. It is well known that they were the pioneers in the establishment of postgraduate training and that they were the main places for fundamental research in the physical, biological, and social sciences. Since their period of pioneering, several state universities have come into the front rank. The universities of California and Michigan and, to a lesser extent, those of Wisconsin and Illinois now stand, in many subjects, among the great universities of the world. This advance of the state universities has not, however, displaced the major private universities from their intellectual preeminence. Harvard, Yale, Princeton, Columbia, Chicago and Stanford universities still have not receded.

Academic opinion in the United States—not simply within the private universities—has repeatedly acknowledged the outstanding merits of the leading private universities. In 1969, a sample survey of the judgments made by academics about leading universities showed that in twenty-one out of thirty-two fields of the humanities and in the social, biological, and physical sciences, four or more of the six leading universities were found to be private. In seven fields, the distinction of being among the first six universities was evenly divided. In only four of the thirty-two fields were there more public than private universities in the first six.[1] In 1964, a similar survey of academic opinion regarding the standing of the universities in twenty-five fields showed that in eighteen of the fields, four or more of the six leading universities were private; in four of those fields, there were equal numbers of private and public universities; and, in three, the public universities among the six leaders outnumbered the private universities.[2] In the twenty-five fields covered in both surveys, the balance remained identical between 1964 and 1969; in six fields the private universities increased their share in eminence; in five, public universities increased their share.

A comparison of the results of the surveys of 1964 and 1969 with two surveys conducted by more or less similar methods in 1925 and 1957 shows that in the fields covered by all four surveys over a period of nearly a half century, the position of the leading private universities has changed only slightly despite the tremendous increase in the size and activity of the public universities.[3]

The eminence of the public universities is in part a result of the accomplishment of the private universities. The members of the five most distinguished departments in each of the fields surveyed by Dr. Alan Cartter were trained predominantly in private universities. Of 372 members of the departments of history, classics, English, French, German, linguistics, music, philosophy, Russian, and Spanish in these universities, 82 percent had their most advanced degree from private universities.

Of the sixty-six Americans who received the Nobel Prize between 1946 and 1971, two-thirds received their most advanced degrees at American private universities, 13 percent in American public universities and 20 percent at foreign universities.[4] Of 479 members of the American Philosophical Society, 71 percent received their most advanced degrees from American private universities, 12 percent from American public universities and 17 percent from foreign universities. Thus, despite the increased eminence of public universities, the leading private universities of the United States have retained their great intellectual vitality without impairment and from among their graduates they have contributed to the state universities scientists and scholars of the highest distinction.

Privateness

Nothing which I have said thus far connects the eminence of achievement of the private university in the United States with its "privateness." For one thing, being private does not mean being wholly different from a public university. Half a century ago, the privateness of a private university as distinct from a public university lay above all in its sources of financial support and in the composition and mode of recruitments of its highest governing body. Nearly all its income came from student fees, endowments, and private gifts and grants. This is no longer the case. For example, in 1965–66, three private universities, of which two, Princeton and Chicago, were of the highest quality and the third, Vanderbilt, was definitely in the next class, drew only 49 percent of their income from private sources—return on their endowments, private gifts and grants and student fees—while just under 46 percent came from government grants and contracts.[5]

The public universities used to receive most of their income by vote of the state legislature and a small proportion from student fees. Now the leading state universities present a different picture. In 1962–63, the University of California, the most distinguished public university in the United States, received 58.6 percent of its income from the state of California, 33.6 percent from grants and contracts of the federal government, 1.9 percent from student fees, 3.5 percent from grants and gifts from private sources and 1.6 percent from endowment.[6] A sample of six state universities surveyed at the end of the 1960s showed none of the six receiving more than 50 percent of its total income by vote of the state legislature; one received 41 percent and the other five received between 25 and 35 percent from the same source. Student fees provided between 20 and 25 percent for five out of the six universities investigated; only one received less than 10 percent of its income from student fees. Public universities now conduct fund-raising appeals among their alumni and other prospective private donors.[7]

Thus the difference is no longer between support exclusively by income from private or from public sources. The patterns of support now overlap to a greater extent than they did half a century ago, but there are still substantial and significant differences in pattern nonetheless.

The great private universities receive much more of their income from student fees, endowments and gifts and grants from private persons and bodies; they receive nothing from state governments. Both private and public institutions receive far more from the federal government than they use to and, in the cases of both the private and the public universities, the proportion of income received from the federal government is a substantial fraction of their total income.

The Sovereignty of the Private University

Legally, the privateness of the private universities of the United States consists in the fact that sovereignty rests with lay governing bodies which are not appointed by the state or chosen through popular elections. The sovereignty of the private university, as in all questions of sovereignty, is no easy thing to locate.

There are certain types of state university which are directly under the control of the national or state ministry of education. The French universities were governed in this way until the enactment of the *loi d'orientation* of 1968.[8] Sovereignty there lay outside the university, to such an extent that it might be said that France had a university system but did not have universities. The budget of each local unit of the Université de France was voted by the National Assembly, decisions about degree courses, subjects to be taught, etc. were made in the ministry and academic appointments were nominally made in the ministry.

There are no private universities in West Germany. Neither with regard to the sources of the financial support nor with regard to the locus of the sovereignty are German universities private. The present-day West German university, which is the heir of the traditional German university of the nineteenth century, is nominally self-governing. Much has been made of *akademische Selbstverwaltung*, but the university section of the state ministry of culture makes all major decisions regarding the establishment of new professorships (i.e., chairs for the teaching of subjects not previously taught in the university); the minister still retains the ultimate power of appointment to academic posts. The ministry makes the regulations regarding admissions policy. The funds come almost exclusively from the state governments; the budget is made by the *Kurator*, an official of the ministry attached to the university to administer and control its financial affairs. There were academic freedom, university autonomy and self-government in the German universities, but within a narrower range than existed in fact and in principle in Oxford and Cambridge at the end of the nineteenth century, or than exists in the modern British universities, where there is an amicable division of functions between the lay and academic strata of the system of government, or than has existed in the leading American private universities since the 1920s.[9]

In Great Britain, there are no private universities in the American sense. Nor are there any public universities in the American sense, either. The universities are all autonomous corporations under royal charter. Prior to the growth in importance of the University Grants Committee to the point where it now supplies practically all the revenue of the universities aside from that provided by the research councils, the modern or civic universities resembled the private universities of the United States more than they did the public ones. Now that their funds come almost entirely from public sources the resemblance has diminished. Their system of government was in broad outlines rather similar to that of the American private universities, with a two-tier system of government, powers being divided between a lay body concerned largely with questions involving major issues of finance and an academic stratum. (There were at one time marked differences in the composition of the academic stratum of government of the two systems; in the United States great powers were lodged in the presidency, in the modern British universities the powers in academic matters lay with the professors.) Oxford and Cambridge were, until the past quarter-century, largely independent of governmental financial support and they were wholly self-governing except for the intermittent influence of the Church of England in earlier times and royal commissions and parliamentary intervention in later times. Now they are almost entirely dependent on the central government for their funds, like all the other British universities. (Their constituent colleges, on the other, hand receive nothing directly from the central government, but the fees which their students pay and which make up in some cases a substantial part of their income are paid by the students mainly from bursaries supplied by governmental bodies.) But, apart from their financial dependence, the British universities are as autonomous as it is possible to be when very large drafts are made upon the public treasury, when there are many other competing uses for funds and when the universities are much in the public eye.[10]

In the last half of the 1960s, Parliament required that university expenditures made with funds supplied by the University Grants Committee be scrutinized by the Comptroller and Auditor General to determine that the money had been spent "efficiently." The word was menacing since it appeared to give civil servants who were not highly educated the power to pass judgment on the purposes for which universities spent their money. Thus far, however, about half a decade later, no complaints have come forth from the universities about any oppressive use of their powers by the agents of the Comptroller and the Auditor General.

The universities are gently nudged by the University Grants Committee to avoid programs of study and research in highly specialized fields which duplicate what is already being done in other British universities. Thus, although the grants are block grants, complete budgetary freedom is somewhat restricted. Nonetheless, British universities, although they have become "state" or "public" universities in a financial sense, have continued to practice a degree of autonomy unknown elsewhere in Europe, and similar in general outlines to what has been enjoyed by the leading American private universities.

American state universities are governed by a combination of representative academic bodies and administrative officers and by boards of regents, popularly elected or governmentally appointed. The American state university system of academic government is in principle more autonomous than the German or the pre-1968 French system. It is closer to that of the modern British university in that it combines corporate autonomy with lay or nonacademic supreme governing bodies. The mode of selection of boards of regents differs, however, from that of the British universities and they are correspondingly more actively expressive of the currents of political and moral opinion outside the universities than their British counterparts; they are more disposed to take partisan political positions regarding academic matters, especially regarding personnel. The universities of black Africa, India, and Pakistan are similar to the British universities in the location of sovereignty in a nonacademic body which is, however, legally independent of the state.[11] Yet, in their responsiveness to currents of political and moral opinion outside the university, they are more like the American state universities, and their governing bodies are frequently much more intrusive into questions of academic appointment.

On the continent of Europe, there were private universities which were entirely free of any governmental control or financial dependence on the state. They were private institutions but they were not autonomous—their governing bodies are appointed by an external body, the church, and their senior administrative officials derived their powers from the ecclesiastically dominated governing body. The University of Louvain, the Catholic University of the Sacred Heart in Milan and the Institut Catholique in Paris were in this category. Recently, Louvain has become increasingly secularized and dependent on the state for its financial sustenance.

Then there are the private universities (and colleges) which are privately owned in the way in which private business enterprises are owned. They are conducted for profit, much as the Berlitz and other language schools or the "crammer" schools which prepare law school graduates for the state law examinations are conducted for the profit of the owners. There are a number of such institutions of higher education in the Philippines.

The famous American private universities today stand at about the middle on the continuum which runs from the university which is run like a division of the ministry of education, where every decision depends on or is made by a nonacademic civil servant and in which all expenditures are foreseen and drawn from the budget of the ministry, to the private university or college which is owned and controlled by an independent extra-academic association such as a church or caste association and, finally, to the entirely private university or college which is privately owned and conducted for the profit of its owner.

The American private universities are private in the sense that they are relatively autonomous corporations—legally independent of the state or government on the one side and of churches and caste or other associations on the other. The locus of sovereignty within the university is not derivative. The legally sovereign governing body within this type of private university might or might not be academic—in America it is not, and in this respect it differs from Oxford and Cambridge. But it shares with them, as with the other British universities, the internal cooptation of its sovereign body. In formal, institutional terms, this is what the privateness of the private university consists in. Derived from this is the fact of budgetary autonomy, that is, it allocates whatever resources are available to it in a given budgetary period in accordance with its own judgment as to what the right allocation should be, unlike those institutions with budgets which must be either drawn up or approved by ministries or legislatures external to them or which are formed under the general guidance of a body making nominal block grants.

Since all American private universities now live beyond their income from endowments, fees and current gifts from private Maecenases, they have become dependent in varying degrees on governmental sources of financial support for current expenditures. In this respect, the private universities have begun to resemble the state universities—in the general sense that their income comes from governmental sources. There is a major difference, however, in that since a substantial part of the governmental income of the state universities comes largely from the state, by an act of the state legislature, the government of the university is more closely bound to the politics and administration of the state government. The condition which is carried by even partial support from the state treasury is that the governing body of the state university—usually the board of regents—should be determined by political processes, for example, appointment by political officials and popular election; in many cases certain state administrative officers sit *ex officio* on the board of regents. In contrast with this, the governmental income of the private universities comes from the federal government, which demands no representation on the governing body of the university. The members of the board of trustees of the leading private universities certainly have interests—many are businessmen, bankers, lawyers, publishers, etc., and they are usually persons of considerable wealth—but they do not represent those interests. The derivation of the board of regents from the political arena brings with it the belief which is inherent in democratic politics—namely, that political action is to a large extent constituted by the representation of interests. Furthermore, the tradition of service to the citizens of the state justifies the political members of the board of regents in their expectation that the university should satisfy the interests of the constituencies which they represent. As a result, the state universities are pressed to undertake many activities which are generally useful but which are not undertaken out of intellectual curiosity or for educational purposes.

The boards of trustees of the private universities exist in a different tradition. That tradition was partly formed from the traditions of Protestant ecclesiastical government in a country where church and state were separate. The trustees of American private universities have often been men of strong convictions about the economic, political, and moral order of society and at one time they attempted—sometimes successfully—to have these convictions observed in the administration of the universities on the boards of trustees of which they served. Nonetheless, they were expected to be disinterested and to serve the university rather than to have it serve them. The Christian overtones of American private higher education prior to the dominance of a secular outlook kept the imperiousness of strong-willed trustees in check; the origins of the student body in the upper classes of society also caused them to restrain their demands. But more important than either of these two factors in forming the traditions of the trustees of the American private universities were the force of character of the great university presidents of the period from 1885 to 1920, the increase in the prestige of science and the growth of the sense of philanthropic obligation among wealthy businessmen.

The trustees of the major private universities thus came to look upon themselves as being called to serve the university's interest rather than to have the university serve their interests and those of their constituents. In consequence, the private universities under consideration here tend to have their centers of initiative and decision within themselves to a greater extent than is the case among the state universities, even the most eminent.

The Quality of Achievement

In general, the greatness of a university as a center of teaching, research, and training can certainly not be a simple function of its being a private university. The German universities at the height of their glory were not private universities; nor are the University of Paris, the University of California in Berkeley and the Universities of Wisconsin and Michigan. The question is not whether state or government universities can be great; the history of universities affords ample evidence of that. The fact remains that, in the United States, the private universities have an edge of superiority over the public ones.[12]

Why is this so? It is not really an explanation to say that the major private universities were the first to develop postgraduate studies and that they established a tradition which is still sustained. The question is why were they able to be pioneers at the turn of the century and why have they maintained their eminence since then. The explanation seems to lie in the larger initiative which the system of internal government of the private universities permitted, in the greater budgetary adaptability which control over the resources they already possessed allowed them, and in their freedom and energy to acquire more financial resources when these were required. These factors, coupled with the prestige, first social and then intellectual, which the major private universities could draw upon, made them more attractive to young and unknown and mature and famous scientists and scholars, as well as to intellectually ambitious and adventurous students.

In courses of study or in methods of instruction at the undergraduate level, private universities in the United States at least have had the great advantage of the power to try out new schemes. They have been able to do this largely because they have had smaller and more rigorously selected student bodies, better staff-student ratios and a greater concern of senior members of the university for the instruction of undergraduates. The major innovations in undergraduate instruction in the United States in the past half-century, for example, in liberal and general education, have been in private universities— Columbia, Chicago and Harvard. In private universities, undergraduate instruction, even where administered separately, is less likely to become an isolated segment of the university and is more likely to be integrated into the university as a whole. This is partly a function of size, partly a function of the high prestige of undergraduate education in the leading private universities of the eastern seaboard. It was also a function of the relatively small size of the undergraduate student bodies and the large number of outstanding scholars and scientists available at these universities which had taken the lead in research and postgraduate training.

Size and Privateness

The state universities, even the best of them, could not provide the same sort of undergraduate education because their student bodies are very large and intellectually more heterogeneous as a result of their necessarily less stringent admission standards. Much of the undergraduate syllabus is intellectually at a lower level than it is at the comparably eminent private universities, and outstanding scientists and scholars are averse from teaching at that level and to such large groups.

Thus the superior undergraduate instruction at the major private universities is partly a function of relative smallness and the more demanding criteria of admission. But these are in their turn functions of privateness. The size of the student body and the criteria of admission which determine that size are much more in academic hands in a private university than is the case in a public university. Of course, this is partly a matter of wealth. If the university does not depend on student fees to eke out its livelihood, it can be as small as Princeton; if it does depend on fees then it might become as large as New York University, which is one of the largest in the United States and very much larger than any of the leading private universities.

State universities seldom have small undergraduate bodies. Even those which have small ones are unlikely to try out new courses of study, intensive instruction and supervision because they are dependent on outside nonacademic bodies as the ultimate locus of their governing authority and of their budgetary decisions. It is not privateness as such, but the smallness rendered possible by privateness, ample financial resources per student and a tradition of concern for undergraduate education which are decisive.

A public university is not necessarily large. All British universities are small by American standards; the greatest German universities of the nineteenth century were so small that, given the overhead and other costs of present-day universities, such a size would be regarded as unnecessarily uneconomic. Furthermore, private universities are not inevitably small. They can allow their numbers to soar indefinitely, but they are under no compulsion to do so unless they conceive of their function as the provision of higher education of some sort for as many young persons as possible, or they might be driven to do so by the need for income from student fees, or they might simply wish to do what they think everyone else is doing. There are private universities in the United States in which there are enrollments of 20,000 and over, but they are not among the leading private universities. A private university has, in the United States, the freedom to restrict its admissions to a number which it believes it can educate and train effectively, and it can do so as long as it has sufficient income.

Budgetary Flexibility

Income which is designated by its donors, private or public, for use for specific purposes imposes rigidity on a university. The growing portion of university revenue in the United States which comes from the federal government by grant or contract is intended for particular projects. A considerable proportion of funds from state governments is also earmarked in a different sense because of the external interests in certain fields of research and teaching. Initiative, therefore, in the creation of new teaching and research departments is deadened by income which is committed in advance.

Income from endowment and gifts and grants which may be used freely for whatever new purposes of teaching and research appear to be appropriate are weighty factors in accounting for the greater initiative of the private university in the United States.

Plurality of Sources of Income

There is one very striking feature of the private American university which is often astonishing to those educated at European universities. This is the scale of the enterprise devoted to the solicitation of funds. It is a continuous headache for those who take on themselves the burden of keeping the university alive. How much easier it is to submit a single budget to a single university grants committee or a single church or a single governor or a single legislature or a single minister of education. It is a great burden but, if it is successful, it confers great advantages.

The plurality of sources of funds is a protection for the university from subjection to a monopoly of influence by an outside body. This plurality of sources—notably private foundations, individuals and families of liberal benefactors, and diverse and separate government departments (other than or in addition to the ministry or department of education)—permits the center of gravity of a university to remain more fully within itself. It is not just that the external monopolist might wish to influence the university's policy since it lies in his power to do so—indeed this has often been the case in American state universities. But even where the single patron is restrained by prudent reason or tradition, the possibility exists. Where that awareness of the possibility is strong within the university, it can also generate a sense of dependence and therewith inhibit self-confidence and adventurousness.

The creation of new professorships in previously uncultivated but promising subjects, the establishment of opportunities for interdisciplinary study and research, the creation of new research institutes, the development of new lines of research which appear promising—all these could obviously occur with a single source of financial support and they have in fact done so. But their occurrence is less probable. For one thing, such single sources tend to develop their own consensus and their own traditions in matters of higher educational policy; they tend also to be more concerned with keeping existing activities going than with expanding their expenditures to provide for new things as well. These tendencies come to be reflected in the expectations of members of the academic staff.

State-controlled and state-financed universities can obviously also have a plurality of sources of financial support. Given the structure of the governmental system of the United States and the multiplicity and munificence of private philanthropic foundations, state universities have indeed, to a certain extent, received financial support from a variety of sources.[13] The tendency, however, is against plurality. The assurance of a single large grant to cover most of the university's expenses has a deadening effect on the disposition to seek out additional sources. It is also a discouragement to those who are potentially to be drawn into the plurality of supporters. If government takes care of so much, why should others who are major taxpayers also use their wealth in that way when they can obviously provide only a marginal supplement. Private universities, however large their endowments and however much help they obtain for specified purposes from the central government, are driven into a perpetual search for funds. This perpetual search is a nerve-racking activity but it is a necessity for keeping the center of gravity of the university within itself. It is thereby an important condition for institutional innovation. A plurality of sources of funds invites initiative in raising funds among academics who wish to do something which they regard as being of great significance and which has not been done previously. It therefore permits new and rewarding lines of research to be developed, and draws into them promising graduate students.

Privateness, Plurality of Sources, and Academic Freedom

There is another advantage of privateness, together with the plurality of sources of financial support, which is especially important in the United States. It is true that American legislative bodies have been, in the Middle and Far West and in Texas, very generous in the financial provision for universities. But it is also true that the American state universities have been recurrently shaken by political controversies in which legislators and regents have disturbed the equilibrium of the universities without any advantage to their teaching, training and research functions. There is probably more respect for the academic profession among legislators today than there was seventy-five years ago, but there is no unilinear trend of improvement in this respect. Seventy-five years ago, the boards of trustees of private universities were not very different from the regents of the state universities in their distrust of the young teacher—or research worker—holding deviant political views, (The question of students' political views had not yet emerged!) But the attitudes of lay governing bodies have changed more markedly and more continuously in the major private universities. Partly in consequence of the more distinguished achievements of the academic staff and the wider recognition of the importance of the university in society, and partly in consequence of the growth of a wider sense of responsibility among bankers, industrialists, corporation officials, lawyers, etc., who have made up the bulk of the membership of boards of trustees, they have come to take literally their obligations as trustees. They have come to regard it as a moral trust on behalf of the intellect and society rather than as a commission by society to confine the intellect. That is why academic freedom in the great private universities has become so well established, while in the great state universities it is extensive but fluctuating in its fortunes.

Of course, the academic intellectual community possesses something like a common intellectual, moral, and political culture and intellectual self-respect has improved throughout the higher educational system. The difference therefore between state and private universities is not a disjunctive one. In general, moreover, the scale of academic freedom has improved throughout the whole university system, state and private. Nonetheless, the occasionally severe constrictions which do occur are almost entirely in the state universities and, in so far as they affect private universities, originate among or are mediated by legislators, state and national.

There is no reason to think that this balance will change in the near future. The political culture of the United States will remain populistic—in fact it is becoming more so. Popularly elected politicians and regents are bound to be more populistic than the kinds of persons who make up the boards of trustees of the leading private universities.

Popularly elected politicians could, of course, become like the passive British member of Parliament was for more than twenty years—voting large sums of money for universities but not inquiring very closely into what was done with them. But this is not the most probable development; in fact the development seems to be in the opposite direction. The British Parliament is moving in the direction of the American legislature; it wishes more and more to set a watchdog over what is being done with the public money which it has voted. As the sums become larger, the likelihood that surveillance will be demanded will increase even more in the United States. The outcomes of scientific research are unforeseeable, the discoveries or new interpretations of social phenomena are likewise unforeseeable and those who engage in these activities must feel that they will not bring down an avalanche of censorious publicity upon themselves if their quest has ramifications or if it ends in views uncongenial to received beliefs and prevailing desires.

Governmental provisions of research funds for specific "missions"—such as has become official policy in the United States in the past few years—is, up to a point, of value to government. It is not so valuable to universities. They have, in addition to the inflexibility of earmarked funds in general, the further disadvantage of being subject to the fluctuations of public and political opinion. The American disposition to operate through "crash programs" means that rapid expansions are followed by sudden "cutbacks."

Universities need continuity, and those which become dependent on this type of support for research are likely to find themselves in difficulties. This has, indeed, occurred among both public and private universities since they have both become dependent on the federal government for the support of much of their research and some of their specialized graduate training. "Cutbacks" disrupt the stability of universities just as much as indiscriminate spending on large-scale "crash programs."

The continuously increasing dependence of the major private universities on the federal government threatens, under conditions of present policy, to annul the advantages of greater flexibility and freedom from political interference which these universities have hitherto enjoyed vis-à-vis public universities. The federal system adds instability of the flow of resources to budgetary inflexibility.

It adds a further disadvantage against which in the past the leading private universities, not being beholden to the federal government, were able to protect themselves. This is political intrusion into the affairs of the universities. In the past, public universities were not infrequently harassed directly by politicians or indirectly by businessmen, bankers, farmers and journalists working through politicians, when they disapproved of the academic or civic beliefs or actions of the academic staff. The private universities, although they had their rough passages around the turn of the century and during the First World War, came generally to be immune from political interference until the student radicals of the second half of the 1960s introduced their own kind of political interference with the working of the universities.

One of the aspirations of the student radicals was to influence appointments. The federal government has now taken over from them and it does so with much more power at its disposal. Under the auspices of the policy which would eradicate discrimination against blacks and women, the federal government now harasses the universities by threatening to suspend payments on contracts made by the government for the conduct of research by the universities. It insists that the proportion of blacks, women, and other groups represented in university teaching and research staffs below their proportion in the population should be given preference until they approximate more closely to that proportion. All universities have been menaced by the bureaucrats who have taken on themselves the execution of this policy; the University of

Michigan, as well as Harvard University, has been explicitly threatened by these actions; Columbia University has actually had its contracts suspended.[14] In many respects the danger to the universities is greater than it was in the time of the first Senator McCarthy because, at that time, the universities did not receive as much of their budgets from the federal government as they have come to receive in the ensuing two decades. Furthermore, at that time, Senator McCarthy did not enjoy the support of the executive branch of government.[15]

As matters stand at present, the leading private universities of the United States have lost a certain amount of their privateness. They did so when the science policies of the federal government were more liberally administered, although the funds passed through the Department of Defense, than they later came to be. They are in danger of losing even more of their privateness unless they can at least maintain, if not expand, the proportion of their support which comes from private sources or unless the federal government adopts a better policy. Not only might they lose a good deal of their privateness, that is, their sovereignty, but they also stand to lose some of their eminence which has been a product of good traditions, affluence, and independence. As things stand now, unless they can gain more private support and render themselves less dependent on the federal government, they might find themselves under an imperious, sometimes fickle, often but inconstantly munificent external power. They might thereby gain affluence while losing their independence. If they lose their affluence, even while retaining or regaining their independence, it will be difficult for them to live up to their traditions, which in the present state of research and given the expectations of students and academic staff have become very costly. In any case, even if they do not become impoverished, they will be able to maintain their traditions of outstanding research, teaching and training only by continence and discrimination in the choice of their activities. This is a condition of the continued privateness and therewith the distinctive high quality of their accomplishments.

Privateness and Expansion

One of the advantages of the privateness of a university if it is also affluent is that it can limit its size. American universities have increased in size during the past quarter of a century, but they have done so very modestly compared with the public universities. In the range and magnitude of their activities, however, the leading private universities expanded greatly. They were aided in this by the convergence of private philanthropy and the continuous growth of federal expenditures on research.

We live in an age in which more is wanted by more people. Affluence has not brought a satiation of wants; it has heightened them. And at a time when the rulers of institutions and the weight of authority are condemned by many, the actions demanded of institutions and the authorities who are charged with their operation have become more numerous, more urgent and more complex. Churches and churchmen are persuaded that they must do more than cater to the religious needs of men; pastoral care has expanded into social action. Governments, however much their legitimacy might be questioned, are driven forward into more and more activities by an unceasing growth of demands for more services, for more provision and regulation.

This expansion of demands has had its consequences for universities. It is manifest in the greatly enlarged student bodies in practically every country in the world. It is manifest, too, in the standards of provision which American university teachers expect in the way of research equipment, library services, secretarial and research assistance. It is manifest above all in their expectations regarding the provision of resources for whatever research interests they develop, for the extension of their departments, for the creation of new teaching posts in subjects which catch their interest. This elaboration and ramification of interests into new fields has been one of the most impressive and generally most fruitful features of American university life, public as well as private, in the past quarter century. In fact, the greatness of the American universities during this period consists in the intellectual progress made through this elaboration and ramification.

The expansion of demands is apparent in the types of activities which universities are called upon to perform. They are called upon, as they have always been, to train personnel for the practice of the well-established and new professions with a basis in systematic knowledge which it is thought only universities can provide. It is also being demanded of them that they contribute directly to the performance of a wide variety of services—urban planning, the rehabilitation of neighborhoods, the provision of low-cost housing, medical services, and legal aid for those who live in their environs, the conduct of courses in police training, in-service training of government officials by special courses as well as by the release of teachers and research staffs for special tasks to be performed for governmental bodies—on a municipal, state, national, and international scale. At one time, services of this type were demanded mainly of public universities; more recently many of them, especially those connected with urban problems, are being demanded of the leading private universities. The demands come not just from outside the university but from inside as well.

The view that a university must be "involved" in the life around it, that it must "serve the people in the urban ghettoes" is given additional force by the fact that the urban universities are in areas where slum conditions are on the increase, in which public order has been allowed to deteriorate and in which slum-dwellers, passive in the past, are now demanding a fuller incorporation into the larger society and a larger share in the opportunities, goods and services it is capable of producing. Hence, in order to save themselves, the private universities have been forced to take on extremely hard tasks of urban renewal.[16]

Some of these demands are intellectual demands central to the chief function of the university. Others are not central or even appropriate and would be more fittingly performed by governmental and civic exertions. The more the university responds to these latter demands, the more danger there is that it will be distracted from the main tasks of teaching, research, and training. The more numerous, diversified, and specialized its activities become, the greater is the danger of the disaggregation of the university. Each activity requires staff and every staff becomes a vested interest, demanding more resources and more freedom in pursuing its interests—in both senses of the word.

The Disaggregation of Sovereignty

The pattern of federal governmental support for university research in the period after the Second World War—a very successful pattern in the production of important scientific results—favored the disaggregation of the university. Any staff member could do almost anything he wished to do, as long as he could obtain the necessary financial resources from the government or a private patron. Many of the projects were on a large scale, requiring large teams of research workers and supporting staff. In many respects they became independent of the university, using its administrative and accounting facilities but otherwise acting in complete independence. In the idiom of the sociologists who welcomed this development, the loyalties of American academics were focused on their profession on a national and international scale, rather than on the institution in which they held their appointment. The former was necessary and desirable. The latter was injurious to the university. The injury lay in disaggregation.

The tradition of learning which lay at the root of the famous intellectual accomplishments of the leading private universities of the United States was precipitated by a group of powerful and enterprising presidents who viewed the intellectual mission of the university with a piety of religious origin. They guided their universities with strong hands and understanding minds. Their universities were sovereign realms and they were sovereign within them. The passing of this notable generation was followed by the devolution of powers to departments. The outcome was a marked degree of departmental self-government. After the Second World War, there was a further devolution of power to the individual members of the departments. The intellectual results, in the period of expansion, were considerable. The universities were, however, weakened as organizations, as was evident from the way in which most of them responded to the student disorders. Internal dissension was the natural outcome of the deteriorated corporate spirit of the academic staff. The sovereignty of the private university, already invaded by the federal government and actively threatened by the extremists among the students and teachers, was in danger of disintegration.

The university—above all the private university—must keep its center of gravity within itself and it must keep itself coherent. This is not said out of any sentimentality about unity, out of a nostalgia for "dear old Siwash," but rather because any academic discipline which loses its sense of connection with the common core of educational, scientific, and scholarly activity will deteriorate. The growth of individual disciplines depends either on their being in a university or existing within the matrix of a university system; the prosperity of an academic discipline depends not only on its own traditions but on the vicinity of the other academic disciplines from which it can draw not only stimulation and technical aid but a sense of the essential standards of scholarly and scientific work, a reinforcement of the ethos which is indispensable to such work.

Of course, a modern university cannot be an Oxford or a Cambridge college, a small sodality in which all the dons know each other, where the junior members know each other and where dons and those *in statu pupillari* know each other. The larger colleges in Oxford and Cambridge have already passed the point where this is possible. But what is essential in the collegiate system and even more in a university is the *sense*—the deeply experienced sense—of being engaged in a common undertaking, with common standards applied to diverse intellectual topics and with a concern for the whole. A university which has become as large as some of the great American state universities or as large as the University of Paris or Calcutta is treading on very dangerous ground. Bigness alone tends to segregate the teachers of undergraduates from those engaged in postgraduate teaching and in the supervision of postgraduate research—although size is not the only cause of this. When departments become very large, they tend to become estranged from adjacent departments, a situation which is aggravated by the specialization of disciplines and narrowness of training. This makes a great difference in the performance of the proper tasks of the university in teaching, training and research. When a university becomes disaggregated, its traditions become attenuated and its main functions are lost from sight; the junior members within the staff come into conflict with the senior members, the students become alienated from both and above all from the senior members. Numerous small sovereignties come into existence; the university becomes like the Holy Roman Empire and particularistic interests grow at the expense of the main functions. Almost anything, however fantastic, appears to be compatible with being a university. This is what has happened in many American universities, in some of the larger private universities and especially in the state universities.

This development is ominous because a university—public as well as private—is more than a statistical aggregate of departments, laboratories, institutes, etc., each of which has its own interests and rules. Every intellectual undertaking depends upon an ethos, and the more specialized and segregated the undertaking, the fainter and feebler the ethos becomes. It is not simply a matter of identity as a member of the university, nor of solidarity, nor of a sense of responsibility for the whole; the ethos is an outlook and a mode of evaluating intellectual activity; it is a sense of responsibility for truth and it is sustained and reinforced by the perception of its wide sway over many minds within a single institution of many disciplines and within a discipline spread over many institutions. It depends on face-to-face contact. The university is thus a whole, with a life of its own on which the constituent parts depend, not merely for common administrative and custodial services, but for moral-intellectual sustenance. The larger a university becomes, the larger the number of its constituent departments and institutes and the larger and more self-contained each of them is, the greater the danger of parochial self-containedness. (Of course, there is the opposite danger in departments being so small that they do not permit enough internal differentiation or sufficient overlapping with adjacent disciplines.) The plurality of sources of financial support—invaluable though it is—accentuates the danger of departmental and even individual self-containedness.

The sudden halting of the post–Second World War expansion brought to the surface the structural weakness of the universities of the United States. The necessary and desirable diversity and pluralism of a university structure was not balanced by a consensus on the tasks and nature of a university, by institutional solidarity and by the strength of the center of the university. This center is constituted by the chief executive officer of the university, his immediate aides and the "saving remnant"—throughout all ranks and generations of the university. The center failed to serve as the locus of a concern for the whole, as the source and intermediary from which a large, comprehensive, and responsible perspective could be diffused through the whole university. The experience of Columbia University, where the center had fallen into neglect ever since the decline of Nicholas Murray Butler, is a somber illustration of what happened to a great private university in which sovereignty became disaggregated. The recent persecution of that university by the Department of Health, Education, and Welfare makes it into a microcosm of the condition of a major private university in which the internal disaggregation of sovereign powers paved the way for the recent governmental encroachment on the sovereignty of privateness.

Sovereignty and Presidency

The good fortune of the private university lies in sovereignty, affluence, and tradition. By the first, the university determines its own course. The second provides the means without which little could be done and with which the sovereign power can be used to good effect. The cultivation of the tradition was in part and fundamentally a product of talent and genius in the academic staff, but it is also in part a product of the exercise of the sovereign power.

In a period of stable resources—or even contracting resources—universities cannot afford the luxury of disaggregation. The disaggregated units are too self-seeking and too concerned generally to perpetuate their kind. The restriction of size, which was once a deliberate choice, is likely in the future to be a necessity imposed by the limitation of financial resources, and a private university which is forced to remain stable in terms of the numbers of its staff against the immediate background of expansion must now husband its resources more parsimoniously. If it is too parsimonious, however, its more attractive members will accept appointments at public universities which can continue to draw directly on the state treasury. All the more need therefore for it to make "hard choices." Its new appointments and promotions must be made more judiciously; its opening-up of new subjects must be more perspicacious. It does not have the surplus of resources to permit the mistakes of appointment and establishment which could be afforded when there were enough resources to permit both good and poor appointments.

Every department thinks it must be larger than it is; few institutes think the general interest would be served by their discontinuance. A strong hand by a central authority, rather than a decision by a "log-rolling" compromise, is called for. What is needed is a strong president.

Critics of the American college and university early in the present century often found fault with the system of presidential autocracy. They were right. It was an unsatisfactory system. At a time when public opinion lacked confidence in the ways in which secular learning approached sacred things and when boards of trustees regarded themselves more as custodians and agents of external interests and watchdogs over the doings of the teaching staff than as trustees of the intellectual and moral mission of the colleges and universities, unhappy results were often produced. The numerous "academic freedom" cases which occurred in the United States in state and in private higher educational institutions from about 1890 to the 1930s were the results of this system. A marked change has taken place since then, particularly in the leading private universities.

The heightened intellectual accomplishments of American universities in the past third of a century, new conceptions of the prerogatives of authority and a new appreciation of the dignity of intellectual creation have much enhanced the degree of academic self-government and, most notably, the freedom of departments and individuals to shape their own teaching and research programs, to choose their members and colleagues and to control their own time-budgets.

As a result, a pronounced devolution of authority has occurred, which has, on the whole, produced very striking benefits. A balance appeared to exist between the center and the periphery. There appeared to be strength at the center and the appearance continued as long as it was untested. There appeared to be consensus between center and periphery and the appearance continued until it was tested. Private universities which have a high standard to observe are more in need of this than public universities because the former are likely to be operating under financially more straitened circumstances.

The formation of a center which is capable of holding and exercising influence is the task of the president, his staff, the formal academic councils, and the informal circles of advisers, gadflies, and busybodies throughout the university who speak for the university as a whole, whether they are asked to do so or not. Their tasks include seeing the university as a whole; the center looks after the interests of the still unborn and the voiceless, and the subjects which have promise but which have no departments of their own, fields of research which have promise, talent, and no resources, and the students who have not yet enrolled in the university.[17] In a well-functioning center, there is thought about the university as a whole; in a well-integrated periphery, there is loyalty to the university, not just to disciplines or departments. The creation of the loose consensus which reinforces the ethos of the university and its derivative virtues is the function of such an institutional center.

One of the factors of the recent crises of the American university is the failure of the mechanisms which maintain the institutional center and which thereby generate consensus. This can happen in private universities as well as in state universities, and it has in fact happened in recent years in both. But the private universities have an advantage—which is at present challenged by ecological difficulties—in that they inherit a stronger tradition of intellectual and pedagogical accomplishment, a more favorable size and structure and a greater sense of freedom. The sense of freedom for the scholar and scientist is vital to creative work and there the private universities have the edge, as is widely attested by those who have worked in both.

The Heart of the Matter

To think about the university as a whole is also to think of its future; a university, a private university, must think of the future. Not just its own future financial position but the future of the university as an intellectual institution. Some persons and groups might think about the demographic, financial, and custodial aspects of the university, but who will think about the intellectual core of all of this if the private universities do not do so? Most public universities need not respond to the urgency of this task because it is a major part of their responsibility—not by any means their sole responsibility—to meet current needs by providing places for students, by providing teachers for them and by providing the desired services for their larger public. The pressures of public demand are the source of their support and custom. Their hands are full. Private universities, which have on the whole been free from the urgency of current demands for services, must think more about the development and enrichment of the university as an intellectual undertaking, as something which transcends the needs and tasks of the moment and which serves the national society and humanity over the course of an indeterminate future.

The demands on the state universities will continue to grow in size and number. The state universities will be occupied with teaching more students, doing all sorts of applied research and recruiting and training persons to do that research within the university and outside. Services will constantly be demanded of them. The higher educational system will become more diversified than it is at present; there will be more different kinds of institutions, teaching a wider variety of subjects at a wide variety of levels, because the kinds of training they will offer will be in demand. All these demands are well justified and our societies will not become what they ought to become if these demands are not met. They are not all, however, wholly harmonious with the idea of a university as an intellectual institution, however tolerably they have managed thus far to coexist with it.

There is a real strain between the maintenance and transmission of the traditions of teaching and training for research in science and scholarship and for the learned professions on the one hand, and the pressing demands of current needs on the other. The systems of public higher education in all countries and not least in the United States are subject to this strain. The demands on higher educational institutions have a powerful constituency which derives its strength from the power of the purse and the force of its moral claims. The maintenance and transmission of the intellectual traditions through teaching and training in science and scholarship have to depend on their own inner force, on the morale of those who are charged with them and on the attractive and radiative power of those institutions and individuals who most effectively embody these traditions. As far as the United States is concerned, these latter functions have been the "calling" of the leading private universities. In the coming decades, it will be their calling to embody those traditions of intellectual work in their daily activities more completely and more unalloyedly than the public universities can. In so doing, the great private universities will not only continue to advance science and scholarship and meet their own immediate responsibilities in teaching, training and discovering at the highest level of quality, but they will serve the higher educational system and society by fortifying the capacity of the public universities to carry on the perhaps more difficult task of serving two gods at the same time.

Notes

1. Roose, Kenneth D. and Anderson, Charles, J., *A Rating of Graduate Programs* (Washington, D.C.: American Council on Education, 1971).
2. Cartter, Alan M., *An Assessment of Quality in Graduate Education* (Washington, D.C.: American Council on Education, 1966).
3. Ibid.
4. These data are drawn from an unpublished paper by Professor James Lorie.
5. Bowen, William G.,*The Economics of the Major Private Universities* (New York: Carnegie Commission on Higher Education, 1968), p. 35. Funds from government grants and contracts had amounted to 1.4 percent in 1939–40, 13 percent in 1948–49 and 24 percent in 1955–56.
6. Betz, Frederick and Kruytbosch, Carlos, "Sponsored Research and University Budgets: A Case Study in American University Government," *Minerva* VIII, 4 (October, 1970), p. 495.
7. Data from a survey by Mrs. P. Rampersad.
8. See "Statement of Principles of the Higher Education Bill" and "The Higher Education Law of 12 November 1968," *Minerva* VII, 4 (Summer, 1969), pp. 706–27.
9. From time to time in the course of the discussion of university reform in West Germany in recent years, a voice has occasionally been heard on behalf of the establishment of a private university. But there has been practically no response. What response there has been has been negative, stressing that a private university would be "elitist" and would also be subject to plutocratic influence. The whole notion was too alien to the German imagination to make any sense, even though at this time the prestige of the main American private universities was at its height in Germany. It did not occur to those who admired them that these universities were private.
10. Some British university teachers, most notably Professor Max Beloff, think that the central government and the University Grants Committee, through their financial power, have begun to have too much influence on the actions of universities. See Beloff, Max, "British Universities and the Public Purse," *Minerva*, V, 4 (Summer, 1967), pp. 520–32. Also see the letters to the editor on this article: Mansfield Cooper, William Paulley, J. W., Correspondence, *Minerva*, VI, 1 (Autumn, 1967), pp. 99–105; also Ashby, Eric, "Hands off the Universities?" *Minerva*, VI, 2 (Winter, 1968), pp. 244–56. The establishment of an independent, that is private university in Great Britain has now been taken in hand. See Mansfield Cooper, William, "A Private University in Britain?" *Minerva*, X, 2 (April, 1972), pp. 332–37.
    The British system has managed to combine in a very far-reaching measure the autonomy and academic freedom traditionally characteristic of British univer-

sities ever since the attrition of ecclesiastical influence with very massive financial dependence on the state. As a result, many British academics do not feel an acute need for anything markedly different from what they have. I once asked a very distinguished British academic, who is also a famous educational reformer and a liberal in the antisocialistic sense, to express his views on the merits and limitations of the private university of the American sort. He excused himself on the grounds that he could not say anything on the matter since he had always lived in a "state system."

11. The best analysis of the governmental system of modern British universities and its assimilation into the university system of formally British territories in Asia and Africa is Ashby, Eric and Anderson, Mary, *Universities: British, Indian and African* (London: Weidenfeld and Nicolson, 1966).

12. To recast the statistics presented above from the two surveys of the American Council on Education, in 1969 private universities appeared in the leading six departments in thirty-two fields in 63.6 percent of the opportunities; in 1964, they appeared in the leading six departments in twenty-five fields in 64.7 percent of the opportunities.

13. The plurality of government sources of financial support in the United States is one of the reasons for the excellence of the greatest American state universities.

14. See "Universities in Danger: The United States Office for Civil Rights *contra* Columbia University," *Minerva*, X, 2 (April, 1972) p. 319.

15. Mr. Stanley Pottinger bears many rhetorical and other resemblances to Mr. Roy Cohn, who was Senator McCarthy's "boy wonder." The real difference is that Mr. Pottinger actually does control the strings of the purse from which the universities draw, while Senator McCarthy and his agents could only threatened to do so. And, in those days, the amount in the purse was much smaller and less vital to the operation of the universities.

16. See Parsons, Kermit, and Davis, Georgia, "The Urban University and its Urban Environment," *Minerva*, IX, 2 (July, 1971), pp. 361–85.

17. One of its tasks, neglected in periods of expansion, is to think about those departments which are losing their subjects and their creative powers but increasing their staffs.

6

Governments and Universities

The activities of the human race may be seen as a triangle. At one angle are those devoted to keeping the physiological organism in being through the gratification of the practical needs of food, shelter, clothing, movement, and so on. They do this through the collection and cultivation of plants, the mining of minerals, the hunting and catching of wild and edible creatures, the husbanding of domesticated ones for food, traction, the use of animal skins and spun and woven fibers, and so on. These activities are susceptible to specialized performance and to coordination into a division of the labor that serves the gratification of these practical needs, although often in a very roundabout manner. At the second angle are those activities addressed to the understanding and interpretation of the vicissitudes and enigmas of man's existence on the earth and in the cosmos, perceiving and assessing the principles and powers that govern human actions and achievements, individual and collective. The activities that attempt to find the meaning and the laws of existence, in large and in small, that attempt to make sense of the world and men and their history are also organized into elaborate institutional forms that are capable of specialization of performance and coherence through a division of labor with unity, and they are sustained by deep and subtle traditions. The third angle subsumes those collectivities that permit and preside over the gratification of physiological, cognitive, and spiritual necessities, that maintain and increase order by regulating conflicts and enunciating rules. These include families, villages, tribes, municipalities, nations, and states.

Governments—legislators, civil servants, judges—universities, churches, the ownership of land, buildings, and machines, the learned professions, and the military together form the center of society, which is a loose agglomeration; they are attended to and deferred to; they preoccupy minds and attract aspirations; they exercise authority and play a dominant part in the allocation of resources and rewards.

The agglomeration of the constituent parts of the center is never wholly harmonious or in an easily stable equilibrium. Each of the constituent elements has its own pattern of values elaborated through long tradition and nurtured within specialized institutions. These traditions are not mutually exclusive of each other in their ends. These traditions contain ends that, although compatible and even mutually affirmative in particular points and on occasion, are not identical. Within the center, the various constituents may be in relationships of superordination and subordination, of consensus, compromise, and conflict.

Governments and churches have coexisted in changing relationships with each other for many centuries. Between theocracy at one rare extreme and real caesaropapism at the other no less rare extreme, with the earthly ruler being effectively and not just nominally the head of the state religion, there are many intermediate points. At present, the relationship between these two central institutions in most liberal Western societies is the far-reaching factual separation of church and state. The state does not intervene into the internal government of churches, it does not attempt to regulate their doctrines, it does not subsidize them, nor does it demand particular services from them. The churches are almost as separate from the state as they could be. They do not claim that the government should use its powers to require that all members of the society subscribe to their particular religious belief; they acknowledge the right of the government to conduct educational and eleemosynary institutions without their own participation. It is true that a complete separation is not attained in any country; the remnants of caesaropapism remain, for instance, in Germany and the United Kingdom; the property of churches is exempt from taxes on real property; in the United States monetary contributions to churches—as well as to educational and charitable institutions—are treated by government as permissible deductions from taxable income. Furthermore, churches are not interested only in the next world. They have always attempted to give ethical guidance to the earthly conduct of their own members, and they have almost always judged the conduct of their earthly rulers. As the preoccupation of the churches increasingly embraced the affairs of this world, the churches became assessors of the moral condition of society, and this too forced them into contact, often censorious, with the government of their societies.

A complete separation of church and state is impossible; so is a complete and harmonious fusion. So too is the complete and harmonious subordination of the church to the state. The same limits obtain for the other institutions of the center. As long as each has its own sphere of activity, and as long as each cherishes its own ends and values, complete harmony between them seems out of the question. Yet they exist in the same society; they are parts, however different from each other, of the same center of that society. They are bound to each other by all sorts of ties of mutual dependence. Nonetheless, despite all these traditional and inevitable interdependencies, liberal Western societies in the latter part of the last century and the first half of the present century have tried to establish a very considerable degree of pluralism in the relations of the different sectors of the center.

From positions of subordination or dominion, the churches were equally removed by the increasing religious neutrality of the states and the universities. The universities enjoyed, within the limits set, the various national traditions and arrangements that obtained in this time; a fairly far-reaching separation from the state. Both churches and universities appeared to be at the same rung on the ladder of autonomy from the state. The churches, however, were moving in the direction of greater separation from the state; the universities were on the verge of a movement towards a diminution of their autonomy. The churches were acquiring greater autonomy as governments became more indifferent to matters of religious belief; on the other hand, the relations of government and universities have become denser and more multifarious because secular knowledge has come to be more highly regarded by governments. Governments have come to believe that secular scientific and scholarly knowledge are pertinent to their own purposes and to the ends they have in view for their societies. The beliefs that scientific and scholarly knowledge such as is pursued in universities is instrumental to the achievement of the ends of economic prosperity, social justice, and military effectiveness, and that the possession of such knowledge should be made available to individuals so that they may increase their incomes and elevate their social status, work against a separation of government and universities comparable to the separation that has come about between governments and churches.

In societies where universities and churches were once allied, the separation of church and state has also been concomitant with the separation of church and university. The close ties which once bound the church and the state have been relaxed while the ties of state and university have been tightened. The separation of church and university was a necessary condition for these two simultaneous and opposite movements.

The universities are not the only arrangements dealing with cognitive tasks, any more than governments are the only institutions concerning themselves with practical tasks. Churches and monasteries, academies, research institutes, and independent private foundations for the pursuit of scholarship are among the variety of institutions devoted to the pursuit of learning. Universities have emerged triumphant over all these alternative arrangements for learning during the course of the past century and a half. The prominence they have achieved in consequence of that triumph has made governments more demanding for their subordination. There is a principle of division of labor among institutions implicit in the ends which each cultivates, but there is also potential conflict among these sets of ends. This division of labor may be so organized that it does harm to one or the other partners of the division, or to the others and the larger society and culture of which they are parts. Each, regarding exclusively its own interest, may frustrate its own intentions and do damage to the other institution and to the larger whole. Such a situation seems to have developed in recent decades as the demands on governments, and the aspirations and self-confidence of government officials, have grown. Politicians and civil servants have come to think of themselves not only as the ultimate arbiters whose task it is to confine conflict within the bounds of the political order, but also as the agents of substantive values. The prudential American concept of "a compelling state interest" that permits the substantive values of institutions to be overridden is indicative of the tendency of the state to regard its own substantive ends as more central than those of all other sectors of society.

The effective equilibrium between universities and governments, which prevailed in most Western countries for about three-quarters of a century up to the 1930s in some of them and later in others, now seems to be under stress.

The relationship between universities and government must be restudied in a wide historical context and with a fresh appreciation of the contemporary situation. There is a pressing need to reconsider what each owes to the other, and what each owes to values inherent in its own distinctive nature and not necessarily harmonious with the values of the other. The objective should be a "constitution of university and state according to the idea of each."[1]

I

The government and the university each owes to the other the acknowledgment, and the performances corresponding thereto, of their distinctive and different obligations to the well-being of their society, their culture, and their civilization—three things which are by no means identical. Government is not coterminous with society; the well-being of society is not always, even in the welfare state, what government decides is the well-being towards which it should strive. The purposes and the values of the various sections of society are never exhaustively protected or pursued by governments, although certain illiberal governments pretend to be able to do so and actually do. Government has many specific purposes that are legitimated by its service of the purposes and values of the individuals and institutions that make up their society, and by its service of the value inherent in that society and its culture. A government may protect the framework of society, it may enable its constituent institutions of society to pursue their respective and distinctive ends. But governments also have purposes of their own which may result in the benefit of particular groups or the realization of a particular form of society. In the advancement of the purposes which are its own, it may attempt to bend the constituent institutions of society so that they will move towards the fulfillment of these purposes.

The values of universities are inherent in their existence as universities. Those who enter them without the deliberate intention of subverting them accept, in varying degrees of awareness, a commitment to these values. The basic commitment inherent in the activities that constitute universities is a belief in the superior value of some cognitive beliefs over others and of some modes of acquiring knowledge over others. The task of the university is the cultivation, extension, and transmission of knowledge as valid as the human imagination, reason, memory, and observational powers can make it. If it does not do that, then it falls short of being a university, even though it carries the name of a university. From this end derives its other activities such as training for the professions where such knowledge is a necessity for effective practice. However devoted many of its members may be to "service" and "practical relevance," there is a particular, pervasive, elusive quality which universities generally seek to have or claim to have. This quality is the furtherance of the acquisition and wider possession of truth—of valid and important knowledge—about "serious" things.

There are many academics who profess to scorn such a formulation; others are outrightly hostile to it, and still others point to higher educational institutions that seldom give explicit thought to such an end. Nonetheless, I think that throughout the academic world, there is a sense that dedication to the acquisition of truth is where universities started from, and that most other things universities do should be derivative from that standard. Despite numerous deviations and shortcomings, this interest in what constitutes a university is apprehended far more widely than among a few idealists who are opposed to the idea that the university should be an intellectual "resource station" for the practical purposes of government, of society as a whole, or for particular groups in society.

The general acceptance of this criterion is evidenced by the recognition of a hierarchy, or as it is called, a "pecking order" among universities. It is recognized in society more widely than in the academic world. The fact that so much lip-service is paid to the standard of being a "great university" and of "the obligation to adhere to the highest standards of scholarship and teaching," shows how widely this standard is accepted, both inside and outside universities. Some institutions of higher education approximate this ideal more closely than others. The state of morale of university teachers depends on some measure of observance of this ideal. Where the discrepancy between the ideal and the reality is seen to be great, university teachers become embittered and demoralized and immerse themselves in rancorous and aggressive disputes.

The quality of the society is believed by many persons to depend on the presence of the institutional embodiment of this ideal. Quite apart from the long-term practical benefits that do in fact often flow from the cultivation of this ideal, its denial of this ideal by the "practical" elements of a society in time leads to a brutalizing of that society. A society without learning, like a society without religion or art would be a society of brutes, however comfortable and well managed. Even bureaucrats and utilitarian and hedonist philosophers would quail at such a prospect. Totalitarian ideologists and military dictators do not seek the obliteration of learning from their higher educational institutions but neither do they care to maintain a pluralistic society.

There are countercurrents to the foregoing. Some persons would say that any institution which calls itself a university, for example, "The University of Islam" in Chicago, is a university or that any institution that receives a charter from the state as a university or that is established by the state is a university regardless of what it does when it acquires the legal right to use that name. More common and more influential have been those who assert that universities are justified not by their dedication to ideals of truth and scholarship but by their relevance to the practical undertakings of society as presently constructed and in their likely future. They cannot see much sense in the study of "useless" subjects. The ideal of a university whose curriculum centers around the study of "useless" subjects is preposterous to them; they believe that universities should be subservient to the powers in charge of the practical tasks of society, and ultimately to "the people."

There is still another countercurrent of criticism to the university as an institution of learning that is rather close to the criticisms by the proponents of practicality. It emanates from the critics who charge the universities with being aristocratically indifferent to the needs and interests of "the people." In the United States where this criticism of the universities for "elitism" became most vehement, it was originally espoused by anticapitalistic, antibourgeois radicals. Nonetheless, it is closely akin to the populistic, practicalistic criticism of politicians, businessmen, and publicists who were not at all radicals. It is not that the latter day critics of the "elitism" of the universities think that they should teach practical subjects exclusively. Their objection places more weight on the fact that the learning pursued in the universities which they condemn, is in its essence not accessible to everyone or is of no interest to everyone. This objection to the allegedly "aristocratic" character of learning is coupled with the "practicalists'" criticism of the "elitist" universities on the grounds that they are "irrelevant" to the tasks of transforming society in a socialistic, populistic direction. The "practical" bourgeois, populistic, and radical critics of universities all seem to believe—although they have never worked their ideas out in any clear form—that societies should be homogeneous in their culture, and that there should not be any differentiation in the quality of culture. The idea of a pluralistic society is fundamentally alien to them.

Nonetheless, the criticisms of the ideal from the practical and popular standpoints and the numerous divergences from the ideal within the universities themselves do not annul the actual existence of the university as a place where, in addition to much else, the ideal is cultivated. The universities that are most esteemed, and the university members who seek to conform with the ideal or standard associated with that status do things that other institutions cannot do to the same extent. They contribute to the deeper understanding of the universe and of man and his works, they train students to do so, and they educate young persons up to the highest level of such understanding. This is one of their main justifications for existence and this is why they are esteemed by so many persons. It is one of the main reasons why they have been supported.

Now it is true that this kind of learning, which is the constitutive idea of the university, has not always been practiced in universities. Universities that have not cultivated this kind of learning have not been esteemed; and at the time, the most active and deepest life of learning went on among private scholars or in monasteries or at royal courts.

There are very few private scholars any more; there are very few royal courts, and they are not major patrons of learning; and the monastic orders could represent, if they were intellectually active, only a very small part of the range of learning. At their present level of sophistication it is difficult to conceive of science and scholarship being carried on as amateur enterprises. They are too intertwined with expensive equipment, large libraries, seminars, students, research assistants, and colleagues to revert to their old form. Learning in its present form requires universities. If the universities exclude it, it will languish and the universities themselves will become something very different from what they have been during the better part of the past century and a half.

Learning is a phenomenon which emerges in every differentiated and literate society. It is an emergent property of the social life of the species, like speech in the individual human organism. Like the economic life of the species, it has come to have an institutional organization that performs the function in a way no individual, unaided by institutions and traditions, could ever do. It is a function which has its own exigencies and laws, just as an economic system has. It has inherent in itself a disposition towards autonomy, but it is not and cannot be wholly autonomous.

II

Universities are not and have never been self-supporting institutions. They have never received payments for their services which were adequate for their maintenance. Greatly esteemed though they have been for their cultivation, pursuit, and transmission of knowledge of the most fundamental and serious things, universities would not have received as much support as they did over the centuries had they not also supplied certain services to the society from which they received their support. The service they rendered was to train young persons for the direct performance of certain vocations and duties.

There are practical activities with high intellectual components of knowledge and skills, mastery of which much be acquired by systematic and disciplined study. The practice of medicine and the practice of law—the traditional learned professions—were among the earliest and most important of these. The cure of souls and their preparation for redemption also fall into this category—a profession in which the practical and the spiritual meet. In the course of the nineteenth and twentieth centuries, the number of occupations with high intellectual components increased; the amount of scientific knowledge incorporated into the practice of the traditional learned professions was vastly expanded. Warfare became more scientific in the sense that the production of munitions and weapons was progressively infused with scientific knowledge. Industrial and agricultural production incorporated scientific knowledge into their procedures. Governmental administration purportedly became more scientific. Record keeping and accounting, necessary to all large organizations, have acquired a more scientific character; social work, librarianship, the detection of crime, and other police work have also acquired intellectual components they did not have in the middle of the nineteenth century. The design and construction of buildings, roads, machines, factories, etc., have all been subject to the same scientific influence. The kinds of knowledge their practice requires and their spokesmen desire as necessary in the training of their practitioners are the kinds of knowledge discovered and taught in universities.

The numbers of persons in these new or minor professions has increased, as has the number of such occupations, and they are now regarded as more important to society than in the past. Their practitioners certainly regard themselves as more important than they used to be and as more entitled to deference by others. Two of the important grounds for this claim are that their practice is grounded on scientific knowledge and that that knowledge has been acquired in universities and has been certified by them. Universities have had assigned to them the power to legitimize the standing of a profession and its practitioners and it has been thought by many that they alone are uniquely qualified to do so. It has not always been so.

Universities have been esteemed in society because they have been the place where knowledge of "serious," fundamental things was discovered, interpreted, and taught. By a circular process they have also been esteemed because they have been progenitors of the professions and occupations that were closely associated with authority and "serious" things like justice, order, life, and death. In consequence, universities have been regarded not only as a link with the order of serious things through the understanding of their nature, but also because they were linked to the most esteemed roles of their respective societies by the training of their incumbents—and their offspring.

III

Universities were supported by churchmen partly because they were institutions that trained for the superior levels of correct understanding of the world central to a Christian civilization or the service of the church. They were supported by princes partly because they trained lawyers, civil servants, physicians, and clergymen for the service of the state, society, and church— and later teachers for the advanced secondary schools—all of which the prince and his government needed for the good order of society. The universities were supported by the state and by private persons, including ecclesiastical patrons, also because intellectual learning as such was esteemed. In the United States, the state universities were supported by the citizenry and by the state governments for all these reasons. In addition, they were esteemed because they placed opportunities for the acquisition of learning and for entry into the socially superior and more remunerative occupations within the range of a larger part of the population than had been the case in Europe. These various grounds for support could coexist because their corresponding functions could be pursued simultaneously in the same institutions. The universities could serve both the demands of learning and the demands of their society for learning at the same time. There was sometimes a tension between the cultivators of these two kinds of learning in the university, not least in the United States where the practical learning of the universities received more attention than elsewhere.

There was an unwritten, unspoken concordat between the universities and the government which maintained this balance. The universities performed the service of training for certain professions that the government regarded as necessary and desirable for its own purposes, as well as those of the society for which it was the custodian. They had this while they cultivated serious learning in a dispassionate way. Governments—and private patrons in the English-speaking countries—supported the universities for these reasons, although they placed the greatest emphasis on the training for the practical-intellectual professions. It was in general accepted without question that universities had tasks apart from the training of young persons for the learned professions and for the service of church, state, and society. Learning as such was esteemed as intrinsically valuable, just as the religious knowledge and ritual of the churches were intrinsically and unquestionably valuable. The universities received and they gave. What they gave was a service that they could give because of their unique possession of advanced knowledge.

The universities were placed in a position something like that of the churches. They were regarded as something very different from business firms or voluntary associations. They were clearly different from political parties or political associations. In certain important respects they were placed apart from the everyday life of society. They were not instruments of public policy. Where they served ends contributory to public policy, they were welcomed and encouraged; they were not to be coerced.

Even in the practical United States, the universities were supported by state governments in the Middle and Far West and by private patrons, because they pursued knowledge in a selfless and dispassionate way. It was accepted that they had to have an internal life of their own, led according to their own standards. Despite the university laws laid down by the German states or by other countries where governments promulgated the constitutions of their universities, efforts were made to assure that the universities would have a realm of autonomy of decision and action, in which they could apply their own standards and act in accordance with their own traditions. Even in the time of the *Obrigkeitsstaat* a sphere of autonomous action was respected by the government. Although professors were civil servants with legal status that entailed rights and obligations of loyalty, they were basically not under the command of the minister or his highest officials. This was what was meant by *akademische Lehrfreiheit* and *akademische Selbstverwaltung*. Comparable principles were not formulated in England because universities were not creatures of the state. Although chartered by the state they were self-governing bodies with a much wider range of autonomy from the state than their continental counterparts. In the United States the situation was not fundamentally different from that in Great Britain. The American pattern was formed in the traditions of Oxford and Cambridge, qualified by the pattern of the colleges of the free Church which had lay governing bodies. The state universities also adopted the institution of a lay governing body so that it was not a part of the executive branch of the state government. In both the state and private universities the principle of the autonomy of the university vis-à-vis the government was respected in principle. In fact, the state universities, wishing to remain on good and fruitful terms with the state legislatures, made concessions by providing courses of study and research schemes that would be pleasing to public and political opinion. In the private universities there were not the same pressures on the substance of teaching and research. In both the state and private universities in the United States, the autonomy of universities in matters of appointment was infringed upon when from time to time teachers were dismissed or threatened with dismissal because of their radical political views.

The structure of university government in the United States was a product of this acceptance of the autonomous character of the state universities. They were not governed by the department of education of the state, nor by the state legislature but rather by a board of regents, popularly elected or appointed by the governor, that intended to act as an autonomous body. In this respect they had the same position as the court of a modern British university. Both were lay bodies like the boards of trustees of the American private universities. They were expected to act as buffers to prevent damaging collisions between the universities and the external world, governmental and private. They were also expected to exercise a custodial solicitude over proceedings within the universities. As the present century moved forward, the lay governing body of the university—both the private and the state university—has left the internal affairs of the university more and more to the president, deans, and the academic staff, out of a recognition of the rightness of academic self-government. (Within the universities, authority has in fact evolved more and more from the central administration to the academic departments, although legally the board of trustees is the ultimate governing body.)

There are many qualifications to be made in this account of the written and unwritten pacts between the universities and government in the United States. Before the Second World War these pacts were sometimes violated by trustees and regents and sometimes by legislators. Most of the infringements touched on the right of the universities to make appointments—particularly reappointments and promotions—in accordance with their own criteria of academic achievement and promise, while the lay authorities insisted that radical political views should be regarded as disqualifications. Such cases were not numerous, however. In matters of syllabi, examinations, degrees, research programs, and in appointments, apart from those in which radical political views were involved, governments remained as aloof as the lay governing bodies. Many changes have occurred since that period.

In different legal settings the Continental universities also developed a considerable degree of autonomy. In appointments the final authority rested with ministers of education, acting on the recommendation of faculties. In most cases, the recommendations were accepted. Although the content of syllabi and qualifying examinations for candidates' entry into the professions (*Staatsexamen*) had official status, they were largely made up by professors; examinations for degrees were entirely in the hands of academics. Syllabi were oriented towards professional requirements in those courses of study that were preparatory to the practice of the profession, but since these were mainly in the hands of academics, the syllabi were also. In those subjects in which students were not preparing for the "state examination," the professor was entirely free to teach those parts of the subject that he himself thought most pertinent to the attainment of a high standard of scholarship. On the Continent as in the English-speaking world, the marking of examinations has been exclusively a matter for the academic staff. The same has been true of programs of research, although as particular research schemes became more expensive, the autonomy of the university was limited by the readiness of external patrons financially to support a particular kind of research. Even there the various institutional arrangements that were invented in Great Britain, Germany, and France, provided for the decisions to be made by juries of qualified scientists who were usually academics. They were not necessarily from the same university as the applicant, but the decision remained generally within the academic profession and thus represented some adherence to the principles of academic autonomy.

IV

Throughout the Western world, a strain has arisen in these traditional patterns of relationship between government and universities. The cognitive expansion of recent trends has been accompanied—when it has not been caused—by the belief that knowledge of the systematic empirical scientific subject matter, such as is sought and transmitted in universities, is of instrumental importance in the pursuit of the ends of government, armies, private and public economic enterprises, schools, and many other institutions. Governments have also acquired through popular desire and consent, greater powers than they have ever exercised before, and they also believe in their own competence. There has also arisen a greater desire in the populace for higher education as a path to higher culture, social status, and monetary returns. Western governments have taken upon themselves the responsibility for the realization of these ambitions. These increases in the activities of research and instruction have enlarged the financial burdens on universities and governments that have on the whole been very forthcoming in meeting most of the demands for increased expenditures. In consequence of all this, universities have become much more visible. Governments are now very much more aware of them than they have been in the past, and are demanding more of them. One result is that governments are now much more concerned with and inquisitive about the affairs of universities.

Long before the disruptions of universities by agitating students and their followers, there was much talk about the new tasks of universities. In Great Britain and the United States, reports on the need for more "scientific manpower" and the increasingly munificent governmental subvention of scientific research in the universities, led the universities to be used primarily as instruments for the service of government policies.

In Great Britain the autonomy of the universities has been respected more than in the other Western countries. This was due largely to the traditions established by the University Grants Committee, which made block grants to the universities for them to spend in accordance with their own conceptions. Meanwhile the universities had become almost wholly dependent on the central government for their financial resources. Private philanthropy, private industry, and municipal government support had dwindled below the level required to meet the rising expenditures needed for conducting university functions under existing conditions. Parliament became more concerned and restive about the universities. As a result the University Grants Committee was detached from the Treasury which had been its only representation to the government, and added to the Department of Education and Science, which already possessed a more direct control over the polytechnic stratum of higher education. The accounts of the universities had within the preceding decade been opened to inspection by the Comptroller and Accountant-General, a relationship that had for several decades been successfully resisted by the University Grants Committee. Most recently, a private members' bill to amalgamate the polytechnics and the universities into a single unitary system of higher education was narrowly defeated.

The *Wissenschaftsrat* in the Federal German Republic was a new step into the relations between government and the universities. Universities had never been the concern of the central government in Germany. Neither the imperial nor the republican government had concerned themselves with the affairs of universities; the National Socialist regime was the first German government to give attention to the universities—with damaging effect. The Federal Republic returned universities to the care of the states but it created the *Wissenschaftsrat* which had only advisory powers. Nonetheless the federal government soon entered into university affairs more directly through a system of grants for capital construction. This in itself did not infringe on the powers of the states, but it did establish the central government as a potential force in the life of the universities. The next step was taken with the preparation of the *Hochschulrahmengesetz*, which laid down the pattern for the university laws of the states that had previously been sovereign in this matter. Meanwhile, most of the states had enacted university laws that changed the composition of the governing bodies of universities to include substantial representatives of students and nonacademic staff. One by-product of this has been a pronounced tendency for the new governing bodies to make recommendations for appointments on political grounds. The state governments have felt it incumbent on them to reject some of these recommendations on the grounds that the nominees were disloyal to the constitution. Laws have been enacted prohibiting appointments to the civil service—which include university teachers—on grounds of disloyalty to the constitution.

In the United States the greatest changes have taken place through the entry of the federal government into the relationship with universities. There had been a thickening of relationships during the First World War, but after that war the situation returned to what it had been previously. The previously existent situation had been one in which there was practically no active connection between the federal government and the universities, other than the very restricted ones contained in the Morrill Act and the relations between the Department of Agriculture and the state agricultural research stations that were often connected with state universities or agricultural and mechanical colleges. State and private universities received no grants of any sort from the federal government; they performed no work contract for the federal government. Education was not a "state-subject." The social legislation of the federal government was very limited and did not impinge on the university.

In the Second World War the universities were drawn into corporate relationships with the federal government through the acceptance of contracts to conduct certain research projects on behalf of the federal government. Various parts of the Manhattan Project were conducted by universities on contract with the federal government and under the security restrictions of the armed forces: the Radiation Project was much the same in this regard. The universities undertook to house and provide instruction for various parts of the Army Specialist Training Program.

After the war, the first impact of the federal government was through the "GI Bill of Rights" which, by providing tuition fees and maintenance for veterans of the armed forces attending universities, caused the size of the student body of the universities to expand rapidly. The Office of Naval Research continued to offer contracts to the universities to "perform" research; the Atomic Energy Commission did the same. The Department of Defense and then the National Institutes of Health and the National Science Foundation, when they appeared on the scene, awarded grants, let contracts, and provided postdoctoral fellowships. Grants and contracts also enabled universities to provide scholarships and research assistantships to graduate students in the natural sciences.

In pursuing this course in relation to the universities, the federal government was not developing anything new. The system of grants for "project research" had been developed in a very rudimentary form by the Bureau of Mines during the First World War, then by the National Research Council and the Rockefeller Foundation in the 1920s and 1930s. The provision of fellowships was developed by the Rockefeller Foundation and the National Research Council in the first decade after the war. The letting of contracts was of course a very old procedure for the purchase of goods and services by governments from private suppliers. The only innovation of the more recent period was that universities became "contractors" like any commercial or industrial firm, which undertook to manufacture military aircraft or to supply typewriters or military books in accordance with agreed specifications and for an agreed payment.

The government has from time to time promoted the teaching of particular groups of subjects, such as oriental languages or medicine. Its interest in the teaching of undergraduates has been restricted to particular subjects for designated periods. It has made funds available by grants and loans for the payment of fees in connection with undergraduate and graduate studies. It has generally promoted the increase in the number of students and the size of the universities.

The federal government has never attempted to support universities in the way in which British and Continental governments have done. It has avoided doing so because it moved into relations with universities in a very piecemeal fashion, and because to do so would immediately raise very difficult political problems. There are more than 1,500 degree-granting universities and colleges in the United States; they vary widely in quality and it would be invidious to discriminate among them. It would moreover rouse legislators to look after the interests of their constituents whose interests and desires would undoubtedly bear little connection with their intellectual merit. But there is a more fundamental reason. It is that the federal government, despite all these programs, does not have what can be called a genuine policy with respect to universities. It has rather intended to achieve certain specific ends for which a number of separate, overlapping policies in the universities are regarded as appropriate instruments.

The federal government in the United States works on an unspoken assumption of the self-maintaining existence of the universities. It is not concerned with the maintenance of the universities; it accepts the fact that they are already there and that it may purchase resources from them at marginal cost. Its various policies have not been accompanied by any reflection or sense of responsibility to the source of the services. It is like a tribe at the level of a hunting and gathering mode of life; it looks upon the university as an already existent resource that came into being without its support and that will go on existing without its support. In viewing the existence of the universities, the government regards them as an instrument to be used for particular purposes as the occasion arises and to be set aside when the occasion passes, as institutions that will continue to exist from their own resources and always available to supply services at marginal cost, when they are so desired.

The government has not developed the concern for the ecology of universities that it has developed for lakes and fishes. It regards the university as a stream which runs on of itself, available to it for particular purposes but of no concern aside from those purposes. It takes no more responsibility for the maintenance of the university than a factory owner, before the period of "environmental" legislation, took responsibility for the replenishment and purity of the stream. As in other spheres of activity, the government of the United States is living beyond its means but manages so far to escape the consequences by consuming the capital accumulated in the past and the capital being accumulated for the future. It is using the capital accumulated by generations of scientists, scholars, and teachers and public and private patrons without any thought for the maintenance and renewal of that capital except sporadically and incidentally to its own purposes.

The Continental and British governments, whatever else they may do, take responsibility for the entire university and at the same time do not demand so many particular services from it. In the British universities Lord Rothschild did attempt to transform a part of governmental support science into a controlled relationship between "customer" and "seller" of scientific services, but that pattern has not come to dominate all of the relationships between government and university in Great Britain.

There is, however, a qualification to be made in this account of the federal government and the universities in the United States. Although the federal government treats the university as it would any other contractor who looks after his own interest and charges accordingly, it has subtly managed to change the nature of the contractual relationship. Whereas traditionally a contract stipulated the good or service to be received, the quality, quantity, time of delivery, and the payment to be made, the government of the United States has now set certain extracontractual conditions to which the contractor must adhere.

Henry Maine's interpretation of legal and social history as a transition from "status to contract" was long regarded by social scientists and historians as touching on a significant difference between modern and premodern societies. The new policies of the government of the United States represent a divergence from this theme. A contract now comprises something outside the terms of the goods or services to be delivered and the consideration offered in return for it; the contractor has now to exhibit qualities which have no connection with the goods or services. In the years immediately after the Second World War, the federal government introduced into its contracts a stipulation regarding the loyalty of the contractor and his employees. In a limited number of cases this stipulation was roughly reasonable where secrecy was necessary; in many cases it was simply irrelevant to the goods or services to be "delivered," which was not bound by the requirement of secrecy. Nonetheless the precedent was established. The contractor had henceforth to abide by conditions external to the substance of the transaction fixed by the contract.

This obligation to affirm loyalty to the government and constitution was of no practical value to either party to the contract; it was only humiliating to academics and academic administrators to submit to it, but since it was a condition of receiving funds from the government for specific purposes, it was accepted. It was easy enough therefore for the federal government to extend the extracontractual condition in the contract for other moral purposes. The contractor had henceforth, as the insistence on loyalty became less pressing, to employ a staff of a given ethnic composition. This innovation in the relationship between the federal government and its contractor originally was not intended to apply to universities. But as the contractual idiom had prevailed in the purchase of services and the rental of facilities, such as buildings and laboratories from universities by the federal government during the Second World War and then persisted thereafter, universities became contractors like any others.

There are however considerable differences between universities as "contractors" and other contractors. These are not just differences in the nature of the "service" provided. They also lie in the capacity to bear the costs of the government's demands. The federal government's social policies, which intend to promote the welfare of the mass of the population, entail the provision of employment for blacks, Puerto Ricans, American Indians, Latin Americans, and women, and the keeping of records to prove that this is being done up to the required standard. The increased payment of taxes for old age pensions, compensation in periods of unemployment, occupational safety and health, environmental protection, and conformity with minimum standards of wages and hours are also required of universities, just as they are for any private business corporation.

The costs of giving statistically persuasive assurance to the government of "equal employment opportunity" and equal pay are not compensated by the federal government. These costs must be met from revenue derived from student fees, the interest on endowment and gifts, and by restraint on the increase of the salaries of their teaching and research staff; the acquisition of books and journals by the library and costs of the extracontractual conditions make the burden all the heavier.

Private business enterprises that have these various charges upon them by the federal government can ordinarily transfer any additional costs of doing business to the consumer by raising their prices. When such a private business enters into a contractual relationship with the government, it does so on terms that will meet all of its costs, including the costs of capital equipment, and provide a profit. Universities have never covered their costs and cannot cover their costs from revenue resulting from the sale of their products. They cannot pass the additional expenses—both those involved in the contract and those that are generally applicable to contractors and noncontractors alike—

imposed by government to anyone except their students and their academic staff, and by drawing on their endowments. They can increase the fees they charge their students, and they can reduce the scholarships available to them; if they are private universities, they can endanger their continued existence by "pricing themselves out of the market" and by liquidating their endowment. They can also allow the salaries of their teachers and research workers to remain constant and thus fall further and further behind the inflation of prices. They can reduce the purchases of books for the libraries and otherwise dilute their quality. Even if universities were not subject to contractual conditions of their agreement, the governmentally engendered inflation would be a burden on them. The costs of the extracontractual conditions make that burden all the heavier.

When the government makes a contract with a private firm, the firm includes in its charges provision for the payment of dividends to its shareholders in return for the capital that they have provided. The federal government in dealing with universities makes no provision for the reimbursement of the capital used in the fulfillment of the contract. Charges for "overhead," about which the government is very grudging, do not take into account the uses of capital by which the government benefits when it enters into a contract with a university.

The capital of a university is much more than its physical plant or its library; it is also more than the stock of knowledge and skills that its academic staff members bring to their tasks. It includes the zeal for discovery, the moral integrity, the powers of discriminating judgment, the awareness of important problems, and the possibilities for their solution that their members possess. These are qualities of individuals, but their stable persistence depends on the existence of an academic community, within departments and faculties in the university as a whole and in the academic community at large—within the boundaries of the country and internationally. These refinements of intellectual sensibility depend on the presence of like-minded colleagues and students, not just within the academic person's particular field of specialization, but over a much wider range.

It is true that it is difficult to apprehend the subtle intellectual product arising from the presence of other persons with similar outlooks and similar propensities. It is nonetheless this presence which keeps these propensities and outlooks alert and constant. The community of scholars who are teachers and investigators at the same time is constituted by these alert and constant propensities and outlooks. The community of scholars who are teachers and investigators at the same time is constituted by this mutual influence and by the identifications formed in consequence of it. This intellectual community and its traditions are what make the physical plant, the library, and the laboratories and the individual members of the university into a university. This is one of the factors that has made universities so successful in the quest for knowledge and in the induction of young persons into the intellectual and moral culture, which the universities at their best can offer.

When it lets a contract or awards a grant for the performance of a particular piece of research, the government is receiving therefore more than the particular activity of the particular persons who receive the money it pays to the university. The government is receiving the benefits that have come to the recipients of its grants or contracts from the presence of many other scientists and scholars, young and old, students and teachers who, separately and all together through the course of their lives, have sustained and incessantly refreshed the atmosphere that each member of the university inhales. Without a stringent standard, without an alert curiosity, without the sense of the urgent importance of discovery, a scientist or scholar, even with a great stock of knowledge of the "relevant literature" and with great ratiocinative capacity, cannot accomplish very much. These dispositions must be kept intense and vivacious. To attain and maintain them at this high level, the presence of colleagues and students with a similar intensity or vivacity is of the first importance. Of course not all colleagues and fellow students are equally weighty; those who are superior contribute more to put the rest of them on their mettle; and there are always some who are resistant or impermeable. But the difference between better and less good universities is that the former have a smaller proportion of their members in the latter category.

All of these considerations should make sense even to persons who think strictly in economic terms, who think that capital should, at the very least, be maintained and that a wise policy of investment would set aside earnings sufficient to maintain the inheritance of capital from which future earnings are to be drawn. Such considerations are no more than an argument that the market must set the price for a good that will cover provision for the replacement and renewal of the capital that has gone into its production; otherwise the good will disappear from the market. It will not be brought back into the market by an increase in price because it has grown over a long time and cannot be re-created by deliberate policy. It can only be maintained if the conditions for its existence are maintained. Its growth and present existence are the result of congenial external circumstances and internal processes and inheritance. They are the products of autonomy with a beneficent matrix.

The long-term interests of government—and of society, if we assume that the interests of government and society coincide, which is by no means self-evident—would be advanced by a policy of action towards universities that acknowledges that universities are institutions of advanced learning with their own distinctive and autonomous traditions. Such a policy will accept that universities have the tasks of discovery and transmission of new and important knowledge, of educating young persons highly enough qualified to assimilate that knowledge and training for the practice of professions that demand the possession of that kind of knowledge for their effective practice, and of training young persons to appreciate and carry on the search for new knowledge. This reasonable policy would accept that the performance of these main tasks presupposes the existence within the university of an ethos that prizes the intrinsic value of such learning. It is primarily in such a setting that the intellectual curiosity necessary for the practical application of knowledge or the acquisition of new knowledge to be used for practical ends can be inculcated and sustained.

These things are the root of a university. A government that wishes to continue to collect their fruits will conduct itself so that the root is not starved. A proper division of labor between universities and government is one that would enable the universities to perform their distinctive tasks and not simply act as an instrument for the execution of the tasks set to it by the momentary or even enduring demands of governments.

Universities have another task which is not met by the fulfillment of their obligations to government and society. This is the obligation to understand what the world in its manifoldness is about. By this I do not mean primarily the understanding of the contemporary world or modern society. I will not say that the universities are identical with churches, but they have much in common with the church in a society of believers. What the universities discover and teach has a status approximate to what the churches have preached. The churches are to be esteemed not because anthropologists say that all known societies have had religious beliefs and a cult of transcendent things; the churches are to be esteemed because what they teach is right and necessary for human beings to know. The understanding and acceptance of the divine order is the obligation of human beings in societies in which that order is acknowledged. The understanding of the world up the edge of the understanding of divinity is the obligation of the university. The monastic community was—and is—the place for those persons whose need to acknowledge the divine order and to live in accordance with it as the highest possible in existence in this world. The university is the place for those who search unremittingly for the rational understanding and appreciation of the order of this world, and for those young persons for whom that search is an essential component of their lives. The fact that not everyone wishes zealously to lead such a life or is incapable of leading such a life is not a criticism of its value. The fact that not all academics are desirous or capable of leading such a life is no criticism of the idea of the university or of the academic ethos which is central to it. The fact that not everyone cares to or is capable of becoming a creative artist or writer or cares to contemplate the works that such artists and writers produce is not a criticism of art or literature. A society without art, or one indifferent to art and literature of a kind that has no use but which is superior to entertainment, is an impoverished and unworthy society. The same may be said of a society which is indifferent to the achievement of an ordered, rational understanding of the world.

The coincidence in the same place and in the same institutions of the search for an improved rational understanding of the world and the acquisition of understanding that has practical utility sometimes renders it difficult to distinguish these two great functions of the university. At the same time the dependence of the latter on the former renders it necessary to see that they are different things. A wise policy would see to it that the former is as necessary as the latter and that the latter could not exist without the former. This should be a fundamental article of the new constitution of state and university.

V

In contributing to the support of universities the federal government of the United States disregards but takes advantage of all this. It "buys" specific services: particular pieces of research and particular "training programs." It pays for the time of those who work directly on its projects; it pays for equipment and supplies. It might also pay for the space it uses and for the administrative expenditures connected with the project. It does not pay for the cost that has gone into creating and maintaining a high level of academic morale, or for maintaining and creating the academic ethos, which is under present circumstances a precondition for understanding and its growth. It is at present obtaining those benefits without charge. It exploits them and does not replenish them; indeed, it runs them down. The system of "project-grants" and "contract-research" has disaggregated the universities of the United States during the period of great expansion. It has led to the self-centeredness of individuals and a disregard for the claims of the institution and of the obligations of membership in it or, as some sociologists have put it, to "placing identification with one's profession above identification with one's institution."

The federal government of the United States by its mode of support for particular activities in the universities has been treating central parts of the universities as a "free good." It does not pay for what its "contractors" or its "principal investigators" receive from their presence as teachers and students in the university and in the national and international community of universities and the knowledge that enters into their service for government and society.

The federal government does not pay for the most fundamental part of what it receives, namely the effect of the long tradition of the universities' devotion to the discovery, interpretation, and teaching of fundamental knowledge about serious things. It is this interior life of the university, this devotion to knowledge as intrinsically valuable that gives intellectual substance to the pursuit of knowledge about things that are of practical importance. Without that intense intellectual discipline and devotion, which is sustained by the tradition interior to the university, there would not be the scientific probity and exactingness and the intellectual sensitivity which goes into research with practical ends in view.

VI

At the beginning I spoke about "a new constitution of universities and state appropriate to the idea of each." The idea of the state is the concern for and protection of the good order of society which includes the material well-being of its members, their diligent support of themselves and their families through paid employment, justice in their relations with each other and with authority, and so on. Government is not everything in society, it is not the "be-all and end-all" of society. It is not the church and it is not the university. The church has almost wholly been deprived of its provision of welfare services and the university, on the contrary, has had more and more tasks assigned to it for the provision of specific services required by the purposes of government.

The cultivation of learning for the purpose of the understanding of the order of nature and of humanity and its works has not, like religious beliefs, been declared a "private" affair. It has however been rudely classified by economists as a consumer's good. Others wishing to praise it, classify it as an aesthetic good, like the ballet or the performance of a string quartet. Still others disparage it as "elitist" or as the useless preoccupation of the occupants of an "ivory tower." The government refuses to acknowledge it as such and supports only particular research projects and training programs "related to national needs."

The government, insofar as it is not using something of the greatest value at no charge to itself—the cost of the capital being borne by state governments and private patrons—is doing so "on the cheap." It is not paying for what it is getting; it is rather demanding and obtaining a great deal more than what it pays for. It is using up and not renewing the intellectual capital of the universities by making their circumstances more straitened than they have been. It is proceeding blithely to starve the goose which lays the golden eggs, assuming that there are others who will breed more geese and who will feed them. It is going further than this and insisting that the universities appoint their staffs with regard to racial and sexual characteristics of candidates, instead of attending to excellency by intellectual criteria. As a result the intellectual capital of the universities is further depleted.

The universities of the European continent have not been faced with this problem, since there their governments take responsibility for the mass of the total budget of the universities. The dangers they face from their governments are however not unlike those faced by the American universities. In Sweden, the central government aims to turn the universities into institutions integrated into the labor market. Their functions, according to its intentions, will be to train students for particular professions and occupations. In effect places of learning will be closed. The other Continental universities have not gone this far in explicitly depriving the universities of their autonomy by making them subservient to the presumably predictable future demand for persons to engage in particular professions and occupations.

The hardest blow that a number of Continental governments have struck against the continuity of the intellectual traditions of universities has been through the provision in the new university legislation for the participation of academically and intellectually unqualified persons in the deliberations and decisions regarding academic appointments. Whereas in the United States, in the pursuit of the ideals of equality and justice, the federal government has imposed sex and race as criteria to be taken into account in appointments, the Continental governments have unthinkingly promoted the application of political criteria. They have done this, in the name of democracy, by aiding the entry into governing bodies of nonacademics, mainly students, whose interests are primarily, if not exclusively political. In consequence, particularly in the Federal German Republic, a number of universities have appointed to their teaching staff persons whose interests and intentions are preponderantly political—usually in a radical direction—rather than intellectual and academic. Thus the interior life of the university is turned into an extension of the political arena.

In different ways, therefore, the equilibrium between government and universities has been out of balance. The universities have been in varying degrees forced to renounce their particularity as institutions of learning and are being made into instruments of governmental and political interests which have their centers of gravity outside of the academic sphere.

A new "constitution" that reasserts the rights and obligations of the universities and of the earthly powers at the center of society is needed. The terms of a new "constitution" must be expressed in words of a general form. It would not even be desirable, at present, to formulate them precisely, even if that were feasible. I begin negatively with the acceptance of the proposition that things will never go back to what they were from the late nineteenth century until the Second World War. It must be accepted that governments and private institutions will continue to regard scientific knowledge as important to them for the construction, assessment, and execution of their policies. For the foreseeable future, government will not be able to have all the scientific research it desires done in governmental research establishments. Even if it could and wished to do so, it would still not be able to dispense with the capacity, distinctive of universities, to do research of high quality on fundamentally important problems and for the inculcation into young persons of the result of that research and of the ethos that is necessary to it. Furthermore, universities will continue to be dependent on governments for financial support to do the research which they wish to do. Unless research were to become as inexpensive as it was a century and a half ago—which is most improbable—universities will remain dependent on governments and, to a smaller extent, private business enterprises and persons for the support of that scientific research. The chances for a "disestablishment of science," which would leave scientists just as well-endowed as they are now, but wholly free of any obligations to government or industry and equally free to pursue only their own interests whatever they might be, become slight to the point of being negligible.

For the foreseeable future, the universities will therefore be under obligation to perform much research in which government has an interest. The universities will continue to be under obligation to train young persons for the learned professions, both the traditional ones and certain newer ones, which have a genuine need for genuinely scientific and scholarly knowledge, such as universities are uniquely qualified to provide. At the same time the universities should be freed from the pressure to accept contracts for the execution of "crash programs" devised by civil servants or the staffs of legislators to provide short time definitive solutions to evanescent problems or to problems which cannot be definitively "solved," and certainly not in a short time. Governments should refrain from tampering with the mechanisms of academic appointment.

The "new constitution of state and university" is not going to be wholly new. Much of the "older constitution" should be retained or be restored. Certain features of the older pattern have been gradually displaced with very few persons being aware of what was happening. Both academics and governments must once more recognize that universities have ends which are not identical with those of government, that are in themselves as valuable as those of government, but are also necessary preconditions to the realization of the ends espoused by government.

Governments must abandon the belief that universities are extensions of the spheres of government and politics. The definitions of the right relationship in this absolutely crucial matter is not easy. A total separation of the proper sphere of the universities from these spheres is impossible as well as undesirable. But the far-reaching assimilation of the universities into those spheres or the movement towards that condition observable in the United States, Sweden, or other countries of the European continent should be halted.

It should be halted because the general direction of this movement is clear. In all countries including Great Britain the governments have been bringing the universities increasingly into a subordinate position. The particular modes of subordination and encroachment vary however from country to country; they vary in accordance with the traditions of the earlier constitutions of university and state. A new constitution would have to have, in addition to a common preamble of principles, a separate text for each country, which takes into account the tradition of that country and the particular setting within which the principles would have to be realized.

The principle is that of a division of labor in the cultivation of the plurality of ends to be sought in a good society. The division of labor should not be one which is organized for the realization of a single end. A good society has a multiplicity of good ends which are not identical or even harmonious with each other. Among the obligations of the institutions that pursue their several ends, one of the most important is the appreciation of the ends inherent in the existence of the others. An adaptation of the principle laid down in Matt. 12:21 "to render unto Caesar the things which are Caesar's and unto God the things that are God's" is necessary. Upon the universities this imposes the task of finding the right combination of obligations within and obligations without. Upon the world of government and society, it imposes the task of defining what it is entitled to ask of and receive from the universities, and what it must recognize as due to the universities in their own right.

Note

1. See Samuel Taylor Coleridge, *On the Constitution of the Churches and State according to the Idea of Each* (London: William Pickering, 1839).

7

Dreams of Plenitude, Nightmares of Scarcity

I

At the beginning of the 1930s, there was no student movement to speak of in the United States. The young people's branches of the socialist and Communist parties—the Young Communist League (YCL), the League for Industrial Democracy, and the Young People's Socialist League (YPSL)—and tiny sects of anti-Stalinists existed as national organizations and as small isolated bodies at the major universities (at, for example, Harvard, Chicago, Berkeley). They were a little stronger in Wisconsin where they were attracted and supported by a strong local tradition; their main activity was at the City College of New York. Although the motives for their radicalism might have been personal and private or abstract and universal, all of them were attached to national organizations under the umbrella of which young persons—not students as such—stood.

In the United Kingdom, some students became communists; pacifism and anti-fascism became moderately widespread at the London School of Economics and in Oxford by the mid-thirties. Despite the notoriety of the refusal, at the Oxford Union, to defend king and country, radical undergraduates at British universities were few, and those few were conventionally radical in their affiliation to the adult "left-wing" political parties.

In Germany, many students supported the National Socialists and the *Deutschnationale*; many fewer supported the Social Democrats or communists. Many students expressed their hostility toward Jewish and socialist teachers by unruliness and rudeness in lectures; much more visible were their frequent altercations with socialist and communist students, their disruption of the latter's meetings and their physical assaults on their members. Whatever they did, they did to express their affiliation with and to promote the progress toward power of their nonuniversity elders. With all their brutality, they were extremely submissive to their masters; they espoused the program of the NSDAP in all things; they denounced Jewish science and those teachers whom, by reason of their humanity, liberality, and lack of xenophobia, they regarded as traitors to the German people; they stood by gleefully when their ringleaders realized the eternal dream of delinquent pupils and burned a pile of books; they marched in parades under the auspices of their adult patrons.

In Eastern Europe, nationalist student organizations created disturbances in lectures of Jewish and liberal teachers and physically assaulted Jewish and socialist students. There, too, youthful delinquency and brutality were coordinated into the movement of adults who carried on the tradition of Polish anti-Semitism. In France, students were members of the Camelot du Roi, which was not exclusively for students; steeped in an old tradition of the youthful upper-class brawler, they joined in the public disorders attendant on the Stavisky scandal. They were youthful ruffians at the disposal of their elders.

There were no university students in black Africa, except for the handful of pious, well-behaved students at the Fourah Bay College. In the Middle East, students were few and, their political activities being radically nationalist, anti-imperialist, and Arabophile, were kept in check by the political elites of that period who lived under French and British influence and who tried at least publicly to conciliate the foreigner. Such public manifestations as they made were a part of a larger nationalistic or ethnic movement of sentiment; students did not act on their own.

In India, at the beginning of the 1930s, the student movement was beginning to rise to the plateau of the decisive years of the independence movement. It had ostensibly one main aim: to bring about the departure of the British so that India could become independent. This entailed the organized truancy called strikes and boycotts; it involved processions and demonstrations and assorted "Jimmy Higgins" services. The political activities of students were practically always under the guidance of the Congress; when students began to become socialists, they did so under Congress patronage; when they became violent, they did so under the leadership of Congress socialists. In China, students were active politically, denouncing the Japanese invaders, the Kuomintang government, and the European imperialists; there, too, students struck, boycotted classes, and demonstrated, but they always did so in close association with adult politicians. In Burma, the small number of students were beginning to be markedly anti-British. Later in the decade they conducted important strikes and published occasionally appearing and short-lived periodicals. Since they were practically the first generation of nationalists, they had relatively little adult collaboration and guidance, but in this they were exceptional.

The varyingly small proportion of students who engaged in the demonstrative, expressive, and always aggressive actions of student politics were always against the existing regime—that is, where they were free to do so and could do so with impunity. (The situation was different in the Soviet Union and in Fascist Italy, where student activities were closely controlled by the government.) Where they were free to act, they always went beyond the existing regime. Where the regime was anti-Semitic, for example, they went further in their anti-Semitism. In most cases, they did not just go further, they actually went against the existing regime. Their beliefs made them oppositional; the urgency and passion of their espousal made them into extremists. They were not just against the incumbent party; they were against "the system as a whole"—either against the "Weimar system," against the entire secularist tolerant culture of the Third Republic, or against the "capitalist system." They were ideologically radical in that sense. Yet although their actions were usually directed against the prevailing system ruled by adults, they practically always had the support and encouragement, guidance and discipline brought by adults. Their organizations were almost always parts of or affiliated to oppositional organizations in which adults were in control. They were, of course, not simply creatures, instruments, and copies of the adults to whom they were affiliated; they added something of their own—resiliency, verve, dramatic actions, and an element of carnival. They were often violent, and they were sometimes courageous in their violent actions—and frequently they were only brutes and bullies. They usually enjoyed engagement in acts of violence, and they sometimes suffered injuries. They could act with more spontaneity than the adults; they had more enthusiasm than their elders; and they enjoyed the excitement of antagonistic encounters with the ruling authorities, who were usually restrained in their treatment of them,[1] and with their antagonists and victims who in Central and Eastern Europe were often weaker than themselves. They acted from a privileged position that radicals of the lower classes did not enjoy, and they had the great advantage of more freely adaptable time schedules. Universities have always been freer than factories and offices, and they could absent themselves from their postponable university duties as the spirit moved them.

Actively and aggressively anti-authoritarian though the relatively small student movements of those days were, their activities were sponsored and legitimated by the authority of elders. They had a tradition that sustained them, but their tradition was not theirs alone; nor was it of their own finding. It was exemplified and embodied in the corporate organizations of their elders, to which their own were affiliated. They accepted the anti-authoritarian authority of adults in the wider movements of which the student movements formed a part. They also accepted in general the authorities of the university system. Although their rebellious activities were often planned and sometimes took place in university buildings or on university grounds, they were seldom concerned with university matters. The university was not the home of their heart; that lay outside. They aimed at the world outside the university although this sometimes involved action within the university, such as the beating of Jewish classmates or the disruption of the lectures of Jewish or socialist or expatriate teachers.

Student rebellions in the present decade are more comprehensively and more fundamentally hostile toward authority than they were three and four decades ago. They are hostile, in principle, toward authority whereas their predecessors were hostile only to particular authorities and submitted enthusiastically to others. They act now without the sponsorship of external adult organizations, and they feel little sympathy with most of them. The innovators in the present generation of student radicals are antinomian; the rejection of authority by their predecessors of more than a third of a century ago was sustained and limited by a legitimating authority. They did not venture so far or so daringly from authority as the most advanced student radicals do nowadays. The present-day student radicals act without the legitimating authority of older figures; their middle-aged courtiers who offer their legitimatory services are offering something that is neither wanted nor needed. Paul Goodman and Sartre provide agreeable but unsought applause. When the student radicals group themselves around an older figure he is of their own creation, as was the case of Senator Eugene McCarthy—who is not a charismatic person but was made into one by the student radicals' need for one. The adults most closely associated with the student radicals are usually young teachers little older than themselves, and they function more to affirm than to guide and legitimate. The "big names" of present day student radicalism—Mao Tse-tung, Fidel Castro, Ché Guevara, Frantz Fanon—are remote in space or dead; they have no commanding power over them, and they all share in the eyes of the student radicals a quasi-bohemian, free-floating, anti-institutional aroma. Even though they govern tyrannically, it is their anarchic element that appeals to the radical students. Castro's period in Oriente province, his conduct of the affairs of his high office in cafés at 3 A.M., and the generally impromptu air of his tyranny attract just as the image of Mao Tse-tung owes much to the period in the caves and the "long march." Neither of these two living amulets is in charge of an organization that the student radicals must obey.

How are these major differences to be accounted for?

II

The turbulence of student radicalism now has the appearance of being worldwide. Alongside the formal international federations of students that appear to be of scant significance for the more dramatic activities of the student radicals, there is a spontaneous and unorganized, or at best an informal, unity of sympathy of the student movement which forms a bridge across national boundaries. In 1968, student radical movements seemed to be synchronized among different countries and uniform in content and technique to an extent reminiscent of the monolithic phase of the Communist International and its subsidiary organizations.

Student radicalism is no longer the possession of small, relatively closed sects within larger student bodies; on the contrary, it can reach out toward the sympathy of a large minority, occasionally even the majority of students, at particular places and for limited times. Its organizations within each country, despite numerous ups and downs, are more persistent in their action and have a larger following than they used to have. They show a self-confidence reaching to arrogance in their dealings with hostile authority, and they are aware of the transnational scale of their undertaking. Nonetheless, the movement is not unified, either nationally or internationally. Synchronization is a function of a generally identical mood, not of concerted organized action.

Nor is the movement uniform internationally. There are major differences between countries and continents. In India, for example, where until the outbursts in Western countries since 1964 the university student population was the most turbulent in the world, the student radicals do not as a rule make the structures of the larger society and of the university objects of a general critique. Indian student radicals declare no fundamental criticism of their society; they have no schemes for the reconstruction of their universities. They do take stands on public issues—for example, on behalf of the construction of a steel mill in Andhra Pradesh or on behalf of or in opposition to the use of English as the medium of instruction in higher education, the nearest they come to espousing a general policy for higher education. The Indian student agitation is "occasionalist"; it responds to particular stimuli, local, regional, or national, but grievances do not become generalized and are therefore not persistent. India, however, is exceptional in its relatively apolitical agitation.[2] In Indonesia, student radicalism is, contrarily to India's, wholly and over the past few years continuously, political. Internal university conditions, terrible though they are, scarcely engage its attention; its interest is in the public realm, where in collaboration with but not under the domination of the army it was important in the ultimate undoing of former President Sukarno.

Elsewhere in Asia—omitting mainland China[3]—in North Africa,[4] and, to a lesser extent, in black Africa, Latin America, and Spain, student agitation follows the conventional nineteenth-century pattern of nationalist agitation against the repressive character of the incumbent government and its insufficient devotion to the national cause (even though the foreign rulers have departed, in some cases very long ago). Their actions are larger, more vehement, and more frequently recurrent than they were in the earlier period, but, except for the magnitude and intensity of the manifestations, they have not changed. They agitate against restrictions on freedom of organization and propaganda and against their government's moral corruption and its alleged subservience to foreign powers—in most cases nowadays the United States. The creed that declares "neo-colonialism" to be the chief enemy is to a large extent a student creed. It is a shoddier version of the Marxist-Leninist analysis of colonialism and imperialism which was a fairly common possession of the nationalistic student movements in Asia during the 1930s or of the African student movements in France and England during the 1940s and 1950s.

Nonetheless, despite these similarities with their earlier outlook, the student movements in most of the countries of the Third World, like those in the advanced Western countries, have broken away from the pattern of their antecedents by becoming independent of adult organizations. They have practically no significant older political figures to whom they look for guidance or inspiration. The leaders of an earlier generation are in power or apolitical, dead or in exile. They are, whether dead or alien, out of the question as the leaders of an effective opposition. Despite some exceptions, aggressive student radicalism is forced to stand alone, to the extent that it stands at all. In India where public opposition is still permitted, the Indian student agitation, too, has by and large lost its connection with a dominant organization of adult politicians. Although in many particular instances, party politicians are able to exploit some of the disruptive capacities of Indian students, the organizational links are loose or nonexistent. In India, too, there is no larger adult political movement of which the students regard their own movement as a part, and this is one of the main reasons why most Indian student agitation voices have no general political demands.[5]

In Eastern Europe, particularly in Poland and Czechoslovakia, courageous students have agitated against tyranny in the larger society and on behalf of the traditional freedoms of thought, expression, and assembly, and for the rule of law—with some of the same nationalist, anti-Russian accompaniment that was characteristic of their nineteenth-century antecedents. And they do these things alone, except for the patronage of a few literary men and professors. Even in the brief periods of liberalization in Poland and Czechoslovakia, the students acted independently with the "liberalizers," not under them. The administration and functions of the university do not worry them, except insofar as party tyranny and favoritism manifest themselves there.

In Western Europe and North America, the situation is both similar and different from the other parts of the world. In their relationship to adult oppositional organizations, Western student radicalism resembles that of the Third World. In Britain, the Labour Party is ingloriously in power; in West Germany, the Social Democratic Party is part of the Grand Coalition. In

France, the socialists are futile and the communists in their odd way, and despite what General de Gaulle claimed, are pillars of the existing order in the face of student "provocation" and "adventurism." In Italy the socialists share government responsibility, and the Communist party has no sympathy with the student radicals whom it regards as Maoist provocateurs. In the United States, the major parties are abhorrent to the student radicals and the only adult opposition to the major parties is a racist know-nothingism. In North America, the bourgeois parties have never concerned themselves with student support, the socialist parties have always been negligible, and the Communist parties have dwindled in size and moral standing. Official Marxism is unaccredited or discredited. There is no ideology ready to hand for student radicalism.

The student radicals have, therefore, no adult political masters; they act on their own. Those sections that maintain organizational relations with adult parties or groups are either in a state of conflict with their elders or are relegated to positions of despised insignificance by their radical contemporaries. The discrediting of the Communist parties, the moderation of the Social Democratic parties, and the eclipse or disappearance of Fascist and Nazi parties in Western Europe have left the students without either a parent organization of elders or an authoritatively promulgated doctrine to which they can give their loyalty or adherence. A "natural" Castroism, amorphous, passionately hostile to organization forms a powerful, profound undercurrent of sentiment and of vaguely formulated belief.

In most of the countries in which there is much radical student agitation, there has been nothing commensurate to it on the intellectual side. In Eastern Europe, liberalism, admirable and courageous though it has been, is no intellectual innovation. In India, *hic et nunc* protests against very particular features of university and college administration and against very particular deprivations represent a retreat from the variety of nationalist, Marxist, and Gandhian creeds and ideologies of the early depression decade. For the rest, the student movements in Africa, Japan, Indonesia, and Latin America have added nothing fundamentally new to the intellectual repertoire of the student movements.

Technologically, there are innovations; students commandeer lorries; they use "bull-roarers"; they confront the police armed in helmets and bearing shields; they have adopted Molotov cocktails from the Russians they despise and the "sit-in" from the American automobile workers' union with which their sympathies are minimal. Nor have they been original organizationally; even the spectre of a worldwide movement—which has been created for them and from which they profit through the heightening of their self-consciousness and confidence—is the work of the bourgeois press and television.

All this being said, the differences between student radicalism at the beginning of the 1930s and in 1968 are greater than the mere differences of organizational independence from adult parties or the criticism of the universities. Far more important are the differences in fundamental beliefs about the self, about authority, about institutions, and about what is "given" by the past and the present. These differences are of the greatest importance and merit close analysis since they refer to serious matters. I will begin from the outside and try to move inward.

III

University students were a far smaller proportion of the population at the beginning of the 1930s than they are now. They were less noticed by the public at large or by politicians, and they did not conceive of themselves as an independent estate of the realm. Even in Latin America where they were constitutionally incorporated into university governing bodies, they did not apparently conceive of themselves in their capacity as students as a "permanent interest." Being a student was thought to be a transient condition, subordinate or derivative from other statuses.

Most university students in most countries came from the relatively privileged classes of their societies. Even in the United States, with its open state universities, students formed a small proportion of their generation, and they came from the better-off sections of American society. They expected to enter into the better-paid occupations and professions. The radicals among them did not regard themselves as "representatives," even if unchosen, of all students, and they did not regard the "student class" as an entity central to their respective societies. Their parental social class, the social class to which they sought entry through their studies, the ethnic group of which they were part, or the political party under whose guidance they acted were the "powers" of their societies, and they drew their significance from those. These collectivities and aggregates are still very important in society, and they are still very important to most students, but they are not so important to student radicals as they used to be. Why?

Students in the late 1920s and early 1930s were at the university for a variety of reasons; some were ambitious to learn more; some wished to ascend in society, to earn more than their co-evals who did not go on to university. Some attended university because their parents had done so and because it was the "normal" thing to do for full membership in their stratum of society. Others attended university for all or any of these reasons, and because it was pleasant and exciting to be there. The pleasures of friendship and discovery and the excitement of games were available there.

It was generally regarded at that time that to be able to go to university was a privilege, an advantage in itself and for the future. It was an experience and opportunity open to relatively few. It was to be exploited for the immediate pleasures of intellectual acquisition, convivial experience, and the prospective rewards that it rendered available. The privilege was of a special kind; it implied no present ascendancy over teachers, officials, politicians, or elders in general; it was a privilege in a subordinate role that adumbrated a more substantial and central privilege at a later stage of life. It was a privilege in an inegalitarian society and in an inegalitarian institution where those at a particular level in the hierarchy accepted the ascendancy of those at higher levels. The privilege of attendance at university was the privilege of entry into the middle classes and perhaps even into the upper class—either to enter it for the first time in the history of one's own family or to enter it as one became an adult at a level approximately similar to that of one's own family. In any case, to be at university was very much a middle- and upper-middle-class sort of thing. The life lived at university was of a pattern thought to be appropriate to the style of those classes, and the completion of a course of studies there was regarded as the qualification for subsequent membership in those classes. Even in India and Germany, where it had become difficult for university graduates to find suitable employment, this conception of the potentialities of university education still prevailed.

Society before the Great Depression and World War II was much less egalitarian than it has since become. Among the main criteria for distinguishing the strata from one another was their respectability, their diligence and dutifulness, their capacity and readiness to persist faithfully in a given task, and their willingness to submit their performance to the assessment of authorities they regarded as legitimate. Most university students, however idle or uproarious or rebellious, accepted this set of arrangements; they thought it just, insofar as they thought about it at all. They expected to enter society and to take superior places in it. Of course, the prospect, except for the minority of the "highly born," was a strenuous one, but the strain was accepted as "given" in the nature of things and as a precondition for the privileges to be enjoyed later.

There were among the students some rebels—nationalists, fascists, socialists, communists, aesthetes, and bohemians—who were not wholly reconciled to the university system. Variously, they thought the larger system unjust or they were appalled by the philistinism of their fellow countrymen or they disapproved of their moral conventions and, insofar as they perceived some of these qualities in the universities, they were against them. The fascists and nationalists usually disapproved of ethnically alien rule or of the presence in the middle classes of ethnically alien elements. They wished to expel the foreigners from their countries or at least from positions of high authority and reward; they therefore criticized the universities where they thought that the aliens were benefiting from them or controlling them. But all of these objectionable qualities did not raise any question concerning the ideal nature or function of universities. Their function as a preparatory stage to the professions and toward the superior occupations was accepted. Their role in the transmission and extension of knowledge and appreciation was accepted. Their methods of government, their use of the resources available to them, the substance of what they taught, the research they did were not regarded by students as "their business"; these matters were the universities' business, and the students were only there as transient, present, or prospective beneficiaries of what they offered. Particular teachers might be disliked, insulted, and in a few cases assaulted; some students might absent themselves from classes and try to prevent other students from attending them. Other students might have little interest in what was taught and would do the minimum of study, but they did not challenge the "system." The university system was unimpugned and its place in society unquestioned. This was so even in Germany and India, where the students were fervid with nationalistic political passions and where Jews and Englishmen held prominent positions in the universities. They wished them to go, but they accepted the structure of the university and its place in society and the modalities which flowed from its tasks. The rebellious students of this earlier period, thus, not only accepted the authoritative structures of their rebellious elders, but they also accepted the university as an institution.

Their beliefs about the nature of society and the rights and privileges of men also showed this same duality. The beliefs of student radicals were received beliefs, shared with those of their elders who led and spoke for the larger movement to which the student organizations were affiliated. They were beliefs that had an authoritative promulgation in the programs of parties and in the writings of doctrinaires. They stood generally in an alienated tradition that heightened the authority of the elders to whom the students looked for guidance. The rebellious students were ideologically disposed, and they had an ideology made available to them. Marxism in one or another of its variants, national socialism, fascism, monarchism, and Gandhism were in their diverse ways the accomplishment of sometimes learned and sometimes genius-like intelligences and of charismatic madmen. None of them was as systematic nor as elaborate as Marxism, but most of them had their literary or theoretical classics and all invoked an intellectual past.

The new generation of student radicalism is by contrast relatively unideological. They might be ideologically disposed, but they have no elaborately and systematically promulgated set of beliefs. They do not accept the ideological services that are offered to them, and they have constructed no ideology of their own. Their own anarchistic inclinations do not lead them to seek the guidance of the writings of Prince Kropotkin or Élisée Reclus. They have affinities with Fourier and Proudhon, but they do not look to them for an intellectual construction of the university. Lukacs is singularly not in demand.

Instead of ideology, they have a mood that a powerful systematizing mind might cast into an ideology. No one has thus far done so.

IV

The great innovation in student radicalism that has occurred in Northwestern Europe and the United States is a moral mood. In a certain sense, the radicals among the students of France, West Germany, Great Britain, and the United States—and increasingly of Italy and Spain—testify to a moral revolution.

The moral revolution consists in a demand for a total transformation—a transformation from a totality of undifferentiated evil to a totality of undifferentiated perfection. Evil consists in the deadening of sentiment through institutions and more particularly through the exercise of and subordination to authority. Perfection consists in the freedom of feeling and the fulfillment of desires. "Participation" is a situation in which the individual's desires and "demands" are fully realized through complete self-determination of the individual and the institutions which such freely feeling, self-determining individuals form. A good community is like Rousseau's; the common will harmonizes individual wills.[6] But the contemporary proponents of participation do not think of the individual will as anything but the concrete empirical will of actual and immediate sentiments, impulses, and desires. The common will is not the resultant of the rationally arrived at assent of its members; it is not actually a *shared* decision making; it is certainly not the outcome of consent to a compromise arrived at by bargaining and exchange. It is not acceptance of anything less than what one initially desired. It is the transformation of sentiment and desire into reality in a community in which all realize their wills simultaneously. Anything less is repressive.

This is why the advance guard of student radicalism is so resolute in its reaction against repression. It is resolute not just against the violent and often brutal repression by the police, but just as much against the moderate repression that is entailed by the application of the principle of *in loco parentis*. It is against the "repressiveness" of the rules of the game of parliamentary politics and of distributions of rewards in accordance with a criterion of merit. It is against "institutional repression" or "individual violence" by which is usually meant the discipline of a practicable consensus in a regime of scarcity. Whatever hampers the fulfillment of whatever happens to be desired at the moment—whether it is a student housing arrangement which stipulates the hours of visiting in halls of residence or an examination or a convention regarding dress or sexual behavior in public places—is repressive. And, as such, it is part of an undifferentiatedly repressive system.[7]

V

The conception of a life in which desires cannot be completely realized at the moment they are experienced is part of a larger view of existence as a realm of scarcity. It is a tradition with the longest history in the moral repertoire of mankind. The acceptance of the fact of scarcity has been an essential element in the outlook of most of mankind over most of its history. Poverty and injustice, illness and the brevity of life, the limitations on the possibility of gratifying desires and impulses have been regarded as inexpungible elements of the situation of mankind, and ethical patterns and theodicies have been constructed to justify or to censure—and to integrate—this ostensibly inevitable condition. The opening of the self and its elevation was confined to festivities, carnivals and rites, but everyday life was marked by constriction imposed by nature, society, and the moral powers of the personality. It consisted in limits on experience, the suppression of experienced impulse, the "avoidance of temptation" to impulses not yet experienced to come forward into consciousness or conduct. Poverty, ignorance, oppression took care of most of the preconditions for the constriction of individuality. A few great personalities transcended these limitations and made their lives into "works of art."

Christianity, particularly in its dissenting Protestant form, the growth of wealth, the spread of literacy, and the gradual recession of the primordial categories and criteria of assessing the meaning and worth of a human being have in the course of centuries worn away some of these individuality-suppressing and -constricting conditions. A profound revolution was worked by romanticism, which spread more widely in intellectual circles the conception of genius that need not regard the laws of society and its authorities and that aimed only to be guided by the inner necessities of the expansion of the self—to embrace new experiences, to enrich itself by the opening of its sensibilities. World War I and the Great Depression were the watershed. The erosion of the bourgeois ethic and the puritanism of diligence, respectability, and self-restraint on behalf of results which rendered one respectable were greatly aided by the Great Depression. The vanity of self-restraint was made evident, saving and striving were discredited; sexual self-restraint had been undermined by psychoanalysis and its literary popularization in the period between the wars. More or less liberal, tolerant, and constitutional political elites had been shown to be incompetent by the prolonged slaughter of World War I and by their failures in dealing with unemployment during the Great Depression. The regime of scarcity with which they were associated was discredited when their own legitimacy diminished. The same happened to the virtues of abstinence and self-discipline preached from the pulpits. Ecclesiastical authority had been under a steady pressure of rational disbelief and indifference; its legitimacy was further undermined in intellectual circles because of the association of the churches with the earthly regimes of external constriction and internal restraint under assault from other sources.

World War II was followed by an efflorescence of material well-being in the advanced countries on a scale never previously experienced. Particularly for the educated classes, there seemed to exist a relatively unbounded vista of opportunity for interesting employment, for travel, and for freedom from the restraints of impecuniousness, boring toil, and confinement. Full employment, the welfare services, and inflation made unrealistic the conception of a rainy day for which to save. At the outermost reaches was the perpetual awful threat of extinction in a war fought with nuclear weapons. The anxiety about the latter accentuated the attachment to pleasures of the moment. The heir of these developments was the generation born after the end of World War II.

In a variety of ways, this was a uniquely indulged generation. Parents who were in a state of unprecedented prosperity were persuaded of the merits of hedonism and were capable of giving some reality to its precepts in the raising of their children. They were convinced of the beneficence of a life free of repression and inhibition, and they treated their offspring with a concern and affection which seemed to confirm the prediction made by Ellen Key at the beginning of the twentieth century that this was the "century of the child." Expanding incomes and unceasing freedom from the threat of unemployment—for the middle classes at least—made for a readiness to believe that scarcity had been expelled from human existence. A life beyond the dreams of avarice seemed to have become accessible to those whom the fortunes of birth—in time and status—had favored. They were an increasingly larger proportion of the population.

The postwar generation has grown up, too, in a society in which authority has lost its sacredness. As the center of society expanded, those in positions of authority acquired a new conception of their obligations. Democratic elections moreover—and a populistic outlook even where there were no democratic elections—have made rulers believe that they have to justify themselves to realizing the desires of their citizenry. The expansion of individuality and the appreciation of the self, intricately related to enhanced self-esteem throughout much of Western societies, have diminished to some extent the arrogance of authority. The range of dispersion between the highest and the quite low has narrowed. It is certainly true that all Western—and all other—societies are far from the fulfillment of an ideal of equality. Power is unequally distributed; wealth is unequally distributed; income is unequally distributed; but the deference-system of modern societies strains toward egalitarianism. Of course, this "moral equality" is far from being realized; the strength of inherited beliefs and the presence of such tremendous concentrations of authority in the state and in great economic organizations—public and private—stand in the way of its realization. Nonetheless, the younger generation—living in the midst of the culturally juvenocentric society which Johan Huizinga discerned already in the 1930s—is experiencing this moral egalitarianism to a far-reaching degree. New methods of pedagogy and exclusion from the labor market—as far as middle-class young persons are concerned—have reduced the amount of experience with severely hierarchical and repressive institutions. But as much as the arrogance of authority has diminished, it has still not disappeared. Its diminution, moreover, has been more than balanced by the increased intolerability of what it seeks to impose. Sensitivity to the impositions of authority has greatly increased, and almost every impingement on it from the outside—unless voluntarily chosen as part of the expansion of individuality—is painful to the point of unsupportability.

Basic in all this is the view that every human being simply by virtue of his humanity is an essence of unquestionable, undiscriminatable value with the fullest right to the realization of what is essential in him. What is essential is his sensibility, his experienced sensations, the contents of his imagination, and the gratification of his desires. Not only has man become the measure of all things; his sentiments have become the measure of man. The growth of the capacity for unconfined sensation is the measure of the value of an institution. The goodness of a life consists in its continuous enlargement of these sensations and of the experiences that give rise to them. Institutions—with their specialized and prescribed roles, their restrictions on individual willfulness, the crystallization of traditions and their commitments that bind the future by the past—are repugnant to this aspiration toward an individuality that creates its boundaries only in response to its internal needs. Authority is repugnant, too, and so is tradition and all that it brings down and imposes from the past.

All this is old stuff. This is what the romantics taught us. But romanticism was only a literary and more or less philosophical movement; it did not become a widely pervasive outlook and style of life for many persons. Writers, artists, and bohemians espoused and embodied it, but its consistent following was small. The desacralization of authority, the productivity of the economy, the growth of moral equality, and the spread of enlightenment and educational opportunity have resulted in the diffusion of a much more consequent romanticism throughout a much broader section of each Western society. The more prosperous classes are the recipients of its diffusion; the offspring of these classes are their purest products.

University students in Western countries, despite an increased recruitment from among the offspring of the working classes, still come largely from middle- and upper-middle-class families. Many of those who have not come from these classes live in a cultural atmosphere of hedonistic expectations for the present and the future as much as do those who have come from families in which such expectations are to some extent realized. Many are supported from the public treasury at the expense of taxpayers. The availability of opportunity to attend university is still interpreted by many students, as it was in the past, as a first step into a less constricted future. Attendance at university, which was once regarded as a stroke of the good fortune of birth or the result of exertion and which offered its beneficiaries a chance to diminish to some extent the rigors of the regime of scarcity, is now, however, regarded by student radicals as itself part of an actual realm of plenitude. Anyone should have it for the asking.

University students, in the view of forty years ago, appeared to be on a straight road into a future which, in the light of the standards of the Enlightenment and in view of the immemorial fate of human beings, seemed to be extraordinarily rich in the possibilities of a better life—at least for themselves, if not for all the other members of their own societies. The student radicals of today have a quite different view of the matter: They do not wish to live in a society in which "the danger of death by starvation is replaced by the danger of death by boredom." The denunciation of the "consumers' society" is the common slogan of the French and West German student radicals; less explicitly but no less pervasively, the same view obtains among the American and British student radicals. They do not wish to be part of a "repressively tolerant society" that seduces by its favors. They wish their universities to be "restructured" to become the microcosms of a total revolution from which, in moments of exhilaration, they think that the rest of the society can be no less totally transformed. The universities must become "participatory," and from there outward their "societies" must become "participatory." They criticize their universities for having become "integrated" into their respective societies, but it is only evil integration which they oppose. They do not believe in the possibility of dispassionately acquired knowledge; they insist that "objectivity" and "neutrality" are simply masks that conceal the intention to serve the "system." They do not wish their universities to become "ivory towers"; they refuse to acknowledge the differentiation of tasks, a division of labor among institutions. There is no task that they would not have their institutions undertake in the transformation of society; only the transmission of knowledge[8] and discovery are left unmentioned by them.

The slogans of "student power" (Great Britain and the United States), *cogestion* (France) and *Drittelparität* (West Germany) disregard the particular tasks of universities and the functions that these tasks qualify them to perform. The idea that there is a measure of inequality which is constitutive in the university's transmission of knowledge from those who possess more of it in particular spheres to those who possess less of it in those spheres is alien to their conception of the right order of life. For the same reason, equally alien is the idea that different institutions have different functions to perform. The very notion of differentiation and specialization in a division of labor among individuals and among institutions is alien to them. They wish their universities to become the centers from which their societies can be forced to become "participatory."

They demand—at least in the United States, but also in France—that their universities cease to be connected with government, except to be supported financially by it. At the same time, in the United States and in France, they insist that the universities take the responsibility—financial primarily—for forming "participatory" communities in their own neighborhoods. They wish their universities to be open to everyone; they are resolutely opposed to *selection*, to *numerus clausus*, and to the restriction on the use of university facilities and amenities to those who are its inscribed members. The "openness" or boundarylessness of institutions for which they contend is paralleled by their insistence on the openness of individual existence to new experience and new sensations. Hence, within their universities, the rebellious minority wish to be rid of all remnants of the institutions that embody the principle of *in loco parentis*. No restraints on their conduct are to be tolerated; neither restraints on their living arrangements, on their sexual associations, nor on their consumption of narcotics. They insist on an expanding series of subsidies for whatever activities they wish to engage in.

These views of life, society, and the university are not shared by any means by the entire generation of students today in the Western countries. Most of the students in most universities still share in the older culture. Nonetheless, the new "communitarian," "participatory" culture—which is really the romantic hunger for *Gemeinschaft*[9] on a more grandiose scale—pervades a substantial minority of the intelligent, sensitive, and hyperreactive students.

VI

Why should all this have come to such a clamorous outburst and in so many of the most advanced countries now? Certain causes were implicitly indicated in what I said earlier. It is now twenty-three years since the end of World War II. Most of today's undergraduates were born in the second half of the 1940s, most of the more advanced or graduate students were born during the war. They were raised during the prosperity of the 1950s; they came to such maturity as they possess after the thaw of the cold war.

In most of the countries of Western Europe and in North America, a considerable state of consensus has been obtained between the ruling party and the bulk of the opposition. Socialist parties of aggressively radical bearing have been lacking; the Communist parties, as in the United States and Great Britain, have nearly disappeared, or in countries where they are strong, they have gradually, as in Italy and France, become domesticated to bourgeois society. Therewith they have lost the attractive power which Communist parties had for young antinomians in the heroic period of the Communist International. The hypersensitive anti-authoritarian student radicals of the past few years came, as they left adolescence, face to face with a "reactionary mass." No adult party has been able to attract their enthusiasm or their loyalty; no adult party could as a result discipline and sophisticate their antinomian zeal. On the contrary, their political relations with sympathetic adults all run in the opposite direction; adults seek to affiliate to them. Abendroth, Enzensberger, Touraine, Mahler, Tynan, Macdonald, and countless others flatter them and assure them of how right they are in whatever they demand.[10] Middle-aged adults seek the ardors of their youth in the vicarious exhilaration of "sit-ins" and strikes. Old memories of revolutions dreamed of in cafés and salons are revived, and embittered disillusionments are dissipated by the thought of the new revolutionaries in the universities. They praise the "sincerity" of the radicals and find in it a vindication of their own benefits from the existing regime. All such elderly enthusiasts can do is to offer confirmation, but they cannot temper or qualify.[11] How could they when they are despised as all weak authorities are bound to be.

Weak authorities occupying the highest positions in authoritative institutions—which must, by their nature and task, exercise authority—do not arouse respect or instill fear. They only generate contempt and hostility, particularly when they themselves seem to believe so little in the authority that they exercise. Split, disunited, temporizing, halfhearted authority that repeats against itself the charges made by the student radicals serves only to encourage more hostility. Its halfheartedness on its own behalf and its readiness, even eagerness, to acknowledge the rightfulness of the charges laid against itself do not reconcile the radicals to a moderation of their demands. It must be said on behalf of the student radicals that they take with a large admixture of salt the flattery and self-abasement of their elderly admirers. But the feebleness of those whom they expect to be strong encourages their hostility. The absence of effective positive models and the faintheartedness of those who oppose them open a free field for their aggressive dispositions.

In all the advanced Western countries,[12] the governments are generally humanitarian in their sympathies and progressive in their domestic social and economic policies. In many particular instances, their conduct diverges from these norms but on the whole, as compared with the constitutional governments of earlier decades—to say nothing of the fascist and communist governments—they are liberal; they respect the freedom of expression; they legislate for the extension of welfare benefits and educational opportunity and submit to the insults and abuse directed toward them. They seldom order security forces to shoot looters and depredators; they generally attempt to restrain their agents in the face of rioters, and they are usually successful in doing so. (Chicago, it is true, was a grave exception, but it would be as wrong to deny its exceptional character as it would be to deny its gravity.[13]) They are even more yielding and conciliatory in speech. They find it hard to refuse the claims to rightfulness of the students who are against them. At most, they denounce the malfactions as the work of a "tiny minority of extremists," while acknowledging in many respects the legitimacy of the demands of the student radicals. What is true of governments is even more true of university administrations.

Despite all this, the existing authorities do not abdicate their authority; they are only liberal in social policy and compliant before the denial of their own legitimacy. Despite their conciliatory statements that the students are right in this and right in that, despite their forbearance, they still go about the business of conducting their governments. They maintain and use their armed forces; they impose burdens of national military service; they administer regimes of scarcity that cannot provide enough for everyone.[14] The same is true in universities; the teachers continue to occupy their professorships (and associate and assistant professorships), to receive their salaries, to set, administer, and mark examinations, pass judgments on dissertations, and grant or withhold degrees and diplomas. Presidents and rectors of universities might make speeches and write articles explaining that much of the criticism which student radicals make of the ideal-less, faltering, contemporary liberal society is just, but they do not dissolve their universities and they do not resign. They continue to operate their universities which, despite permissiveness and flexibility and flattery, continue to be selective institutions in a world of scarcity.

The radical students are opposed to competition and the scarcity which necessitates it. Their ethos is the ethos of a regime of plenitude, but they know, too, that their societies are regimes of scarcity. They know, too, that if they do not accept the rules of the regime of scarcity, they will go to the wall. Dean Marc Zamansky said to the striking students of the faculty of sciences in Paris when they were debating the boycott of examinations that even "a socialist society must be selective." How much more so a bourgeois society! Honors are scarce, first places are scarce, research grants and stipends are scarce, professorships are scarce. They are, of course, all more available than they used to be, but the student rebels do not know the past any more than most other young persons, and they do not take seriously what little they do know of it. They are entranced by a vision of plenitude of which they disapprove when they conceive of it as the "affluent society" or *société des comsommateurs* or the *Konsumentengesellschaft*, but which has nonetheless become an essential part of their construction of reality. Nonetheless they also know that they live in a world of scarcity run by adults whose legitimacy they do not acknowledge and whose ascendancy they hate; they deny the inevitability of the realm of scarcity and at the same time they know that they will not be able to avoid it. The examination system is the focal point of the repugnance for the regime of scarcity, particularly in the European universities where they are so concentrated in comparison with the dispersion of the American examination system; but in the United States, as if to compensate for the attenuation of strain from the concentration of examinations, there is the other strain of having to obtain marks high enough to qualify for admission to an eminent graduate school—and the radicals among undergraduates are also those disposed to go on to graduate school for no other reason than that it is less obnoxious than the bourgeois world outside.

It is not for nothing that the French "revolutionaries," once they occupied the Sorbonne and distracted their minds from examinations by the exhilaration of action committee meetings and fighting on barricades, soon began to worry about their examinations. Nor is it for nothing that the German student radicals—sprung from a breed famous for putting off the dreaded examinations—should demand that students sit on examining bodies and that the examination system be "transformed."[15]

It is to those better universities with famous graduate schools, which are also more liberal and therefore more popular with student radicals, that admission is sought. Places in such universities are scarce, and their regime is severe for those who succeed in entering. For those who are successful, life turns out to be very hard. In American universities, postgraduate studies are densely organized; many of the students are married and feel the pressing proximity of philistine life—family, job, routine responsibilities, and assimilation into the great machine where ideals are only a fragrance and hard decisions in the allocation of scarce resources to alternative ends must be made. The long, drawn- out proceedings of acquiring a postgraduate degree—several sets of examinations and an elaborate research dissertation—and a real or imagined dependence on the good will and sponsorship of one's supervisor for financial support and then for appointment to a teaching or research post on completion, add to the strain. All this underscores the discrepancy between the ideal of a regime of plenitude and the "hard facts of life" so often and so rightly referred to by older critics of student radicalism. It all comes at the worst possible time—at the point of passage that separates the open life of the expanding individuality from the dreaded knuckling under to authority.

It does not, therefore, seem to me to be accidental that the outbursts all over Europe and the United States reached their height in the spring of 1968 just at the time when students normally begin to prepare themselves for examinations. It was fitting that within a short time after the occupation of the Sorbonne, examinations—whether they should be put off, abolished, transformed, or, in the last resort, taken—came to occupy the center of the revolutionaries' attention.

I do not contend that examinations and examinations alone are the causes of the present student unrest,[16] nor that they provide an exhaustive explanation of why the disorders occurred on such a grand scale in the first half of 1968. The examinations are causes; they do not often become issues. As far as Europe and America and other countries are concerned, some of the issues on which the radical students confront authority so aggressively are really— and sometimes justly and reasonably—felt by them as genuine grievances. Some of the issues have become more urgent in the past year. University facilities and amenities in France and Italy are extremely insufficient, and grievances about this have accumulated. The Spanish government has been unjustified in its obstinate insistence on a monopoly of all student activities by the official student organization, and the persistence of unyieldingness on both sides has led to intensification and politicization. The West German universities have been plagued by the haughty self-righteousness and rigidity of the professorial oligarchy, and the conflict between this and the "Berlin model" has become more patent during the past few years. The internal domestic regulations and disciplinary arrangements of British and American universities are certainly irksome to some students, as are the arrogation of power and its unthinking use by professional university administrators (for example, the withdrawal of the "speakers corner" at Berkeley a few years ago), and sensitivity to this has always become sharper and more reactive in the past few years. Above all, there is the war in Vietnam with all its cruelty and its unending ineffectiveness and the menace of conscription into the most individuality-constricting of environments. Finally, there is the race problem in the United States, more severe now than it was four or five years ago. (The preoccupation of white students with it is less now than it was while it was still the "civil rights movement.")

In addition to these issues that obtrude, there are the issues that an issue-seeking desire for confrontation discovers. For British radical students there are Rhodesia, the supply of arms to Nigeria, and the tacit, uncomfortable, and negligible support of the British government for American action in Vietnam. For German students, the Springer concern, the Shah of Iran, the alliance of the federal government with the United States, the recognition of the German Democratic Republic and the legalization of the German Communist party. For French students, there has been little since the end of the war in Algeria, except for anti-Americanism and unlimited visiting between the sexes in university cities. From time to time specific issues like the free distribution of cours polycopiés arose but passed away. There were also fights with the extremist Occident, but these did not lead to large-scale demonstrations or strikes.

In Italy, there were many fights between antagonistic extremists of various designations, but these did not precipitate a "confrontation" with the authorities on a broad front. In Spain, the conflict between students, on the one hand, and the authorities in government and the university has been unremitting, and the original domestic issue of "free student syndicates" has been increasingly supplemented by anti-Americanism (Vietnam, American aid to Spain) and overtures to the illegal workers' syndicates.

Now all these issues are very disparate and do not tell us why they should have broken out with such an uproar this year. The earth is a vale of tears, but it is certainly not much worse this year than in other years in the past century and a half. Nor does the general analysis which I have offered in this paper of the horrified resistance of those attached to visions of the regime of plenitude in contact with the oncoming pressure of the regime of scarcity explain why the outburst occurred this year.

The only explanation I can give for the approximate simultaneity of the outbursts of the present year is one that combines the general distressfulness of the student situation with a number of accidental coincidences and the working of the "demonstration effect."

VII

We are far from living in a single world community, but the rudiments of a world society do exist. The international scientific community is the most international of all the elements of this rudimentary world society. Learned and scientific periodicals, international scientific societies, and the universities are the most elaborated and most internationally coherent parts of this rudimentary worldwide network of institutions. They do, at least at their peaks, have common standards, common heroes, and a unifying sense of affinity. Students, through their membership in universities, share in some of this, and their sense of sharing is accentuated among a fluctuatingly small group by an acute sense of generational identity. Although international student organizations are of little significance in the concert of action of 1968, and although students have nothing like a major scientific or scholarly press which creates a common focus of attention and a common awareness of leading accomplishments and personalities, it has an effective surrogate in the mass media—the newspaper press, wireless, and television. Information flows rapidly without a student international, without the use of a cumbersome system of couriers and coded messages such as international revolutionary organizations once had to use. The radical students have not created this organ of their movement, but they have been responsive to it and indeed, being aware of its value, direct their actions to it. They value television publicity as much as do the figures of the entertainment world or politics.

The international society is no more egalitarian in fact than are the various national societies. This is as true of scientific distinction as it is of wealth and political power. The scientific world has its centers and its peripheries just as any national society has and so does the sphere of student radicalism. What happens in the periphery does not radiate to the center; the movement is in the contrary direction. When the Indian students erupt as they have been doing quite continuously for about twenty years, student radicals do not attend to that. They attend to it even less than their teachers in biochemistry or sociology attend to what is being done in biochemistry or sociology by their colleagues in the Indian universities. Even a more powerful country like Japan produces little demonstration effect. When the *Zengakuren* went on a rampage to prevent President Eisenhower from visiting their country, the facts become known, but they did not become exemplary. When the Indonesian KAMI's helped to bring down the unspoken coalition of Sukarno and the PKI, what they did was admired, but not attended to. When the gallant students of the *Po Prostu* circle helped to bring about the short-lived and now dead Polish October, the students of Berkeley and London found no inspiration there. But when the Berkeley students and then after them students in many other American universities began their "revolution," the radiation from the center outward began. It was like the radiation of the revolution of February from Paris in 1848, when all of Europe felt the repercussions.

The Berkeley model was diffused to West Berlin. It was perhaps no accident that one of the original instigators of the events of West Berlin was Ekkehard Krippendorf who had been a graduate student in political science in the United States at the crucial time. From West Berlin, the movement spread later to the rest of West Germany; from Berkeley, it spread to the London School of Economics and to a much smaller extent to other British universities. From West Germany, it spread to Nanterre through the personal embassy of Daniel Cohn-Bendit and—with a reinforcement of inspiration from Columbia in April, 1968, and from the riots which followed the attempted assassination of Rudi Dutschke in the same month—from Nanterre to the Sorbonne. For a time, in a way not pleasing to General de Gaulle but in conformity with the main direction of his desires, Paris once more became the center of the world. (He would have been even less pleased than he was, however, had he reflected that the technique of those who made Paris momentarily into the center of the world of *chienlit* had been imported from the United States where it had first been used by working men and later by blacks.) From Paris it spread to such peripheral academic backwaters as Brussels, Rome, Florence, Milan, and Dakar.

Was there a coincidence of issues in the various countries that would help to explain the speed and intensity with which the demonstration effect operated? I doubt this because most of the issues on which the radicals seek "confrontation" are factitious and not imperatively obtrusive in themselves. There are really and deeply felt issues among those I listed earlier. The

Vietnam war and the draft overshadows all others in the United States, but on the whole this is a secondary matter in other countries. There are scarcely any other issues than those connected with the war in Vietnam that do not seem to be contrived by those who are bent on confrontation.

Most of the issues that arouse the passions of the radical students are not serious in the sense of being well grounded in fact or deeply cared about. The accusations of antiblack prejudice against the newly appointed director of the London School of Economics, for example, were baseless. The accusations of antiblack prejudice or of indifference to black needs on the part of the Columbia University administration were a little better based, but they were not quite as the SDS alleged. The insulting of M. Missoffe, the minister of sports and youth, when he opened the swimming pool in the faculty of letters and human science at Nanterre was a confrontation pure and simple; it was not an issue. The protest against the visit of the Shah of Iran which was the occasion of the death of Benno Ohnesorg at the hands of the police was not a serious issue for the West Berlin students; it was the occasion for a confrontation. The striking thing about all of these precipitating issues is how soon they disappeared under the onrush of subsequent responses.

At the London School of Economics, the merits and demerits of Dr. Adams were forgotten in favor of resistance to the disciplinary actions threatened by the authorities of the School following the death of the porter; the long "sit-in" disregarded Dr. Adams. At Columbia, protests against the action of the university administration in summoning the police and against the police for their unnecessarily harsh action dwarfed protests against the university's policy to build a gymnasium in Morningside Park and even against its relationship to the Institute of Defense Analysis. At Wisconsin, protests against the university's use of police and against the conduct of the police placed the prior protests against the Dow Chemical Company in the shadows. In West Berlin, the agitation following the death of Benno Ohnesorg consigned the Shah of Iran far into the rear of the student radicals' memory. In Paris, even the issues of visiting rights of the two sexes in university cities and of the disciplinary proceedings against Cohn-Bendit and his colleagues were put aside in favor of amnesty of those arrested during the demonstrations and skirmishes of the nights of May.

VIII

This transience of initial issues does not testify to the forgetfulness of the student radicals and the unseriousness of their original complaints. The transience of many of the issues is a function of the more important fact that they are the occasions for confrontations with authority.

It is authority that the radical students wish to confront and affront—and almost any stick will do for the camel. This brings us back not only to the general predisposition with which we dealt earlier, but also to the immediate precipitation of this year's outbreaks. In West Germany, Great Britain, and the United States, this has been a poor year for governments. In the United States, in particular, the image of the ineptitude of President Johnson—exemplified in the faltering and failing conduct of the war in Vietnam, the inability to bring the disturbances in black districts of the big cities to an end, the enfeeblement of urban public order in other respects, and the lack of spectacular results from the poverty program—has made government authority an easy target. The possibility that he could be succeeded by Senator McCarthy made for an even greater aggressiveness against incumbent authority. In Great Britain, the recurrence of the crisis of sterling and the devaluation, the failure to compel admission into the Common Market and powerlessness in the face of the Smith regime in Rhodesia, as well as the flagrant impropriety of the government's treatment of the East African Asians who held British passports have darkened the visage of the Labour government. For different reasons, the federal German government is in the same position. In France the mounting criticism of General de Gaulle from the ineffective opposition parties and the immobilism of the General's government as well as the small majority by which he was returned in the general election which preceded the crisis had similar consequences—which were aggravated, too, by the absence of the two most powerful figures in the government (General de Gaulle in Rumania and M. Pompidou in Afghanistan) when events were cascading— have all replaced the image of a strong and effective authority by one of feebleness and abdication. Where authority abdicates through failure, ineptitude, and weakened self-confidence, it invites aggression against itself. That is what happened this past spring.

If this complex of factors accounts for the concert of confrontations in the advanced Western countries, how do we account for the magnitude and especially for the speed with which movements of *groupuscules* became "mass movements"?

Wherever authority is confronted and takes aggressive but limited counter-action, there are victims. The repressive actions—police action and intra-university disciplinary proceedings—always enlarge the size of the student group drawn into the confrontation of the second stage. The students whose moral sensibilities are affronted by repressive action are much more numerous than the student radicals; they are drawn into confrontation on an issue which is quite different from those on which the smaller group of radical pioneers took the initial steps of challenging authority. The issues become quite different and the newly involved protesters are drawn from a different stratum of opinion among the students. This is when amnesty becomes the main issue.

Why is the second and usually much larger group drawn in? Originally they were more moderate and kept their distance from the extreme, particular, and often fairly specific demands of the pioneering nucleus of disturbance. Yet when the action changes its character, they become as involved, as adamant, and as daring as those whose initial confrontation was the prelude to their own involvement. It is also usually among these somewhat more responsible elements that demands for *cogestion* and *Drittelparität* obtain their strongest support.

The rapidity with which repressive measures by authority galvanize a larger support among previously inactive students seems to indicate that there is moral consensus within the student generation deeper than that about the particular issues the tiny minority of extremists invoke. In one form or another, this consensus centers on the value of the unconstricted expansive individuality, free in its movements, determinative of its own fate. The strength of the demand is not so great that it is continuously prominent, but constrictive and repressive activities by authorities shock it into prominence. This aspiration toward the romantic ideal of the ego is the bond that unites the extremist *groupuscules* and the larger circle around them. The difference between them is that in the former it is intense and continuous, while in the latter it is attenuated, only intermittently intense, and easily subsided.

Nonetheless, the expansive power of individuality and the dream of a regime of plenitude have opened up in the world. They cannot be conjured away, and they cannot be gratified by flattery by elders. In the United States, the war in Vietnam will be brought to a halt, the blacks will be treated with a greater measure of indifference to their color. The universities will be somewhat reformed in France, Germany, and Italy, and the Spanish government might allow students to have their own unions—it is already moving haltingly in that direction, although perhaps the moment has passed when it could do it without cost to anything but its obstinate pride. If the parents who are still legally responsible for their offspring agree that university should not stand *in loco parentis*, then that feature of Anglo-American university life will be modified. Students everywhere outside the communist countries are likely to be granted consultative powers in certain university decision-making bodies, and in some matters they will be given full responsibility. All these changes, desirable in themselves, will not, however, resolve the deeper tensions between a cultural tradition that fosters individuality and the vision of a realm of plenitude and a society the institutions of which require efficiency, competence, selection on the basis of past and prospective accomplishment, and differential rewards.

Notes

1. The late Professor Tawney once told me that when in the late 1920s he was in China on a League of Nations educational mission, he and his colleagues were forced to wait at a railway station for several hours. On enquiring of the stationmaster as to the cause of the long delay, the stationmaster told them it was because students had squatted on the track several miles up the line. Professor Tawney asked why the students were not removed by the police; he was told the students would resist. But, he said, could not their resistance be overcome by the police. The answer was that it was inconceivable because some students might be hurt.

2. Commentators on the indiscipline of Indian students often explain the dissatisfactions of the Indian students by saying that the political leadership presents no acceptable ideal to the student generation, that it is corrupt and purposeless, and that it is therefore unable to inspire the students. The students themselves, however, seldom refer to the general features of contemporary Indian society.

3. The recent form of the student movement in China appears to be a more moblike variant of the youth movements of the Soviet Union, Fascist Italy, and other countries where state authority dominates the student scene.

4. The countries of the Maghreb still, as in colonial times, have the seat of the most virulent oppositional student organizations located in the former metropolis.

5. This is true even for West Bengal where, considering the aggressive restlessness of the students, relatively few of them are willing to subordinate themselves to the Moscow or Peking communists.

6. The SDS in the United States spoke about "participation" long before General de Gaulle's recent proposal of the participatory solution as an alternative to the solutions of "totalitarian communism" and "competitive capitalism." Lucien Lévy-Bruhl spoke about it before either, and he referred to the extension of the boundaries of the self—among other things—to include within it objects apparently alien to it. Contemporary student radicals base their criticism of modern society and its institutions, particularly the university, on an aspiration to an expanding individuality. Lévy-Bruhl's idea of participation entailed a transcendence of individuality. Yet the two apparently contrary conceptions converge in the seamless unity of the community of expanded individualities or egos.

7. Student radicals in France, Germany, and the United States do not know that their frequent denunciations of the "system" are evocative of the Nazi abuse of the Weimar "system." But why should they know it when all of the past and practically all of the present is "little more than the register of the crimes, follies and misfortunes of mankind." But the similarity is there, and it bespeaks an affinity of outlook.

8. They seem to think so poorly of the transmission of knowledge as a university task that they insist that all learning must be through "dialogue" and "contestation." They assume that the past has accomplished nothing and that those who are ready to transmit the fruit or record of its accomplishments are simply repressive of the essential individuality of each student.

9. I should like to take this opportunity to call attention to a forgotten book which deserves to be recalled and studied for its sober assessment of an earlier form of the present *Gemeinschaftsschwärmerei*. It is Professor Helmuth Plessner's *Grenzen der Gemeinschaft: Eine Kritik des sozialen Radikalismus* (Bonn, 1923).

10. The moral self-abasement of a large part of the French literary and academic

intellectual class in May and June, 1968, expressed a disposition which is to be found in nearly every Western country. The students have for the time being replaced the "working classes" in the highest point of the pantheon of the "progressive" intelligentsia.

11. When one of the middle-aged sympathizers of the student radicals has the courage and good sense to attempt to qualify their views as Professor Habermas has done, the result is denunciation.

12. In October, 1968.

13. The roughness of American and French police is notorious, but in all of the student demonstrations in Paris last spring only one young man was fatally wounded during an altercation between demonstrators and police, and he was the victim of a knife wound which has not been attributed to the police. In the United States, the behavior of the police in Chicago in front of the Hilton Hotel in August was utterly incommensurate with the provocation, but the recollection of American police conduct in labor disputes and toward radicals over the past century would soon disclose the relative domestication of the police in the past few years in dealing with "dangers to public order." All I contend above is that the agents of public order are much less harsh and repressive than they were during the 1930s in Western Europe and North America—and in many other places in the world.

14. The ineffectiveness of authority is a stimulus to aggressiveness against it. A deprivational, scarcity-administering authority puts itself into a difficult position when it acts ineffectively. If the United States government had been able to fight the war in Vietnam successfully, even using the same technology it is now using in fighting without a positive outcome, I venture to say that it would not have aroused the animosity among student radicals which it has done in the past few years. I say this while agreeing with many criticisms which student radicals make of the war, and particularly about the need to bring it to a halt.

15. Examinations and their appurtenances are among the main occasions of student disorder in Indian higher education. The confrontation of a kinship-dominated culture of diffuse expectations such as that of the student in his familial *foyer* with the culture which demands specific performances as conditions for prospective rewards such as examination marks, appointments to particularly desirable positions, and so forth creates much tension.

16. I have dealt elsewhere with the whole range of causes in the Indian situation. Compare Philip G. Altbach (ed.), *Turmoil and Transition: Higher Education and Student Politics in India* (New York, 1969).

Part III
Academic Freedom

8

Academic Freedom

The Idea of a University and the Right to Academic Freedom

A university possesses an image or images of what it is and should be. At the core of this collective self-image is the interest in truth; the university's primary task is to transmit and discover truths about important matters. These images contain or imply norms for the conduct of the members of universities, their tasks regarding each other, and their responsibilities toward the society outside.

If a university is conceived as an institution that transmits definitive truths that cannot be improved upon and that cannot be modified or revised without diminishing their truthfulness, the norms governing the activity of teachers would stipulate the complete abstention of the individual teacher from critical intellectual efforts and limit him to the repetition of what has already been accepted as truth. If, however, as is the case of modern universities, the objective is the attainment of the best possible truths, with the best possible interpretation, and the best critical improvement of truths already attained, then the governing norms of conduct, method, and theory will require the attempted improvement of truths, already attained, their critical and methodical reassessment, and the search for better truths more in accordance with methodologically sound observations and rational interpretation.

The imperfection of any existing theory and the need to improve it do not make it permissible to regard all propositions as equally valid. The absence of finality is not grounds for believing that any proposition about a given subject is as true as any other: some propositions are definitely truer than others. Cognitive traditions, whether scientific or scholarly, are not to be lightly discarded, although all must be regarded as susceptible to improvement. The improvements cannot be foreseen with any certainty. As a result, at any given time, there is an acknowledged zone of indeterminateness as to what is valid. The substance of the improvement cannot be determined in advance. There are always a number of claimants to the improved or more certain truth. Each believes that he or she is right. In such situations, usually no sufficiently reliable consensus emerges to accredit some claims and to discredit others. The range of "reasonable disagreement" is the range over which academic freedom entitles individual academics to be free to investigate and to enunciate in spoken or written form the results of their investigation.

Academic freedom is a situation in which individual academics may act without consequences that can do damage to their status, their tenure as members of academic institutions, or their civil condition. Academic freedom is a situation in which academics may choose what they will assert in their teaching, in their choice of subjects for research, and in their publications. Academic freedom is a situation in which the individual academic chooses a particular path or position of intellectual action. Academic freedom arises from a situation in which authority—be it the consensus of colleagues in the same department, the opinion of the head of the department, the dean, the president, the board of trustees, or the judgment of any authority outside the university, be it a civil servant or a politician, or a priest or a bishop, or a publicist or a military man—cannot prevent the academic from following the academic path that his intellectual interest and capacity proposes. Academic freedom is the freedom of individual academics to think and act within particular higher educational institutions, within the system of higher education institutions, and within and between national societies.

The range of academic freedom is not identical with the range of human cognitive beliefs. Astrological propositions about the determination of the fortunes of individuals by stellar configurations, or assertions that the British Isles were originally settled by the lost tribes of Israel, or beliefs that the cosmos and the human species were created within six days are not generally acknowledged as falling within the legitimate range of ideas that academics are free to assert. Such propositions do not come under the protection of academic freedom.

The criterion of truthfulness of assertion in teaching and research and the associated method of attaining it confer a right to freedom in academic matters; these in turn impose a set of obligations. The right to freedom in the search for and the assertion of truth not only confers a right on academics to seek the truth by methods of acknowledged validity and to assert the truth orally and in writing but it also imposes obligations on colleagues and on university administrators to acknowledge that right to freedom in the search for truth and its assertion. It also imposes obligations on nonacademic persons and institutions to acknowledge that right to freedom and to respect the institutional arrangements through which that free search and free communication are carried on.

Academic freedom exists where academic persons (i.e., persons who are members of academic institutions) are free to perform their academic obligations (i.e., the actions to which they are committed to perform by virtue of their being members of academic bodies).

The first obligations of an academic are to teach and to do research; each of these entails many subsidiary obligations. There are also obligations regarding proper conduct with pupils, with institutional colleagues, with administrators, and with colleagues in academic institutions other than one's own. These are the rules of the academic profession and of academic institutions that provide the context for the pursuit and transmission of truth through study, reflection, and research.

There is a second sphere to which academic freedom pertains: the sphere of political and social contention. Academic freedom has long come to include the civil freedom of academics. This has to do with the freedom of academics outside their freedom and obligation within the university. It is different from academic freedom proper in its content and in the place in which it occurs. These two kinds of academic freedom share certain features. The freedom of teachers or researchers is the absence of any compulsion or dangers that would cause them to depart from the path laid out before them by the academic norm regarding the respect for and the pursuit of truth.

The Constitution of Academic Freedom

The existing extent of academic freedom might or might not be congruous with the extent of legitimate academic freedom. Academics often have less academic freedom than they ought to have; but they also sometimes have more academic freedom than they ought to have for the optimal transmission and pursuit of truth and for the optimal functioning of a university as the institutional setting of that pursuit.

Academic freedom, in the sense in which it is used here, is the freedom of individual academics to teach and to conduct research in accordance with their intellectual inclinations and standards and to espouse in their academic activities, through spoken discourse and through written or printed publications, propositions that they have, on the basis of their studies and research, concluded to be true. It embraces the freedom of academics to form learned associations and to be free to participate in them. It is also the freedom to communicate through publication, oral communication, and correspondence with other academics within their own university and in other universities, within their own society and with academics in other societies.

Academic freedom is not just the freedom of individual academics holding appointments as teachers and as research workers to teach and to do research in accordance with the standards that obtain in the academic community; it includes the freedom to express their views on public questions with impunity and to join learned societies, national and international, and to participate freely in those societies.

Academic freedom is also the freedom of students to study the subjects and to pursue the courses of study that appeal to their intellectual and vocational interests in universities that they themselves have chosen to attend, and to form associations in accordance with their intellectual, political, and convivial interests.

Academic freedom does not exempt individual academics from the obligations that are incumbent on them as members of academic institutions. Thus, the requirements for the award of a degree should not be at the discretion of any individual academic unless the power to decide has been assigned to him by his department or by some other authority in the university who is empowered to do so. There are many activities necessary for the good functioning of a university as an institution that should not be decided by each individual academic at his own discretion. No single academic, for example, has the right to decide the number of hours he or she will teach or the standard by which A's should be granted in examinations. Such matters must be a collective academic decision.

Academic freedom is the freedom of university teachers to perform their academic obligations of teaching and research. These are obligations to seek and communicate the truth according to "their best lights." Academic freedom is not the freedom of academic individuals to do just anything, to follow any impulse or desire, or to say anything that occurs to them. It is the freedom to do academic things: to teach the truth as they see it on the basis of prolonged and intensive study, to discuss their ideas freely with their colleagues, to publish the truth as they have arrived at it by systematic methodical research and assiduous analyses. That is academic freedom proper.

It has a number of corollaries. One is the obligation to maintain academic institutions and the academic profession and its traditions, as well as the traditions of the particular fields, disciplines, and subdisciplines. This entails the obligation of assessing academic things academically, judging academic/intellectual works according to academic/intellectual criteria, regardless of the author's political or religious beliefs, his or her sex, ethnic origin, personal qualities, kinship connections, friendship with or enmity toward the individual or work assessed. It entails also the obligation to assess candidates for academic appointments in accordance with their academic qualifications; this in turn entails conformity with academic standards in the procedures for appointment.

Academic freedom does not extend to all the activities that academics might do or might neglect to do. An academic is not free to falsify the record of his observations; he is not free to forge or misrepresent the content of documents and inscriptions. He is not free to disregard in his reports or in his teaching observations of data that call into question or negate his assertions in teaching or in reporting the results of his research. He is not free to teach propositions that are contrary to the prevailing tradition unless he can support his contentions with evidence from his own research, from his own rational analysis of the traditional proposition that shows that those traditional propositions are erroneous or insufficient.

Academic freedom of individuals may legitimately be limited by institutional requirements. An individual academic is not entitled to the freedom to absent himself frequently from the classes that he has undertaken to teach or to refuse to examine a dissertation that he had previously agreed to examine. He is not free to refuse to conduct or mark examinations if such tasks are among the terms of his appointment. An academic is not free to refuse to teach certain subjects or courses that he is qualified to teach and that must be taught by members of his department. An academic is not free to change his discipline pronouncedly, deciding on his own that he will teach astrophysics even though the department of astrophysics did not appoint him to do so and even though he was appointed to teach constitutional law or Greek tragedy.

The Political Freedom of Academics

Academic freedom includes the political freedom of academics. The political freedom of academics extends to the espousal of the teacher's own political, economic, and social beliefs in teaching where these beliefs pertain to the subject matters that are to be properly expounded in classes within the university or in books, articles, and other forms of publication and where the teacher makes clear that his exposition of his political or ethical views is distinct from his analysis of the facts or his exposition of a theory about those facts. In general, it is desirable that teachers should not expound their own political or moral preferences and values in their classes, but if they do so they should take care to distinguish their evaluative judgments from their statements of facts concerning empirical observations.

The political freedom of academics extends to political activities outside the university, such as contending for public office on behalf of one or another political party. It extends also to representations of their political beliefs in public, nonacademic organs. It extends also to membership in political associations.

The political freedom of academics does not extend to activities or memberships that are prohibited by law, such as collaboration in terroristic activities. It does extend to the espousal of views that are not prohibited by law; it does not extend to the public espousal or defense, directly or indirectly, of illegal actions by others, such as justifying political assassination.

Academic freedom does not extend to actions that are contrary to public morality. The sexual activities of academics are not among those things covered by academic freedom. Likewise criminal activities by academics are not among those activities that academics are free to perform under the protection of academic freedom.

Political Declarations in the Course of Teaching

Since academic freedom is the freedom to do academic things, it is proper to enquire whether it is permissible for a teacher to attempt to win his students to his own evaluative convictions and particularly to his own political convictions. (No question is raised here about the rights of a teacher to declare and to attempt to propagate his own political or moral convictions outside the classroom.)

It is obvious that for a teacher of chemistry or physiology to expound his own political convictions or his own views about sexual morality or his own views of the moral value of an economic system based on the private ownership of property would be a defection from his obligation to teach chemistry or physiology. A teacher of those or similar subjects who in many of his lectures devoted a considerable fraction of his time to a partisan—or even an objective—analysis of the current political situation would not be entitled to claim the protection of a legitimate academic freedom against sanctions by his departmental colleagues or the superior authorities of the university. He could not reasonably say that he had been performing his academic duty as a chemist or a physiologist by lecturing on the current political situation in the Middle East or in the United States. In this instance it is clear that the right to the exercise of academic freedom cannot be validly invoked to protect actions that are contrary to academic obligations, stipulated and accepted explicitly or implicitly at the time of appointment.

But what about a professor of history or economics who uses a large amount of time in his lectures and seminars to denounce or to praise the policies of the United States government regarding abortion or the consumption of narcotics? The matter is not so simple here. If he is teaching the history of the United States in the twentieth century or is conducting a seminar on price control, in connection with which he has to discuss black markets, reference to these subjects does not breach academic obligations; indeed, it might even fulfill them. If he were threatened with sanctions for teaching these political topics, he could claim the protection of a legitimate academic freedom, saying that the course that he was teaching required discussion of abortion or the sale of drugs. I think that he would be justified in doing so.

But what if he also introduced into his lectures a brief statement of his own moral evaluation of the practice of abortion or of the consumption of narcotics? If he did these things only in passing and made clear that he was expressing his own moral preference and was as objective as it was possible to be in describing existing attitudes to policies regarding abortion or drugs, he would be justified in invoking his right to do as he did under the principle of a legitimate academic freedom. But if he spent a considerable portion of his class time in denouncing or affirming passionately, in hyperbolic language, the policies of the government or certain currents in public opinion, it could be justly said that he was exceeding the prerogatives afforded by a legitimate academic freedom.

There is a categorical difference between statements of fact and evaluative propositions. The main body of teaching should be concentrated on statements of fact, on empirical statements, concrete and descriptive, on unique events or on abstract and generalized events. But we must recognize the difficulty of preventing evaluative statements on moral and political issues from intruding, and we must grant that it is permissible to utter them. But it is desirable for the teacher to state at what point his own personal evaluations enter and to make clear that they are different in character from the description and analysis he is rendering.

At the Margins of Academic Freedom

University Autonomy

University autonomy is frequently associated with academic freedom. University autonomy is the freedom of the university as a corporate body from interference by the state or by a church or by the power of any other corporate body, private or public, or by any individual such as a ruler, a politician, government official, ecclesiastical official, publicist, or businessman. It is the freedom for members of the university, acting in a representative capacity and not as individuals, to make decisions about the affairs of their university. Sometimes it is said that these two freedoms are the same, but they are not. They can, in principle, exist independently of each other, although they have come in modern times to appear together. In the Middle Ages there was considerable academic autonomy but little academic freedom.

No university has been or could ever be wholly autonomous. Historically, the right to award degrees has been a privilege conferred through a charter granted by church or state. The activities of universities, for the most part, take place within the territorial boundaries of states; states in various ways must therefore take some responsibility for universities, whether by authorizing their existence or by supporting them financially. A degree received from a university is a claim for public acknowledgment (i.e., by the public at large or by an employer). Those who acknowledge the degree believe that it has been authorized by the highest authority in the society, be that authority the church or the state. Increasingly over the past century the state ultimately legitimizes the institutions that offer the degrees. This legitimation is represented in the charter granted by the state.

But the provision of a charter does not necessarily entail government penetration into the internal or academic affairs of a university. In some societies the government also promulgates the statutes and by-laws of the universities. In others, it delegates that power to a board of trustees, a court of governors, or a board of regents whom it appoints (or who are elected) and who are empowered under the charter to draw up the constitution or statutes and by-laws of the university. Thus the major constituent parts of a university—the faculties of philosophy, medicine, law, and theology; or the colleges of arts and sciences; or the undergraduate colleges and the graduate and professional schools—can be determined by the state or the church, or by the board or court to which the powers of such determination are delegated by the ultimate authority, whether that ultimate authority be the state or a church. The state or church may also determine what subjects will be taught and by how many professors. But powers such as these do not necessarily entail the prescription of the content of what is taught, or of the points of view from which it is to be taught, or of decisions that may be delegated to heads of departments or to individual teachers.

Universities require revenues to remunerate teachers, to construct and maintain buildings, to run libraries and laboratories, and to provide various services for staff and students. The fees paid for tuition and examinations provide some of these revenues; revenues are also obtained from the performance by contract of certain services or by the licensing of patents owned by the university. There are some cases where the higher educational institutions depend on the fees paid by students for their main source of income. Otherwise universities are largely financed by the state or by private patronage or by both.

This condition of financial dependence can lead to infringements on the autonomy of the university. If the state or private patrons prescribe not only the fields but also the substantive content of what is taught, or the point of view regarding the subject matter taught, or the conclusions of research, it is infringing on the autonomy of the universities and it is also infringing on the academic freedom of individual teachers and research workers.

In the admission of students, in some societies, universities are by law required to admit all candidates who can present certificates to demonstrate that they have completed certain courses of study in secondary schools. This is not a universal practice but it is the rule, for example, in American state universities, in Germany, and in some other countries. (Indeed, in present-day West Germany, universities are required to admit any student who is assigned to them by a central admissions office.) This practice is a restriction of the autonomy of the universities because it deprives them of the right to make a decision on an important matter affecting them.

In matters of appointments, the autonomy of the universities is sometimes limited by the fact that professiorial appointments are made by the state through ministerial officials from short lists of acceptable candidates submitted by the faculty in which the professorship is located; in many instances the entire list is rejected and the university is recommended to submit another list of acceptable candidates. In some cases the ministry has imposed on the university a candidate of its own choice. The German universities are subject to this system. In contrast, in Great Britain and in the United States, autonomy in this respect is complete; the state abstains from any participation in the process of academic appointment or in the appointment of administrators. In France and Italy the appointive body is national but not governmental; it is made up of academics from all the universities of the country who decide on appointments to vacant professorships. In France the appointed person must accept the given vacancy or he loses his position on the list; thus the particular university does not have a free choice of who is to become a member of its teaching staff. This is an infringement on the autonomy of the universities. In Italy the candidate has the right to await an opening that is to his taste and the universities have a similar freedom regarding the candidate or candidates who are available to them; the autonomy of the Italian universities, thus, is a little greater in this respect than that of the French universities.

In the determination of the content of courses of study, societies vary in the degree of autonomy of their universities. In some societies, such as Great Britain and the United States, universities are nearly entirely free to decide on which subjects are to be studied as qualifications for degrees and likewise to determine the content to be mastered and the standard to be achieved in order to earn a degree.

The independent determination by the university itself of the arrangements for the conduct of its internal affairs is the heart of university autonomy. There are two aspects to this conduct of internal affairs: one is the institutional pattern of university government and the other is the decisions made by those internal institutions.

The statutes laying down institutional patterns of university government reveal variations among national academic patterns. In the United States the statutes governing internal arrangements lie almost entirely within the powers of the governing body of each particular university; the same is true in Great Britain. In Germany, up to the beginning of the 1970s, statutes regarding the patterns of internal university government were laid down by the separate states. From that ...ne onward, these provisions were brought into uniformity by the federal *Rahmengesetz*, although legally the determination remained with the states. Within the *Rahmengesetz*, which was adopted by the states, the composition of the governing bodies was fixed by the university laws enacted by the states. The situation has been similar in the Netherlands.

European universities and those that follow their pattern still enjoy to some extent the autonomy conferred on them in the Middle Ages. Many of their privileges and liberties were related to the disciplinary powers of universities over their members and the universities still retain these for the most part, although diminishingly.

The Right to Appointment as an Academic Freedom

The exclusion of particular categories of aspirants for entry into the academic profession or of individuals who, from the standpoint of the proper criteria for academic appointment, would normally be given serious consideration, has been an occasional failing of modern universities. In the German universities in the time of their glory up to the outbreak of World War I, socialists and Jews rarely became professors in most faculties. In British universities up to 1865, it was prohibited for anyone to become a fellow of a college at Oxford and Cambridge unless he subscribed to the thirty-nine Articles of the Church of England; dissenters, Roman Catholics, and Jews were thereby excluded. In American universities, until the 1930s, there was unwillingness to consider Jews and African-Americans for appointment. In all these countries it was difficult, if not impossible, for a woman to gain an academic appointment. Insofar as particular persons would have been, apart from the particular disablements of political outlook, religion, race, or sex, better qualified for appointment than the candidate chosen, an impropriety was committed. The improprieties were clearly infringements of the academic ethic, one of the chief constituents of which is the rigorous adherence to intellectual criteria in academic appointments. Respect for academic freedom of colleagues and subordinates is one of the important obligations of the academic ethic but it is only one of them. The academic ethic includes very important obligations and rights that fall outside the boundaries of academic freedom; the application of strict academic criteria in appointment is one of these obligations.

Membership in National and International Learned Societies

Learned societies are corporate bodies; they have their own criteria and procedures for admitting new members. The qualifications for admission to membership are specified; they usually include specific academic and professional qualifications. Not everyone can claim the right of admission to a particular learned society because not everyone has the specified academic and professional qualifications. But if an individual is refused membership on other than academic and professional criteria, if he or she is refused membership on grounds of color, religion, sex, or political views, for example, this refusal represents a clear breach of the academic ethic. (A distinction must be made here between learned societies like the American Anthropological Society which anyone with the necessary qualifications and readiness to pay the fee can join and honorific societies like the United States National Academy of Sciences or the British Academy where the quality of achievement is the primary criterion—at least in principle.) And once an individual becomes a member of a learned society, to refuse to allow him or her to participate in its intellectual activities on political, national, racial, or any other grounds, is clearly an infringement on that person's academic freedom.

Freedom of Publication

Freedom of publication derives from the freedom to conduct research because it represents the culmination of research efforts. A discovery is not complete until it is published and has entered into the body of collectively shared knowledge. Most learned journals do not have a formal membership that delimits their contributors, actual and potential, from those who cannot be or become contributors. The submission of manuscripts for publication is sought by editors without regard to formal membership, even where the journal is officially the organ of a learned society. Anyone may submit a manuscript for publication. The refusal of a manuscript on the grounds of the author's ethnic or national affinity, political association or attitudes, or sex is certainly a breach of the academic ethic. But is it an infringement on the author's academic freedom? Since there is no explicit criterion of membership in a formally organized body as a condition of publication and since the right of publication is an extension of the freedom to do research (which requires publication for its completeness), I believe that it is an infringement on the author's academic freedom. (Similarly, any political censorship, either by a formally constituted office of censorship or informally by an editor, who has received instructions from a governmental office or by a political party, is an infringement on academic freedom.)

It must be emphasized that the right to the academic freedom of publication does not extend to writings that are intellectually inadequate. Similarly, the dismissal of a teacher for the inadequate quality of his/her teaching or research is not an infringement of his/her academic freedom.

The application of the criteria of intellectual quality in decisions regarding appointments, promotions, and acceptance for publication is a sine qua non of academic activity. Academic freedom and the academic ethic postulate the meticulous application of such criteria. (Of course, it is very difficult in some cases to demonstrate with rigorous persuasiveness that intellectual incompetence exists.) The claim to academic freedom cannot override criteria of intellectual quality of achievement in matters of appointment, promotion, continuation of appointment, or publication.

Infringements on Academic Freedom

Preemptive and Punitive Infringements on Academic Freedom

Academic freedom may be infringed in many ways. Academic freedom may be infringed by legal enactment or by administrative decisions—governmental or ecclesiastical or academic—that expressly prohibit the assertion of specific beliefs that are intellectually legitimate. These include laws and administrative orders forbidding the teaching of certain doctrines or particular topics, or requiring the teaching of certain doctrines or topics while explicitly or implicitly forbidding the teaching of other doctrines or topics. This type of infringement on academic freedom does not strike at a particular person for an action already performed. It is intended to forestall actions not yet performed, although it can be invoked to punish individuals who have performed such actions. I call these infringements on academic freedom "preemptive infringements."

Academic freedom can also be infringed by actions or statements of persons in authority against a particular person who is alleged to have already performed the sanctionable action. This type of infringement is preemptive as well as punitive. In addition to punishing a particular person, it functions to forestall—and indeed might be intended to have this effect—disapproved actions by academics in the future. It punishes the individual, but it also intimidates the academic community by explicit or implied threats, inhibiting faculty from acting freely in their subsequent performance of academic actions. Whereas the first type of infringement looks to the future, the second type of infringement looks both to the past and to the future.

Censorship prior to publication prevents the completion of a particular academic action already partly complete. In a modern society with a large academic population, censorship of all works prior to their publication is extremely difficult. Governments overcome this difficulty in part by dispersing the activity of censorship over many editorial offices of learned journals, periodicals, and publishing houses. By creating fear of government disapproval and even punishment, such a dispersion of censorial activities can be quite effective.

Sanctions take many forms. Imprisonment is an extreme form which is usually not applied to academics for academic actions, but is applied for political infringements. Physical violence, wounding, or murder for academic actions or for political actions by academics do occur. But the most frequently employed sanctions by authorities are dismissal from academic posts; variants include the withdrawal of the right to teach while retaining title, salary, etc.; the withholding of promotion; censure, oral or written; withholding of research funds, income, honors, opportunity for publication; refusal of perquisites such as leaves of absence; restrictions on travel within or outside the country; etc.

The most common or at least the best-known sanction against a particular academic is dismissal. Because dismissal has been the most common mode of infringement of academic freedom, it is quite understandable that academic freedom has come to be regarded by many persons, especially in the United States, as very intricately intertwined with or even synonymous with permanence of tenure. This particular coupling of academic freedom with permanence of tenure has usually not been asserted outside the United States. Recently, however, in response to the prospective abolition of permanent tenure, the coupling has been asserted in Great Britain; there it has recently been said that the permanent tenure is a guarantee of academic freedom and hence of independence of thought in academic matters.

The prospective withholding of financial patronage has not infrequently been a ground for justifying infringement of academic freedom. It is the apprehension of such action on the part of possible patrons—governmental or private—that has caused university administrators to exercise sanctions against particular academics whose beliefs or actions, inside or outside the university, might offend such patrons.

Loyalty Oaths

A required oath of loyalty to the existing regime is a preemptive restriction on the political freedom of academics. In Italy under the Fascist regime such oaths were required of academics from the late 1920s onward. In the United States during the decade after World War II, when the government was preoccupied with the danger of communist subversion, loyalty oaths were required of university teachers in many public institutions, most notably California, and even at many private institutions.

Is a loyalty oath that foreswears the performance of subversive actions an infringement of legitimate academic freedom? Taking the narrow view, academic freedom is not defined so as to include the illegal subversion of public order as one of the actions that an academic should be free to undertake. But during the period when oaths of loyalty were being demanded of academics, many academics and nonacademics opposed such oaths. They argued that the

loyalty oaths were an infringement of academic freedom. The question remains: is the legal requirement that an academic subscribe to an oath of
loyalty to the existing constitutional and public order an infringement on his
or her academic freedom? While loyalty oaths were ostensibly intended to
limit the political freedom of academics to commit acts of subversion, they
had overtones that went far beyond such limiting intentions. They were offensive to the dignity of the academic profession because they intimated that,
without subscription to the oath, academics would commit or encourage acts
of subversion. They were further offensive to the academic profession because it was singled out as particularly inclined toward subversion; loyalty
oaths suggested that academics were more inclined toward subversion than
the members of other professions. Again taking the narrow view, these asper-
sions are, in themselves, not restrictions of the freedom of academics to
perform the wide range of intellectual activities that are legally permitted in a
liberal order.

Yet the requirement of such loyalty oaths was intended to restrict the
freedom of academics, and it is true that they did in some instances inhibit the
will to exercise academic freedom.

The Incidence of Infringement

Not all subjects are equally susceptible to infringements on academic freedom. In the Middle Ages and the Renaissance, when all European universities were under the dominion of churches, theological studies and philosophy,
insofar as it was applied in theology, were subject to preemptive and punitive
restrictions. The prominence of Bible criticism in the nineteenth century,
especially in Germany, but also in other Western countries, often placed that
particular part of religious studies under scrutiny and restriction. At Oxford in
1863 Benjamin Jowett was brought before the Court of Arches for his biblical commentaries; he was exonerated, but only after disagreeable harassment.
W. Robertson Smith was compelled to resign from his post at the Free Church
College, Aberdeen. Julius Wellhausen resigned his professorship in Greifswald
in 1882 to escape from the censure of his studies of the composition and
dating of the Old Testament. Ernest Renan was dismissed in 1863 from his
professorship in the College de France for his reference to the humanity of
Jesus and the clearly implied denial of Jesus' divinity.

There were similar happenings in the United States although the victims
were not such famous scholars. Geology and cosmogony likewise came under critical scrutiny. Since Charles Lyell, the greatest geologist of his time,
was not an academic—he was professor of geology at King's College London for only two years—his research, which caused consternation among
academic devotees of the Christian account of the age of the earth, escaped

from the sanctions which might have confronted him had he followed an academic career. Darwin, whose ideas raised questions about the traditional biblical view of the creation of man, was likewise not an academic and he too escaped from any constriction of academic freedom. Nevertheless, especially in the United States, lesser followers of Lyell and Darwin were subjected to the various kinds of sanctions that single out individuals who have acted freely in intellectual matters. But by the end of the century academics were able to attain a high degree of freedom in the teaching of subjects which impinged on the biblical account of the creation of the world and of the human species as well as on the history of the Jews as portrayed in the Old Testament.

By and large, the natural sciences have been relatively immune from restrictions on academic freedom. Physics, chemistry, astronomy, and mathematics have for several centuries been left untouched by infringement on academic freedom. But teaching and research in genetics and the teaching of the theory of relativity were severely constricted or prohibited for many years in the Soviet Union.

With the coming of World War II the physical sciences in the United States and Britain experienced one kind of restriction that was unprecedented in the history of their universities. For the first time academic scientists working in their own universities, but with the financial support of government, had to renounce their freedom of publication and even free discussion with colleagues of their conduct of research and their results. After World War II, research in American and European universities on scientific-military matters under contract with departments of defense was typically "classified" (i.e., its results could not be published). Since very little of such "classified" research is now conducted in universities, many questions about such restrictions of academic freedom have lost their urgency.

It is possible that the growing collaboration between private industrial firms and universities in scientific research, especially in microbiology and genetics, which provides for the patenting of the results for the benefit of the private industrial partners in the collaboration, will restrict the freedom of the academic collaborators to publish the results of their research directly after completion.

The traditional humanistic disciplines—classics, philology, Oriental studies, modern languages, literature, and history—have generally been spared any restrictions of academic freedom. But in countries where the government imposes a central ideology on all people and all institutions, as in the Soviet Union and National Socialist Germany, academic freedom in the humanistic subjects has not been spared restriction.

Historically, the most common victims of sanctions have been teachers of law, history, philosophy, and social science. There was only one natural scientist among them. In the dismissal of the Göttingen Seven from the University of Göttingen, of Edward A. Ross from Stanford University in 1892, of Theodor Lessing from the Technische Hochschule of Hannover in 1925, of Leo Arons from the University of Berlin in 1892, Emil Gumbel from the University of Heidelberg in 1926, the dismissal of Louis Levine (later, Lorwin) from the University of Montana in 1912, of Scott Nearing from the University of Pennsylvania in 1912, of Leon Fraser and J. McKean Cattell from Columbia University in 1917, of Moses Finley from Rutgers University in 1946, the activities which were made into the grounds for sanctions were not activities in teaching or in research but in public declarations or activities regarding public matters. (The dismissal of Finley was occasioned by his claim to the protection of the Fifth Amendment of the United States Constitution before the Un-American Activities Committee of the United States House of Representatives which was enquiring about his presumed membership in the Communist party.)

Indeed, over the past century, the chief object of restriction on academic freedom—and above all, of the political freedom of academics—has been the social sciences. Academic social scientists frequently devote their attention to current social problems and policy issues. In their academic teaching and research they often deal with conditions and situations that have been publicly controversial. They often espouse in public beliefs that are critical of existing social arrangements, and at least by implication, critical of the government. Their scientific investigations often concern conditions, situations, etc., about which there has been public contention. Thus, social scientists often draw the attention and anger of government authorities, even when they themselves have not engaged in public controversy, and even when they have scrupulously avoided the assertion of political preferences in their strictly academic activities. Nevertheless, their critical attitude often results in restrictive measures.

It was relatively seldom, if ever, that the sanctions were responses to whatever the academics in question had asserted in the reports on their research. A little more often but not very frequently, they were accused of teaching in a manner hostile to the existing society. However, by far most of the actions for which sanctions were taken were for expression or activities in the public sphere. The reasons why there have been very few instances of academics who have suffered sanctions for their teaching or research and publications are not far to seek. For one thing, teaching and research are not easily visible. Teaching is invisible even to most colleagues; published writings reporting on research are hidden from most colleagues, especially those in other fields of study. Persons outside the university are not likely to know of either unless an aggrieved student informs them or unless an informant has been posted in a class. This has been common in totalitarian societies but is practically never done in liberal-democratic societies. That is why teaching and research in themselves have been fairly immune from infringements on academic freedom.

Academic Freedom and the Expectation of Orthodoxy

By and large there seem to be relatively few instances where genuine academic freedom has been restricted. Naturally, it is impossible to know of the cases in which intimidation caused a university teacher to avoid some topics, interpretations, etc., which he otherwise might have pursued. Most of the known cases of infringement of academic freedom, in the strict sense of curtailment of freedom in academic matters, have occurred in connection with religious matters. The dismissal of W. Robertson Smith from the Free Church College, the discomfiture of Julius Wellhausen at Greifswald, and the dismissal of Alfred Loisy from the Institut Catholique in Paris—all had to do with their scholarly publications about the Bible. The dismissal of Ernest Renan from the College de France in 1863 for his lecture in which he referred to Jesus as "that wonderful man" also was a harsh infringement on academic freedom in the strict sense.

Robertson Smith and Loisy were teachers in colleges conducted by religious bodies. There were more or less clearly promulgated doctrines with which the teaching in the colleges was to conform; the governing bodies made no pretense of respecting academic freedom. It is indeed a question as to whether it is legitimate to discuss the state of academic freedom in higher educational institutions which make their appointments with the expectation of orthodoxy. The removal of Professor Hans Küng from the chair of Roman Catholic theology at the University of Tübingen was similar to the cases of Loisy and Robertson Smith. Professor Küng's appointment was dependent on the approval of the Roman Catholic archbishop, as agreed in the Concordat between the German republic and the Holy See.

When orthodoxy is one of the conditions of appointment, it is wrong to expect academic freedom. It is not promised by the appointive body since orthodoxy is at least overtly expected by the person appointed. Yet, it is perfectly clear that academic freedom does not exist in these instances.

Agents of Infringement

Infringements of academic freedom have usually been instigated by rulers, politicians, government officials, ecclesiastical dignitaries, ecclesiastical administrators, and zealous members of religious communities; more recently, they have also been instigated by businessmen, publicists, and ordinary citizens. Whenever they originate outside universities, they must operate through persons occupying positions of authority for or within universities; they must stir members of the governing body of the university and higher administrations who have appointive powers. They must, before they can be successful, persuade some persons who exercise legitimate authority over academic institutions to infringe on the academic freedom of individual academics. There is seldom an infringement of academic freedom that does not have the collaboration of academics or academic administrators.

Sometimes the infringement originates within the academic institution, sometimes at a high administrative level, sometimes within the academic teaching staff itself. Those infringements initiated within the academic institution itself are sometimes intended to preempt or forestall infringements that might otherwise emanate from some powerful body, office, or individual outside the university. These infringements, like those that have been instigated externally, are of the usual sort; they range from discontinuance of appointment, refusal of promotion, assignment to uncongenial tasks, avoidance, etc. Internally instigated infringements on academic freedom add to the usual motives for infringement personal antipathies, political antagonism, religious and ethnic repugnance, etc. It should not be thought that academics always desire and strive for the academic freedom of their colleagues.

The Consequences of Infringements on Academic Freedom

One of the arguments in defense of academic freedom is that it helps to maintain the morale of the academic profession which is in constant danger of entropy and that it thereby maintains their creative power. Obligatory oaths of loyalty, for example, diminish the self-confidence and self-esteem of the academic profession and promote the belief among academics that they are generally disesteemed and distrusted by society outside the universities. It is unknown whether the loyalty oaths had such consequences. It is my impression that the impact of the loyalty oath despite the agitation was neither deep nor prolonged in the decade after World War II. It is most likely that they caused some discomfiture, remorse, and resentment but that they did not really damage the creative powers of those who submitted to them. It should be remembered that the same decade was one of exceptionally fruitful intellectual activity at the University of California.

The gravest case of infringement of academic freedom occurred in Germany in 1933 and thereafter when all persons of Jewish ancestry or who were socialists or Marxists were dismissed from their academic posts. About one-third of the body of university teachers was dismissed. This damaged German universities very severely by depriving them of some of their most outstanding scholars and scientists. It caused great distress to its victims, many of whom suffered for an extended period after they went into exile, since most of them did not find appointments of comparable status to those from which they had been expelled. Yet most recovered their intellectual power in the free atmosphere of the English-speaking universities and made many very important contributions to learning.

Not all those who remained in the German universities approved of the dismissals or thought that the Nazis were good for the universities. But most were intimidated. The fear of dismissal and even more severe sanctions inhibited the intellectual activities of some of the better scientists and scholars who remained. The German universities declined very markedly during the Nazi period and it has taken them a long time to recover.

Much the same is true of the universities of the Soviet Union, where the dismissals and voluntary departures began in the early 1920s. The far-reaching denial of academic freedom that began after the Russian Revolution obliterated whole fields of academic work in the humanities and social sciences. It seems reasonable to say that the universities of the Soviet Union declined from their previous level in many fields. This was party a result of the exile of many persons of great intellectual powers and partly the result of the intimidation of some of those who remained. Soviet policy also brought about the appointment of many timeservers, who even in a regime of academic freedom would probably have been just as sterile. The remarkable thing is that a subterranean intellectual life of considerable merit seems to have continued. Official publication was denied or not even sought by many of these scholars, but many persisted in their studies against the most appalling obstacles.

The exercise of sanctions against an academic to the point of dismissal for the expression of political views outside the main course or for corresponding political activities usually has not aroused much sympathy among his colleagues. As far as I can find out, there generally has been no apprehension that similar injury might be inflicted on them. In such instances, it cannot be said that the morale, self-esteem and self-confidence of academics was damaged by the penalties imposed on one of them for attempting to exercise his legitimate academic freedom. Little thought that "there, but for the grace of God, go I," seems to be stirred among the colleagues of the victim. Such freedom in their research and teaching as they thought they needed they could take without apprehension that a fate similar to that of their colleague could befall them.

There is nevertheless some truth in the assertion that infringements on academic freedom have an intimidating effect on some members of the academic profession. Those who shared the political views or political activities of the victim do seem to have been intimidated, but whether that dulled their intellectual creative powers or made them less curious and imaginative in their research cannot be said.

It seems doubtful whether infringements on academic freedom do severe damage to anyone except to the victim. The one striking case of a victim who rallied and became a famous scholar is that of the late Moses Finley, who made a distinguished career at Cambridge University after having been expelled from Rutgers University in the United States. M. I. Rostovtseff, A. D. Momigliano and other great scholars were surely wounded severely by their need to leave their native countries and to go into exile but that did not prevent their prodigious intellectual achievements; the same is true of other exiled great scientists and scholars. Persecution and the obliteration of their academic freedom in their own countries did not prevent them from ascending to great heights. It is true, of course, that they went from totalitarian to liberal-democratic countries; they did not have to continue to live in the atmosphere of brutality in their native countries.

It is, however, not to condone infringements on either academic freedom, strictly understood, or academic freedom in the loose sense of political freedom of academics, to say that the infringement is not fatal to intellectual life. Even if it had no consequences whatsoever, it would still be reprehensible.

The Conditions of Academic Freedom

The first condition of academic freedom is the separation of church from society and the separation of religion from learning. The Roman Catholic church before the Reformation and the Protestant churches at the height of their powers after the Reformation contributed greatly to learning, but they contributed very little directly to the tradition of academic freedom. But it is from this period that the tradition of the autonomy of the universities comes, as well as the tradition of the cultivation of the pursuit of truth. These traditions have been the greatest inheritance of modern universities from the Middle Ages and their greatest contribution to academic freedom.

The separation of church and state in France and in the United States after the French and American revolutions did not help universities or colleges greatly. In France, the church lost its influence over universities , but the state became more influential.

In the United States the early separation of church and state had little influence on the formation of academic freedom. Religious congregations remained very strong, their outlooks were pervasive in their respective communities, and they were frequently very insistent in the observation of their own particular orthodox beliefs and practices. Nevertheless, the separation of church and state has left, over the long run, a considerable mark on the condition of academic freedom. The separation of church and state was one element of a more comprehensive pluralistic liberal outlook. It was a step in the renunciation by the center of society of a claim to complete ascendancy.

Universities had previously been deeply marked by their subordination to state or church or both. Under the new regime of pluralism, universities became subcenters of society with their own traditions and a sense of their own autonomy vis-à-vis other centers and subcenters.

Thanks to the medieval inheritance of the ideas of autonomy and the quest for truth, and the Enlightenment ideas of pluralism and individual freedom of expression of belief, academic freedom has by now gained great respect in most Western countries—although with definite reverses in the totalitarian regimes. Totalitarian regimes, authoritarian regimes, and tyrannies of all sorts have practiced severe, comprehensive, and continuous preemptive and positive infringements on academic freedom in the narrow sense. Of course, the political freedom of academics was entirely abolished in these societies as was the political freedom of all their other members.

Since the disappearance of the National Socialist and Fascist regimes in Germany and Italy, a high degree of academic freedom and of the political freedom of academics has been restored. The relatively strong position of academic freedom in universities in Western countries in the past four decades is attributable to the widespread liberalism or pluralism which has survived the growth in the powers of the central government and the very wide extension of policies of welfare.

In this period since the Second World War the deference accorded to science and to research generally and to the universities as their proper site, and the recognition of the fact that the universities are the main source of certification for entry into higher occupations and for higher remuneration and status, have strengthened the position of the academic profession and therewith expanded the range of academic freedom proper and of the political freedom of academics. The partial evaporation of the puritanical ethos and the recession of most of the Protestant churches with middle-class membership have also enlarged the sexual and social freedom of academics. The religious freedom of academics, except for the great catastrophe in Germany and Italy and the territories conquered temporarily by Germany in the Second World War, has grown almost to the point where it has ceased to be an issue. Of course, theological seminaries and faculties and ecclesiastical universities have continued to limit the religious freedom of academics in those higher educational institutions.

Academic freedom may also be sustained by the constitution of a society and by the body of judicial decisions. It is guaranteed in the Fundamental Law (*Grundgesetz*) of the German Federal Republic as it was in the constitution of the Weimar Republic. Some students of the United States Constitution and of the body of constitutional law claim that academic freedom is guaranteed by the Constitution of the United States. (I think that this assertion has not been demonstrated.)

The Demand of the Academic Profession for Academic Freedom

When sanctions are inflicted on individual academics as infringements on their academic freedom—usually their political freedom—there are few colleagues who come to their support. When E. A. Ross was dismissed from Stanford University by the then President David Jordan, under unceasing pressure from Mrs. Stanford, the widow of the founder, seven other professors resigned in protest but thirty-five signed a declaration in support of the action of the president. When in 1917 Charles Beard and James Harvey Robinson resigned from Columbia University after the dismissal of J. McKean Cattell and Leon Fraser, no other professors resigned or even, as far as I know, protested to the president of the university. In contrast with these situations, in 1894, fifty-three professors of the University of Berlin protested very emphatically against the action of the Prussian Ministry of Religious Affairs to withdraw the right of Dr. Arons to teach. They had previously refused to act on the request of the ministry to revoke Arons's *venia legendi*. The protestors included many of the greatest scholars and scientists of the century.

When the freedom to teach was attacked by radical students in the late 1960s by picketing outside of classes, some teachers did insist on conducting their classes, but many submitted to the students' demands that they desist from teaching. There were many teachers who showed no concern at all about the interference with the freedom of teaching and research when it was carried on by radical students who interrupted classes, demonstrated against and menaced certain scientific investigations and those who conducted them.

The mass of university teachers are not concerned most of the time with academic freedom, and they are particularly unsympathetic toward it when it is invoked on behalf of colleagues whose political views are distasteful to them; they are also usually indifferent to the freedom of their colleagues in strictly academic matters.

It is not my contention that academics initiate restrictions on the academic freedom of their colleagues, more particularly their political freedom. If they do it at all, they do it against their specifically academic freedom and they do it with the justification of a description of the desire to maintain high standards of teaching and research. As I said above, disapproval of the distinctive feature of a colleague's research might be a consequence of jealousy or animosity or it might be from a genuine conviction that the research is unacceptable according to strictly intellectual standards.

Corporate Academic Pride and Academic Freedom

The attitudes of the academic profession itself are connected with academic freedom. It is not so much that academics of high quality have demanded academic freedom in an explicit and audible way. It is rather that they have taken it for granted in their work and in their relations with university administrators. They regard academic freedom, that is, the absence of intrusion into what they teach and what they investigate, as a patent necessity for their work.

The growing intellectual achievement of academics from the third quarter of the nineteenth century was accompanied by a growing self-confidence and self-esteem in the academic profession. Administrators, academic and governmental, came to be in awe of them. The academics thought that what they were doing was important, and influential laymen outside universities and outside government came to share that view. This is the way in which things developed in the United States in the present century and that is why, after World War II, when academic self-esteem and pride in scientific and scholarly achievement were higher than ever before, American universities finally reached the condition of *akademische Selbstverwaltung*—faculty self-government.

Academic freedom was the beneficiary of this change. But alongside those who invoke the principle of academic freedom to justify actions that are contradictory to it, there are many academics who are not interested in academic freedom. They are content to go on doing what has been done before, to teach what has become well established, and to affirm the widely accepted and dominant political outlook. They think they have no need for academic freedom; they are unsympathetic toward those who do need it to protect their political freedom. If they think of academic freedom at all, it is usually in the context of the political freedom of other academics whom they do not favor.

Academic freedom is in danger of becoming an object of lip-service to which everyone alleges to subscribe without thinking of what it really entails. It has come, in some academic circles, to be used to justify any action, academic, political, personal, etc., in which academics may at any moment wish to engage. They do not see that academic freedom is primarily the freedom to do serious academic things without obstructions imposed with other intentions in mind.

Academic freedom goes beyond the freedom of expression and action, and even beyond the freedom of expression of opinion. Academic freedom is justified when it contributes to the growth of the body of truthful propositions and to this body's transmission to contemporary and oncoming generations.

Under more ordinary circumstances, there are nearly always some uncertainties, contrary voices, and diverse currents of opinion within the circles of the authority that is considering the restriction of the academic freedom of a particular individual or group. The decision to infringe on academic freedom under ordinary circumstances is seldom wholly free from hesitation and disagreement. Those who make such decisions are encouraged by confidence in

their rightness, in the practicability of their decision, and by their confidence
that the infringement will be accepted by the colleagues of the individual or
individuals against whom sanctions are being considered.

These assertions are difficult to demonstrate. Nevertheless, it may be observed that both in Germany in the nineteenth century and in the United
States in the twentieth century, as the academic profession became consolidated, and as it acquired a clearer collective self-consciousness and as it
manifested more collective self-esteem and more self-confidence in its importance and its powers, instances of infringement on academic freedom
became less frequent and less prominent.

Respect for academic freedom by external authorities is partly a function
of their respect for the academic profession and for the universities of their
own country. When they regard the academics as no less a part of the center
of society than they think themselves to be, academic freedom is likely to be
less often violated than it is under other circumstances.

The Historical Vicissitudes of Academic Freedom

Academic freedom is not a constant of the history of universities. Academic freedom has had its ups and downs. Though now accepted as a matter
of course in liberal-democratic societies, it has been practically abolished in
Communist countries and in other totalitarian and authoritarian countries around
the world. It has varied from society to society, from epoch to epoch, and
from subject to subject. In some modern societies, like Nazi Germany, Fascist Italy, and the Soviet Union, it has been highly restricted. The professoriate has been prohibited from expressing certain academically acceptable beliefs, and have been required to profess certain academically unacceptable
beliefs. They have lacked civil academic freedom, the freedom to express
themselves in speech and writing about matters of public significance. (In
this respect, of course, they have not been any different from their fellow
countrymen.) They have not been permitted to form their own learned associations, or to participate freely in international learned associations. Even
their informal communication with colleagues within their own universities
has been restricted by suspicions about informers in their midst—frequently
their own colleagues—even in fields that seemed to be outside the scope of
the ruling doctrine.

After the French revolution of 1789, the Christian churches lost most of
their power over European universities. But in the United States many small
colleges continued to be affiliated with and supported by Christian denomina-
tions and sects, who were on continuous alert against religious unorthodoxy,
sexual unconventionality, public declarations in support of governmental intervention into economic life, and criticism of private business enterprise.

Even in societies in which church and state have been constitutionally separated from each other—in the United States above all—the academic freedom of individuals appointed to university posts, in the present century in the United States, has been infringed by religious bodies or more frequently by individuals strongly attached to their respective churches or religious communities.

It was only the gradual subsidence of the power of the churches in society that conferred on academics a degree of academic freedom such as they had never had before.

In the liberal conception of the state, provision was made for the autonomy of private corporations. The universities on the continent were not private institutions but they too benefited from the establishment of the pluralistic pattern of society.

In consequence of the growth of the belief that universities should be left to run their own affairs—best expressed in von Humboldt's idea of *akademische Selbstverwaltung*, that is, academic self-government—the idea of academic freedom, within limits, became firmly established, even where monarchical governments retained much power. Liberalism was conducive to the belief in the rightfulness of academic freedom. Along with the idea of the autonomous, self-governing university, there emerged a fairly high degree of self-consciousness with the universities about the absolute value of academic freedom as a part of academic life.

Infringements on academic freedom of one sort or another have occurred in liberal-democratic societies. The universities and colleges of the United States were especially subjected to these occasional constrictions on academic freedom. Political demagogues and publicists in the United States have from time to time demanded a greater degree of conformity with their own outlook which sometimes verged on ideology. Excitable businessmen took action against academics who favored governmental intervention into the operations of private business enterprise, or who, they thought, wished to abolish the capitalistic economy. Extremist nationalists and religious zealots and sometimes well-established churches have been sensitive to critical attitudes toward their own orthodoxy and have in response sought to constrict the academic freedom of particular individuals or whole universities. Throughout the 1920s to the 1950s, American universities were repeatedly criticized by conservative elements for "harboring" radicals or for propagating disloyalty to the then existing American society. The attempts of communists to sway academic opinion, although generally an abysmal failure, did lead to the formation of very small communist groups, mostly younger teachers, in a few universities and thus gave a false appearance of a basis for the rabid accusations which were, in fact, far wide of the mark. The accusations, if not always utterly baseless, were usually much exaggerated. They intimidated many not very brave academics, left a bad taste in the mouths of many and in some cases, precipitated the dismissal of a teacher.

Nevertheless, despite these intermittent flurries, it has been in liberal-democratic societies such as those prevailing over the past century in Western and Northern Europe, North America and the English-speaking countries of the antipodes, that academic freedom has most widely prevailed.

Academic Freedom and Academic Standards

The right of academic freedom does not extend to charlatans, forgers, plagiarists, or cranks. It does extend to the honest but less-gifted scientist or scholar. But to refuse to the latter reappointment, promotion, or the publication of their works is not an infringement of their academic freedom, as long as the refusals are based only on a strictly academic or intellectual assessment of their works, and are not based on considerations of their political attitudes, their religious or ethnic connections, their race, or their sex.

There is one obvious similarity between the prohibitions and prescriptions by external powers that infringe on academic freedom and those actions that enforce conformity with minimal academic standards: both apply sanctions. However, the grounds for these sanctions are totally different. Universities are institutions oriented toward the discovery and communication of truth and their members must adhere strictly to that obligation. That objective requires freedom of action in the search for and exposition of truth, and also, as a corollary objective, the refusal to continue to support the activities of those who are grossly incompetent in that search and those who deliberately contravene it. Academic freedom entails the absence of sanctions; academic incompetence or willful failure and even obstruction requires the imposition of sanctions but only on strictly intellectual, academic grounds.

Nevertheless, it must be admitted that the assessment of conformity with exigent academic standards is a difficult task. When it is a matter of dealing with a scholar or scientist who moves far from the beaten path, there is the danger that the generally conservative ethos of the university may be jeopardizing a legitimate exercise of academic freedom. There are times when it is not easy to distinguish a crank from a really gifted person who is striking out on an idiosyncratic but potentially very fruitful path. There is sometimes a danger that an individual is deprived of his rightful academic freedom on what appears at the time as appropriate academic grounds.

The Justification for Academic Freedom

The right to academic freedom is not identical with a human right that is a right of all human beings. Academic freedom is a much narrower right. It is a right that exists only for academics, and it is a right hedged about by obligations and conditions. It is a right that sometimes might be in conflict with other rights.

The right to academic freedom is not tantamount to the right of free expression which is subject to few obligations other than the avoidance of the immediate precipitation of public disorder and the demonstrated eschewing of deliberate untruthfulness. Academic freedom is the freedom to seek the truth by reliable methods and the freedom to communicate the truth through teaching and publication. The truths that academics are concerned with are propositions methodically achieved by observation, that are based on the best possible evidence, and that do justice to contrary evidence. A crank and a demagogue enjoy the right of freedom of expression, but even if they are academics, academic freedom does not protect their right to make arbitrary assertions without regard to the evidence, methodically and critically assessed.

Academic freedom in a narrow, professional sense cannot be justified simply by the invocation of human rights; the relationship of human rights to the political freedom of academics is much closer.

Human rights and academic freedom are not necessarily in conflict with each other but they can be because they may apply different criteria of evaluation. For example, the human right to equality of status—equality of treatment regardless of performance, intellectual capacity, and intellectual achievement—would conflict with the academic obligation to assess the works of individual academics according to the criteria of the truth of their assertions and the adequacy of the evidence they adduce. All human beings, regardless of the quality of their academic intellectual achievement, are entitled to equal political rights, equal status, equality before the law, and so on. They are not by virtue of these rights entitled to equal academic status. Once they become academics, however, they are entitled to equal academic freedom within the limits of the obligations that are appropriate to academics. They are not entitled to immunity from sanctions if they fall short of their academic obligations or exceed their legitimate academic freedom.

Academic freedom is not identical with intellectual freedom and its justification is different from the justification of intellectual freedom. Academic freedom certainly includes intellectual freedom, but within the academic setting; academic freedom entails the obligation to perform certain duties in teaching, to act collegially with other academics, and to maintain and protect the internal order in which academic activities can be effectively performed. Intellectual freedom has traditionally entailed no institutional obligations; academic freedom does entail such obligations.

The justification for academic freedom places the value of rationally and methodically achieved truth about the world, man, and his works at the center. This is the value from which all else flows. It asserts that truth is of fundamental value in human existence and that its possession is one of the chief conditions of human dignity. Academic freedom is above all the freedom to seek, discover, and assert important truths.

The justification for academic freedom goes beyond and sometimes against certain human rights. Insofar as it is an extension into the academic sphere of the principles of human rights, it must qualify some of those rights by more specific and perhaps narrower criteria. The justification for academic freedom derives from a quite different value, namely, the value of truth in human life as a good in itself and as a good that leads to other goods, such as a more rational understanding of the world, insofar as it can be rationally understood, and a more rational ordering of the conditions of life and society.

Yet it is necessary to avoid an overblown and grandiloquent way of thinking about academic freedom. Most of its beneficiaries do not discover much that is important and many of them do not live up to the standard that the existing state of knowledge permits. Many of those who speak most about academic freedom—meaning usually the political freedom of academics— make little use of it, being very conventional in their research and in their teaching. Those who do make use of it because they do things in teaching and research that are off the beaten path often take for granted the academic freedom that they enjoy and from which they benefit. Nevertheless, for them academic freedom is genuinely necessary.

One need not say that academic freedom is the highest good and that there might not be moments when academic freedom might be justifiably abridged. There might be brief periods when national security and the peace and good order of society might render it desirable to abridge academic freedom. It is, however, not easy to conceive of any situation in which what one scientist or scholar, in dealing with his academic concerns, says to his colleagues or his pupils might endanger such valued conditions as the integrity, peace, and good order of society.

Intellectual achievement in a university requires academic freedom. The fruitful choice of important problems, the choice of the best methods of studying them, and the most independent and imaginative interpretation and analysis are indispensable to intellectual achievement. The free interchange of opinions is part of academic freedom. Free access to publications and the freedom of publication both contribute to the stimulus to intellectual achievement. Not all academics benefit from academic freedom; they do not need it and they do not want it because what they do conforms completely with the prevailing tradition. At the same time, it should be remembered that the great efflorescence of scholarly and scientific learning that occurred first in German universities from early in the nineteenth century, and then in British, French, and Italian universities, and later in American universities was paralleled by a pattern of the expansion of academic freedom in those countries.

These countries were also becoming more liberal in their political life and in their public institutions. Without that liberalization, however partial and hesitant, the universities might not have prospered, academic freedom would not have expanded, and ordered and sound knowledge would not have grown as it did.

9

Academic Freedom and Permanent Tenure

The Question: Is permanent tenure a guarantee of academic freedom?
The Answer: Yes and no.

I

Dismissal or denial of renewal of appointment is, short of incarceration, torture, or murder, the most severe sanction against individual academics whose academic and civil activities are displeasing to their academic and administrative superiors and peers—and in some countries, to their governmental authorities. This severe sanction of dismissal is rendered much less practicable where the academic person in question has been appointed on permanent tenure. In this respect and to this extent, appointment on permanent tenure is a protection of academic freedom. The abrogation of the contractual obligation undertaken by a university in making an appointment on permanent (or indefinite) tenure places the university in a difficult situation; it renders it subject to legal action and public obloquy. In the United States, it might even call down the censure of the American Association of University Professors, which university administrators try very hard to avoid. University administrators in the United States nowadays are usually reluctant to face such embarrassment.

If dismissal or refusal to promote were the only sanctions against persons whose views on intellectual, religious or political matters were offensive to their superiors, academic or governmental, then the academic freedom of the persons in question would be effectively protected by appointments on permanent tenure. (I do not deal here with discrimination against women or African-Americans, except in so far as their beliefs and actions are concerned. Discrimination on grounds of sex or race or ethnicity *per se* are not considered in these pages.)

Academic freedom however is subject to restraint or restriction by numerous sanctions short of dismissal or the refusal to reappoint. The refusal of promotion in rank and the refusal of rises in salary are examples of such sanctions; so are the denial of a teacher's proposal or application to teach certain courses which he (or she) is qualified to teach and which fall within the syllabus of the department. There are other ways of injuring a teacher who is disapproved of because of his (or her) intellectual, political or religious attitudes or activities. Boycotting a teacher socially, not inviting him (or her) to "faculty parties," assigning office space more inconvenient in location and size than the average office, steadily refusing recommendation for a distinction which is merited and desired, while other, no more worthy or even less worthy, persons are granted the distinction, are all sanctions which can be applied to curtail a teacher's academic freedom.

Thus, short of dismissal, there are many ways to act injuriously against a teacher who is disapproved of for the expression of views or for the performance of actions, which the laws of the country and the prevailing conception of academic freedom permit, and which the teacher in question should therefore be free to express or perform. This is why I say that protection from dismissal such as is afforded by permanent tenure does to some extent protect the academic freedom of particular individual university teachers who hold appointments on permanent tenure. Such an appointment is, however, no guarantee that teachers who offend their superiors by their intellectual, political or religious views or actions will not have other sanctions inflicted on them.

II

The principle of "anything goes" is inadmissible in academic actions. There are rules of proper teaching and proper research. It is difficult to articulate these rules but it is clear when they are being infringed upon.

Each field or subject has its own substantive and methodological traditions and these must be observed or, if they are departed from, there must be rational grounds for doing so and there must be evidence of careful study. Where traditional rules and substantive propositions are not adhered to, the divergent methodological procedures and divergent substantive propositions must still meet certain rules of reliable evidence and rational criticism. The teachers or research workers who follow these deviant lines must do so with adequate knowledge of the traditions from which they deviate and they must be able to explain in a rational way why they do not accept these traditions.

Where academic activities are legitimately performed, then academic freedom is called for. Academic freedom is the freedom to perform academic actions. Academic actions are teaching, research, and the publication of the results of research and reflection.

The need for academic freedom is not pressing for most academics, who in the substance of their teaching and in the results of their research conform with the consensus formed around the prevailing tradition. The need for academic freedom arises in the case of those who do not conform with that consensus. But it is not just any nonconformity with the consensus that is entitled to the right of academic freedom.

The right to academic freedom is for the protection of the rank and file of the academic profession who wish to tell the truth as they see it in their teaching and research within the university. It is also for the protection of those who wish to speak or act outside the university for some political or religious cause which is entirely legal, even if distasteful to their administrative superiors, academic peers, external journalists, and politicians.

The justification of academic freedom is that it protects the moral and intellectual integrity of the teacher. It protects the teacher's exercise of his (or her) intellectual powers in the search for and the exposition of truth. Even if he only rediscovers already known truths and understands them better as a result of his own studies, he is responding to the academic calling and should be free to do that. If permanent tenure helps in an honest search and exposition, that is its chief, but not its only, justification.

There are certain claims made on behalf of academic freedom and hence of appointment on permanent tenure which are illegitimate or irrelevant. It is, for example, frequently said that originality of discovery and analysis is inhibited or suppressed where there is no right of academic freedom, reinforced by appointment to permanent tenure. I think that this is not straightforward. Most cases of infringement of academic freedom have nothing to do with original thought or discovery. Most academics are not capable of original thought or discovery, but they are nonetheless entitled to academic freedom as long as they are concerned with truth.

Genuine originality really does not need the protection of academic freedom. It can scarcely be suppressed. Genuinely original minds are irrepressible. It is not for the protection of the intellectual freedom of original minds that permanence of tenure in academic appointments is justified. Originality is really beyond the protective and strengthening powers of academic freedom. This does not mean that original minds should be refused appointment on permanent tenure.

The situation in the present century is different from what it was in the nineteenth century. Genuinely original scholars in the field of biblical studies did suffer sanctions for their substantive scholarly work.

In Europe in the nineteenth century there were infringements of the academic freedom proper of great scholars like Ernest Renan, who was dismissed from the chair—a chair on permanent tenure—at the Collège de France for saying that Jesus Christ was "a marvelous man." One of the greatest scholars of modern times, William Robertson Smith, was dismissed from the Free Church College of Aberdeen—a Presbyterian theological seminary. Another, Julius Wellhausen, in 1882 resigned his professorship of Old Testament studies at the University of Greifswald to become an associate professor of Oriental languages at the University of Halle because he felt himself to be under censure for his work on the Old Testament. Wellhausen was not dismissed; he suffered lesser sanctions which infringed on his academic freedom.

There are at present in the United States colleges and universities where adherence to a particular religious doctrine is expected of students and teachers. Teachers who accept appointments at such institutions forswear the right to academic freedom in subjects touched on by the obligatory doctrine.

It is not given to many minds, academic or nonacademic, to be original. Although originality is highly desirable, it cannot be expected that most academics will be original. But they can and must be truthful, that is, they must seek and tell the truth in their teaching and try to discover it in their research. Academic freedom should protect the efforts of academics to be truthful in their teaching and research. That is its justification.

There are certain activities performed (or not performed) by academics which are not entitled to the right of academic freedom. These include repeated and unauthorized failure to meet one's scheduled classes, teaching classes without adequate preparation, falsification of the results of research, telling falsehoods in teaching, plagiarism, claiming to have made observations which were in fact not made, improprieties in relations with students, deliberate distortion and favoritism in marking examinations, teaching subjects which one is not qualified or authorized to teach—for example, a teacher of sociology who devotes many sessions in a course nominally on the family to mathematical genetics, Egyptology, or cosmology. Entering into demonstrated sexual relations with students, or conducting a full-time private business which has no connection with the substance of the subject which he has been appointed to teach, or organizing students to boycott all classes or the classes of particular teachers are clearly not among the activities which an academic should be free to perform. When a teacher is clearly and demonstrably guilty of such derelictions from academic obligations, he (or she) is legitimately subject to sanctions, even though on a permanent appointment. Criminal activities, revolutionary activities, which are proscribed by law are also not to be protected by the right of academic freedom.

The maintenance of what is regarded as an acceptable level of accuracy, of reliability of observation in research, and of rationality in analysis are not protected by the right of academic freedom. A teacher, scholar, or scientist who is censured for very poor quality of performance, cannot legitimately claim against critics the protection of the right of academic freedom.

III

Thus far I have dealt mainly with the right to academic freedom to protect the honest performance of academic actions which diverge from the prevailing academic consensus. Now I shall deal with academic freedom in the sense of the civil freedom of the academic. This variant of academic freedom is justified by the perfectly obvious proposition that academics are citizens. They have the same rights and obligations in the political sphere as ordinary citizens have. They must be perfectly free to express political and other beliefs which other citizens are free to express. They must be free to enter into political association which other citizens are free to enter into. They do not have any obligations which ordinary citizens do not have, except for one, arising from their academic role, which is to speak the truth and not to use the devices of the demagogue. But this is not mandatory.

The right to civil academic freedom does not extend to propaganda for legally prohibited political associations, to membership in prohibited political associations, or to the performance of espionage on behalf of foreign states. In other words, an academic must be as free politically as any other citizen, not more so or less so. Only those actions which are prohibited to other citizens are to be prohibited to academics.

Most of the infringements on the right to academic freedom in the United States have been aimed at the expression of political views and the performance of political activities outside the university but falling within the law. Those who have infringed on the civil freedom of academics have usually been concerned with these extra-academic beliefs and actions.

Most of the cases known to me of infringements on academic freedom were infringements on the civil freedom of academics, and not on their academic freedom proper. I cannot recall any one being dismissed or handicapped in consequence of his (or her) performance as a scientist or scholar for anything published in a learned journal or book. The situation has been slightly different with regard to teaching in the case of teachers lecturing on the theory of evolution in small evangelical Christian colleges.

Harassment of university teachers for their political activities and the use of severe sanctions against them by persons in positions of superior authority—academic administrators, including heads of departments, journalists, politicians and governmental and ecclesiastical authorities—has become very rare in liberal-democratic countries.

It is, however, not because of the existence of permanent tenure that such harassment or constriction has become so rare in liberal-democratic societies. It is rather because universities and scientific knowledge have come to enjoy high esteem in these societies, and because intellectual originality is so highly and widely esteemed that the right to freedom for less original thought, and utterly unoriginal thought as well, has been accorded to academics. This is as it should be.

IV

It is to protect the academic in his freedom to perform activities within the university and outside the university that permanent appointment on tenure is justified. There are other arguments for appointment on permanent tenure which will be dealt with later.

During the period of congressional investigations into communist associations and activities, a small number—larger than it should have been—of academics were accused or suspected of communist associations and activities and were dismissed from the colleges and universities where they taught. They were mainly rather young and most had probably not been appointed on permanent tenure. Perhaps a few were on permanent tenure. However, they were in some cases summarily dismissed by the president of their respective institutions. As far as I can recall, none of them claimed that the institution had acted in breach of contract. No conclusive evidence can be drawn from these instances as to whether appointment on permanent tenure would have protected the academic freedom of the persons in question. I myself doubt it.

The protection of academic freedom is not the only justification for permanent tenure. There are reasonable arguments for permanent tenure which have little to do with academic freedom.

One such argument for permanent tenure is that it gives an academic a sense of security which enables him to devote himself with less distraction to the performance of his proper academic activities, that is, teaching and research. It makes it easier to perform duties of academic citizenship, such as serving on administrative committees, without an uneasy sense of neglecting other academic duties which the academic is under equal obligation to perform. It makes a teacher more self-confident, more self-respecting in his role as a university teacher, in departments where other members have permanent tenure, *de facto* or *de jure*.

Appointment on permanent tenure weakens the impulse of sycophancy. A teacher on permanent tenure is protected from his own tendencies towards cravenness. But one should not overestimate the benefits of permanent tenure in this regard. It does not make silk purses out of a sow's ears any more than it makes creative minds out of persons of middling potentialities.

It is unfortunately true that appointment on permanent tenure often provides protection for the academic who performs improper activities, none of which he is entitled to perform in accordance with the right to academic freedom. There might or might not be good reason for the administrators of the university to inflict sanctions—even very severe ones, such as dismissal—on such a teacher. They are in any case not protected by the right of academic freedom. Such actions by teachers and their toleration by administrators give both permanent tenure and academic freedom bad names.

Permanent tenure is not absolute. Those who are granted it receive it under certain conditions. Its grant presupposes a corresponding obligation. It can be abrogated on "cause," as the letters of appointment at many colleges and universities state. Permanent tenure is not often abrogated because, although there are many abuses or fallings-short of academic obligation, they are difficult to specify and to demonstrate. As a result, many abuses are permitted. They should not be permitted; and where there are good grounds for suspecting that such abuses or fallings-short of academic obligation are occurring, they should be meticulously investigated and assessed. Where they are clearly established and are not rectified, appointment on permanent tenure may legitimately be abrogated.

It is reasonable to assert that permanent tenure actually has negative results.

One argument against permanent tenure is that it allows its beneficiaries to "slack on the job," that is, to take their academic duties lightly. According to this view, if permanent tenure were abolished whole universities and single departments would have more flexibility in their efforts to attain a higher standard of education and research and in their adaptation to new interests, new fields and to new budgetary constraints. It is also said that if there were no permanent tenure, many teachers would not be so ready to neglect their teaching and to do little or no research. It is argued that teachers would be forced to show their mettle. Colleges and universities would be well rid of these idle characters. So it is said.

There is something to this. Teachers who think that their teaching is being closely scrutinized, and that the renewal of their appointments depends on their visible exertions, might indeed try to meet their obligations more adequately. They might spend more time in preparing for their classes; they might be more inclined to keep up with the literature; they might demand more of themselves and their students.

Along the same lines, it is said that the abolition of appointment on permanent tenure would compel persons who do no or little research to do more research and hence to publish more. I think that this argument for abolishing permanent tenure might be true. The amount of research done if permanent tenure were abolished might indeed increase. Nevertheless, I think that the argument is ill-considered. It does not show any understanding that it is high quality in research that is desirable, not just "busy work." A person who does research because of external compulsion is unlikely to do a good job of research. There seems to me to be little sense in compelling persons to do research if they have little appetite and aptitude for it. Research which is done without driving curiosity, without passionate intellectual interest, is not likely to be good research. Such persons would use their talents better if they improved their teaching by preparing their courses better, by "keeping up with the literature," and by revising their courses each year, and so on. But if they are not interested in teaching either and will not exert themselves to improve their teaching, their colleges or universities would be better without them. It may be argued that if they already have permanent tenure, they should be deprived of it. They should be deprived of it not because they cannot do original research or produce original ideas for their students, but because they are not giving their students an adequate account of the body of knowledge for which they are responsible.

It is clear that this has nothing to do with academic freedom. A teacher, as I have said earlier, cannot claim the protection of the right of academic freedom for his neglect of his academic obligations.

The economic argument against permanent tenure has also to be considered. A staff without permanent tenure would be less expensive because it would have fewer older members who are in the higher ranges of salary simply as a result of their long service and automatic increments in salary. This is usually not mentioned by administrators who would like to abolish appointment on permanent tenure for their academic staff. They speak of "greater budgetary flexibility." Nevertheless, despite my suspicion of hypocrisy on the part of administrators, there is something to be said for their contention.

V

Now, if permanent tenure were abolished, so that no new appointments which provide permanent tenure were made after a certain date, there would, in the course of time, be no teachers holding appointments on permanent tenure. This would correspond to the ideal of those who wish to make the universities like free markets in which the most productive benefit and the failures go to the wall. But would this really happen? And if it did happen, would it be desirable?

The result of the system of short-term appointments, if it works as desired by its protagonists, would perhaps be a younger, fresher department in which the newest ideas would have enthusiastic spokesmen, sometimes more enthusiastic than wise. There would be numerous young persons "on the make," eager to get ahead, looking further afield for new and better opportunities for entry into the "major league," as the small number of major universities are called by the ambitious persons who are not content with being in the "minor league."

Would this be beneficial to the departments in which it might take place? There would undoubtedly be more interest in the latest developments which are often, but not always, no more than terminological fads. There would be more enthusiasm and more energy in research and more productivity in research. It might not have the same benefits for the students, who must learn the fundamentals of their subjects as well as "the latest wrinkles."

There is another aspect of the matter which ought to be considered. Most colleges and universities have a small core of devoted teachers who care especially about the institution, its reputation, and its standards. They play an important part but it is a part which is difficult to state explicitly. It is made up of numerous components. One is concern for the well-being of the entire institution; another is the maintenance of a tradition, a recollection of important moments and persons in the history of the institution. These traditions can often be a drag on the adaptation of the institution to new circumstances, but where the institution had in the past some noteworthy moments and some outstanding intellectual figures, it can be a stimulus to striving for the achievement of a higher standard.

In the recent development of American universities—perhaps also the universities of Great Britain and Western Europe—these institutional traditions have been much weakened. Distinctiveness is lost in the process. This has had the result of making the universities more homogenous within each country and internationally. If the academic world is made up of a large number of more or less identical universities, all of them pursuing or being dominated by the same ideas, that will not be beneficial to the teaching of students or to scientific and scholarly activities. (At the same time, it might foster some striking achievements arising from collaboration between scientists in different universities and in different countries.)

VI

Is it desirable in the light of what I have said earlier to abolish appointments on permanent tenure?

My answer to this question is negative. If appointments were for five-year periods and every department had from fifteen to twenty members, there would have to be from three to five reviews each academic session. If the reviews were done thoroughly and conscientiously by committees of about five members each, and if membership in the committees were annually rotated among the members of the department, each member of the committee would have from three to five major reviews each session, to say nothing of the reviews of candidates for new appointment. If the smaller committees made recommendations to the department as a whole, and if some of the members of the latter wished to render a judgment of their own on the recommendations of the smaller committees—which they should do—assessments for the renewal of appointments would make up a larger part of the work of each department.

If assessments are seriously and responsibly carried out, they will entail much reading of the candidates' writings, published and unpublished, interviewing students, and reading the writings of other teachers in the same specialized field in order to have a basis of comparison. In other words, a review of any single candidate would take from two to three weeks of hard work—assuming it were well and conscientiously done.

Meanwhile, the candidates considered in that academic session would be biting their fingernails, waiting for the decision of the committee and the department. Such anxiety is not conducive to the serenity of mind needed for the performance of intellectual tasks. Such anxiety might become pervasive throughout the department. Not only would the candidates be placed in a state of anxiety, but so would the members of the assessment committees—who will naturally want to avoid causing damage to colleagues whom they might like personally and by some of whom they themselves might be judged in the coming years.

In view of the work and nervous strain of the system of quinquennial assessments on both the assessors and the assessed, the system would be difficult to maintain at a high level, year after year, without any prospect of cessation. It would become an unpleasant burden. One response to the strain would be to allow the process of quinquennial assessment to deteriorate into a perfunctory operation which would be taken seriously only occasionally. Most of the reviews would result in almost automatic renewals. Only in a small number of cases in which the candidate was found to be extremely deficient would he (or she) be removed.

If this hypothesis is correct, the departments would not be much improved by the new system. The amount of financial savings, and the flexibility of which academic administrators speak as among the benefits of quinquennial assessment or something like it, would not be very great. Most of the deplored vices of the old arrangement of permanent tenure would remain, and new ones would be added.

VII

All these miscellaneous reflections lead to the conclusion that the unqualified retention of appointments on permanent tenure is not an unmixed good. They lead also to the conclusion that the wholesale jettisoning of appointments on permanent tenure has drawbacks.

I would therefore recommend the retention of appointment on permanent tenure, with a provision for reviews in a small number for individual cases where it seems necessary for the well-being of the institution. In the cases of teachers who have shirked their duties in an arrant way over many years, who have fallen utterly out of touch with their subjects, who do not study and who if they do publish, publish very little and that of very poor quality, even though they have the time and the resources of laboratory space and equipment, libraries, etc., there should be the possibility of creating committees *ad hoc* to review the achievements of the persons in question and making recommendations regarding dismissal or retention and, between those two extremes, intermediate measures such as warning, probation, etc. There would probably not be very many cases requiring such review, but it is certain that there will be some. However, the review of such cases will occur only if administrators, heads of departments, deans, provosts, academic vice presidents and presidents have the strength of character to bring the necessary action.

Hence appointment on permanent tenure should be retained with some of the indicated modifications. The retention of permanent tenure does offer one obstacle to the most severe infringement on academic freedom, which is dismissal. Retention of permanent tenure is, however, no guarantee of the protection of academic freedom from sanctions less severe than dismissal but injurious nonetheless.

Academics must be free to express their views, rationally formulated and based on reasonable evidence, even if they depart from the prevailing tradition. Furthermore, outside the university, they should be as free as any other citizens in a liberal democracy to express their views, orally and in writing, and to join associations and assemblies.

I do not think that either the maintenance or the abolition of permanence of tenure can protect universities and their teachers from the politically motivated sanctions which radical teachers nowadays impose on some of their more traditional academic colleagues in the departments of the humanities of American colleges and universities. The retention of permanent tenure might protect the traditional academics from dismissal—of which I know no instances—but it does not protect them from harassment. The abolition of permanent tenure might render them more vulnerable.

The abolition of permanent tenure would impose unwelcome burdens on academics who would have to assess and be themselves assessed. For that reason, these quinquennial assessments would be likely to degenerate into perfunctory actions in which the appointments of most of the teachers being reviewed would be renewed as a matter of course. For this reason, I anticipate no marked improvement in the effectiveness or conscientiousness of teaching, or any increase in the amount of important research which it is said would result from the abolition of permanent tenure.

What the American academic profession needs is an improvement in its observance of the academic ethic. But that is a different matter—more fundamental and very difficult to bring about. It is unlikely to be brought about by the abolition of permanent tenure. Nor is the retention and expansion of permanent tenure likely to do it.

What might be the effects of any such changes on academic freedom? We know more or less what are the effects of appointment to permanent tenure on academic freedom. In principle, but only in a limited way, it protects the academic freedom of serious teachers, scholars and scientists in their specifically academic activities. It also protects indolent teachers who default on their obligations. It would also have protected the civil freedom of the academics of four decades ago, practically all of whom as communist sympathizers or party members were still within the law.

Would the abolition of appointment on permanent tenure and their replacement by appointment for five-years terms, continuously renewable, make any difference to academic freedom? As far as the universities in Western liberal-democratic countries are concerned, I think that there probably would be no gross differences. It is possible that there would be more pressure for conformity with the dominant intellectual and political views in a department in which assessment is recurrent. In this respect, the proponents of retention of the system of appointment on permanent tenure have an argument in their favor.

At present there is, except in certain departments of universities, a general spirit of toleration. Heads of departments, deans, provosts, presidents, and trustees who used to be very forward in harassing teachers who availed themselves of the civil freedom which other citizens enjoyed, but who did so in a radical direction, are nowadays indifferent if not sympathetic to such expression. And even if they are not indifferent or sympathetic, they are too cowardly to take any repressive initiative which they anticipate would result in a storm of protest by their teaching staff and the local and national press. Given this widespread tolerance, perhaps academic freedom does not need the very limited support it obtains from appointments on permanent tenure.

For one thing, the atmosphere of tolerance such as exists at present might not last. Recently "enfranchised" groups such as emancipationist radicals, African-Americans, homosexuals, deconstructionists, quasi-Marxists, etc., might fall into disfavor once more. They might feel themselves to be constrained to conform with the more traditional ideas in their respective fields. It is possible that their academic freedom—in so far as they do serious academic things—might be somewhat diminished in such a new, at present unforeseeable situation. But as things stand at present, and are likely to stand in the near future, with or without permanent tenure, their freedom to do the kinds of things they are now doing in teaching and publication and in the determination of academic appointment is not likely to be curtailed. This is, I think, deleterious to universities.

In certain departments of the humanities in the United States, at least in the leading universities, the more likely victims of infringement on academic freedom—infringement taking the forms of nonrenewal or harassment—are the exponents of traditional views about the proper objects and procedures of education and research in the humanities. Under present circumstances, those persons are found mostly in the older generation. Newly appointed staff seldom come from this generation. If they are appointed, they are under strong pressure to conform with the now dominant emancipationist outlook. If they do not conform with that outlook, they are also less likely to be granted promotion and permanent tenure so that the protection of academic freedom through permanent tenure would not be available to them.

VIII

There are good arguments for retaining appointments on permanent tenure, but they have to be strengthened against challenges by the recognition that permanent tenure is a bilateral matter. It entails costly and weighty obligations on both sides.

The traditional discussion of academic freedom in the United States and Europe has located the dangers to academic freedom in the administrators of universities and in certain parts of society outside the universities—church leaders, politicians, businessmen, governmental officials, and newspaper editors or publishers. Historically there is much truth in this account. In recent years however the threat to academic freedom has lain largely within the academic staffs of the universities themselves. I refer to the application of political criteria in assessments regarding retention and promotion. (Decisions regarding new appointments are also affected, but they do not come under the right of academic freedom.) New criteria are now being asserted, namely, sympathy with certain views of the third world, class conflict, race relations, sexual differences, and a critical attitude towards the traditions of the Western European-North American "canon" of outstanding works. It is especially in the departments of modern literature and languages, and to a lesser extent in history and social sciences such as sociology, political science and anthropology, that it is now regarded by academics as appropriate to apply political criteria in the assessment of the merits of works and of the scholars who write them and who write about them. Candidates for retention and promotion are assessed by the criteria of "political correctness" as it is called in the United States today. (The introduction of these political criteria in appointment bears a close relationship to the application of political criteria in restrictions on academic freedom. In both instances intellectual criteria are being set aside.)

It is possible that the present dominant groups would be just as offensive to academic freedom were they subjected to periodic assessments as conditions of reappointment as they are under conditions of permanent tenure. Since they are the most energetic and aggressive in the setting forth of their views and in declaring their enmities, it is likely that they would dominate the committees and protect their own kind. They would be infringing on the postulate of academic freedom, in which the concern for truthfulness in teaching and research is fundamental.

What about the academic freedom of those with whose views they disagree? As regards the ultimate sanction of dismissal, no cases are known to me of the dismissal of a proponent of the views they dislike. But they would not necessarily desist from the infringements on academic freedom which fall short of dismissal. After all, they contend that there is no validity in the criterion of truthfulness; therefore they nullify the entire category of academic freedom proper. Nor would their own persecutory conduct be diminished by the knowledge that they were themselves to be subjected to review every fifth year. Their like-minded colleagues would see to it that they were protected. Their more traditional colleagues, if their present conduct offers any guidance, would not have the courage to insist that the radicals conform with the traditional academic ethic. Furthermore, university administrators being what they are—most of them are Benito Cerenos—would not have the courage to countermand the actions of politicized review committees.

In those institutions in which there is some approximation to "faculty self-government," I doubt whether the abolition of appointments on permanent tenure would make much difference to the extent of academic freedom. As far as administrators are concerned, they are in the major universities so subservient to the desires of the teaching staff, so fearful of aggressive criticism, that they could not be counted upon to act against the wishes of their teaching staff. The abolition of permanent tenure would therefore not restrict the academic freedom of the dominant group. But, on the other side, it might diminish the academic freedom of the minority of traditional teachers of English, German, history, and so on.

10

Limitations on the Freedom of Research and Teaching in the Social Sciences

I

The central interest of this essay is in the use of sanctions against social scientists in colleges and universities in the United States whose scientific and pedagogical work runs counter to the evaluations dominant in their institution or in the wider community. Restrictions on the *public* utterance and activity of the social scientists, however widespread and important these restrictions are, are not of direct concern, and come in for consideration only as they have a bearing on teaching and research activities. Nor are we to deal with the numerous disputes in academic life arising out of questions of tenure, advancement, rivalry among the faculty, and administrative conflicts, except as they are directly relevant to the freedom of research and teaching. Heavy teaching burdens, inadequacies of staff and equipment, and financial hindrances, though they are certainly very significant as obstacles to research in the social sciences, will not be brought into this discussion unless they appear as consciously used implements of a policy oriented toward the prevention of the investigation and the pedagogical exposition of certain subject matters and problems.

In short, we shall treat here only one segment of the broad complex of situations designated as academic freedom, namely, restrictions on the freedom of research and teaching in the social sciences in the higher schools, understanding by the freedom of research and teaching the probability of the noninvocation of sanctions against persons treating particular subject matters, propositions, or problems at the level of average competence obtaining within the discipline in question. *

II

In a society lacking an inclusive consensus, numerous groups strive to create a consensus which will guide the actions of the other members of that society in a manner conforming with the values of the groups in question. Practically all of the politically, economically, and culturally relevant values of the validity of which they attempt to persuade nonmembers are based not only on certain ultimate valuations but on certain assumptions about the factual structure of the social world. It is the peculiar situation of the social sciences that the objects of their investigations are those very conditions and relationships toward which, in a variety of ways, a central part of the program of every group is evaluatively oriented. This is true whether the group has already "arrived" and is seeking to maintain or to consolidate its position, or whether it has not yet attained the status or goods which it desires. Purely factual propositions, established with the best techniques now available and asserted with the most impartial intentions are subject to attack from interested parties who feel that some of their claims have been shown to be either less practicable or less legitimate than they had hitherto claimed because the facts are not as they say they are.

Every scientific proposition which has a bearing on practical issues tends to become "someone's" proposition. A scientific analysis of the structure of a political party will soon enter public circulation, either through the channels of that party itself, if it happens to discover and present facts which will make that party the object of favorable evaluations, or through the channels of the opposing parties if it presents facts which are likely to cause the analyzed party to be judged negatively by the public for whose support the parties compete. Analyses which reveal the impracticability of certain norms are fortunate if they pass unopposed.

The same is true of scientific analyses which diverge from certain conceptions concerning historical personages or events, from an identification with which certain groups believe that they derive their status and moral value as well as the security of their economic position. "Facts" have indeed become all the more crucial, since with the more or less universal acceptance of a system of hedonistic humanitarian values as the ultimate source of legitimization, conflicting groups (insofar as they do not resort to violence) must appeal to the "facts" to legitimate their divergent immediate ends.

It is for these reasons that the reprisals, obstructions, and criticisms which have been directed by various groups against the social sciences throughout their existence as academic disciplines in the colleges and universities of the United States, have by no means been aimed exclusively at the assertion of value judgments which many social scientists have felt were included in their pedagogical and civic obligations. They have been aimed equally at the factual analysis of situations, particular conceptions of which are regarded by interested parties as essential to the validation of their preferences and the fulfillment of their "factual" expectations or plans. Of course, often the allegations about pernicious doctrines taught and obnoxious objects investigated were in fact instigated by disapproval of statements made in public places outside academic confines.

III

Restrictive action may be taken in almost any social science field, but the highest concentration of such cases has, in the last years, occurred in such fields as the sociology of the family, social disorganization, social psychology, labor economics, race relations, and social origins (social evolution). Restrictions motivated by dogmatically held values such as those involved in religious beliefs and sexual and racial attitudes are likely to be directed not only against specific propositions but against a subject matter as a whole. Restrictions motivated by pragmatically held values, on the other hand, tend to disregard subject matters, and to be alert for specific propositions within the subject matter field, and the way in which they are asserted. Depending on the social context, objects which are responded to on a pragmatic basis at one time and place, may be treated dogmatically at another.[1]

The more dogmatic the manner in which the values touched on in a given field of scientific work are held, the greater is the probability of interference. Furthermore, it might safely be said that the greater the dogmatism of the social environment, the earlier in the process of intellectual production will be the interference. Thus, for example, in cases where inquiries into sexual attitudes were interfered with, the restrictive action took place immediately upon discovery; whereas in economics, toward which usually a more pragmatic attitude is maintained, restrictions largely occur after several years or at the point of publication (as in the Levine-Montana case discussed below).

Economics

Economics, thanks to the increased explicitness of ethical neutrality in the field and the increased capacity for instrumental as over against dogmatic thinking on the part of influential businessmen, has experienced a decrease in the proportion of attacks made in response to threats to the mores. Pragmatic interest in the teaching of economics has led to attempts at restrictive action whenever the position of the predominant groups in our society has been so threatened that vigorous defensive measures were deemed necessary by them. The limitations on academic freedom in economics have passed through three high points: (1) the first great attack on the plutocracy at the end of the last and the beginning of the present century (Populism and muckraking); (2) the post–World War period when the fear of communism was at a maximum; and (3) the deepest period of the post-1929 depression and the years immediately following, when the plutocracy organized against the New Deal reforms.

Since the labor situation has been continuously in the forefront of attention, it has been the social scientist specializing in labor problems at whom sanctions of varying degrees of severity have most frequently been directed.

However, monetary and other problems have frequently been the center of discord. In the period of public concern with the bimetallism issue, proponents of free silver coinage did not escape unscathed. The cases of Professor Edward A. Ross at Stanford University, President E. B. Andrews at Brown University, and Professor John R. Commons at Syracuse stand as testimony to the severity with which the dominant classes of the period met this challenge.

Similarly, economists dealing with public utilities in a manner which, given the reigning values, would be conducive to an unfavorable judgment have often found themselves in unpleasant situations. Professor E. W. Bemis in the first decade of the existence of the University of Chicago and Professors Leo S. Rowe and E. J. James at the University of Pennsylvania at the end of the last century were among those whose conclusions regarding public utilities stimulated sharp opposition. (The late Professor J. L. Laughlin denied that the Bemis case was one of reprisal for statements within his principal sphere of competence, and other informants have agreed that it was not just a case of interference with freedom of research and teaching. What is relevant here, however, is that the personal issues involved would probably not have risen to the surface had Bemis not held the views that he did about the Chicago traction franchises.) Recent instances of reprisal for assertions on this subject have not come to the attention of the investigator.[2]

The fiscal policies of governments as objects of study have also met with resistance when the policies which research implied were regarded as dangerous. Illustrative of this type is the case of Professor Louis Levine and the University of Montana in 1919. Professor Levine had completed a series of studies on state tax problems which indicated that the mining enterprises bore a disproportionately small share of the state tax burden.[3] Although he had had the support of the university administration and a promise of university assistance in publication, he was informed that it would be inadvisable to publish the results of his research. Although no evidence can be given as to the precise number of such cases, there can be little doubt that the treatment of fiscal problems has been relatively free from extrascientific control.

Sociology

Perhaps because of the diversity of attitude among members of the academic profession and between the academic and the layman as to what is factually correct and politically practicable in sociological analysis over the country as a whole, there are more instances of interference in that field than in economics. Sociology is as yet a discipline in which professional consensus is rather restricted and in which there is a great divergence between what is generally accepted within the field and what is insisted on by lay persons whose conceptions of society are derived from traditional definitions of the situation or from interests which are still too unsophisticatedly viewed.

Thus, while economists are usually attacked (for pragmatic reasons) by businessmen and by groups supported by businessmen or those who identify themselves with businessmen such as politicians and university administrators, sociologists are open to attack from any individual or group which abhors what is taught in sociology and fears that it will bring about a departure from established ways of thinking and acting (dogmatic and pragmatic considerations).

Further, since there is such a great cultural difference between city and country, between metropolis and small town, and between the North and the South, it is not surprising that sociologists trained in advanced departments of sociology in the great private and state universities should encounter difficulties when they take up posts in the less liberal areas. Professor Howard K. Beale has observed that "in many communities conservatism, either religious or economic or political, is so strongly intrenched that no graduate of a liberal university can obtain a position. This has long been true of the University of Chicago in fundamentalist parts of the South, because it allegedly destroys the religion of its students."[4]

In this connection we may cite the complaint of one sociologist teaching in the South, that a book which is completely acceptable in the North was objected to by his superior. Classical sociological works such as W. I. Thomas' *The Unadjusted Girl*, Shaw's *The Natural History of a Delinquent Career*, and others have created tense moments for some sociologists. Teaching institutions are dominated by strict mores regarding the mentionability of sexual subjects.

What is taught about blacks and about race relations by the best contemporary sociologists has not been acceptable to every part of certain Southern college communities, and at least one teacher of sociology has been "put on the carpet" for the assertion that there was no evidence of biological deterioration due to intermarriage between blacks and whites. The pedagogical procedure of student tours through various sections of the city for purposes of sociological observation has contributed to the dismissal of at least two well-known sociologists and has embarrassed others.

Sex

Inquiry into sexual attitudes has frequently been an object of repressive measures. Thus, two persons were dropped from the faculty of Oklahoma Baptist University for using a questionnaire containing what President W. W. Phelan called "a vile set of questions on sexual life."[5] Similar action was taken against members of the University of Missouri faculty for participation in the distribution of a questionnaire on sex mores.[6] A specialist on the family, preparing a work on divorce, encountered the displeasure of his colleagues because he interviewed divorced persons. Another sociologist, at a large privately endowed institution, found his situation becoming difficult due to his prosecution of a study of homosexuality. When he finally published it in a foreign journal, resentment rose even higher. The author of a reputable book on prostitution was regarded uneasily by the administration of the eminent Southern university where he taught, and the chancellor insisted on examining the reading lists for his course on social disorganization. The author of a highly competent book on divorce was the object of suspicion at a large Western state university.

> The president has objected to any discussion of sex matters in my courses on "Social Pathology" and "The Family." For example I was asked if I could not omit the chapters in the text by Queen and Mann, *Social Pathology*, entitled "Prostitution" and "Illegitimacy." The President took out of the College Library last year several books which I had the Library order for parallel reading in connection with these two courses, because he considered them improper for students, especially girls.

So writes a professor of sociology in a small college in the South.[7] The number of illustrations could be multiplied.

Social Evolution

Social scientists whose activity involves a relativization of modern beliefs and institutions, as is, for example, required in the study of social evolution, have at times been subjected to severe attacks. This is notably the situation in the South and in small denominational schools where the attachment of the administrators, the trustees, and the community at large to the biblical version of the early history of human society is still intense.

The case of Professor J. M. Mecklin at Lafayette College provides an especially pointed illustration. Professor Mecklin was dismissed in 1913 from his Presbyterian college for applying the "genetic and functional method" to the history of religion.[8] One trustee stated that the objection to Dr. Mecklin's teaching was based upon his use of the doctrine or theory of evolution in his discussion of the growth of religion.[9] A correspondent said that the president of the college had declared, "the doctrine set forth in certain textbooks adopted by Professor Mecklin, viz., Angell on Psychology, Dewey and Tufts on Ethics, McDougall on Social Psychology, and James on the Psychology of Religious Experience, were a departure from the doctrines that had been taught in the college."[10]

The consequences of this cultural differential are nowhere more clear than in those instances where conformity with the tenets of a particular theology is demanded, either explicitly or implicitly, of all staff members. Conflicts over the early course of social development are especially likely in denominational schools,[11] although it should be recognized that many denominational schools do not require a rigid adherence to their theological principles. Nonetheless, the study of the early condition of mankind and of the morally relativistic analysis of the moral codes of non-Christian societies has often caused teachers to be brought to book. One has the impression that as late as the 1920s college teachers were still being warned to desist from such views. The incidence was especially great in the South and in undenominational colleges in the Middle West.

It seems safe to say that within the larger universities, this attitude, which was characteristic of the nineteenth century, has already been transcended, so that interference on such grounds is now highly improbable. At the same time, the increased secularization of the formative centers of public opinion in the metropolis makes outside interference in this respect almost negligible.

IV

Thus far we have considered taboos erected out of moral, religious, political, economic, and "personal" considerations. Quite different in characteracter are those taboos which are exercised on intellectual-doctrinal grounds. In a university where metaphysical first principles are espoused by the controlling administrators, empirical research such as has been carried on in the social sciences in the past two decades is frowned upon. In social science faculties where historical and general speculative work is carried on, precise statistical investigations limited to rather specialized subjects of a contemporary character do not meet with favor, and in other faculties where exact quantitative research is favored by those in authority, broadly conceived studies not relying exclusively on statistical procedures are discouraged.

Such situations are perhaps generally infrequent and are most improbable in disciplines which have developed to the point where the various contending methodologies and techniques have had an opportunity to demonstrate their fruitfulness in such a way that consensus obtains among the recognized leaders in the field. In the less well-established disciplines, where a methodological anarchy tends to prevail, this situation is more likely to emerge. It may also be expected where personal rivalry exists. The operation of sanctions that maintain these "taboos" does not culminate in dismissal or threat of dismissal or in intimidation. The sanctions consist, however, in the creation of an "atmosphere" and in the provision of models to which students who seek advancement conform.

What is taboo in one type of institution is, as has been seen, by no means necessarily taboo in all others. And the same type of research or teaching or publication is not always equally outlawed in all departments of a given institution. The threshold of prohibition fluctuates in height from one situation to another. A large state or private university with a liberal tradition, such as Chicago, Harvard, or Minnesota, will only rarely invoke sanctions against members. Yet during crisis situations, as in war time, persons who have been a minor source of irritation to the administration or to civic groups during peace time will be proceeded against under justification of the emergency situation. The level of instruction is also a relevant factor. Prohibitions are almost always confined to the undergraduate level of instruction, so that teachers of the social sciences feel less constrained and apprehensive in graduate instruction.

A large city, and especially a metropolis, is more favorable to freedom in the social sciences than a smaller community. The research activities of the social scientist are much less likely to become the object of off-campus gossip in a big city where the college or university is not in everyone's eye than in a small town where most of the population is in one way or another connected or familiar with the school. The larger the city, the greater are the opportunities for off-campus contact for the faculty, and the fewer are the opportunities for that particular form of intrafaculty surveillance and gossip which has an inhibiting influence on the study and teaching of unpopular subjects. But on the other hand, the large cities offer the threat of sensation-mongering or red-baiting press campaigns, such as those to which the country was treated by the Hearst papers in 1935.

Among the conditions which are relevant in determining whether or not sanctions will be invoked against a given utterance, is the manner of exposition. The cultivation of special forms of obscurity which permit the assertion of what would otherwise cause consternation seems to have been pursued by Thorstein Veblen. Other persons have succeeded in escaping restriction through a careful avoidance of the dramatic. Matter-of-factness and absence of rhetorical emphasis seem to be indispensable accompaniments of the maintenance of freedom of teaching and research in certain institutions.

V

No discussion of the varying conditions under which prohibitions are made effective may disregard the "mixed case." Reference has already been made to cases in which the research or pedagogical activity in itself would not alone have led to punitive action. Persons who transgress in only one way, and who are entirely respectable in every other phase of their activity, are still relatively secure. A Marxist who teaches sociology and who is a "good fellow" has a more secure position than a Marxist who is equally scholarly and competent as a teacher but who is not so pleasing socially. A Marxist who participates in outside organizational activities is less secure than one who attends exclusively to his academic concerns. A man who investigates taboo subjects can less well afford to disregard the moral or social conventions of the campus community than those who do not.

An associate professor of economics in a Southern university was engaged in a study of liquor consumption during the twenties. There was originally some resistance to his appointment and later a threat of discharge because of this investigation, but the threat was suspended when an agreement was reached that his title as a member of the university in question would not appear in the printed report. Certain students who wished to avoid his course started rumors about him, and this revived the threat of dismissal. A colleague summarized the situation as follows:

> I am also of the opinion that the officers of the University were greatly biased by the prohibition study and that they were to a degree awaiting an opportunity to dispose of Mr. X. . . . An overt act not appearing, they decided to take advantage of the manufactured student unrest, and expressed it in terms of not "fitting in." I am also of the personal opinion that the failure of Mr. X's wife to "fit into" the women's community was a prejudicial factor. Mrs. X has been teaching at a Negro School in the community, and she is lacking, apparently, in certain social qualities that faculty wives demand.[12]

Professor E. A. Ross's caution to the independent-minded academic seems to provide an adequate characterization of the situation:

> You'll have to live much more straightly than your harmless colleagues. You'll have to pay your bills promptly, be content with your wife, shun "wild" parties, give your students the best you have, meet your classes with clock-like regularity, avoid rows with your colleagues, conform to all the university rules, tell good stories, be able to laugh at yourself, and stand "razzing" good-humoredly.[13]

In brief, the degree to which one may deviate from accepted viewpoints or interests varies with the standing of the particular person. The higher the scientific, personal, or "social" status, the greater the range of freedom in specifically intellectual activities. For those who do not have the requisite esteem of their colleagues and the community, statements which would pass unremarked in the case of more widely accepted persons might well lead to disaster.

VI

In the "mixed cases," the precipitating factor often also provides the necessary public justification for the sanction when it is thought inadvisable to make explicit the original and central consideration. In denominational schools or in other institutions where the administrators are not entirely devoted to the freedom of research and teaching, they feel no necessity for dissembling their motives by claiming that the person in question did not conform with standards the binding character of which is conceded by everyone.

Where administrators do feel an obligation to refrain from interference with heterodox research or teaching, or where they perceive the existence of such an attitude in influential sections of the community, they attempt to avoid charges which point at nothing more than intellectual heterodoxy. Under these conditions, the application of sanctions is likely to involve charges that the person is "incompetent," "a troublemaker," presents "personality problems," does not have a "scholarly attitude," is "disloyal" and "generally disharmonious." Curtailment of the budget also can offer a justification for dismissing teachers who are not entirely agreeable.

On the whole, however, it appears that the more dogmatic the manner is in which values are held, the greater the probability is that restrictive actions will be legitimated directly in terms of those values. On the other hand, when values are held pragmatically or instrumentally, and scientific assertions are regarded as pernicious not in themselves but rather in their repercussions, there is greater probability that restrictive actions will be legitimated in terms of other values (masking).

Masking is especially probable when the repercussions of a scientific investigation or classroom statement are likely to be distasteful to a special group but not to the public at large. In such cases, those who feel their interests threatened and consequently seek to invoke sanctions against the investigator or teacher are especially apt to disguise their motives by an attack on other matters about which the public can be aroused. Recourse to pretexts which are actually of secondary importance is likely in areas where attitudes of intellectual tolerance are widely diffused in the relevant sections of the public, and where accordingly restrictive actions against intellectual activity would arouse some resistance and ultimately a withdrawal of support.

Another factor which influences the chances that the justification for restrictive action will be masked rather than avowed is the degree of ethical neutrality prevailing in a field. Where ethical judgments are explicitly asserted in the classroom, the administrator might feel a greater justification in taking action against a teacher than where the teaching is purely analytical, even though distasteful. In tolerant communities, there is apt to be an especially strong aversion for the invocation of sanctions against strictly analytical work, and the administrator who wishes to take action must find a legitimation which will be more acceptable publicly. Accordingly, charges like "incompetence" and "administrative necessity," which find a universal acceptance, are the ones most likely to be used.

When masking is required, the "incompetence" charge is preferred where the degree of intellectual consensus within the field is relatively low, while "administrative necessity" is chosen where consensus is high and where accordingly charges of incompetence would soon be denied by an important section of the profession.

VII

Every effective prohibition involves a sanction. This section of the report will analyze the various types of sanctions (*methods*) and the *agencies* by which they are initiated and administered. Steps taken against social scientists may be classified into (a) primary, that is, those which operate directly on the individual in the sense that they represent official or unofficial punitive measures of the administration or faculty of the school directed against the "guilty" one, and (b) secondary, that is, those which are initiated by groups other than administration or faculty, but which operate directly as sanctions through intimidation and indirectly through transformation into primary sanctions. Secondary sanctions, which comprise newspaper agitation, complaints of individual alumni, parents, and students, and the activities of civic, religious, political, and legislative bodies, usually aim at the initiation of a primary sanction.

Dismissal

Of the primary sanctions, dismissal is the most decisive. Dismissal is especially likely to occur when pressure from outside sources is very great. Agitation from outside the institution for punitive measures almost always calls for dismissal. The period elapsing between the time at which the decision to dismiss the faculty member is arrived at and the point at which his connection with the institution is completely severed varies from a few days to several years. A rather frequent procedure is to inform the person to be dismissed that his teaching duties are to cease at the end of the current academic year, but that his salary will continue through the following year.

This type of consideration seems usually to be reserved for those who have attained a rank beyond instructorship and who have accordingly already served for a number of years. It is highly likely, furthermore, that such financial considerateness is a luxury which more impecunious institutions cannot afford, and these, therefore, simply notify the person in question that his services will not be required after the current academic year.

Abrupt dismissal in mid-term is a practice which can be indulged in only by administrators who have no reputation for judiciousness and liberalism to maintain. Accordingly, such dismissals are most infrequent in the large, wealthy institutions with established positions as centers of intellectual eminence and administrative restraint.

Finally, in institutions which would seem otherwise immune from the practice of precipitous dismissal, a severe crisis which is thought to threaten the entire society is likely to be the condition for dismissal without more than a few days' notice.

Threat of Expulsion

The threat of expulsion is also employed as a means of silencing a particular viewpoint. Instances of this which have been discovered are confined to small institutions which are not outstanding for either their educational or their scientific standards. Such procedures are usually followed only by tactless administrators lacking in experience. They usually involve teaching, since the institutions in which such actions are taken do not allow much time or opportunity for research by their faculties. In none of the more important universities which are famous for the social research done under their auspices has such a barrier been encountered. Intimations that it would be tactically unwise to investigate certain aspects of homosexuality and divorce have been found in one large university, but the sanctions did not proceed further than general social unpleasantness.

Schools like the University of Pittsburgh, which maintain a system of annual reappointment delayed until some time after the customary date of reappointment, use this system as a means of keeping their faculty members in leash. "As is to be expected, the evidence shows that it (the obtaining system of reappointment) has brought into the lives of the men and women of the faculty . . . acute anxiety, worry and fear."[14] This insecurity is aggravated by the fact that the renewal notification sometimes has appended to it a very menacing and ambiguous note which says nothing specific but which intimidates that the coming year may be the recipient's last year at the University of Pittsburgh.[15]

Nonpromotion

The blocking of the normal course of the teacher's and investigator's career by withholding promotion and financial advancement is an additional technique. This technique has precedence over dismissal in institutions where attitudes of toleration are not entirely absent in matters of intellectual disagreement or where there is an intense aversion for the unpleasant type of publicity which usually accompanies dismissals. Where neither of these preconditions is present, it is necessary that the degree of heterodoxy should not be extraordinarily large if nonpromotion is to be preferred to dismissal as the sanction.

Promotions may be either refused entirely or granted only after a much longer lapse of time than is customarily the case. In both cases, but especially in the former, nonpromotion is to be regarded as an implicit notification to modify one's intellectual conduct in the direction of greater conformity with orthodoxy or to look elsewhere for employment. While nonpromotion and the perception of the possibility of nonpromotion are important factors in extending the academic territory ruled by orthodoxy, they are not infallible devices; for if an instructor or an assistant professor decides that the results of his analyses or the problems that interest him are worth more to him than a promotion to a higher position, and if the school which employs him, though obviously intolerant, is not so intolerant as to dismiss him for his pertinacity, he may continue to expound his views and to investigate conventionally unapproved subjects or problems.

Selection

The process of determining what ideas shall come to expression and what shall remain unexpressed is, moreover, at work even before the teaching stage of the career is attained. From the stimulation and recognition offered in the first year of graduate studies to first appointment as a faculty member and subsequent promotion, a process of selection goes on which, other qualities being equal, offers the best chances for ascent to the man whose ideas are in conformity with those held by his superiors. The choice of graduate fellows and the distribution of assistantships always provide the possibility for eliminating the student who deviates from some of the intellectual conventions of the academic social sciences.[16] When new appointments to a faculty are to be made, it is only to be expected that the candidates will be carefully scrutinized and that those who promise to be embarrassing to the institution will be looked upon less warmly.[17] In consequence, very many teachers in American colleges are able to feel that their freedom is unlimited, simply because the process whereby they and their colleagues arrived at their present positions operated in such a way as to select out persons to whom the intellectual actions which might lead to sanctions do not have the slightest appeal.

Intimation of Sanctions

Intimidation of sanctions rather than their actual application is another method which frequently produces compliance. Taking the form either of *warning* or of *counsel*, it is often sufficient to remind a transgressor of the dangers involved in his present tendency in order to secure greater conformity. This is sometimes done through a conference in which either an order to desist is issued by the administrator or the matter is merely discussed by the administrator indicating the sources of his uneasiness and advising a certain moderation. The degree of formality can, however, be much slighter and the sanction no less effective. A remark from the head of the department or from an older colleague who is in no way officially inspired by who has had long experience in the academic world, may sometimes suffice, and a word of caution from a friend on the staff who points out the fate of a more recalcitrant person at the same or another institution, may be all that is necessary to increase conformity. The following statement by Dr. Louis Levine, in connection with the prohibition against publication of his taxation study, is illustrative of this procedure:

> Chancellor Elliott did not claim that his new policy gave him the right to forbid me to publish my monograph privately. He argued with me that it would be better for me not to publish it. He told me that "The Interests" were determined to crush out all liberal thought, and that if I published the monograph, an attack would be made on me generally: that the newspapers of the State would not give me a fair hearing . . . that the very fact of my being brought up for trial would ruin my professional reputation and would make it impossible for me to get another position anywhere in country. . . .The chancellor claimed that he wanted to keep me at the university and that he was advising me not to publish my book in order to protect me.[18]

Uncordiality

A general "social unpleasantness" manifested toward those who have broken the taboos is an occasional instrument for obtaining conformity. In one university the members of a department of sociology were advised to shun one of their colleagues who had investigated a forbidden subject. The one person in the department who refused to follow this advice endangered his own position. This lack of cordiality sometimes takes the form of open though unofficial hostility when the man's colleagues feel that his failure to conform to the values of the community has placed the institution in a difficult situation and made their own positions less secure against outside attacks. The boycott is not likely to be applied to persons who enjoy high status among their colleagues. Naturally, the extent to which this uncordiality does silence the transgressor depends very much on the psychic dependence of the person involved, on the environment, and on his devotion to his scientific views.[19] Accordingly, the chances for the success of a boycott are affected by the size of the community and the opportunity which it affords for convivial relations outside the faculty.

Obstructions

Of a more official sort among the primary sanctions, and likewise more substantial in character, are those actions coming under the head of obstructions. In research, this appears chiefly as a withholding of funds. However, it so happens that the institutions in which funds are available for social research are probably the most liberal in the country. In the limited investigation possible for this report, only one attempt to withhold funds from an applicant on extrascientific grounds was discovered.[20] Decisive action by an influential member of the committee quickly quashed this attempt. Here too the possibility exists for repressive measures based on doctrinal or scientific-theoretical considerations,[21] the chances for such withholding being greatest in those fields or disciplines where professional consensus is slightest. The monopolistic attitudes of individuals or departments toward research on certain subject matters sometimes presents a danger to freedom of research on these subjects by younger colleagues or by persons in neighboring disciplines.

Heavy teaching schedules are sometimes mentioned in popular discussion as a type of obstruction to interfere with research on taboo subjects. No evidence of this has been turned up, and the presumption is against it, since in the larger universities where considerable research is carried on, obstructions to research activity rarely occur, while in the smaller colleges very little research work is done, and teaching burdens are usually heavy for other reasons.

There have been cases where courses teaching "unsound doctrine" have been scheduled for hours inconvenient for students or have been made to run at exactly the same hours as certain courses required of all students. The consequence of this is of course exactly as intended: the students are kept from "infection," and the instructor comes to appreciate that he is not one of the favored sons of the institution.

Secondary sanctions are effective either by galvanizing into action the formal administrative machinery of the college or university or by bringing into play the more informal "coordinating" procedures such as counseling, cautioning, avoidance, intimidation, and "self-coordination."

Patriotic Organizations

The most forceful form of secondary sanction is the campaign waged by civic, religious, business, and patriotic organizations. Of these campaigns there is no scarcity. Patriotic organizations are perhaps the most vehement and energetic. These organizations react even in situations where the trustees of a small denominational college would find no cause for alarm. Stimulated by and stimulating the sensation-seeking press, these organizations seek to focus the attention of the authorities—be they state legislators, the trustees, or the university administration itself—on what they consider derelictions within the institution.

The movement for loyalty oaths, although by no means aimed exclusively or even primarily at research activities, is only one phase of the repressive activity of such groups as the Daughters of the American Revolution, the American Legion, the Veterans of Foreign Wars, and other patriotic organizations.[22] A protest by the Sons of the American Revolution against Professor R. E. Turner was a contributing factor in bringing Chancellor Bowman to a decision to dismiss him.[23] Professor William Schaper was dismissed from the University of Minnesota on the basis of "information" supplied by an informant of the Public Safety Commission, a patriotic society of the war period.[24] Veblen's *Nature of Peace* was assailed by Henry A. Wise Wood, chairman of the Conference Committee on National Preparedness, who declared that "professors like Veblen must be driven from the colleges."[25]

Other Outside Forces

Other important outside sources of interference are to be found in the parents of students and in alumni and businessmen and ministers unattached to the school. Chancellor Bowman of Pittsburgh charged that the complaints which caused him to dismiss Professor Turner came principally from parents and ministers.[26] When Professor H. A. Miller was dismissed from Ohio State University, the recurring complaints of parents and others were put forward as among the reasons for the action. "From his very first year here, complaints were received from parents of students in his classes and from others about his teaching on the relations between classes and on domestic relations."[27]

The Illinois State Legislature investigation into the University of Chicago in 1935 was precipitated by a prominent local businessman and the zeal of the Hearst press. Businessmen who feel that the bases of their existence are being questioned at the university, and ministers, especially fundamentalists, who become agitated by the naturalistic analysis of social development and social organization, are among the most sensitive to any laxity in the reinforcement of conventional social ideas. They are quick to bring their misgivings to the attention of the authorities of the institution, as well as to carry on an outside agitation. Alumni whose induction into the detached scientific outlook during their student days was left unperfected are also to be included in the list of those who have at times demanded the silencing of teachers and investigators in the social sciences. The businessmen alumni of one of the greatest American universities were so perturbed by the economics taught to the undergraduates that they organized a committee to prepare a textbook to be used in undergraduate instruction there. The economics department of that institution is, however, still governing itself.

There is no evidence as to whether the alumni tend to be more sensitive to deviations in institutions which are located in large cities and where consequently a larger proportion of the alumni are quite close to the school after graduation, or whether they are more responsive in schools in smaller "college towns," from which they are usually further removed but to which they are often bound by primary group ties.

VIII

Movements for sanctions initiated outside the college or university vary in the extent of their success. Occasionally some are able to bring about dismissal; others have been instrumental in the decision of legislative or administrative bodies to conduct inquiries into the content of faculty teaching. The Walgreen-Hearst Illinois Senate investigation of the University of Chicago in 1935 was of this character, and on this particular occasion the president of the university and some of the professors made very pronounced statements in defense of their teaching practices and emphatically denied the charges made against them. The university was exonerated, but two of the professors were censured. What was significant here was the action of the president and administrators of the university in defending its staff members. In contrast with this situation was that at the University of Missouri, where neither the president nor the administration attempted to defend several members of the staff who were attacked by the press and civic bodies.

A similar differentiation in response is to be found in the treatment of complaints coming from individuals. In some schools they are taken at their face value and made the basis of censure or even more far-reaching action by the authorities of the school. In a small college town in New England the members of the board of trustees received an anonymous letter charging several of the economics instructors with radicalism. One member of the board of trustees sent this to the president suggesting that one of the men in question be silenced or dropped from the staff. The president advised the instructor to avoid such utterances in the future. In another school an extrauniversity complaint was made the basis for immediate action without even an adequate hearing being given to the accused faculty member, or any serious examination being made of the reliability of the complainant.

In some schools, in contrast with the above, complaints from the outside are carefully sifted[28] and, when considered worthy of answer, are brought to the attention of the person complained about, who then has the opportunity of vindicating himself. In other instances, the head of the department himself prepares a statement to meet the charge. An excellent example of a statement in which the chairman of the department comes to the defense of his younger colleagues is contained in the following excerpts from a letter written in response to a request by the university president for information relative to a complaint which had reached his office:

> You say that "sometimes an instructor is criticized as being very loose in his thinking and very irresponsible in his statements and sometimes even immoral." All these terms are, of course, relative, and in the absence of definite charges, with accurate quotation of the instructor's remarks, can only be set aside as "loose talk" on the part of irresponsible citizens. No citizen who is himself judicially minded and free from prejudiced sentiments will make vague charges of this kind, since he knows or should know both that they may be unfair and that they cannot be substantiated if specific evidence is lacking.
>
> I wish very much that when you get any complaints about an instructor in economics, or about what is taught or said in an economics class, you would refer the complainant either to the Dean or directly to me. . . . it might in a measure discourage irresponsible and uninformed complainants if they knew that they had to make good their criticisms directly to the Dean and the department head concerned. In most cases, I believe, a tactful conference with the complainant would help him to see that no instructor is perfect, that many things will necessarily have to be talked about in the classroom and many views expressed of which he would not approve from his own point of view, that he cannot have education in the social sciences at all unless both teacher and student—and student's parents—are tolerant and "reasonable," that in the social sciences we are not "teaching," that is inculcating, any specific doctrines but are trying to get the student to think for himself and to give him data as objective and unbiased as we can on which to do his thinking, and that our fundamental aim is to give the student opportunity to choose his own values.
>
> The sad part of this whole question of propriety in the classroom and of "outside" complaints that this or that instructor is "radical" in his teaching is that so few of the middle class public, from which college and university students preponderantly come, have an intelligent idea of what a college or university is for.[29]

Factors Affecting Sensitivity

In connection with all such actions by private individuals or civic groups, it would seem that the intensity of their influence depends to a large extent on the intimacy of contact between themselves and the school administrators. Close personal acquaintance between university or college authorities and persons who are concerned about the contents or the problems of teaching and research is apt to increase the effectiveness of complaints. This is especially likely to be the case in municipal colleges and in state universities which are located in the capital of the state, where the higher frequency of personal contact between the administration and those who control its funds creates a high sensitivity to complaints.

A further factor which helps to determine whether a given complaint will be heeded is the status of the complainant and that of the institution to which the complaint is made. Thus, whereas a complaint from an individual small businessman might be disregarded, one from a leader in the economic life of the community would probably be looked into. Correspondingly, while a given complaint to a smaller less opulent institution might find a respectful audience, a complaint coming from a person of the same status would, in the case of a more wealthy institution, have a good chance of being passed over with no more than a courteous acknowledgment.

The trustees are important in so many of the methods of applying sanctions that it is worth-while to single them out from the other agencies for special attention. They are in the first place the only authorities in the institution whose major occupational activities are regularly nonacademic, and because of their economic position they may well be regarded as the representatives, in the councils of the college or university, of the dominant strata. They are furthermore, as we have seen, not merely representatives of their stratum, but also continuous channels through which protests can pass from the various centers of influence in the larger society to the administration of the school itself.

But despite the extensive class homogeneity, considerable variation in attitudes exists among trustees. These variations are probably functions of educational experience, family tradition, and urbanization. The larger, wealthier, and more eminent schools recruit their trustees from the higher ranks of the plutocracy and from those segments of the professions which are closely associated with the plutocracy. Schools of the second rank in wealth and prestige draw their trustees from the lower fringes of the wealthy classes, depending much on local business leaders.

The longer the lapse of time between the first acquisition of a sizable fortune and service as a trustee, the greater is the likelihood of an attitude of tolerance and sympathy for intellectual values. The schools which are most successful in obtaining as trustees persons on whose families wealth has resided for several generations are accordingly less likely to have restrictive measures emanating from the board of trustees. In parts of the country where such trustees are more difficult to obtain the chances for such interference are correspondingly greater.[30]

But whatever the characteristics of the trustees themselves, the traditions of the institution itself as a center of science and scholarship and of tolerance toward intellectual variety are of prime importance in restraining the actions of trustees who in other roles are rather more conservative.

IX

One other phase of repressive action arising from outside complaints which merits attention is the hypersensitivity of university administrators during fund-raising campaigns. The possible alienation of potential donors because of unorthodox teachings of members of the faculty is a constant source of worry to university presidents, and in periods of straitened finances this fear and, consequently, the tendency to comply with imagined demands are especially great. Whatever sanctions might be imposed here are not necessarily consequences of intellectual or doctrinal intolerance as such, but rather of a concern for the financial well-being of the institution.

Nor is the apprehension itself always necessary, since it appears probable that in some cases, at least, the administrator projects his own intolerance on the environment.

> It is not necessary to maintain that wealthy patrons of educational institutions attach service conditions to their gifts. It is a notable fact that this is rarely the case. It is much more commonly the fear on the part of faculty and managing boards that frank utterance will lessen the income from gifts which really impairs the freedom of teaching.[31]

An outstanding liberal American educator with many years of experience as a fund gatherer stated that in his opinion many donors of large sums would not be pleased if they knew of the restrictive measures taken by administrators in order to assure themselves of the donor's favor. The wealthier a school is, and accordingly the less its dependence on any single donor, the lower will be the degree of anticipation of assumed demands for compliance. With this, the probability of freedom is considerably enhanced.

X

Restraints are maintained not only by the punishment of those who have already deviated. Self-intimidation or *self-coordination*, by which we mean the more or less deliberate renunciation of any intention to investigate or teach subjects which are forbidden or which are thought to be forbidden,[32] operates against those who have not yet deviated.

A decisive action, as for example, dismissal or a state legislative inquiry against a colleague at the same university or at another university, has often produced conformity among persons who under less dangerous conditions would have presented the views they actually held. There are, furthermore, numerous instances of the feeling that it is necessary to "soft pedal" the treatment of certain subjects. In schools where there is a strong and clearly formulated student opinion on public issues, there may exist a tendency for instructors who do not like to face opposition to accommodate themselves to the prevailing outlook, and sometimes out of no other consideration than that of student popularity, an instructor may find himself enunciating views which he did not previously hold. This is especially true in the smaller schools and in the less urbanized communities, where an incautious or misunderstood statement might give rise to distasteful gossip and ultimately perhaps to direct sanctions. Continued avoidance of potentially embarrassing issues renders self-restraint easier to bear. After a time the insight and interest which had to be repressed are lost, and the teacher comes to regard his situation as totally free from restriction.

There is no indication that self-coordination is extensive in the sphere of research, since the institutions which are large enough and wealthy enough to provide time and money for research are also likely to be sophisticated enough not to interfere with the research done by their staff members. There is occasional self-coordination of interest by applicants for financial assistance in order to make a grant more probable. There is also self-coordination in the choice of research subjects by candidates for the doctorate, although again no evidence is available as to the extent to which it obtains. There is usually a wider range of political viewpoints among graduate students as compared with faculty members, and consequently a feeling that it is necessary to find a thesis subject which will be agreeable to the faculty members, on whom, of course, their academic career frequently depends.

XI

We now turn to a brief examination of the possible consequences of restrictions on the freedom of teaching and research. Insofar as they affect teaching, restrictions obviously limit the range of knowledge and of possible interpretation which is made available to the student, and whether one believes that the function of the university or college is to educate "whole men," citizens, specialized technicians, or humanistic scholars, this cannot be looked upon as other than a serious deficiency. Restrictions which are peculiar to the undergraduate level and to smaller schools are negated in some measure if and when the student continues his studies as a postgraduate student at one of the larger and more outstanding institutions.

On the side of research, limitations on freedom do not seem to play any very significant role, since the great centers of research are on the whole quite free. But the sanctions which deter teachers from dealing with "dangerous" subjects in the classroom carry their force over into the research field by focusing the attention of the student and future research worker and channeling his interests in such a manner that when he begins his research career he will out of "trained incapacity" skip over important problems requiring investigation which he would be quite free to work on if he so chose. It is not far from correct to say that a considerable amount of the narrowness of many American social scientists is the result not of any explicit restrictions or fear of possible sanctions, but rather of the narrow undergraduate training which they received (in less advanced institutions) at the hands of teachers who themselves were trained in a period when even the greatest of the American universities were considerably less free than they are today.[33]

Notes

*Editor's Note: It should be borne in mind that this article was written before the Second World War. In the period dealt with, the social sciences, including economics, did not enjoy the prestige within universities or in American society at large which they later came to receive. The older American tradition of imperious presidents, interfering ecclesiastical and lay governing bodies, a callow orthodoxy, and a considerable touchiness among businessmen regarding the sanctity of the existing order of things combined to place academic social scientists in a weak position.

1. It should be noted that objections rooted in highly affectively toned attitudes and "final" values (as in the case of sexual and religious matters) may be expressed and legitimated in very pragmatic terms. We shall, nevertheless, consider these as instances of dogmatic, rather the pragmatic, obstructions to teaching and research. This does not, of course, exclude recognition that such objections may at times have a distinctly pragmatic motivation in addition.

2. In the twenties, agents of the public utilities seem to have shifted their tactics from protests to university authorities, once objectionable statements were made, to a more aggressive preventive type of action. The National Electric Light Association solicited textbooks which presented the "facts" as they preferred to have them seen. One of these texts by Professor M. G. Glaeser of the University of Wisconsin was "submitted to the National Electric Light Association, which suggested extensive emendations. Glaeser testified that he had made some 'corrections and changes of argument' after receiving the utility criticisms, but only such as were deemed valid. He denied that he had submitted the manuscript to the N.E.L.A., and accused Prof. Ely or Macmillan of having done so." H. K. Beale, *Are American Teachers Free?* pp. 556, 562–63; cf. also Jack Levin, *Power Ethics* (New York, 1931), pp. 81–86.

3. American Association of University Professors, *Bulletin*, vol. 5 (1919); *New Northwest*, March 14, 1919. Cf. also Louis Levine, *Taxation of Mines in Montana* (New York, 1919).

4. *Are American Teachers Free?* p. 518.

5. *New York Evening World*, April 25, 1929.

6. American Association of University Professors, *Bulletin*, vol. 6 (1930), pp. 143 ff.

7. Letter to L. B. Milner, March 28, 1933.

8. *Journal of Philosophy, Psychology and Scientific Method*, vol. II, no. 3 (Jan. 29, 1914), pp. 76–77.

9. Ibid., p. 77.
10. Ibid., pp. 75–76.
11. President E. D. Soper of Ohio Wesleyan University, one of the more liberal denominational schools, has said that a member of the faculty of such a school "should be a Christian in the essential meaning which is conveyed by the word. . . . A Christian is a man of deeply reverent spirit whose God is the one personal creative spirit at the center of the universe, a God who can be in significant contact with personal beings through prayer. He is one who has caught the meaning of Jesus Christ and who sees in him and his ways of life the hope of social righteousness and the assurance of personal emancipation." *Schools and Society*, vol. 30 (Oct. 19, 1929), p. 525. When a faculty member can no longer accept these views, President Soper believes he should leave the institution.
12. Letter in A.C.L.U. files.
13. E. A. Ross, *Seventy Years of It* (New York, 1936), p. 86.
14. American Association of University Professors, *Bulletin*, vol. 21 (1935), p. 256.
15. Occasionally these notices of appointment carry with them an ominous postscript which in effect conveys to the recipient in rather vague terms the information that at the expiration of his present appointment he may not be reappointed. There is evidence that a large number of professors find such disturbing postscripts added to their regular letter for the annual reappointment. Many of the professors testified that these postscripts are usually phrased and worded in such an equivocal manner that it is impossible to construe their real meaning.

    Thus in the case of Prof. C. Professor C. has regularly been reappointed and promoted. . . . Then one year he received his renewal contract with the following postscript: 'Further, in view of the probable decrease in the attendance, a reduction of the number of faculty may be imperative. The administration, therefore, wishes to notify you at this time that you may not be reappointed to the faculty at the expiration of this appointment.'" Ibid., pp. 257–58.
16. It should be remarked that this possibility is somewhat reduced by the fact that the main centers of graduate training are also the main centers of research, and are in general characterized by the highest degree of tolerance to be found anywhere in the country. Consequently, the selection of fellows is made by the men whose capacity for detached judgment is more than average.
17. "There is one even more important question which hardly comes under the name of academic freedom. It refers to the fact that while a man is fairly well protected once he has gained a permanent position in a first-class university, it may easily be true that men whose opinions are unconventional are handicapped in securing such positions. If university teaching is in general biased on the side of conservatism—and I do not grant that it is—it is because of the way in which selection rather that elimination works." From a letter from the late Professor Allyn A. Young to Roger T. Baldwin, April 25, 1924. Cf. also Norman Foerster, *The American State University* (Chapel Hill, 1937), pp. 166–67.
18. *New Northwest*, March 14, 1919.
19. A professor who was dismissed from the University of Minnesota during the First World War summarizes the process of intimidation as follows: "Usually the intimidation of a professor is so veiled and vague that he hardly knows what is wrong. A certain significant remark, dropped at the right time, a certain coldness of attitude, failure to be included in certain social affairs, a certain slowness to get well-earned increases, granted with gusto to others, many other little hints that his views do not meet with favor in certain quarters serve to curb many a man with

wife and babies to provide for. For instance there were a score or more called before the regents at the time I was. . . . Some of these men told me they had to lie or starve their wives and babies, and they took the easier road." Letter quoted in Upton Sinclair, *The Goosestep* (Pasadena, 1923), pp 214–15.

20. The applicant in question had written several authoritative studies the conclusions of which may be regarded as conducive to an unfavorable judgment of the reigning system of economic organization.

21. The determination of the extent to which funds have been withheld from research on "dangerous" subjects would necessitate an analysis of the decisions on every request to research committees for financial assistance. Such detailed investigation was not possible in this report.

22. Cf. *The Gag on Teaching* (2d rev. ed., New York: American Civil Liberties Union, May 1937), pp. 22–26; *Depression, Recovery and Higher Education* (New York, 1937) pp. 445–46.

23. American Association of University Professors, *Bulletin*, 1935, p. 228.

24. Letter from Governor Elmer Benson of Minnesota to Mr. Lewis Lohman.

25. *New York Tribune*, February 25, 1918.

26. American Association of University Professors, *Bulletin*, 1935, p. 233.

27. From a statement by President Rightmire in *Columbus Evening Dispatch*, May 27, 1931.

28. The president of a large university writes regarding rumors and criticisms circulating on the outside: "When I have endeavored in the past to get substantial evidence from an individual, the complaint melts away and no one has given me any definite statements which he would be willing to stand for. Loose talk apparently is carried on outside, but something tangible is brought forward only on the rarest occasion." "Economics and Sociology in the University," *School and Society*, vol. 42, no. 1096 (December 28, 1935), p. 893.

29. Ibid., pp. 893–95. The compliance of the administration with pressure from the outside is perhaps greater where appointments, dismissals, and other matters of academic policy and administration are centralized in the president or dean than in those institutions where there is a high degree of decentralization of authority among the various departments.

30. There is no evidence that there has been much improvement since the time when the late President Charles W. Eliot wrote: "In the newer parts of our country, it has of course been impossible to find at short notice men really prepared to discharge the difficult duties of educational trusteeship; and it will take generations yet to bring these communities in this respect to the level of the older states and cities." C. W. Eliot, *Academic Freedom* (Ithaca, 1908), p. 7.

31. Elmer C. Brown, "Academic Freedom," *Educational Review*, March 1900, p. 230.

32. It is, of course, necessary in this case to draw a careful line between conformity with intellectual standards on the basis of intellectual conviction, and conformity or self-coordination out of career-consideration. It is only the latter that concerns us here.

33. These remarks do not pretend to offer a complete explanation of the range of selection of research problems which obtains today in American social science.

**Part IV
Policy**

11

The Criteria of Academic Appointment

I

Since university teachers retire or resign, or die before doing either, they have to be replaced, assuming that their departments are not contracting in size. Every decision about a replacement is a determinant of the intellectual direction and quality of the university. Every decision to promote an already appointed teacher is similarly a determinant of future direction and quality. Decisions about the appointment or promotion of those persons who are to teach and do research as members of the academic staff of a university over the ensuing decades do more to fix the quality of the intellectual life of the coming generation than any reform of university government or any modification of syllabuses and courses of study. The decision to appoint or promote is a decision which cannot be rendered inconsequential by increased budgets; decreased university budgets render appointive decisions particularly fateful.

In most liberal countries, these decisions are nowadays mainly in the hands of the existing generation of teachers. In a number of continental countries which wished to advance towards meeting "the needs of the times," that is, who wished to satisfy the desires of a transient but clamorous generation of students, this power is in varying degrees shared with students, secretaries and other custodial, service and administrative employees of the university. In most liberal countries, the final decision rests legally with the ministry of education, or with the lay board of trustees or governors, or with the president, director or provost acting on their behalf. Only in Oxford and Cambridge is there no higher authority than communities of teachers and sometimes other experts. But whatever the formal differences between uni-

versities in which the power rests legally entirely with the academically constituted appointments committee, and those in which it remains legally in the
hands of a body of laymen, whether they be governmental officials or private
persons, it is the teachers on the appointments committees, sometimes hin-
dered and less frequently helped by student members, who make the effective
decision. There are occasions when a minister or the official to whom he
delegates the task refuses to confirm an appointment proposed by a faculty or
department. There are cases where he appoints a person who is not first on
the list submitted to him by the academic body, but by and large it is the
academics in the faculty or department or committee who make the decision.
Even where students have a part allotted to them by law, they are usually
influenced in their preference by one of the teaching members of the appointments committee. In the United States it used to be different. In recent decades, however, the boards of trustees or regents seldom do other than confirm the proposal which has been made to them by the academic staff, acting
through an appointive body made up of academics.

Hence with all the limitations on academic autonomy which arise from the
external location of the purse-strings, from the demands of professional bodies, from the educational standards of the secondary schools, and from many
other external conditions which universities have to heed, in one of the several things which are most decisive for their future intellectual quality and
effectiveness, university teachers hold the future fortunes of their institutions,
their subject and their profession in their own hands. They have the effective
power of appointment of their colleagues and their successors.

II

This power has not been uncontested. About a decade ago, students began
to demand a voice in the appointment and promotion of teachers, and in some
countries they were given what they demanded. In the United States, the
federal government has in the past decade intruded into the process of appointment by making its financial support contingent on, among other things,
the appointment of women, blacks, and persons of Latin American origin.[1]
There has been much contention about this but the federal government has
nonetheless been successful in obstructing the appointment of white males of
European ancestry on the basis of their academic qualifications, in favor of
the appointment of blacks, Latin Americans and women on the basis of their
ethnic and sexual qualifications. The establishment of trade unions among
teachers in higher education in the United States is also in part an effort to
inhibit or restrict the application of intellectual criteria in the process of
appointment, and particularly in matters of reappointment and promotion.
The characteristic concern of trade unions with security of tenure and with

seniority as the criterion of right to promotion is alien to the proper criteria of academic appointment.

In West Germany, and indeed in nearly all Western countries, the introduction of political criteria in academic appointments has become common. This is so particularly in the social sciences and certain humanistic disciplines such as philosophy and literary studies. No comprehensive study of this introduction of politics into academic appointments has been made and it would be very hard to make such a study. Nonetheless, many instances come to mind of appointments which have been made in which political criteria were applied; they are almost always suspensions of academic criteria in favor of politically radical candidates. This occurs particularly in appointments to posts of lower rank, but it also occurs in the appointment of full professors. It happens less frequently at that level simply because there seems to be a somewhat lower incidence and a lower intensity of political radicalism among the older academics. Nonetheless, there is no rank which is immune from his introduction of considerations of a radical political sort into proposals for academic appointments. This is not a result of governmental intervention and it is not a result of "student power"; it is done by university teachers themselves.

The gravest menace to the process of appointment comes from within the teaching staffs of the universities. It is graver than the menace brought by students, greater than the menace brought by governments and politicians in liberal countries. Not that these are by any means blameless!

Ever since the beginning of the rapid expansion of the budgets and student bodies of the universities, a correspondingly steep increase in the size of their teaching staffs also occurred. The demand for university teachers had to be met with corresponding speed. It was not always easy to find persons who were well trained for all the junior, intermediate and senior posts which were being created, or who had dispositions which would enable them to exercise the sense of intellectual and institutional responsibility which was more common in universities when they were smaller, less prominent, more isolated and more earnest in the secular, quasi-religious way characteristic of Western universities since the last quarter of the nineteenth century. The enlargement of the student bodies with new types of students, new in their aspirations and in their backgrounds, made teachers a little less meticulous and less solicitous about teaching them. Carelessness in appointment became a bit more common. The continuous increase in students, financial resources and teaching posts meant that even if more persons of indifferent intellectual quality were being drawn into the academic profession, there would still be room for the person who really was of the first class in quality. Senior academics sometimes justified their negligence in such terms.

The growth of numbers which gave birth to this negligence also gave rise

288   The Order of Learning

to the roaring wave of political passions of the second half of the 1960s. The tide has receded since that time but it has left a heavy sediment. The universities have become infested with teachers who think that their first duty in the university is not to teach their students conscientiously up to their best abilities and to stretch themselves in their research, but to look to the propagation of their political beliefs and to work towards the "destruction" of the existing order of society. For them academic standards are "merely an ideology"; they are nothing more than the "point of view" of a certain generation and of no intrinsic validity. For many, science is "only an ideology." The politically radical academics assert that social science is even more an "ideology" than science. The autonomy of the university and the freedom of science are regarded by at least some of them as no more than slogans of the "cold war," created primarily with the intention of putting communist countries in the wrong. Such persons have no understanding of what universities have been in the past and should be in the future.

Nevertheless, contemptuous though they are of the university as an institution and faithless though they are to the academic ethos, they are insistent that they have a place in the university. Any frustration of that insistence is immediately denounced as an infringement on their academic freedom and of their right to the freedom of expression.

Their conception of academic freedom is not the freedom to do academic things; it is the freedom of the academic to do nonacademic things. It is perfectly right that they should defend the right of academics to follow their own lights in politics. That, however, is a very different thing from meeting academic standards and obligations. The radicals in the universities have little regard for these, so little indeed that when one of their fellow-believers is taken to task for his deficiencies in research and teaching they immediately set up a hue and cry about "infringement on academic freedom." If they are taxed with these deficiencies, they argue that "methodological pluralism" should obtain, that is, that there is no generally valued intellectual standard to which all academics, regardless of their political attachments, must be faithful. This view is reinforced by the argument that since "bourgeois approaches" are already very well represented, "critical approaches" should be given a place. Thus they progress, from appointment to appointment.

In all this, they would not be so successful if they were not sheltered by the complaisance and negligence of other members of appointments committees and by their decent and thoughtless liberalism.

III

The University of Geneva stands out among universities through the presence there for so many decades of Professor Jean Piaget and the original and far-ranging school which he has built about himself. It shares in the minds of academics everywhere the good repute of the Swiss universities, and of Swiss institutions more generally, for probity, sobriety, painstakingness and solidity.

But this idea of the University of Geneva does not correspond to the way things actually are; at least the idea and the reality part ways in the faculty of economics and social sciences. Since December 1976, that faculty has become an exhibit, in microcosm, of some of the more ominous developments in the contemporary academic world. An associate professor of sociology, Dr. Jean Ziegler, is the neuralgic point.[2] Although his achievements are very slight, he is a radical politician—what is now called an "activist"—and his activities, aside from the fact that he is a member of the Swiss Bundesrat, are like those of his opposite numbers across the border in Germany and France. His analytical powers are meager, his research is light-hearted. He was nonetheless appointed first as an associate professor, then reappointed, and before his second term as associate professor had run its full course, he was proposed, recommended and then—after an acrimonious public dispute about the rights and wrongs of his position—appointed to a full professorship by the government of Geneva, acting on the recommendation of the legally constituted appointive bodies of the University of Geneva. There the matter now stands. It is instructive to look into the "Ziegler affair," as it has come to be called in Switzerland, because it is one instance of a class of situations which are to be found in many universities of Western countries today.

IV

The university authorities have insisted on their correctness in adhering to the legally required procedures. There seems to be little doubt that they acted within their powers in recommending his promotion. But at the same time it is hard to believe that they attended seriously to the matter of M. Ziegler's intellectual achievements and prospects. It is hard for me to believe that any scholar who read M. Ziegler's main sociological work and compared it with other work in the field could have come to a favorable conclusion. There is no indication that Professor Jeanne Hersch's charges against M. Ziegler's intellectual merits were taken seriously enough for a serious investigation to be conducted. To its credit, the appointive body did not say that he was an outstanding sociologist, even in the field of the study of underdeveloped countries. But if it had no expert in its own ranks, it could have sought the opinion of qualified scholars elsewhere, either in Switzerland or abroad. At least it said nothing about this; nor did any of M. Ziegler's partisans, who obviously had access to confidential documents and probably also to unwritten accounts of confidential discussions and who were not reluctant to divulge these confidences to the press, make any reference to the opinions of well-established authorities in the field. The rector in his statement after the decision of the Conseil d'état again said nothing about the intellectual achievements of M. Ziegler.

It is true that, ultimately, the authority to decide rested with a governmental body, the Conseil d'état, and it seems to be the case that it made the decision primarily without regard to intellectual merits. That is fairly evident from the statement issued by the two Christian-Democratic councilors who also avoided any reference to intellectual merit.

Why was it this way? It is certainly not that Swiss universities have a tradition of disregarding intellectual distinction in the making of academic appointments. The many illustrious figures in the history of Swiss science and scholarship render it very clear that it has not been a Swiss tradition to disregard intellectual merit in deciding whom to appoint, promote or discontinue. The letters of Professors Hersch, Lüthy, and Trappe are indications that not all Swiss university teachers are indifferent to intellectual merit. The letters show that not all of them think that an appointment, once proposed, should be made primarily because the candidate is sympathetic with one political standpoint or the other or because it will be to the advantage of one's own political party or faction if one supports his appointment. Indeed the university appointive body in this case knew that it was wrong to appoint a person on grounds other than his intellectual merit. That is why they emphasized the propriety of their procedure, to show that they did not allow themselves to be affected by the political qualifications of M. Ziegler. The protestations of the rector do not show that intellectual standards were in the forefront of the minds of the members of the appointive bodies, or that they sought the judgment of persons qualified to say whether such standards were met by M. Ziegler's work.

V

I know how difficult it is for the members of an appointive body to arrive at unanimity on every aspect of the intellectual merits of a candidate. It is very difficult for a member of an appointive body to put aside his personal sympathy or repugnance for the candidate, to expunge from his judgment every trace of sympathy or distrust of his political or religious views or his views about contemporary culture or whatever it is about which partisan sentiments and attachments are formed. It is difficult to arrive at a judgment of the academic merits of a candidate. About his teaching practically nothing can be known, except indirectly. Members of appointments committees have seldom been pupils of the candidate under consideration. Sometimes they have heard him lecture at a meeting of a learned society, sometimes they have been in a seminar which he has addressed, but in so far as they consider pedagogical merit, they have to proceed on hearsay. This is one of the reasons why accomplishment in research is so highly prized in universities. Young scholars and scientists, quite apart from their intellectual zeal, know that when they are being considered for appointment to a post in a university, their research will be scrutinized much more carefully than their teaching or their academic citizenship. Research is something which can be much more rigorously assessed than can accomplishments in teaching. But even the assessment of research is not a simple operation.

Why should not the assessment of the research of a candidate for a university post be rigorous and reliable? After all, the most significant aspect of the research is right there in front of the members of the committee. Scientific and scholarly papers and books can be read by members of appointive committees just as they are read by scientists and scholars who use them in their own research. So it would seem. Perhaps the situations are not equivalent. A scientist or a scholar reading the work of someone else working in his field can assess its merit with respect to particular points in which he himself in interested, has worked on, and knows a great deal about. A scientist or scholar reading the results of research is seldom interested in assessing the work as a whole unless he is writing a review of it; he is interested in what it contains for his own use in his own research and speculation. He is practically never interested in assessing the entire body of the work of another person unless he is writing an obituary or a testimonial or is sitting on a appointments committee. In writing an obituary, one does not have to estimate the prospective accomplishments of the deceased scientist or scholar. Even if the obituarist speculates on what the deceased might have done had he not done what he did, he can do so without causing harm. It is a speculation without serious consequences.

Testimonials are another matter. There we come into the heart of the process of appointment. A scientist or scholar has to be evaluated, comprehensively and briefly, on the basis of what he has done in the past, and his capacity for accomplishment in the future has to be estimated. Although it is not easy to render a just summary of past achievement, it is easier than estimating the probability of achievement in the future. How can one say with complete confidence that a productive and imaginative scholar in early middle age has not already "shot his bolt," will cease to be productive and will no longer have any new ideas? The responsibility of a referee is considerable, but he is, after all, only an adviser; the responsibility in the end rests with the individuals who make up the appointive body. Sharing in making the decision reduces somewhat the individual's responsibility, but it might also reduce his sense of responsibility.

There are honorable differences among equally well-qualified scientists and scholars in the assessment of a particular paper or book. They might differ in their estimate of the degree of originality which the particular results of another worker in the field has shown, or they might disagree about the extent to which he has demonstrated his contention. All the more is it possible to disagree, honestly, disinterestedly and with goodwill, in the evaluation of the work of a particular person taken as a whole.

With all these obstacles in the path to a valid judgment of a person who is to be appointed, it certainly can be made. It is done. It is not an accident that certain departments within a university remain outstanding over many years. It is true that the tradition which a newcomer confronts when he becomes a member of an outstanding department constrains him to exert himself so that he can meet the high expectations of his colleagues. But it is not only the tradition of work in teaching and research, it is also the tradition of exigency in assessing prospective members of the department. If members of a department will not appoint a person unless they are convinced that he is one of the very best in his generation in his field, and if in countries where salary scales, libraries and other resources differ among universities, the candidate is the best whom the intellectual and economic resources of the institution can attract, then the battle is partly won.

The obstacles to rendering a sound judgment of the merits of a candidate are less obstructive to good appointments than indifference to making good appointments on the basis of stringent academic standards. A sense of institutional inferiority, being content with persons who will go through the routines of teaching, who will do some mediocre research, who will be congenial, harms not only the university where such criteria are accepted, it also harms the entire university system of the country.

Indiscriminateness, negligence, insensitivity to the intellectual standards which must be observed if universities are to justify themselves by their intellectual accomplishments, all entail abdication. The zone emptied by abdication can be filled by the criteria which prize friendship, loyalty, intellectual discipleship, fashionableness and other qualities which can be mistaken for those vitally needed in universities. The "need to keep the institution going" is another criterion which makes for mediocrity, especially in universities in which established positions are not allowed to remain vacant.

VI

Expectations of mediocrity were no barrier to the rush of political radicalism into the universities. Teachers encouraged students in the disturbances of the troubled decade; radical students encouraged their teachers into radicalism. Both demanded a more "engaged" or "committed" university, meaning thereby the elevation of political considerations to primacy in the direction of studies and in the appointment of teachers. Political criteria had to be applied positively and openly.

Political criteria had been effective previously by intermittently and mainly negatively. Socialists were frowned upon in Wilhelmian Germany and obstacles were placed in the way of their "habilitation," but few sought to make academic careers and so the universities were spared the problem of actively rejecting socialist candidates. In the United States, the situation was a little different; socialists and populists did obtain junior appointments in the period from the 1890s to the 1930s but there were resistances to promoting them and they were sometimes dismissed. Nonetheless, a considerable number of progressivistic and collectivistic liberals did obtain appointments in American universities but they succeeded in doing so because political criteria were not applied. In France and Great Britain political criteria were utterly in abeyance; the situation was approximately the same in Italy.

Ethnic and religious criteria had been of some significance in the maintenance of restrictions against Jews. These became catastrophically severe in Germany in the 1930s and then, following the German example, Italy expelled Jews from universities, while in the United States and France and Great Britain, religious criteria receded to insignificance. Ethnic criteria were also less regarded in the American universities in the 1930s. But it was only after the Second World War that a handful of blacks were appointed in the major universities. The number of plausible black candidates had certainly been very small in the 1930s but they were passed over.

The great expansion of the universities in the United States practically eliminated negative ethnic, religious and political criteria. The general affluence made for slovenliness. The leading universities sought to appoint very outstanding persons but they were also willing to turn a blind eye when inferior candidates were appointed on grounds of convenience and out of unreflective indifference. The demand for teachers and the availability of the funds to pay their salaries encouraged disregard for stringent standards; had they been observed, not enough teachers could have been appointed. As a result of this "openness" of appointment, almost anyone could be appointed and even the leading universities nodded.

This easing of requirements coincided with the increased population of the social sciences and the more permeative diffusion of the belief in the primacy of politics, especially or radical politics.

VII

The task of arriving at a reasonable assessment of a candidate requires competence and scrupulousness in fields where standards are high and where political, religious and social views are clearly distinguishable from the facts and theories which are currently accepted in the field. In fields like the social sciences where standards are not so high or clearly defined and where political, religious and social views overlap in their objects with interpretations, observations and theories, the exclusion of political elements from assessment is more difficult than it appears to be in fields like solid state physics, classical archaeology or microbiology.

Despite these difficulties—which I do not underestimate—the task is certainly not beyond human powers. It is certainly feasible to distinguish between good and poor intellectual quality in a person with whom one disagrees politically. Just as one might disagree with the conclusions reached by another scholar and still find him estimable in the range and depth of his erudition and the subtlety of his analysis, so it is no less feasible to separate one's political preference from one's judgment of the intellectual merit of another person. It requires a concern for one's university and department, a concern for one's subject and a willingness to take pains to study the candidates' works carefully and impose a strict surveillance over one's own baser impulses. It also takes time which intellectually active academics often do not like to give at the cost of their own research. Even under favorable circumstances there will always be hard cases.

Worse, however, than the hard cases are those academics who care only about the political views of the candidates they are to assess and who try very strenuously to persuade their colleagues that their fellow-believer among the candidates is just the right person for the appointment. Such academics often try to arrange it all beforehand by organizing a bloc of like-minded colleagues on behalf of their candidate. This practice has become one of the blights of academic life. The social sciences and the humanities are especially prone to it.

Those members of appointments committees who have political intentions would not get very far if they did not have willing helpers. The willing helpers are the negligent, the self-preoccupied and the intimidatible liberals; of these the negligent are the most important. Even if the field is one like physics with high and relatively ambiguous standards of accomplishment, the members of appointments committees in those subjects might be indifferent to the standards, even though they know what they are and would not on their own initiative ever say anything against them. They might not care about the future of the university or the department to which the appointment is to be made; they might want to appoint a particular person whom they like or whom they think might be useful to their own purposes but whom they know not only to be mediocre but clearly less meritorious intellectually than another candidate. These negligent guardians of the future of the university might be interested primarily to obtaining the appointment of a friend or protégé, or less frequently of a person who shares their political, religious or social views. They acknowledge the right standard and they might know that the candidate in question falls rather below it. They do not care enough. A good university is strong enough to withstand a carelessly made appointment—so they think—and if they think that their university is poor, then what difference does a mediocre appointment make?

The glaring defects of the academic profession in matters of appointment are just of this sort. However scrupulous a scientist or a scholar might be in his own work, he might not wish to take the trouble to read the writings of the person about whom a decision has to be made. Those members of appointments committees who take lightly their responsibility to maintain or raise the quality of the subject and the department to which an appointment is to be made become the accomplices of those who are interested in promoting a particular outlook or ideology. The latter are not behindhand in seizing the opportunities this lays open.

VIII

The recent passage of events at the University of Geneva could provide the text for a sermon on the lines of the foregoing analysis. It is clear that the appointive committees and the assessors were negligent in assessing M. Ziegler's intellectual accomplishments, or did not care for the quality of teaching and research in the university to which M. Ziegler was to be appointed. His main work in the field to which he has devoted himself through most of his academic career is *La Sociologie de l'Afrique nouvelle*. Having read this book when it first appeared at a time when I was working in that field myself and was fully abreast of the literature in it, I was struck at once by the paltriness of M. Ziegler's contribution to the subject. It was a superficial summary of a small number of not very well chosen books decorated with political and philosophical stereotypes. It was neither meticulous in its descriptive aspects nor imaginative in its interpretation. At that time, I knew nothing about M. Ziegler and I concluded that he was one of those dilettantes of Marxist pretensions who were so common in France in the early 1960s; he certainly was not one of the scholarly Marxists who has mastered the literature of his subject and who knows something of it at first hand. I was surprised when I learned some years later that he held a post in a Swiss university.

Sociology is certainly not a subject in which the average standard is high either in Switzerland or in the world at large. It is also a field in which there is disagreement about the best techniques. Nonetheless, even in sociology, with all its ambiguity, there is a tangible difference between merit and mediocrity and between mediocrity and slapdash incompetence. Why should the committee of rectors and deans of the University of Geneva have proposed

M. Ziegler for a full professorship with such unanimity and persistence in the face of criticism by serious academics? Indifference, desire to keep the peace, the desire not to appear to be illiberal, and outright political partisanship must each have played their parts in this.

IX

One should not take the Ziegler affair too tragically. After all he is only one of many such persons strewn over the universities of Western countries. Geneva is only one of about ten Swiss universities and advanced technological institutes. Switzerland is only a small country; and sociology in almost every country has many agitators and unscholarly, intellectually frivolous teachers. The heavens will not fall because M. Ziegler has been made into a full professor.

Nonetheless it is very regrettable as a sign of the times. There are strong forces now at work in universities aiming to destroy them as institutions of learning, of disinterested science and scholarship. Wantonly, the blissful unthinking, well-intentioned academics allow themselves to be edged in the direction of intellectual unscrupulousness and rancorous partisanship.

The churches have become more partisan and more enmeshed in the current conflicts of society. Parliament and political parties are by their nature the scenes of partisan conflict. Yet all societies need some detachment from daily concerns and from partisan espousal of particular interests or ideologies. The higher judiciary is one of these centers; universities should be the other. The high standing of the universities has depended on their disinterested concern for truth, however general or however specialized. If the universities do not give an example of the disinterested, patient, honest and occasionally brilliant application to the tasks of sober teaching and serious discovery, of the example of devotion to things higher than the passing fashion, to things superior to the interests of a party or a sect and to holding a pleasant and well-remunerated post, they will lose the respect which, despite all the troubles of recent years, they have still not wholly forfeited. Every careless or nepotistic or willfully political appointment made in a university is that much of a diminution of the intellectual capacity and of the standing of that university in the future. Every time a professor is appointed by carelessness or by willful disregard of criteria of past intellectual achievement and promise of future intellectual achievement, the university is committed to about twenty-five years more of intellectual mediocrity and professional irresponsibility. It is wasting its future. With every appointment of a lecturer or an assistant professor simply because he is committed to political activity and to the use of his academic post for political ends, the university assures itself in that measure of about a third of a century more of mediocrity and irresponsibility.

Notes

1. See Reports and Documents, "Academic Appointment, University Autonomy and the Federal Government," *Minerva*, IX, 2 (April 1974), pp. 161–70; and "The Criteria of Academic Appointments in American Universities and Colleges: Some Documents of Affirmative Action at Work," *Minerva*, XIV, 1 (Spring 1976), pp. 97–117.
2. See "Reports and Documents," "Criteria of Academic Appointment, I: Switzerland," *Minerva*, XIV, 3 (Winter 1976), pp. 530–69.

12

The Invitation to Caesar

I

The traditional conception of academic and scientific freedom presupposed that academic and scientific institutions were capable of governing themselves. The argument for this freedom has been an argument that there was a sphere in which the authority of Caesar—the external authority of the state—had no place, even though, as in the case of the state universities, the state itself defined the boundaries of the sphere within which academic freedom was to prevail. In the universities, academic freedom has comprised the freedom, *de facto*, to appoint new staff members, to teach in accordance with intellectual conviction, to select and conduct research schemes in accordance with scientific standards. In the Anglo-American academic world, academic freedom has covered a wider range than on the Continent, where governmental ministries retained certain ultimate rights in appointive and budgetary matters and in the arrangement of certain examinations. The scope of academic freedom has been wider in American private universities than in the state universities. Still, whether Continental or Anglo-American, private or state, a far-reaching academic freedom was established in principle and in practice in the major Western universities. It was always a freedom from external authority seeking on its own initiative to intrude into the affairs of the universities.

In the freedom of science, while the right to prescribe in one form or another the topics or problems of applied or technological research was generally acknowledged, the power of decision as to the problems to be investigated in basic or fundamental research was regarded as uncompromisably the right of the individual scientists and of the scientific community. The assessment of results, together with the choice of research procedure, were even more vital and even more insisted upon. This was one of the grounds why even such devoted supporters of the Soviet Union as the late Professor J. B. S. Haldane could not accept the ascendancy of "Michurin biology." Correspondingly, the scientific community demanded and generated the right to decide the merits of the accomplishments of individuals and to attribute to them the appropriate credit and honor. What could be more an affair of the scientific community than the determining of whom it should honor. Honors attributed by bodies external to the scientific community were accepted only if they confirmed the assessments of the scientific community; otherwise their recipients were regarded as nothing more than court favorites with no claim to superior standing in the scientific community.

The main danger to this freedom was believed, and usually rightly, to originate outside the academic and scientific communities. The state, private business, the Church and the press were regarded as the potential instigators and agents of infringement upon academic freedom and generally, in varying patterns and degrees in the different countries, this view was correct.

II

To keep the external powers at arm's length in these fields of activity which are so much at the heart of teaching and research, it was necessary that those who had preponderant influence in the academic and scientific communities should act justly and that they should have been thought to act justly by those members who did not ascend to the peaks of their respective sectors. Internal consensus was a precondition for self-government whether hierarchical or equalitarian. It was especially important that the most eminent members of these communities and those who occupied positions of authority enjoyed a general respect for honesty and goodwill.

This was all the more necessary in view of the inevitable vagueness of the criteria to be applied in specific cases, especially in appointment and assessment. There is nothing like a body of tort and contract law governing the fulfillment of obligations and the observance of rights in academic and scientific institutions. There is a necessary looseness in many of the terms of appointment; a great deal of the judgment as to the merits of scientific achievement lies in the realm of what Professor Michael Polanyi has called "tacit knowledge." The assessment of quality of scholarly and scientific accomplishment is not of the same standard of precision as the determination of accomplishment in athletics, for example, in the determination of championship in the 100–meter sprint. The assessment of pedagogical accomplishment is even more difficult than the assessment of accomplishment in research. Scrupulous goodwill on the one side and confidence in the scrupulousness and goodness of will on the other are indispensable. Deficiencies in the one side must be made up by surpluses on the other.

There is ample evidence that this consensus regarding fair-dealing has become frayed—at least at the peripheries, and not only there. The student disturbances were the first and most dramatic instances of this fraying within the universities; the role of assistants, teaching assistants, junior lecturers, and assistant professors in these disturbances provides further instances of this rent in the fabric of mutual trust. The fraying has spread from the peripheries closer into the center in the Western German, French, Italian, and Japanese universities. It has advanced least in the English-speaking universities—except for those of India, if they may still be regarded as belonging to the universities in which the English language is the medium of instruction and publication. (The issue does not arise in the university systems of communist countries because the conventions of academic freedom usually do not obtain there.)

In the English-speaking countries, it is advancing more in the United States than in Great Britain. There too, however, Caesar is receiving invitations to attend to aspects of academic life to which he had previously been indifferent and might still continue to be indifferent if his attention and intervention had not been sought. I refer here particularly to the applications for injunctions which several universities have actually made or threatened to make to the courts over the past few years to aid them in the restoration of internal order.

In the United States, the matter has gone somewhat further. One very striking case is that of David Roth, an assistant professor of political science at the University of Wisconsin at Oshkosh. Professor Roth was appointed for a one-year term without any reference whatsoever in his notification of appointment to continuation beyond the end of the academic session. The university law of the state of Wisconsin—the University of Wisconsin is a state university—is very explicit in its statement that those state university teachers who have not been awarded permanent tenure are employed on probation.[1] It is equally explicit in its assertion that "During the time a faculty member is on probation, no reason for nonretention need be given. No review of appeal is provided for in such case."[2] Nonetheless Professor Roth brought suit in a federal district court

alleging that the decision not to rehire him for the next year infringed his Fourteenth Amendment rights. . . . First he alleged that the true reason for the decision was to punish him for certain statements critical of the University administration, and that it therefore violated his right of free speech. Second, he alleged that the failure of University officials to give him notice of any reason of non-retention and an opportunity for a hearing violated his right to procedural due process of law.[3]

The district court ordered the university to provide him with reasons and a hearing; the court of appeals affirmed this judgment. The board of regents appealed against this decision before the United States Supreme Court, which, in response to the question of whether Professor Roth "had a constitutional right to a statement of reasons and a hearing on the university's decision not to rehire him for another year,"[4] held that he did not have such a right.

I refer to Professor Roth's suit, not with the intention of passing judgment on the merit of his charge against the board of regents but only to illustrate my contention that the consensual basis for the internal adjudication of disagreements is weakening. With it is weakening one of the necessary conditions for academic self-government. The weakening has many causes but the most immediate is distrust and animosity among the various strata and sectors of the academic community. This is deeper than the juridical inadequacy of university rules and statutes. Universities, as has often been pointed out, live and regulate themselves by a set of accepted even if explicitly unacknowledged conventions.[5] Generally, in the quarter of a century since the end of the Second World War, they have fared reasonably well under this arrangement. They have avoided, despite the great increase of *paperasserie* connected with their financial and householding affairs, the imposition of very precise rules on their academic staff. But even in the instance cited, in which the rules of the board of regents were very explicit, the explicitness was not extensive enough to absorb the grievance of Professor Roth and so he turned to Caesar.[6]

Another affair, this time in the scientific community, is now transpiring in the United States. It is by no means as commonplace as Professor Roth's affair. This time it reaches to the very pinnacles of eminence of the scientific community.

In 1959, Professors Emilio Segre and Owen Chamberlain, of the Lawrence Laboratory of the University of California at Berkeley, were awarded the Nobel Prize in physics for their discovery of the antiproton in 1955. On June 14, 1972, Professor Oreste Piccioni, of the University of California at San Diego, filed suit in the Superior Court of Alameda County against Professors Segre and Chamberlain. He charged that he "was responsible for originating [their] research and for furnishing the basic experimental ideas which were used in its execution." He claimed that in 1954 he had communicated to Professors Segre and Chamberlain the idea of using magnets to focus streams of sub-atomic particles and that his two colleagues agreed to use his idea in their research. They, according to his account, proceeded to do so, and publish the results in October, 1956, without acknowledging his contribution. As compensation for what he alleges was improper conduct, Professor Piccioni demanded damages to the extent of $125,000 and a public acknowledgment of his contribution.

This is not the first time in the present century that there has been contention about the attribution of credit for a scientific discovery. It is, as far as I know, the first time that such a claim has been argued in a civil court. It is therefore the first time that Caesar has been invited to enter into the heart of the scientific community to settle a question of the type which has always hitherto been regarded as an exclusive prerogative of the scientific community.

III

These are straws in a rising wind. We are living in a world full of aggrieved persons. There have always been grounds for grievance about the way the world works. Scarcity is at the root of it but growing plenitude is not a cure since scarcity is unexpungible from human existence. Even the most just order is bound to have patches and moments of injustice. It was always the pride of the scientific community that within the injustice of the world, and with respect to the narrow band of activity—however broad its intellectual objects—for which it took responsibility, it came as close to justice as it was possible for human beings to come. There were always aggrieved persons in the intellectual community. They were, however, willing to suffer their grievances in silence or to count on the ultimate justice of their colleagues and superiors. This is no longer so.

Especially in the United States, where grievances tend to be more vociferously expressed, the aggrieved are now using whatever resources are available to them to right the wrongs they think they have suffered. Their loyalty to their intellectual communities and the authorities who operate within them is too attenuated to deter them. The "demonstration-effect" of aggrieved women working on the United States Department of Health, Education and Welfare, and many others who believe themselves to be oppressed, could not fail to penetrate the academic and scientific communities. Bitterness against the "establishment," manifested throughout the world where it is permitted to intellectuals to criticize those who rule, has a great resonance.

Governments are arrogant—when have they not been?—and they are constantly expanding their sphere of jurisdiction. They do it on their own initiative, on the initiative of bureaucrats who think they can do everything and politicians who do not reflect on the limits of the practicable. They do it under the pressure of the demands of the electorate or some sections thereof. It is unlikely that when invited to extend their jurisdiction further, governments will refuse the invitation. As they do so, they come to take it for granted that it is right for them to go on doing so.

If the autonomy of the academic and scientific communities is to avoid being able to survive only in the catacombs, they will have to cease issuing invitations to Caesar and cease, too, to tempt him. To do this, they will have, on the one hand, to act justly in those matters which are their responsibility. They will have to define rights and obligations more clearly and try to adhere with strictness to their definitions. On the other hand, they must give more thought to the conditions of a rehabilitated consensus within themselves. With all that this entails, the task is far from easy and the time available is not unlimited.

Notes

1. "All teachers in any state university shall initially be employed on probation. The employment shall be permanent, during efficiency and good behavior, after four years of continuous service in the state university system as a teacher." (*Wisconsin Statutes* 1967. C. 37.31 (1) quoted in *Board of Regents of State Colleges et al., Petitioners v. David F. Roth, etc.*, on writ of certiorari to the United States Court of Appeals of the Seventh Circuit. *Supreme Court of the United States.* No. 71–162 (June 29, 1972).

2. Rule II, promulgated by the Board of Regents in 1967.

3. *Board of Regents of State Colleges v. Roth* (—U.S.—, 33 L.Ed. 2d 548, 92 S.Ct. 227).

4. Ibid.

5. See the wise reflections of the Stanford University advisory committee report on the case of Professor Bruce Franklin, *Minerva*, X, 3 (July, 1972), pp. 452–83.

6. Another case illustrating the same tendency to turn to Caesar to right wrongs allegedly suffered within an academic institution was decided on the same day by the United States Supreme Court This was the case of *Charles R. Perry et al., Petitioners v. Robert P. Sindermann.* Mr. Sindermann had taught for ten years in several institutions within the Texas state college and university system. His appointments were on annual contract. He claimed that he had by his service of ten years acquired permanence of tenure. The offical *Faculty Guide* of his college stated: "Odessa College has no tenure system. The Administration of the college wishes the faculty member to feel that he has permanent tenure as long as his teaching services are satisfactory and as long as he displays a cooperative attitude toward his coworkers and superiors and as long as he is happy in his work." (Quoted in *Perry v. Sindermann* [—U.S.—, 33 L.Ed. 2d 570, 92 S.Ct. 267].) *Policy Paper I*, issued on 16 October, 1967, by the Coordinating Board of the Texas College and University System, referred to a probationary period of a maximum of seven years of full-time service within the system. The United States Supreme Court affirmed the decision of the appeals court which had ruled that the plaintiff should be granted "a hearing . . . where he could be informed of the grounds for his non-retention and challenge their sufficiency."

13

The Confidentiality and Anonymity
of Assessment

I

In the past few years, there has been intermittent expression of dissatisfaction with the conventions of treating assessments as confidential and of withholding the names of their authors from the person whose achievements are assessed. There are allegations that under the covers of confidentiality and anonymity untruthful statements are made which do injury to those whose performance is assessed and hamper the progress of science and learning. Criticisms have been directed against the confidential assessment by referees of papers submitted for publication in scientific and scholarly journals.[1] Similar criticisms have been made of the assessments of proposals for research submitted to bodies which allocate funds for the support of particular projects.[2] It is also claimed that improprieties are hidden in the confidential files of universities. Reforms in the practice of confidentiality and anonymity are demanded. The disclosure to the interested parties of the text of the assessments and the names of the assessors are demanded. In various institutions of higher education, students and others have broken into the files and have thus infringed on these conventions.[3] Most recently, the Congress of the United States has hastily enacted legislation which abrogates the confidentiality of assessments in universities.

II

Some of those who are dissatisfied with confidentiality in science charge that a small circle of scientists with well-established reputations and positions in major universities dominate the assessment, and permit only papers issuing from their own circles and congenial to their own standpoints to reach the point of publication. Papers by aspirant contributors and proposals by scientists who are not well connected or whose views diverge from those of their well-established assessors are at a disadvantage—so the argument goes. The evil here lies, it is said, primarily in the anonymity of the assessors. The text of the main points of the assessment is quite often disclosed to the authors and applicants but this does not seem to be a sufficient guarantee to the critics of the present system. If referees are allowed to remain anonymous, they will assess papers and proposals without the regard for the standards which they would exercise were they aware that what they do would be known by their peers. As a result, the critics of anonymous assessment believe that papers which deserve publication and proposals which deserve support are indiscriminately and unjustly rejected while others, no more, or even less deserving, are recommended for acceptance. The remedies which are put forward to undo the noxious effects of anonymous assessment do not go as far as to recommend the elimination of assessment as a condition of publication or support.

The tradition of assessment in the light of exigent standards in the scientific and scholarly communities is too strong to be swept aside by the present discontent. The critics only say that, as a result of anonymity and confidentiality, these exigent standards are unevenly and prejudicially applied. Rather, a measure less radical is proposed as a remedy. This is the divulgence to the author of the assessed paper or proposal of the name of the referee or assessor, together with the text of the assessment. The assumption is that referees would be more just if they were held publicly responsible for their assessments.[4] They would be more scrupulous; they would not take such liberties if they knew that they would have to answer for what they say. Usually, the critics discuss the problem in a matter-of-fact way. Sometimes, however, the idiom of contemporary political polemics is introduced.[5] The disinterestedness of the scientific profession is called into question.[6] The situation is interpreted as one in which the author of the paper or the applicant for a grant which is assessed stands in the relationship of an adversary to the referees and those whom they advise. It sometimes appears as if an assessment is equated with an accusation. "The establishment" is the accuser; the accused is therefore entitled to the right to confront his accuser and to refute the accusation. Seen from such a standpoint, the argument against confidentiality and anonymity of assessment makes some sense.

III

Something tantamount to circumvention of assessment as such does occur in the widespread practice of the distribution of papers prior to publication.

This distribution of "preprints" is justified, according to those who practice or recommend it, by the speediness and lower costs of this mode of distribution of the results of research. It does not necessarily entail a denial of the moral integrity of the "refereeing system" as such. In certain fields of research where there is intense competition for the establishment of claims to priority of discovery, and where the queues of papers awaiting publication are very long, the circulation of "preprints" of papers which have already been accepted for publication is a useful device, and it by no means contravenes the principle that prior assessment by a professionally authoritative, competent and disinterested body is a precondition of any claim on the attention of the scientific community. The long lapse of time between submission of a paper and its publication, once accepted, in a journal, is the only, and quite reasonable, ground for an independent widespread distribution prior to publication.[7]

In contrast with these departures from the conventional pattern of distributing the results of research, the demand for the divulgence of the text of the assessment and of the names of the assessors does imply that there is something morally wrong with the present practice of assessment. It implies that meritorious scientists are treated carelessly and unjustly and that valuable scientific knowledge is at the same time prevented from coming into existence and from reaching its proper audience.[8] Sometimes, this judgment of the present mode of assessing the worth of papers and proposals submitted for publication and support is part of a more comprehensive distrust of the reigning authorities in science and scholarship as a whole and in particular fields, and in the various institutions which accord recognition and influence careers. The anonymity of authority seems intolerable. Authority itself has become repugnant; the repugnance is one of the motives of contemporary "antielitism." Anonymity only compounds the wickedness of authority.

Anonymity is contrary to the prevalent belief that everything should be out in the open and that only sinister interests are the beneficiaries of anonymity. There is a more fundamental feeling that anonymity is anomalous; it makes for uneasiness. Anonymity as such, quite apart from its practical consequences, is disliked. There is a belief that malevolence is hidden by anonymity. Anonymity is manipulation; anonymity is a derogation of the dignity of the human beings who are subjected to its baffling presence. Things which are seen are subject to control or can be rendered neutral. Those which cannot be seen are capable of doing harm.

Why should there be anonymity in science, which is the realm of empirical knowledge and of rational criticism? A scientific proposition becomes established only through its acceptance by other qualified scientists. Scientific knowledge is, as Professor John Ziman has said, "public knowledge." Book reviews are signed by their authors; critical reviews of current literature in the various fields of science and scholarship are signed. "The scientific literature" is publicly accessible, and a good part of it is made up of the public assessments, positive and negative, of the results of the research of others persons. In most fields of social life, referees are visible and known. For example, in sporting events and in the law courts, referees and judges are known. Reviewers of scholarly works in learned journals and critics of works of art in newspapers and periodicals sign their names to what they have written. Why, it is asked, should assessors of papers submitted to scientific and scholarly journals wish to continue the practice of anonymity and even of confidentiality?

IV

There has been a parallel movement against anonymity in higher education. Ever since the student disorders of the 1960s, there has been a flickering belief among radical students that their teachers in universities and colleges secretly compile dossiers on them for some unspecified but damaging use in the future. This is one of the grounds on which students who occupy administrative offices and purloin documents from the files justify their misdeeds. They wish to demonstrate that, with sympathetic exceptions, teachers and administrators are their enemies and are intent on doing them damage behind their backs. They believe that is why observations and assessments are kept secret.

The thought of "secret files" fascinates, and on occasion even obsesses, some persons outside universities as well as within them. The thought of being known—not famous but just known—to someone else when one does not know what that person knows about oneself is often disquieting. Although radical students have often criticized the universities for their impersonal and bureaucratic indifference to students and for not "knowing and appreciating them as human beings," the same radical students who make these criticisms are sometimes uneasy at the thought of being known to their teachers. They seem to think that being known lays them open to danger; the danger is enhanced when they do not know what it is that is known about them.

In Great Britain and the United States, there is still a tradition of personal concern for students; it is what is left of the now generally discarded belief that university and college teachers should stand *in loco parentis* to their students. As a result of this surviving tradition, many teachers in American and British universities actually take an interest in their students and come to know a certain amount about some of them. Their knowledge of their students does not end with knowledge of their results in examinations. Deans' offices, sections of the universities concerned with helping students to find employment, tutors, supervisors, and advisers, expect to receive assessments of a student's intellectual propensities and accomplishments beyond what is conveyed by the record of marks on examinations. Teachers are expected to report in confidence their assessments to tutors and advisers so that the latter may have as well rounded view as possible. Thus, files are created. Most students accept this without thinking about it. The more distrustful students believe that teachers must be inimical to them and that their reports about them must necessarily be damaging.

Assessment, examinations, marks, and grades have all aroused a lot of sentiment and bitterness in the years of turmoil in the universities. Assessments deal with fateful matters; failures and poor passing marks are humiliating and portend a harder path into the future. That is why assessments and examinations have been under such fire from student radicals during the past decade. The burden of apprehension which examinations impose and the affront to egalitarian beliefs which grading presents account in part for the resentment against examinations in most of the countries where student disturbances have occurred. But, in addition to this there is something abhorrent in being known and assessed unilaterally.

Continental students, who have been not less rebellious and not less critical of examinations than American and British students at their worst have been, have not paid much attention to "secret files" and "confidential reports." That has been an Anglo-American specialty. It is a by-product of the residual tradition of acting *in loco parentis*. Events at the Universities of Warwick[9] and Lancaster[10] and the North London Polytechnic[11] are instances of this concern about "secret files" in British universities.

The preoccupation with confidential or "secret" files has more of less faded in Great Britain. It flares up from time to time, but it is not supported by any deeper currents of opinion in the larger public, or even among students.[12] The press has been critical of governmental secrecy in Great Britain and to some extent there has been concern about the storage in computers of information about individuals. On the whole, however, there has not been a widespread public commotion about the secretiveness of authority.

The situation has been rather different in the United States. The concern, in one way or another, with governmental secrecy has been prominent over much of the past three decades. It has been far more intense than anything in Great Britain. In the decade after the war the United States government and a sufficiently large part of the American political public has shown themselves to be so solicitous of secrets that persons who were thought disposed, for whatever reasons, to divulge governmental secrets were denied employment in the government; foreigners of allegedly communistic sympathies were denied visas for entry into the United States on the ground that they might acquire and abscond with American secrets. Since the second half of the 1960s "secrets" have continued to be at issue. The tide was, however, by that time running in quite the opposite direction. In the first part of the postwar period, "secrets" were sacred. In the more recent past, "secrets" have been the devil's own work.

The "right to know" has become enthroned as one of the most sacred of American values; governmental secrecy has been cast down.[13] Dr. Daniel Ellsberg became a hero in intellectual circles within the United States by disclosing to the press a vast miscellany of "classified" documents. The federal government has come to demand more and more information from its citizens; the press and some academics have come to demand that more and more of this information about citizens and about government itself be made available to them. The press has not abated any of its long-practiced intrusiveness into the private affairs of individuals, both famous and obscure.

All these latter developments have coincided with widespread declarations of allegiance to the principle of privacy. Some of these declarations deal with what are genuinely issues of privacy, in the sense of an inviolable sphere in which the individual is free from observation and control by others.

The "right of privacy" has been very broadly defined. It has come to include the protection of the rights of human subjects in bio-medical experimentation, the protections of criminals from being recognized as formerly criminal after release from imprisonment, the protection of school children who might do poorly in intelligence or other psychological tests from having the results of those tests disclosed, the protection of the right of abortion, the protection of homosexuals from discrimination in employment. The protection of the individual from having various, previously scattered, bits of information about himself brought together into a single, composite portrait hitherto nonexistent has also been one of these concerns. It is implied that no one should know anything about an individual unless he himself knows it and has authorized its becoming known. The "right of privacy" is construed to include the "right to know" whatever others know about oneself.

These assertions of the "right of privacy" entail the denial of the "right of others to know" particular things about the particular individual; they do, however, entail his right to know what these others know about him. The "right to know" includes the right to know what others know about oneself. It does not include their right to know about oneself, or if they do know something about oneself to keep it confidential.

V

All this is taking place at a time when more and more information is being gathered about individuals by governments, hospitals, psychiatrists, psychologists, sociologists, teachers, journalists, television interviewers, credit-rating establishments, unimaginative novelists, and private detectives. Some of this information is necessary for the government's performance of its functions; some of it is necessary for the restoration or protection of health, mental and physical. Some of it is necessary for the furtherance of intellectual understanding. Some of it is sought because it has value as entertainment or as "human interest stories." Some of it is sought for the conduct of business enterprises and some of it is sought in order to put those investigated into difficulties. Many of these information-gathering activities are legitimate and some are necessary for worthwhile ends, but the fact remains that they are made possible only by intrusion into the private sphere of the persons known.

The "right to know" and the "right of privacy" are antithetical to each other. The right to know is the right to know about another person's actions or state of mind. The right of privacy is, among other things, a right not to have one's actions or state of mind known by others. The right to know is the right to infringe on the privacy or confidentiality of other persons.

VI

The right of privacy in the sense of freedom from being the object of another person's knowledge cannot be fully realized. To assess the actions of another person and to record and retain the record of that assessment is an infringement, according to the principle thrown up by this new sensibility about being known and assessed, of the right of privacy understood as immunity from being known by others and from the sharing of what is known by those others with a still wider circle. There are some actions and states of mind which are inevitably, if unwittingly, disclosed by the mere fact of living in society. In entering into certain undertakings or relationships, a human being thereby accepts that he will be perceived and assessed. In certain instances, the condition of entering into a particular role is the disclosure of certain information about oneself. Especially where an individual claims benefits which are supposed to be apportioned in accordance with achievements, he must assent to the assessment of the merit of his achievement. He must indeed, in such instances, supply information about himself to the assessors. Assessment is a precondition of justice.

Both the assessors and the assessed have an interest in the information and the assessment which is made of it. The assessed individual is interested in having as favorable an assessment as possible; the other individuals and institutions, for example, prospective employers, institutions of more advanced training, other scientists, and "the larger public" have an interest in a truthful assessment. These several interests do not always coincide. Where the assessment is favorable to the person assessed at the cost of truthfulness, society or the larger public or the particular field in the scientific community—that is, the other individuals and institutions—is inevitably injured. Where the assessment is truthful, society benefits but the individual who is assessed might be frustrated in his aspirations.

VII

Assessment is indispensable where proficiency of achievement is to be maintained in any field of activity. It is not simply a matter of justice in the allocation of rewards but of the maintenance and improvement of the level of proficiency in that field. Of course it does not mean that all privacy is renounced; only that some privacy is renounced. Assessment is an integral part of university education, as it is of the workings of the scientific community. In both, it is necessary for justice to individuals and to the quality of performance in the professions and in society at large.

A scientist who performs an experiment and prepares a paper does so with the expectation of placing it before other members of the scientific community and with the anticipation that they will assess it for its scientific worth. The very act of undertaking a scientific work is a commitment to publication and assessment. The assessment of the manuscripts by referees of journals— or of publishers—is a preliminary sifting to assure that what reaches the wider public is at least of a minimal standard. Since not all the manuscripts which are submitted can be published, assessment is necessary to assure that those published are better than those not published. If this is not done properly, authors of merit are sacrificed to the advantage of those with less merit. The scientific community is damaged and society, in so far as it depends on the products of the scientific community, would also be damaged by wrongheaded and irresponsible assessment.

Students come to university to learn and to obtain degrees or diplomas. They come with the expectation that if their performances reach an appropriate standard in the substance and level of their achievement in learning, they will be qualified to enter certain occupations or to continue their studies at a more advanced stage. They enter, therefore, with the expectation of being observed and assessed; it is inherent in the acceptance of admission to university. In order to avoid assessment, they would have to abstain from examinations and this would contradict much of their rationale for being at university. They would have to forswear the anticipation that what they do at university will qualify them for subsequent steps in their careers. (This does not mean that there are not students and teachers who think that assessment of some persons by other persons is "elitist" and hence to be done away with as soon as possible.)

Examination results are sometimes posted in public—although this has been criticized recently—and sometimes they are held confidential, with only the student and the institutions which he wishes to be apprised of his achievements being given that information. Assessments of qualities of performance supplementary to the assessments embodied in examination marks have been made for a long time in universities, and above all in the universities and colleges of Great Britain and the United States and in those countries which share the same traditions of university life. These supplementary assessments have always been regarded as necessary by other institutions in which the student seeks admission or employment or from which he seeks an award. Being directed to features of the student's qualities which do not lend themselves easily to satisfactory quantitative description, they have the properties of "tacit knowledge." They cannot be demonstrated in the way in which scientific propositions can be demonstrated. Yet they are rightly regarded as indispensable to the working of educational and scientific institutions and to the effective collaboration of higher educational and other institutions. The necessity of these assessments have been accepted by students and teachers ever since universities and education became linked with entry into professional careers.

These assessments—including testimonials—have invariably been regarded as confidential by the assessors and by the institutions to which they have been transmitted on the initiative of a student, for example, a medical school to which the student seeks admission upon completion of his premedical course. Again, confidentiality has generally been regarded by students as acceptable. There has been very little criticism of this feature of academic life until recently. Students have not questioned it, and teachers, although they might have complained about the number of testimonials which they must write every year, have accepted the task as one of their responsibilities to their students.

There has been a similar long-standing tradition of confidentiality governing the assessments which are made by teachers which are intended to give information to deans, advisers, and tutors and to remind them of their own judgments of particular interviews and discussions. Such assessments, intended primarily for internal use, are also drawn upon in the preparation of assessments which, on the student's initiative, will be sent in confidence to external bodies. The confidentiality of the communication has bound its recipient not to divulge it to anyone else without the agreement of the person with whom it deals and the agreement of the person who has written it. Until recently, this pattern of assessment has been universally accepted. The only criticisms one used to hear were that assessments tended to be more favorable than subsequent experience justified. Occasionally—but very rarely—one encountered a hostile testimonial; it was usually discounted.

VIII

The reasons for confidentiality, as well as the reasons for anonymity, are not matters of principle. They are matters of practical advantage to all parties concerned. The function of confidentiality and anonymity is to make it possible to obtain the truest possible assessments and hence to do more justice to individuals and to serve society better.

The necessity for confidentiality derives from the occasional necessity of making statements which, however tactful and circumspect, might be injurious to the self-esteem of the person assessed if the obligation of being truthful to the person or institution addressed is to be fulfilled. Some teachers would find it difficult to speak with the same frankness and truthfulness to the pupil about whom these statements are made. It is not that anything harshly disparaging is common in these confidential letters, but rather that a differentiated assessment is made which might wound the pride of a sensitive young person. A conscientious and devoted teacher will seek to guide his pupil around the shoals of his defects without describing them explicitly. Yet in writing to a potential employer or a grant-awarding body or a professional school, a teacher would do less than his duty if he does not write the truth as he sees it. If he fails to do so, he will impose disadvantages upon the better qualified student for the benefit of the less qualified one.

Would a student benefit from having access to the files of letters and other assessments I have written about? There are some instances where a purely factual error has been made, for example, a wrong grade entered, an omission of some distinction, etc. Since examination marks and transcripts of marks are not withheld from the student who has received those marks, the need to correct such errors raises no question of an infringement of confidentiality. But the record of courses studied and marks received, where errors are clearly definable and tangible and hence easily corrigible, is different from a series of letters and memoranda in which the qualities of the student's accomplishments and shortcomings are described. Such assessments are not in the nature of the case clearly corrigible in the way in which a record can be. To make such assessments requires much experience, a keen power of observation, and the capacity to articulate impressions gained in numerous different situations.

The reading by the student of such assessments and testimonials, however truthful, might well give rise to a sense of injury if the student happened to think that his merits were insufficiently appreciated, and that his defects should not have been mentioned at all. If human beings, especially young ones, were insensate machines, completely rational and without pride and without a need for self-esteem and appreciation by others, the scrutiny of such documents could cause no injury. But they are not such machines and a sense of hurt which might have been avoided is a likely consequence of divulgence to them of assessments made of their work. This is another, no less important, argument for confidentiality.

Furthermore, quite apart from the corrigibility of assessments and the wounded feelings to which divulgence might give rise in the student, confidentiality is necessary to the truthfulness of assessments and hence to justice, in the sense of the equivalence of rewards and merits.

If there were no scarcity in the world, if there were places in every law and medical school for all those who wish to enter, if there were fellowships and scholarships for everyone who wished to have them, and if there were no limits on the numbers of the highly desirable and remunerative appointments in the most esteemed institutions, there would be no need for truthful testimonials. But there is a scarcity of such valued objects, which our sense of justice requires to be allocated in accordance with past achievements and the prospect of future achievements. Without truthful testimonials or without testimonials at all, the distribution of such prizes would be much more arbitrary and much more unjust than the present system, with all its defects.

IX

Nonetheless, the confidentiality of assessment in American universities and colleges has just been abolished by the United States Congress. On August 21, 1974, an amendment to the Elementary and Secondary Education Act of 1969, to be called the Family Education Rights and Privacy Act of 1974, conferred upon students over the age of eighteen years—and upon parents, where the students are younger than eighteen years—the right to examine records and documents bearing on, or referring to, them in the files and archives of the university or college in which they are inscribed. Following severe criticism by the universities and colleges of the country, Senator Buckley, who proposed the original[14] amendment of August 21, submitted with Senator Pell on December 13 a further amendment which modified several of the features of its predecessor. Like its predecessor, it still requires that students, present and past, are to have "the right to inspect and review the education records" referring to themselves.[15] Students must be provided with an "opportunity for a hearing . . . to challenge the content of [their] education records, to insure that the records are not inaccurate, misleading, or otherwise in violation of the privacy or other rights of students, and to provide an opportunity for the correction or deletion of any such inaccurate, misleading, or otherwise inappropriate data contained therein. . . ."[16]

The failure of universities or colleges to comply with these requirements will result in the withholding of funds which the United States Department of Health, Education and Welfare might otherwise grant to the institution in question. Given the important part which such funds for research, educational programs, and scholarships occupy in the budgets of the major universities, public and private, of the United States, the pressure for compliance is great.

As far as the records of universities and colleges are concerned, the significant documents are the assessments of the student from the time of his application for admission and the assessments of his performance as a student during the course of his studies at that particular institution. These assessments, like the assessments of papers submitted for publication in scientific and scholarly journals, have almost always been written with a tacit understanding or an explicit assurance of confidentiality.[17]

The original amendment left it uncertain whether it would be retroactive; the new amendment stipulates that no documents placed in a student's file prior to January 1, 1975, with the understanding or assurance of confidentiality, are to be open to inspection by the student under the rights guaranteed to him. But subsequently to that date, former students will have the same right of access as currently inscribed students.

In the future, as in the past, the students' files will contain testimonials by secondary school teachers, principals and advisers, which the student submitted when he or she sought admission. There will be confidential reports written by teachers and advisers regarding the student's performance while at university or college. There will also be testimonials addressed to prospective employers; copies of many of these were placed in the files of the individual teachers, but many have in the past been kept in the files of the employment or appointments office of the university.

The second amendment is ambiguous as to whether the copies of testimonials which were sent directly by a teacher to a prospective employer and which are retained in the file of the teacher in his own room will be regarded as falling within the student's right of access. It would be only a logical extension of the provisions of the law to require that the documents in the private files of teachers and of prospective employers must also be made available to any student who wishes to know what has been said about him.

The second amendment is also ambiguous as to whether reports about a student written by a teacher or tutor to a dean, adviser, or department head within the same university are to be open to the student's inspection. It is explicit in granting to teachers the right to circulate such reports to other members of the same university without the express consent of the student, but it does not say whether the student is to have access to reports prepared only for internal distribution and use. Given the general tenor of the law, it appears likely that such documents will be regarded as open to the student's inspection.

The new amendment provides a right of waiver for students. A student may state that he will forgo the inspection of testimonials bearing on him in the files of the university. It is not clear whether the waiver will be general and comprehensive for all his years in the university or whether he can at one time waive the right to inspect and rescind that waiver at a later date, or whether the waiver will be made only for particular testimonials at the time when he requests them.

X

The abrogation of confidentiality and of the teacher's right of privacy raises no questions about the continued necessity of assessment. The law seems to accept the continued necessity of assessment. In these respects, the new American law runs parallel with most of the criticisms of the present practice of assessment of scientific and scholarly papers submitted for publication and of applications for the support of research. They both accept the necessity of assessment; they only wish to make it more truthful by getting rid of confidentiality.

Assessment will indeed continue to be necessary for as long as there is a scarcity of resources and a need for justice, and for as long as the adherence to intellectual standards is required in science and scholarship and in society at large. But will these great ends be attained if the assessments which are instrumental to them are not truthful? The question is, therefore, whether the elimination of anonymity in the assessment of manuscripts and applications for grants, and the elimination of confidentiality in assessments of students, make assessment more truthful or less truthful, more reliable or less reliable.

It is possible that referees refuse to serve as advisers to editors of journals, and that they do not wish to lose time and energy by becoming involved in acrimonious correspondence with authors of whose papers they have disapproved. After all, service as a referee is an unpaid service, and persons who are good enough in their work to be invited to be referees usually have more than enough to do, without spending their time studying unpublished papers.[18]

It is possible that university teachers decide that rather than risk a suit in court they will henceforth write perfunctory assessments which only repeat examination results, or that they will refuse to write any testimonials at all. (Even though a student might waive his or her "right to know" in order to persuade the teacher to write a testimonial, there can be no assurance that the student will not undergo a change of mind. And if there is such a change of mind, what would be the legal status of the student's waiver?)

What might be the repercussions of such refusals to assess papers and pupils seriously, or to assess them at all?

XI

There are already too many papers of little consequence being published, and if there were no stringency of assessment there would be a larger proportion of inconsequential and even poor papers published. The stream of intellectual life in science and scholarship would become even more turbid than it is at present when too many trivial and wrong things find their way into the public forum. The average level would deteriorate. The scientific or scholarly fields in which this occurred would sink in their accomplishments, and the oncoming generations would have no unambiguous standard by which to set their sights. If no austere and demanding standard is held before the oncoming generations, and if it comes to be thought that one can get away with anything, authors of papers will become more slipshod and indiscriminate in their procedures and analysis. The moral discipline which is imposed by anticipation of discriminating assessment in the light of stringent standards will be relaxed.

It would become impossible for colleges and universities and particular departments within them to maintain a high standard if they were to admit students and appoint teachers and allocate grants and research fellowships on the basis of "first come, first served," or some other criterion having nothing to do with intellectual accomplishment and promise.

Since the propositions contained in assessments are often a type difficult to prove to a person without an intimate knowledge of the subject, one likely outcome of the end of confidentiality would be greater care to avoid writing anything which could be interpreted as negative and which could be the basis for a demand for rectification, leading in some cases to litigation and claims for damages or to the withholding of governmental funds from the university. A few cases of litigation by an aggrieved student, applicant, or author would become well known. They would serve as warnings to those of discriminating judgment not to be subtle or differentiated in their written assessments.

This is what might well happen if assessment becomes perfunctory. The simulacrum of assessment may be maintained, but honest assessment will be discouraged. It will be discouraged if an assessor thinks that he will be dragged through long "grievance procedures" and perhaps even litigations in court. Assessments will become noncommittal if they are written at all.

Of course, those who wish to have an end to confidentiality of assessment do not say that they wish to bring about these conditions. They deny with horror the suggestion that their reforms will make selection and reward more arbitrary than it is at present and that they will foster publications of a lower standard than those which are now published.

Those who would reform the assessment of papers for learned journals and of applications for the support of research, and the legislators who enacted the legislative abrogation of confidentiality in the United States, think that their reforms will only make assessment more truthful.

The service of assessment is a work of supererogation. If assessment is to take time and is to offer the prospect of disagreeable and even acrimonious correspondence—and the no less disagreeable possibility of becoming involved in "grievance procedures" or in legal action as a defendant, or in financial loss to the university—the simplest resolution of the problem would be to refuse to act as an assessor or to write assessments which say nothing of consequence. Written assessments would, in consequence, lose some of their credibility. Those who receive them would be more skeptical about their truthfulness. They would seek other means of discerning the merits of those who apply to them. The telephone, which has already done so much to destroy the epistolary art, would add another conquest to its list. The assessments which count would be oral assessments. A sort of black market in truthful assessments would come into existence alongside the official market of bland, uninformative assessments. Those who sought to exercise their "right to know" would find little of interest in the files of their universities or in a referee's report, but the assessments which determine their next step in life would probably still be made. Being made orally, they would be more subject to divergent interpretations, they would vary as they passed from one person to another. The work of appointments committees and grant-awarding bodies and editors of scientific and scholarly journals would become more difficult, especially where the applicant has no prior publications to provide independent evidence of his merits.

Assessment would cease to function as a basis of just decisions. The abolition of the confidentiality of assessment would undermine assessment. The aims of the reformers, in so far as they genuinely believe in the necessity of assessment, would be undone.

XII

There is an irreducible fiduciary element in the working of all institutions and of all societies. A certain amount of willingness to accept the bona fides of colleagues, partners, collaborators, teachers, students, and correspondents is no more dispensable than assessment itself. The progress of science and scholarship rests on confidence that other scientists and scholars are not liars or forgers. The traditional ethos of science and scholarship reduces the likelihood of lies and forgeries, and the mechanisms of assessment of unpublished works and of the criticism of published works sustain this traditional ethos. The traditional ethos of universities, especially in the English-speaking world, has always involved solicitude for students and the desire to help them to make their way in the world, while at the same time upholding standards of scholarly and scientific integrity and of responsibility for the maintenance of proficiency in the learned professions. This has been accepted by students and employers alike.

This fiduciary element is indispensable. Not everything and not everybody can be checked and controlled on every occasion. Fear of being unmasked is useful, but it is insufficient. It must be sustained by devotion to truth and by the confidence that other persons are also devoted to it.

It is reasonable, certainly, to believe that, from time to time, errors are made in the assessment of candidates for grants or admissions or appointment. No human enterprise could ever be wholly free of error. Yet, by and large, the system has worked remarkably well. Referees who are known to be "hanging judges" are avoided, as are those who would carry on vendettas. Teachers who blacken the character of their students become known, and their testimonials are put aside by colleagues. Moreover, students do not ask them to write to prospective employers. Furthermore, as long as there is a plurality of journals, grant-awarding bodies, teachers, and employers, the victim of a mistaken assessment has a reasonably good chance to avoid being broken by a mistake. Pluralism is a protection to the person who is assessed; it is also a reinforcement of the integrity of the assessment process itself. Pluralism helps to make assessors worthy of this confidentiality.

The recent criticism of the anonymity and the confidentiality of assessment postulates the superfluity or inadequacy of the fiduciary element. The principle of the "right to know" is intended to replace this fiduciary element by something better. It will not improve the process of assessment. It is more likely to damage it.

The "right to know" first came into effect when it began to be believed that the reigning authorities in political institutions could be made to act more in accordance with the public interest if their actions were open to public scrutiny and criticism. The Benthamite maxim which asserted that "the eye of the public is the virtue of the statesman" was a great contribution to the civilization of politics. Its value is still very great. It is not, however, capable of universal application. It cannot supersede the confidentiality of certain deliberations and transactions. It cannot do so in the scientific, scholarly, and educational spheres any more than it can in the political sphere. Publicity, the abrogation of confidentiality, and the "right to know" cannot replace probity and the truthful and discriminating application of exigent standards of assessment.

Confidentiality, and where it obtains, anonymity, are not ends in themselves. They are practical solutions to the task of obtaining truthful assessments to enable the meritorious to be rewarded, and to enable society to benefit by proficiency in the practice of the professions for which universities train young persons. Compared with other spheres of life, for example, business and government, the world of science and learning has had very few scandals. This good record is partly a product of the traditions of assessment in which confidentiality and anonymity have, in different ways, played a very great part.

Notes

1. Some of the recurrent criticisms of the confidential assessment of scientific papers are discussed in an editorial article in *Nature*, CCXLIX, 5,458 (June 14, 1974), p. 801.
2. See, for example, Horrobin, D. F., "Referees and Research Administrators: Barriers to Scientific Research?," *British Medical Journal*, II, 5,912 (April 27, 1974), pp. 216–18, and the ensuing correspondence in *British Medical Journal*, II, 5,915 (May 18, 1974), pp. 381–82.
3. See, for example, the Campbell, Frank, "Letter to the Editor," *Times Higher Education Supplement*, 155, (October 4, 1974), p. 10.
4. Recent assertions of this view may be found in Fraenkel-Conrat, Heinz, "Letter," *Nature*, CCLXVIII, 5,443 (March 1, 1974), p. 8; Reid, George C., "Letter," *Nature*, CCLXIX, 5,454 (March 17, 1974), p. 206; and Horrobin, "Referees and Research Administrators." Professor Fraenkel-Conrat is a member of the Department of Molecular Biology of the University of California at Berkeley. Dr. Reid has been editor of the *Journal of Geophysical Research* (*Space Physics*). Dr. Horrobin is reader in physiology at the University of Newcastle upon Tyne. The positions occupied by these three recent critics of anonymity show that the critique is not to be explained away by the statement that dissatisfaction with anonymity is simply a function of an unsuccessful scientific career.
5. Dr. Horrobin, for example, refers to "a closed system, operated by faceless men with vested interests in the status quo." Horrobin, "Referees and Research Administrators," p. 218.
6. Dr. Horrobin declares that "the myth which sustains the scientific establishment—namely, that all scientists are honourable and interested only in scientific progress—must be rejected." Ibid., p. 218.
7. A variant of this mode of distribution has been proposed by Professor Michael Moravcsik in the field of high-energy physics. Professor Moravcsik has argued for the distribution of papers immediately on completion without waiting for editorial acceptance. But again his main consideration has been greater speed and lower cost; the moral aspect of confidential assessment has not played any part in the justification for his scheme. Moravcsik Michael, "Some Modest Proposals," *Minerva*, IX, 1 (January, 1971), pp. 58–59.
8. Such evidence as exists indicates that there is no monopoly of assessment by the "establishment" of science. That evidence also indicates that the "establishment" does not use its power of assessment to promote its own interests. See Zuckerman, Harriet and Merton, Robert K., "Institutionalized Patterns of Evaluation in Science," *Minerva*, IX, 1 (January, 1971), pp. 66–100 reprinted in Merton, Robert K., *The Sociology of Science: Theoretical and Empirical Investigations* (Chicago: University of Chicago Press, 1973), pp. 461–96.
9. A detailed account of the opening, reproduction, and distribution of confidential files at the University of Warwick in 1970 is contained in Thompson, E. P. (ed.), *Warwick University Ltd.: Management, Industry, and the Universities*

(Harmondsworth: Penguin Books, 1970).
10. The "Craig case" at the University of Lancaster was partly conducted by Dr. Craig's supporters through the disclosure of "confidential" papers. This affair has been reported in detail in the *Times Higher Education Supplement.*
11. Mr. Frank Campbell, the author of a book entitled *High Command: The Making of an Oligarchy at the Polytechnic of North London,* 1970–1974, said in a letter published in the *Times Higher Education Supplement* (155 [October 4, 1974], p. 12) that some of the documentary evidence used in his book consisted of "letters and other things taken from administrators' offices by students." In a letter to the same journal, Mr. Terence Miller, director of the Polytechnic of North London, wrote that "during the October 1973 'occupation' a filing cabinet in my office was broken open and many letters, memoranda, and other papers were stolen. Some were subsequently returned after having been photocopied." *Times Higher Education Supplement,* 157 (October 18, 1974), p. 12.
12. The apprehension concerning "secret files" is, nonetheless, capable of being quickly aroused. In his observations about the events at the University of Warwick and their repercussions at other British universities, Mr. E. P. Thompson wrote: "The speed with which the agitation to 'open the files' spread to other universities recalled a *grande peur.* Like all such infectious social fears, it revealed not so much an accumulation of hard particular evidence (I don't myself believe that the more obnoxious items in the Warwick files are 'typical,' although such items might be found in a few other places) as a general condition of insecurity and lack of confidence." Thompson, *Warwick University Ltd.,* p. 152.
13. See the Freedom of Information Act, Public Law 89–487, July 4, 1966, An Act to amend section 3 of the Administrative Procedure Act, chap. 324, of the Act of June 11, 1946 (60 Stat. 238) "to clarify and protect the right of the public to information and for other purposes." United States Senate 1160, 5 United States Code 1002, *United States Statutes at Large,* vol. 80 (Washington, D.C.: U.S. Government Printing Office, 1966), pp. 250–51; Public Law 90–23, June 5, 1967, United States House of Representatives 5357, *United States Statutes at Large,* vol. 81 (Washington, D.C.: U.S. Government Printing Office, 1967), pp. 54–56; and Executive Order 11652, March 8, 1972, "Classification and Declassification of National Security Information and Material."
14. United States Congress, Educational Amendments of 1974, "Protection of the Rights and Privacy of Parents and Students," Public Law 93–380, 93rd Congress, United States House of Representatives 69, 21 August, 1974. 20 United States Code, 821, 88 *United States Statutes* (Washington, D.C.: U.S. Government Printing Office, 1974), pp. 88–91. The second amendment, enacted on December 13, 1974, bears the same title as its predecessor. My comments are based on the final version printed in Department of Health, Education and Welfare, Office of the Secretary, "Privacy Rights of Parents and Students," *Federal Register,* 40, 3 (January 6, 1975), p. 1,208. It is rumored that the original amendment, introduced by the conservative Republican senator, Mr. James Buckley of New York, was not subjected to the usual scrutiny or reflection. It was proposed by Senator Buckley, as drafted by one of his legislative assistants, and was an extension to universities and colleges of a measure intended to protect school children from becoming the unprotected objects of psychological and sociological tests and investigations. All this may be true, but the content of the amendment corresponds closely with certain currents of American opinion. It is, in other words, not simply an accident without a past and without a future.

15. Ibid., section 438 (a) (1), p. 1,208.
16. Ibid., section 438 (a) (2), p. 1,208.
17. While writing this comment, I have also been requested by one of my students to provide a testimonial in support of his application for a grant from the United States Department of Health, Education and Welfare (USHEW). The testimonial is to be submitted on a printed form supplied by the USHEW; the form contains an explicit assurance that my testimonial will be treated as confidential. What would be the status of my testimonial if I placed a copy in the student's file in the office of the registrar of my university or of the department in which the student is inscribed? Would the copy of my letter in the files of the USHEW be confidential while the same letter at my university is deprived of the confidentiality assured me by the USHEW?
18. Occasionally one hears it said that referees sometimes make off with some of the data or ideas contained in manuscripts or proposals which they have been asked to assess. I myself have heard of only one authentic case: the grant-awarding body required that the faithless referee make public acknowledgment of his inspiration in a subsequent publication. But the elimination of confidentiality and anonymity gives no guarantee against plagiary. Plagiary is just as possible from published works as it is from unpublished ones.

Part V
Reflection

14

The University: A Backward Glance

Fifty years of universities! This just about corresponds to my own lifetime in universities. When I entered the University of Pennsylvania, except for Saturday afternoons in the autumn, the university was a quiet place, apart from the world. The teachers did their teaching as seriously as it was in their nature to do so; they told no jokes in their lectures. Some of them had written books and edited texts; only one of them had written a textbook, one had edited an anthology, none had compiled a book of "readings." They seemed to me to be a priesthood, rather uneven in their merits but uniform in their bearing; they never referred to anything personal. Some read from old lecture notes—one of them used to have to unroll the dog-eared lower corners of his foolscap manuscript and then haltingly decipher the thumb-worn last lines. Others lectured from cards that had served for years, to judge by the worn and furry edges, which were visible to students like myself who sat in the front of the lecture room. The teachers began on time, ended on time, and left the room without saying a word more to their students, very seldom being detained by questioners. There were about two or three lecturers who were admired by the middling and lower grade of student because they entertained the students by quips or eloquence or by personal references to their own experiences. They were the "characters" of the university.

Some of the students studied continuously; some, not always the case, read widely and continuously; some idled; and most did what was more or less the required minimum, took each course as seriously as they could without allowing it to interfere too much with their youthful pleasures, except for a few weeks or days before examinations. Almost all male students wore suits; all wore neckties. The students in the school of business administration wore well-pressed suits, and when they sat down they pulled up their trouser legs in order not to blunt the sharp creases.

The more serious students—among whom I counted myself and a few of my friends—thought it was the duty of the teachers to do their work with passing conscientiousness. They all seemed to do this. I never heard it said that so and so had not prepared his lecture. Once one of the teachers delivered the wrong lecture—that is, a lecture for another course that he was teaching that term; he became aware of it about three-quarters of the way through, smiled in a sweetly sheepish way, and continued with the wrong lecture. But it was certainly a properly prepared lecture! Those who did research and who wrote books or scholarly or scientific papers were admired, but in a distant and detached way. No student expected to become friendly with his teachers, and the teachers took little personal interest in their students. I and almost all of my friends were commuters; we arrived between 8:00 and 9:00 A.M. and stayed until 10:30 or 11:00 P.M., mostly in the university library and, when not there, in the Horn and Hardart cafeteria across the street from the center of the campus. We occasionally saw our teachers in the library, but nothing more than a nod passed between us.

The classes were not large, yet there was no discussion. No questions were raised in class, and there were no office hours. Students were addressed—if they were addressed at all—by their surnames; no student, if asked his name, would answer "Bill" or "Jack" or whatever his intimates might call him. Few of the teachers had a room to themselves where they worked on their research; those who did made no arrangements to meet their students. I cannot recall ever having heard of a student who had been invited to the home of a teacher. Teachers lived in remote suburbs, mostly, I think, in the Main Line.

It all worked fairly well. The students did not complain about the distance between themselves and their teachers. The teachers kept to themselves and so did the students. There must have been neurotic students and dropouts among us, but I did not hear about them. The library was there and the laboratories were there and the museums were there. These were the places where those students who were interested in their subjects educated themselves. They read the journals, became acquainted or, in some cases, intimate with a wide range of literature, took copious notes, and prepared to write the papers that were required in almost all courses. Cranks like myself wrote long and probably outrageous—and sometimes unsolicited—papers, which were graded with scarcely a comment, even when they received exceptionally high marks.

We never thought about Harvard or Columbia or Princeton. Nor did we feel inferior to them. We were not proud of our university. Nor were we ashamed of it. We were, of course, not ignorant of other universities.

We, or at least I, knew of the works of professors elsewhere. I used to read Irving Babbitt, whom I definitely associated with Harvard. We knew of Whitehead at Harvard, Dewey at Columbia, Rostovtzeff, who had gone to Yale, Lancaster at Johns Hopkins, and so on. The fact that we did not have such eminent scholars at Pennsylvania never caused any of us to feel inferior. Each university was sui generis. We did not have any sense of competition among universities, and I surmise that most of our teachers had none either.

We commuters—mostly Jews—never felt that we were outsiders. None of my friends ever thought that the distance between the teachers and ourselves had anything to do with anti-Semitism. The question did not arise. The teachers appeared to be just as distant from the Christian students.

II

When I came to the University of Chicago it was all rather different. There the teachers seldom lectured from old notes, although Professor Ogburn once read the wrong superscript of a statistical formula from an excessively used card. Questions during lectures were accepted. The more interested students flocked round the teacher at the end of the class, and the most interested or ambitious or sycophantic might walk with the teacher to his room and perhaps be invited in to sit down, surrounded by shelves full of books and amidst tables and chairs piled high with manuscripts and notes. Many of the teachers not only spent the whole day at the university but could also be found there in the evenings and even on Sundays. There were departmental student societies, and teachers sometimes joined them for dinner or attended their meetings.

The University of Chicago was a quiet place and a grave one as well. The country was well into the depression by then, and that had an additionally sobering effect. The students and the research assistants, of whom I was one, occasionally discussed politics—something we had never done at Pennsylvania despite our interest in political and social philosophy and European intellectual history and literature. But there were never any harsh discussions about politics.

At Chicago, the students were much more self-conscious about being at Chicago than we had ever been at Pennsylvania. Harvard, Columbia, California (Berkeley), and Yale were more on our minds. We were much more alert to the standing of the University; and since we were closer to the teachers, we could also sense that they were aware of the standing of their respective departments in the country.

When I was a student at the University of Pennsylvania, its name never appeared in the newspapers except in connection with athletic events and games. There were some very good scientists at Pennsylvania in those days and at least one distinguished economist, but I cannot recall ever having seen their names in newspapers. Even magazines such as the Nation and the New Republic only rarely referred to universities. At Chicago it was quite different. For one thing, the president of the university was Robert Maynard Hutchins, a remarkably quick-witted, sharp-tongued, and handsome man, then in his early thirties and able to stir up—and enjoyed stirring up—controversies.

The teaching at Chicago was more informal and sometimes more eccentric than it had been at Pennsylvania. The titles and substance of courses changed frequently; the teachers spoke from the heart of their research and reflection. With all the informality, however, the students were very deferential and seldom complained among themselves about their teachers. Even teachers who deserved to be were rarely criticized. Most of them had established reputations as scholars, but even those who had not were respected by the students as promising young men who would ascend to the heights once they reached the proper points of their careers. There were few lists of required reading and ample lists of suggested reading. Teachers often said in response to a query: "I often wonder about that," or "I can't answer that question."

Neither before nor after I ascended to the rank of instructor, from having been a research assistant, did I hear any of my colleagues speak of tenure. The verb to tenure and the adjective tenured had not yet come into common usage, partly because the older generation of social scientists was still not confident of its capacity to improve the English language, and partly because the idea of the university's fixed and permanent obligation to them had not yet appeared. My colleagues at Chicago, if they though about it, never spoke about it. Each of us was glad just to have an appointment. For one thing, teaching at a university, and at the University of Chicago in particular, was thought by us to be a privilege. We did not think that we had been predestined for distinction, and having appointments—however lowly in the academic hierarchy, but so high by comparison with what the world generally seemed to offer—was a sufficient boon for us. I did not think that far into the future, anyway; nor did my friends at Chicago.

There was a vague sense of the hierarchy of universities, but it was not acutely felt. A person who had a doctorate from Chicago did not think that he was exiled from the Elysian Fields if he took a post at Vanderbilt or Utah. The hypersensitivity to rank, which is characteristic of the "anti-elitist" decades in which we are now living, had not yet appeared. Fifty years ago, our country and our universities were all too "elitist," according to the passionate conviction that, in the last two decades, has seized the intellectuals of this country. Yet fifty years ago it was not regarded as a mortification to be appointed to a university located somewhere else than "where the action is," to use another of the phrases of the egalitarian anti-elitists!

III

The professors at the University of Pennsylvania taught comprehensive courses for undergraduates and more specialized courses for seniors and graduate students. The former courses were given every year, the latter usually every other year. The specialized courses were taught by men who had specialized in the subjects of the courses, who had covered all the literature on them up until fairly recent years. I cannot recall any new courses except for those brought in by newly appointed professors or associate professors, and they were required to be on subjects well established in the field. There was no demand for innovation.

There is now. As a result, new courses proliferate, new subjects appear, especially in the social sciences and humanities where there is little corresponding growth of knowledge to necessitate them or to supply them with substance. There is nothing wrong with new courses. The mind does not stand still any more than does the stock of knowledge, and it is proper that students should benefit from these developments. It is desirable that a canon should be revised from time to time to accommodate genuine accomplishments in academic disciplines and, on rare occasions, to institute a new discipline. It also is desirable that a canon should exist, because there is a real hierarchy of works and genres, and students should not be made the victims of indiscriminately introduced novelties. A canon is, however, repugnant to the academic culture of the present day.

IV

One of the achievements of American universities at the end of the last century was the introduction of a departmental pattern of organization. Each department covered a discipline—or two if they were close to each other and if one or both were not sufficiently attractive or intellectually strong enough to justify building up a separate department. Each department had a chairman. To be a chairman was a distinction; it was regarded as an honor by the person who was selected for the position. His term was often of indefinite duration. A man could become known as a chairman, loved and respected or hated and feared. I never came across a case of a person who was offered the chairmanship and refused to accept it—although things being as they were, junior teachers and research assistants were not included in the circle of confidentiality. The chairman was appointed by the dean or the president and was usually, through not always, a relatively eminent scholar. He had great authority—he was listened to and obeyed. Some chairmen were imperious, some soft-mannered and considerate. In most universities, the chairman initiated and carried through appointments to his department in conjunction with the dean and the president. Sometimes he consulted all the other professors; sometimes he consulted only those who were in his confidence; sometimes he discussed a prospective appointment with the whole department. This was at his discretion. The situation did not always produce happy relations within the department, but at the University of Pennsylvania, and generally at Chicago as well, the students knew nothing of this. Academics tended to treat such matters as confidential and did not unthinkingly or spitefully disclose to graduate students or journalists what had been discussed in confidence within the teaching staff of the department.

The chairman had great power. Sometimes he did harm to a department by his favoritism or even persecution. But aside from doing occasional ill, the department chairman usually kept the balance of his department, saw to it that legitimate points of view and modes of thought were represented in the teaching of the department, and that the traditions of his discipline were duly respected and departed from only with good reason. A good chairman know on how long a leash some of his professors should be held and what justified the tolerance of departure from the canon.

Both of these things have changed. The chairman is no longer the ruler of his department; sometimes he does not even stand in a relationship of primus inter pares. He has become executive secretary with little or no discretionary power. The amount of administration has increased greatly, and there is little deference given to the chairman. One of his main tasks is to listen to the complaints of his colleagues—to their angry demands for higher salaries and promotion, to their efforts to persuade him privately of the desirability of appointing one of their protégés or political companions. The chairman can control very little; his former sovereignty has seeped away into all the ranks of the department. It is not always easy in some departments to find a senior person willing to become chairman. It threatens to be five years of absence from one's own research. It means the renunciation of nearly complete freedom and the assumption of a role in which one is both a powerless bystander and an errand boy between his departmental colleagues and the administration.

V

Universities are more competitive now than they used to be. The worry about "league tables" has become a sort of mania. The two surveys by Cartter and by Roose and Anderson are often mentioned; these surveys of the rankings of departments and universities have aggravated a state of mind that had already existed. It is not accidental that three such rankings were published within the dozen years between 1957 and 1969 and only one before that in the preceding half century. One of the ways of assuring that a university is in the "big leagues" is to see to it that it is "nationally visible."

The press paid little attention to universities fifty years ago, and this is one of the reasons why universities gave an impression of quiet and gravity. Accounts of accomplishments in games or occasional scientific achievements did appear in newspapers, but in general, universities were not news. University teachers were not pundits; they did not appear on the radio and were not interviewed by newspapers. University teachers did not become involved in litigations against their universities. The main concern of the public relations office of a university was to keep out of the newspapers, not to get into them. There was nothing like the Chronicle of Higher Education or Change.

The work of academic scientists in the production of the atomic bomb probably had a great deal to do with setting the stage for the expansion of publicity about universities. Academics were almost as prominent in the McCarthyite denunciation of communist spies. Both the atomic bomb and McCarthyism persuaded journalists to begin looking upon universities as the objects of newspaper stories. The student disturbances of the 1960s and early 1970s also caused the volume of publicity about universities to leap upward. University teachers in the social sciences study current events now more than they did half a century ago; more of them are willing to express their opinions about these events; and there are several publications eager to print their opinions. Many teachers want publicity and vie for it; and some of those who receive little of it are jealous of those who receive more than their share.

Less dramatic but perhaps as important has been the fact that the federal government has become involved in university affairs by supplying most of the funds for academic scientific research. As government intrudes more into the affairs of universities, the more spectacular instances of this intrusion appear in the press. The universities rather like much of this publicity. It seems to be the normal thing, and even old-fashioned scholars who do not seek publicity are convinced that the universities must make themselves appreciated by the public, which supplies the funds for their continued existence. In the course of all this hullabaloo, the universities have lost much of their necessary self-enclosure.

VI

At the beginning of the century, the universities studied the past and the timeless. They studied history, classics, literature, oriental subjects, and the physical and biological sciences. When they studied the past, they stopped their studies well before the threshold of recent events. They did not study contemporary literature or contemporary history. Fifty years ago American universities were just beginning to move into the present. This was especially the case at Chicago where sociology and political science were concerned with the present. It was less so at more old-fashioned universities where the past still held its own, in uncongenial circumstances.

The social sciences were the first point of entry of the universities into the contemporary world. The reports and opinions of university social scientists are frequently reported in the press. They are "news" because they are concerned about the same things that concern newspapers and television. University social scientists are inextricably entangled with creating news for the press through their research and through their own opinions on current affairs.

The politicization of academics has contributed to the interpenetrating of the inner world of the universities and the outer world of current contention. Academics have become more occupied with contemporary politics and have been taking partisan positions in political issues to the point of giving political ends precedence over intellectual ones—sometimes doing so under the cover of teaching and scholarly research. Politicization is not the study of contemporary politics, although it is encouraged by that; it is the infusion of contemporary political partisanship into universities.

Certainly the social scientists of the late 1920s often had political sympathies and affiliations. For the most part, however, they held these views in check, and the traditions of academic rhetoric required temperateness of expression. Where they were partisan, the arrangements they desired did not demand a far-reaching transformation of the fundamental constitution of society, nor did their political expression require melodramatic rhetoric. There was also a convention that teaching should be confined to facts. This made for fairly dull teaching, but it also contributed to the maintenance of the cool tone that prevailed in classrooms and in universities generally. Now, after a half century, it is widely believed among the younger generation of social scientists that "objectivity" and "evaluative neutrality" are mare's nests or deliberate deceptions, and impossible as well as undesirable. What the younger and middle generations vehemently deny, the older generation lacks the strength of conviction or strength of character to affirm. This is an invitation to partisan agitation in classrooms; although many teachers of the social sciences, especially those who are more mathematically able, do not avail themselves of the privileges afforded by this license, many in fact do. In any case, few are willing to speak out forthrightly on the possibility of separating statements of fact from evaluative statements.

Until the very beginning of our period, most academics were Republicans and Democrats; a very small number were socialists; and there were a few sympathizers with the Industrial Workers of the World (I do not know whether there was even one Wobbly in the academic world). In the 1920s there were a few (certainly not many more than would crowd a small broom cupboard) who were members of the Communist party. Of the vast majority who regarded themselves as Democrats or Republicans, very few took active part in politics. The academic profession was, even in the robust hog-butchering Middle West, a genteel profession—perhaps a rather shabby genteel profession—and American politics in those days was not a place for the genteel.

The national political arena could be entered mainly through service in the local and state political machines. The latter were filled with Bathhouse Johns and Hinky Dinks, lively and clever and not very scrupulous or refined.

This did not mean, however, that academics were indifferent to politics. Professors of economics tended toward the Republican party, although they disapproved wholeheartedly of protectionism. Sociologists and political scientists leaned to the reformers' movements.

In the 1930s the mass of American academics—especially in the humanities and social sciences, but elsewhere, too, outside the professional schools—embraced the New Deal with enthusiasm. From about 1932 onward, the long political silence began to give way to clamorous politics in American universities. The Communist party set about in right earnest to recruit students and teachers to the party and to the flourishing crop of para-party or fellow-traveling organizations. They made some progress at Harvard, City College of New York, the University of California at Berkeley, and perhaps at the University of Wisconsin.

The fifty years through which we have passed have been fifty years of academic political zeal, enthusiasm, frenzy, alarm, excitement. At first this zeal was concentrated in a few universities; by the last decade and a half of our period it has spread through the entire system, although unevenly.

VII

The intensified political interest and activity of American academics over the past fifty years have taken place in a situation in which administrators and the lay governing bodies of universities have renounced much of the disciplinary authority that they once exercised over their teaching staffs. The half century preceding this last one saw sanctions not infrequently imposed against university teachers for exercising their civil freedoms.

Members of boards of trustees used to take affront very quickly when university and college teachers spoke in public from a standpoint that was called "socialistic" or "syndicalistic" or "communistic." This did not happen at Chicago or Harvard or Columbia, or if it did, the affronted ones were calmed or suppressed by their colleagues or by the president of the university. It did happen in lesser private colleges and universities as well as in state universities. Some state legislators were very excitable about such things in those days. They really had very little to be excited about: there were no revolutionaries of a dangerous kind in the country—certainly not in the universities—but it was only a little more than a decade after the Russian Revolution, and there had been communist uprisings from Hamburg to Shanghai.

This was the time when the elites of small towns had been shaken by the cultural changes wrought by the First World War. Puritanical, pious, workaday, ambitious, patriotic America seemed to be under attack. The appearance of sympathy with bolshevism upset their inexperienced eyes. They were about the last generation of trustees who took their trusteeship in the narrowest and most literal sense of the word. The result was that provincial newspaper editors, dentists, merchants, and petty local politicians fanned each other's sparks of distrust of Europe and the eastern seaboard, of bohemianism and agnosticism.

In the late 1930s I read through all of the reports of infringements on academic freedom reported in the Bulletin of the American Association of University Professors. (I was refused access then to the archives and was refused again a few years ago.) I also read through the academic cases in the archives of the American Civil Liberties Union. Most of them had to do with sanctions exercised by presidents and boards of trustees against university teachers for political activities outside the university. The political activities were mostly of a rather mild socialistic tendency. There were practically no cases that had to do with political agitation in lectures or classes within the university. There were no cases of disrupting the college or university in its normal functioning. There were no cases of agitating students to go on strike, to boycott classes, or to hold sit-ins in university buildings. There were no charges that the teacher had neglected his classes; research was not an issue in most cases because the incidents occurred in institutions in which research was not expected of teachers. There was at least one case of a sociologist who, in his teaching about the family, had either spoken too plainly about sexual matters or expressed skepticism about the value of the monogamous family; there were very few such cases, and those that did occur were mainly at minor undergraduate colleges often under denominational sponsorship.

Most of the cases had to do with the civil freedom of academics, that is, their rights to express political views, within the framework of the law and outside the university, in the same way as any other citizen could. The issue at stake was the political freedom of the academic—not academic freedom, which is a different thing. The American Association of University Professors was certainly right to attempt to protect academics from the restrictions of their rights as citizens. It called these rights "academic freedom" and left it at that; it practically never concerned itself with the obligation of academics to perform certain tasks and their freedom to carry them out. Not very long before he was murdered, Charles Frankel told me that he recalled having been told by John Dewey that when the American Association of University Professors was founded, it established two committees: one on academic freedom and tenure, the other on academic obligations. Dewey told him that the latter committee had not met for about three decades, while the former committee was almost continuously active.

VIII

The first decade of the half century of American academic life through which I have lived was a period of exceptional academic freedom in the sense of there being the freedom to do academic things. Research was not so expensive then; the departmental system gave opportunities to younger staff members to do research. Departments were beginning to be autonomous in the choice of colleagues. Administrators and heads of departments, especially in the more eminent universities, gave every faculty member the freedom to do what he thought he should be doing. Imagination and initiative in research were appreciated and rewarded to the extent that was possible with restricted resources. The federal government had not yet appeared on the scene to try to regulate the conduct of research or to police appointments.

Once the Second World War was out of the way, the universities resumed the course on which they had been moving with greater verve (as a result of the stimulating experience of war) and with the greater amplitude conferred by the affluence that increased the size of departments and permitted more and larger research projects. The McCarthyite harassment certainly alarmed and intimidated academics of leftist connections, and it seems to have curtailed their civil freedom; but I doubt whether it had much restrictive effect on academic freedom in teaching and research. The invocation of the Fifth Amendment did result in the dismissal of Moses Finley, who later became an eminent figure in Great Britain; but the activity about which he refused to testify was not his research and teaching. There were very few such cases in the American academic world. There might have been academics who were intimidated into refraining from deeper investigations or from teaching what they wanted to teach or who asserted beliefs that did not correspond with what they really thought. I myself never came across anyone who said that this had happened to him. Both academic freedom and the civil freedom of academics flourished in the United States in this past half century—the former without fluctuations and the latter once the McCarthyite intimidation ceased.

From the middle of the 1960s, however, infringements on academic freedom became at least as common—insofar as such things can be estimated when no statistics can be reliably assembled—as the infringements on the political freedom of academics had been in earlier periods, perhaps more so. The lead in public was taken by aggressive, not very brave students, encouraged by floods of favorable publicity in press and television and spurred by the knowledge that their elders were praising them for demonstrating moral elevation. The most impressive thing to me—having lived through the depression and the McCarthy period and having observed as closely as I could from a distance the behavior of German professors in the face of the Nazis— was the faint-heartedness of the American academic profession and how little it understood or cared for academic freedom.

IX

American students had almost always been pleasant and deferential young persons who had invariably accepted the universities as they were. It was therefore a shock that sent their teachers reeling when the students went against their institutions with criticisms that were, however outlandish, asserted with an unthinkingness called "sincerity." When the rebellious students demanded the reconstitution of the syllabus, the liberal academics found themselves speechless before the challenge. When it was demanded that students share in "hiring and firing decisions," this too seemed right. When it was demanded that "pluralism of standpoints" be admitted into teaching—meaning that radicals must be appointed to the teaching staff—that contention also appeared undeniable. Prudence and timidity supported the view that some of the new staff members should be appointed on grounds of their political convictions. When after a few years, the federal government entered the scene to insist on the suspension of intellectual criteria for academic appointment in the name of affirmative action, the position from which academic standards could be defended had already been evacuated. The federal government did not insist on the appointment of radicals; it required the appointment of blacks, Puerto Ricans, Mexicans, American Indians, and women. Aside from equity and justice and amends for past injustice, the argument of "pluralism of standpoints" came in again; sociology contributed the idea of "role models." Blacks and others would introduce new standpoints; they would also be role models for their own kind.

Only a handful of academics rejected such preposterous statements. Most of them accepted the demands for the application of intellectually irrelevant criteria because they thought it would not affect their own work or because they were afraid not to do so because they had never really thought of the matter. Once state legislators and boards of trustees and imperious presidents gave up the field, McCarthy, student radicals, and the federal government all found it just as easy to intimidate the academics.

University administrators in most universities have gone along with the federal government's deforming demands, not wishing to have trouble and above all not wishing to endanger the large federal payments in grants and contracts for research. Most of them capitulated with little public complaint to the demand for a further renunciation of intellectual standards in academic appointments. Academic biomedical and physical scientists who had not yielded to the demands of radical students because they did not have so many were not worried that they would be forced to appoint unqualified members of ethnic groups or unqualified women. Their first interest was to get on with their research; they were confident of the importance of their research and they were confident, too, that the federal government would not compel them to adulterate their standards. They had no sympathy with administrators and members of those very few humanistic departments who, exceptionally, resisted the bullying of the federal government. The attitudes of the scientists, particularly those in the medical schools, gave evidence of their professional self-centeredness and of how lightly they had taken their responsibilities for the university as a whole.

X

How strange this all would seem to a professor who passed into the next world in 1930 and underwent a premature resurrection fifty years later. Mild and restrained in expression, moderate in his political interest and sympathy, and used to a stilles, friedsames Gelehrtenleben, he might well be alarmed by the noisiness and busyness of a contemporary university. The breezy bad manners of his colleagues might disturb him. He would be frightened, not reassured, by the large number of security officers, the university's own police force, patrolling the campus and the university's buildings. The consumption of food and drink in classes and seminars might startle him, and the state of the language spoken by his colleagues and pupils would confound him. The size of sums requested and granted for research would surprise him as would the number of administrators, high and low, and their secretaries. But what he would be least able to comprehend would be the presence of the federal government at every turn of the corner.

In the late 1930s the presidents of the leading American universities, then as ever in severe financial straits, agreed that they should not seek or accept financial support from the federal government—none was being offered—because they feared that such acceptance would be followed by the intrusion of the government into strictly academic matters. Brave words when there was neither temptation nor threat! After the Second World War, large sums of money were offered by the federal government, and the presidents of universities—probably not the same presidents who had so proudly and honorably turned their backs on the money that was never offered—accepted with enthusiasm. The result has been as their impecunious predecessors predicted.

The acceptance of large sums for research has greatly changed the universities. The growth in the size of universities is partly a result of this; so is the relegation of undergraduate teaching to the status of something to be done by junior teachers, graduate students, and old fuddy-duddies who do no research. The activity of applying for grants has become a pervasive preoccupation. Even in the humanities, in which research can still be done with very little money, it has become common to apply for, and sometimes to obtain, a grant for research. Political science and sociology, having become ostensibly more scientific, need larger sums of money to conduct sample surveys and to deal with the larger qualities of data. The natural sciences where the wedge first entered, require, it goes without saying, more money to pay for more refined and more powerful instruments and more assistants and technicians to attend to their machines and to analyze the data that are generated through their use. All these activities and all this equipment depend on funds from the federal government. The number of students has also depended on the government's provision of grants and loans for the payment of tuition fees, cost of maintenance and other expenses, and the provision of funds to employ students as research assistants.

But this is not all. The federal government never developed a tradition of understanding what universities are, unlike the state legislatures and departments of education of the Middle West. It discovered their utility for military purposes during the Second World War, and since that time it has looked upon them as instruments and objects of policies concerned with ends other than the ends intended by universities. The federal government has put the universities in an extremely expensive iron maiden, through its demand for, and its surveillance of, the universities' conformity with "affirmative action," "rights of human and animal subjects," "access for the handicapped," "accountability," and other policies. These contracts and grants and the consequent surrender of the universities to the government's intrusive bureaucracy have compelled the universities to enlarge their own bureaucracies to meet all these demands for the keeping and submission of records, which the government requires to aid its surveillance of the universities' "compliance" and to enforce their "accountability." There are more administrators in universities than ever before, more paperwork, more reports, more committees, and more meetings to discuss business, more sensitivity to the government's policies.

XI

Wilhelm von Humboldt, whose memorandum of 1810 started universities on their modern course, said that universities need Einsamkeit and Freiheit. Einsamkeit—solitude, separateness, being alone in a small room—is one of the main absentees from the universities of the United States as theAmerican Scholar celebrates its fiftieth anniversary. It might have been a shy guest at the journal's christening fifty years ago, but now it is hardly to be found. The Freiheit, which was to enable the individual to benefit from his Eisnsamkeit, is also more hedged about now than it used to be, but it still exists and is in some respects greater than it used to be, both in ways that are in conformity with the best interests of intellectual life and in ways that are injurious to those interests.

In certain areas of academic life, scholars and scientists are very free, especially in the major universities. Presidents and boards of trustees are very much in awe of them. Some of them have used their freedom to great intellectual advantage, made great discoveries, and written works of great learning and insight. Many of them have misused their freedom by their deficient academic civility.

The misuse of academic freedom is a consequence of the belief that the universities are primarily instruments of ends other than intellectual ends. The utilitarian conception of the university about which Irving Babbitt and Abraham Flexner used to complain is still with us, but it has come to an accommodation with learning and is not all-pervasive. More noxious to universities is the political and emancipatory conception of the university that has become crystallized over the past fifteen years.

Until about a quarter of a century ago, it was thought that academic studies should be carried on without prejudice and with an appreciation of the intrinsic value and attainability of truth. Philosophers of science, theorists of historiography, and social scientists have now concluded that all intellectual activity is "ideological," and that objectivity is neither a worthy nor a feasible ideal. There is therefore no canon of major works in the humanities; there is no difference between political contention and social science. Some of these theorists also undertake to undermine the natural sciences with such methodological and sociological analyses, but they do not succeed in reaching the work going on in those fields. They do not succeed wholly in social sciences and the humanities either because many who assent to these anti-intellectual, anti-academic theories do not really assimilate them.

Nevertheless, the various forms of politicization of the universities, the intrusion of bohemianism into the universities, and the highbrow disparagement of objective knowledge form a tremendous pressure on the heart of the universities. The pressure emanates from the academic profession itself. The academic profession of fifty years ago was a relatively small corps of persons who regarded themselves as serving an intellectual tradition that was a postulate of their existence, however ineffectually they served it. The academic profession was a corps that accepted institutional and intellectual traditions perhaps too unreflectively, but also dutifully. The academic profession of fifty years ago was in many respects rather mousy; it did not seek confrontation. It had relatively few demands except to be left alone so that it could carry out its duties. Many of its members were intellectually mediocre and performed their tasks in a routine and unexacting way; they lived withdrawn lives and did not seek to dominate their society. Some of its members were great scholars and scientists; others were obstinate eccentrics, some of whom did excellent work, and some of whom did very little. Some of them soldiered on the job, but they did so quietly and did not try to justify their indolence and evasion of their tasks by large theories.

Today the academic profession is a very different entity. It is, for one thing, very much larger. It is more heterogeneous culturally and in its social origins. It is much more animated, more excitable, more voluble, more impolite, and much more political. The academic profession is much more demanding today. It wants more resources. Enough of its members to make a difference want more freedom to do whatever they want to do, even though what they want to do is not academic and not intellectual. The academic profession today wants more influence in society; it wants political influence and it wishes to exploit for its political purposes the academic positions to which it has been appointed—to teach and to do research and to contribute to keeping the university functioning effectively. There are, of course, many academics who do not share these unbridled aspirations and this passion for expressive and ideological politics.

The university of fifty years ago will never come back. It could not be brought back into existence, and even if it could, it would not be desirable that it should be brought back in the way in which I knew it as a youth. But it had a very sound core; it had the traditions of science and learning and of the academic ethos, together with much that was adventitious and unnecessary. Those traditions managed to withstand the force of the utilitarian outlook that was inimical to them.

There are many things occurring in universities nowadays that are inimical to these traditions, but traditions are tough plants. They have even insinuated themselves into the minds of those academics who have allowed themselves to be made into enemies of academic life. The emancipationist antinomianism and egalitarianism that continue in a different way the utilitarian outlook of an earlier period have had much influence on the contemporary American university—nearly all of it pernicious. Nevertheless, they are less deeply rooted than the traditions of science and scholarship and of the academic ethos which will, despite all, withstand them.

Bibliography of the Published Works of Professor Edward Shils

Christine C. Schnusenberg and Gordon B. Neavill

The published works of Professor Edward Shils reflect an extraordinary range of intellectual interests, an international perspective, and an enormous productivity extending over a period of six decades. His writings have appeared throughout the world and have been reprinted and translated widely. We have tried to make this bibliography as inclusive and accurate as possible, but there is no doubt that we have fallen short of our objective. There are published works that remain to be identified, reprints and translations that we have missed, and manuscripts that are likely to be published in the future. The bibliography is arranged chronologically. Within each year books are listed first. Next are journal articles arranged alphabetically by journal, followed by chapters in collective works. A handful of sound recordings of lectures and panel discussions that have been identified are listed last. Several items that could not be verified have been omitted; most of these are probably bibliographical ghosts that were projected for publication but have not yet appeared.

The bibliography has been compiled over a period of years and reflects the contributions of several hands. The first part, covering the years through 1983, was originally compiled by Christine C. Schnusenberg, Assistant to Professor Shils, with the help of the following students: Liah Greenfeld, Michel Martin, John Mulholland, Peggy Rampersad, and Henrik Verest. It was presented to Professor Shils on the occasion of his seventy-fifth birthday at a dinner at the House of Hunan in Chicago on 1 July 1985 and was subsequently distributed as a working tool to students and colleagues. In 1993 Professor Shils expressed interest in bringing the bibliography up to date, and Dr. Schnusenberg promised to have it ready for his eighty-fifth birthday. After Professor Shils's death on 23 January 1995, Gordon B. Neavill, a former student and now a member of the faculty of the Library and Information Science Program at Wayne State University, offered his assistance in completing the bibliography and preparing it for publication. Working from drafts provided by Dr. Schnusenberg, he was able to add a number of new entries and to supply bibliographical details missing from entries in the original version and subsequent drafts. He was aided in this work by his graduate assistant at Wayne State University, Charles Barney Sands, who devoted himself to the project with exceptional dedication and persistence. Christine C. Schnusenberg and Gordon B. Neavill assume full responsibility for the errors and omissions that remain.

1936

(tr. with Louis Wirth) Mannheim, Karl. *Ideology and Utopia: An Introduction to the Sociology of Knowledge.* International Library of Psychology, Philosophy and Scientific Method. London: Kegan Paul, Trench, Trubner & Co.; New York: Harcourt, Brace & Co., 1936. 318pp.

1938

"Limitations on the Freedom of Research and Teaching in the Social Sciences." *Annals of the American Academy of Political and Social Science* 200 (November 1938): 144–64. Reprinted in *The Intellectuals and the Powers and Other Essays* (1972), pp. 307–32.

1939

(with Herbert Goldhamer) "Types of Power and Status." *American Journal of Sociology* 45, no. 2 (September 1939): 171–82. Reprinted as "Power and Status" in *Center and Periphery: Essays in Macrosociology* (1975), pp. 239–48.

1940

(tr.) Mannheim, Karl. *Man and Society in an Age of Reconstruction: Studies in Modern Social Structure.* London: Kegan Paul, Trench, Trubner & Co.; New York: Harcourt, Brace & Co., 1940. 469pp.
"The Bases of Social Stratification in Negro Society: A Research Memorandum." Prepared for the Carnegie-Myrdal study, "The Negro in America." New York: Carnegie Corp, 1940. Typescript. 69 leaves. Available in the Schomburg Collection, New York Public Library, and on microfilm.

1941

(tr. with Edith Lowenstein and Klaus Knorr) Fraenkel, Ernst. *The Dual State: A Contribution to the Theory of Dictatorship.* New York; London: Oxford University Press, 1941. 248pp.

"A Note on Governmental Research on Attitudes and Morale." *American Journal of Sociology* 47, no 3 (September 1941): 472–80.

1945

"Britain and the World: The Position of the Labour Party in Foreign Policy." *Review of Politics* 7, no. 4 (October 1945): 505–24.

1946

"Some Political Implications of the State Department Report." *Bulletin of the Atomic Scientists* 1, no. 9 (April 15, 1946): 7–9, 19.

"Atomic Energy in the House of Commons." *Bulletin of the Atomic Scientists* 1, no. 10 (May 1, 1946): 13–15.

"A Soviet Comment on American Atomic Policy." *Bulletin of the Atomic Scientists* 1, no. 12 (June 1, 1946): 16.

"Social and Psychological Aspects of Displacement and Repatriation." *Journal of Social Issues* 2, no. 3 (August 1946): 3–18.

(with Thomas Finletter and Harold Urey) "The United Nations and the Bomb: A Radio Discussion." University of Chicago Round Table (Radio Program). Chicago: University of Chicago, 1946. Transcript. 28pp.

1947

(with Bruno Bettelheim and Morris Janowitz) "A Study of the Social, Economic, and Psychological Correlates of Intolerance among Urban Veterans of Enlisted Rank" [abstract]. *American Psychologist* 2, no. 8 (August 1947): 323.

"British Atomic Energy Debate." *Bulletin of the Atomic Scientists* 3, no. 2 (February 1947): 52–54.

"The Atomic Bomb and the Veto on Sanctions." *Bulletin of the Atomic Scientists* 3, no. 2 (February 1947): 62–63.

"A Critique of Planning in Science: The Society for Freedom in Science." *Bulletin of the Atomic Scientists* 3, no. 3 (March 1947): 80–82.

"American Policy and the Soviet Ruling Group." *Bulletin of the Atomic Scientists* 3, no. 9 (September 1947): 237–41, 246.

"Atomic Energy Control." *Discovery* 8, no. 4 (April 1947): 114–17.

"Karl Mannheim." *Erasmus* 1, no. 4 (February 15, 1947): 193–96.

"Political Science and Sociology." Review of *Democracy and Industry*, by Constance Reaveley and John Winnington (London: Chatto and Windus, 1947). *Erasmus* 1, nos. 13–14 (August 1947): 693–97.

"Displacement and Repatriation: A Sociological Analysis." *Left News*, no. 127 (January 1947): 3755–61.

"Human Nature in Industrial Societies." *Listener* 37, no. 961 (June 26, 1947): 1005–7.
"European Letter: 1." *University Observer: A Journal of Politics* 1, no. 1 (Winter 1947): 37–41.
"Socialism in America." *University Observer: A Journal of Politics* 1, no. 2 (Summer 1947): 96–102.
"The Present Situation in American Sociology." *Pilot Papers* 2, no. 2 (June 1947): 8–36.

1948

The Atomic Bomb in World Politics. Peace Aims Pamphlet. London: National Peace Council, 1948. 79pp.
The Present State of American Sociology. Glencoe, Ill.: Free Press, 1948. 64pp.
"The House of Lords Debates International Control." *Bulletin of the Atomic Scientists* 4, no. 4 (April 1948): 122–24.
"The Failure of the U.N. Atomic Energy Commission: An Interpretation." *Bulletin of the Atomic Scientists* 4, no. 7 (July 1948): 205–10.
"The Next Phase of International Control Discussions." *Bulletin of the Atomic Scientists* 4, no. 12 (December 1948): 359–62.
"Some Remarks on the Theory of Social and Economic Organization." *Economica*, n.s., 15, no. 57 (February 1948): 36–50.
"The Failure of Atomic Control, Part 1: Russia's Responsibility." *Manchester Guardian*, no. 31,764 (August 3, 1948): 4. Reprinted in *Manchester Guardian Weekly* 59, no. 7 (August 12, 1948): 5.
"The Failure of Atomic Control, Part 2: The American Responsibility." *Manchester Guardian*, no. 31,765 (August 4, 1948): 4. Reprinted in ." *Manchester Guardian Weekly* 59, no. 8 (August 19, 1948): 13.
"The Atomic Problem: Professor Blackett's Book." *Manchester Guardian*, no. 31,845 (November 5, 1948): 4. Reprinted in *Manchester Guardian Weekly* 59, no. 20 (November 11, 1948): 12.
"Russia and the Atom." *New Commonwealth* (London) 9, no. 7 (December 1948): 150–52.
(with Morris Janowitz) "Cohesion and Disintegration in the Wehrmacht in World War II." *Public Opinion Quarterly* 12, no. 2 (Summer 1948): 280–315. Reprinted in *Center and Periphery: Essays in Macrosociology* (1975), pp. 345–83.

1949

(tr. and ed. with Henry A. Finch, with a foreword) *Max Weber on the Methodology of the Social Sciences.* Glencoe, Ill.: Free Press, 1949. 188pp. Later printings as: Weber, Max. *The Methodology of the Social Sciences.*
"Blackett's Apologia for the Soviet Position." Review of *Fear, War, and the Bomb,* by P. M. S. Blackett (New York: Whittlesey, 1949). *Bulletin of the Atomic Scientists* 5, no. 2 (February 1949): 33–47.
"Social Science and Social Policy." *Philosophy of Science* 16, no. 3 (July 1949): 219–42. Reprinted in *The Calling of Sociology and Other Essays on the Pursuit of Learning* (1980), pp. 259–88.
"The Relevance of Sociology." *Universities Quarterly* 3, no. 2 (February 1949): 584–92.

(sound recording with Martin Avrams and Alan Simpson) "The British Welfare State: What Is It?" Radio discussion on University of Chicago Round Table (Radio Program), August 28, 1949. 1 sound tape reel (30 min.). Copy in Michigan State University Library.

1950

"Primary Groups in the American Army." In *Continuities of Social Research: Studies in the Scope and Method of "The American Soldier"*, ed. Robert K. Merton and Paul F. Lazarsfeld (Glencoe, Ill.: Free Press, 1950), pp. 19–39. Reprinted in *Center and Periphery: Essays in Macrosociology* (1975), pp. 384–402.

"Georges Sorel: Introduction to the American Edition." In Georges Sorel, *Reflections on Violence*, translated by T.E. Hulme and J. Roth (Glencoe, Ill.: Free Press, 1950), pp. 13–29.

"Society." In *Chambers's Encyclopædia* (London: George Newnes; New York: Oxford University Press, 1950) 12:670–71.

1951

(with Henry Dicks) *The Soviet Army*. Santa Monica, Calif.: Rand Corporation, 1951.

(ed. with Talcott Parsons) *Toward a General Theory of Action*. Cambridge, Mass.: Harvard University Press, 1951. 506pp. Reprinted as *Toward a General Theory of Action: Theoretical Foundations for the Social Sciences*. New York: Harper Torchbooks, Harper & Row, 1962.

"The Soviet Elite: Analysis of a Legend." *Bulletin of the Atomic Scientists* 7, no. 3 (March 1951): 77–80.

"Congressional Investigations: The Legislator and His Environment." *University of Chicago Law Review* 18, no. 3 (Spring 1951): 571–84.

"Informal Organization and Formal Organization." In *Human Relations in Administration: The Sociology of Organization, with Readings and Cases*, ed. Robert Dubin (Englewood Cliffs, N.J.: Prentice-Hall, 1951), pp. 49–51.

(with Herbert Goldhamer) "Types of Power." In *Human Relations in Administration: The Sociology of Organization, with Readings and Cases*, ed. Robert Dubin (Englewood Cliffs, N.J.: Prentice-Hall, 1951), pp. 182–87.

"The Study of the Primary Group." In *The Policy Sciences: Recent Developments in Scope and Methods*, ed. Harold D. Lasswell and Daniel Lerner (Palo Alto, Calif.: Stanford University Press, 1951), pp. 44–69.

"L'etude du groupe elementaire." In *Les "Sciences de la Politique" aux Etats Unis*, ed. Harold D. Lasswell and Daniel Lerner (Paris: Librairie Armand Colin, 1951), pp. 65–104.

1952

"America's Paper Curtain." *Bulletin of the Atomic Scientists* 8, no. 7 (October 1952): 210–17.

"Lo stato attuale della sociologia americano" (translation of *The Present State of American Sociology*). Parts 1–4. *Quaderni di Sociologia*, no. 4 (Spring 1952): 179–90; no. 5 (Summer 1952): 3–10; no. 6 (Autumn 1952): 90–108; no. 7 (Winter 1953): 155–67.

1953

(with Talcott Parsons and Robert F. Bales) *Working Papers on the Theory of Action.*
Glencoe, Ill.: Free Press, 1953. 269pp. Reprinted, Westport, Conn.: Greenwood
Press, 1981.
(with Michael Young) "The Meaning of the Coronation." *Sociological Review*, n.s., 1,
no. 2 (December 1953): 63–81. Reprinted in *Center and Periphery: Essays in
Macrosociology* (1975), pp. 135–52.

1954

(tr. with Max Rheinstein) *Max Weber on Law in Economy and Society*, ed. by Max
Rheinstein. Cambridge, Mass.: Harvard University Press, 1954. 363pp.
"Conspiratorial Hallucinations." Review of *The Secret War for the A-Bomb*, by Medford
Evans (Chicago: H. Regnery, 1953). *Bulletin of the Atomic Scientists* 10, no. 2
(February 1954): 51–54.
"The Scientific Community: Thoughts after Hamburg." *Bulletin of the Atomic Scien-
tists* 10, no. 5 (May 1954): 151–55. Reprinted in *The Intellectuals and the Powers
and Other Essays* (1972), pp. 204–12.
"Scientists Affirm Faith in Oppenheimer" [statement]. *Bulletin on the Atomic Scien-
tists* 10, no. 5 (May 1954): 189.
"The Slippery Slope." *Bulletin of the Atomic Scientists* 10, no. 6 (June 1954): 242,
256.
"Scientists, Administrators and Politicians: The Report of the Riehlman Committee."
Bulletin of the Atomic Scientists 10, no. 10 (December 1954): 371–74.
"Populism and the Rule of Law." In *Conference on Jurisprudence and Politics* (1954),
ed. Scott Buchanan et al. (Chicago: University of Chicago Law School, 1955), pp.
91–107.
"Authoritarianism 'Right' and 'Left'." In *Studies in the Scope and Method of 'The
Authoritarian Personality'*, ed. Richard Christie and Marie Jahoda (Glencoe, Ill.:
Free Press, 1954), pp. 24–49.

1955

(ed.) "Secrecy, Security and Loyalty" [collection of articles on this theme]. *Bulletin of
the Atomic Scientists* 11, no. 4 (April 1955): 106–69.
"Security and Science Sacrificed to Loyalty." *Bulletin of the Atomic Scientists* 11, no.
4 (April 1955): 106–9, 130.
"The Intellectuals: Great Britain." *Encounter* 4, no. 4 (April 1955): 5–16. Reprinted as
"British Intellectuals in the Twentieth Century" in *The Intellectuals and the Powers and Other Essays* (1972), pp. 135–53.
(contributor) *Science and Freedom: The Proceedings of a Conference Convened by
the Congress for Cultural Freedom and Held in Hamburg on July 23rd-26th,
1953* (London: Martin Secker & Warburg, 1955), pp. 48–49, 174–175, 180.

1956

The Torment of Secrecy: The Background and Consequences of American Security

Policies. Glencoe, Ill.: Free Press; London: Heinemann, 1956. 238pp. Reprinted, Carbondale: Southern Illinois University Press (Arcturus Paperbacks); London: Feffer & Simons, 1974. Reprinted with an introduction by Daniel P. Moynihan, Chicago: Ivan R. Dee (Elephant Paperbacks), 1996.

"Milan Conference." *Bulletin of the Atomic Scientists* 12, no. 2 (February 1956): 38–40.

"Two Patterns of Publicity, Privacy, and Secrecy." *Bulletin of the Atomic Scientists* 12, no. 6 (June 1956): 215–20.

1957

"Primordial, Personal, Sacred, and Civil Ties: Some Particular Observations on the Relationship of Sociological Research and Theory." *British Journal of Sociology* 8, no. 2 (June 1957): 130–45. Reprinted in *Selected Essays* (1970), pp. 37–52; *Center and Periphery: Essays in Macrosociology* (1975), pp. 111–26.

"Freedom and Influence: Observations on the Scientists' Movement in the United States." *Bulletin of the Atomic Scientists* 13, no. 1 (January 1957): 13–18. Reprinted in *The Intellectuals and the Powers and Other Essays* (1972), pp. 196–203.

"The Intellectuals, Public Opinion, and Economic Development." *Economic Development and Cultural Change* 6, no. 1 (October 1957): 55–62.

"Daydreams and Nightmares: Reflections on the Criticism of Mass Culture." *Sewanee Review* 65, no. 4 (October-December 1957): 586–608. Reprinted in *The Intellectuals and the Powers and Other Essays* (1972), pp. 248–64.

1958

"The Intellectuals and the Powers: Some Perspectives for Comparative Analysis." *Comparative Studies in Society and History* 1, no. 1 (October 1958): 5–22. Reprinted in *The Intellectuals and the Powers and Other Essays* (1972), pp. 3–22; *The Constitution of Society* (1982), pp. 179–201.

"Tradition and Liberty: Antinomy and Interdependence." *Ethics* 68, no. 3 (April 1958): 153–65.

"Ideology and Civility: On the Politics of the Intellectual." *Sewanee Review* 66, no. 3 (July-September 1958): 450–80. Reprinted in *The Intellectuals and the Powers and Other Essays* (1972), pp. 42–70.

"Intellectuals, Public Opinion, and Economic Development." *World Politics* 10, no. 2 (January 1958): 232–55. Reprinted in *The Intellectuals and the Powers and Other Essays* (1972), pp. 424–44.

"The Concentration and Dispersion of Charisma: Their Bearing on Economic Policy in Underdeveloped Countries." *World Politics* 11, no. 1 (October 1958): 1–19. Reprinted in *Selected Essays* (1970), pp. 53–71; *Center and Periphery: Essays in Macrosociology* (1975), pp. 405–21.

1959

"Old Societies, New States: A Dialogue at Rhodes." *Encounter* 12, no. 3 (March 1959): 32–41.

"La Metropolis y la Provincia en la Comunidad Intellectual." *Revista de Ciencias Sociales* 3, no. 4 (December 1959): 493–508.
"The Culture of the Indian Intellectual." *Sewanee Review* 67, no. 2 (April-June 1959): 239–61.
"The Prospects for Intellectuals: Reflections of a Sociologist." *Soviet Survey*, no. 29 (July-September 1959): 81–89.
"Ideology and Civility." *Twentieth Century* 166, no. 989 (July 1959): 3–12.
"Social Inquiry and the Autonomy of the Individual." In *The Human Meaning of the Social Sciences*, ed. Daniel Lerner (Cleveland, Ohio: Meridian Books, World Publishing Co., 1959), pp. 114–57. Reprinted in expanded form as "Social Inquiry and the Autonomy of the Private Sphere" in *The Calling of Sociology and Other Essays on the Pursuit of Learning* (1980), pp. 421–51.
"Resentments and Hostilities of Legislators: Sources, Objects, Consequences." In *Legislative Behavior*, ed. John C. Wahlke and Heinz Eulau (Glencoe, Ill.: Free Press, 1959), pp. 347–54.

1960

(ed. with Talcott Parsons) *Koi no Sogo Riron o Mezashite* (translation of *Toward a General Theory of Action*, pts. 1–2). Translated by Nagai Michio, Sakuta Keiichi, Hashimoto Makoto Kyoyaku. Tokyo: Nihon Hyoron Shinsha, 1960. 445pp.
"The Moral Relationship between the Investigator and His 'Data'." *Bollettino del Centro per la Ricerca operativa* 2, no. 1 (1960): 15–23.
"Political Development in the New States." Parts 1 and 2. *Comparative Studies in Sociology and History* 2, no. 3 (April 1960): 265–92; 2, no. 4 (July 1960): 379–411.
"Mass Society and Its Culture." *Daedalus* 89, no. 2 (Spring 1960): 288–314. Reprinted in *Culture for the Millions? Mass Media in Modern Society*, ed. Norman Jacobs (New York: D. Van Nostrand, 1961; Boston: Beacon Press, 1964), pp. 1–27. Reprinted in expanded form in *The Intellectuals and the Powers and Other Essays* (1972), pp. 229–47.
"The Traditions of Intellectual Life: Their Conditions of Existence and Growth in Contemporary Societies." *International Journal of Comparative Sociology* 1, no 2 (September 1960): 177–94. Reprinted in *The Intellectuals and the Powers and Other Essays* (1972), pp. 71–94.
"On the Eve." *Twentieth Century* 167, no. 999 (May 1960): 445–59.
"The Intellectual in the Political Development of the New States." *World Politics* 12, no. 3 (April 1960): 329–68. Reprinted in *The Intellectuals and the Powers and Other Essays* (1972), pp. 386–423.
"The Traditions of Intellectuals." In *The Intellectuals: A Controversial Portrait*, ed. George B. de Huszar (Glencoe, Ill.: Free Press, 1960), pp. 55–61.
"The Prospects for Lebanese Civility." In *Politics in Lebanon*, ed. Leonard Binder (New York: John Wiley & Sons, 1960), pp. 1–11.

1961

The Intellectual between Tradition and Modernity: The Indian Situation. Comparative Studies in Society and History; Supplement 1. The Hague: Mouton, 1961. 120pp.
(ed. with Talcott Parsons, Kasper D. Naegele and Jesse R. Pitts) *Theories of Society:*

Foundations of Modern Sociological Theory. New York: Free Press of Glencoe, 1961. 2 v. (1479pp.)

"Scientific Development in the New States." *Bulletin of the Atomic Scientists* 17, no. 2 (February 1961): 48–52.

"The False Prospero: Observations on Mrs. Elspeth Huxley." *Encounter* 17, no. 1 (July 1961): 82–87.

"Indian Students: Rather Sadhus Than Philistines." *Encounter* 17, no. 3 (September 1961): 12–20.

"Further Observations on Mrs. Huxley." *Encounter* 17, no. 4 (October 1961): 44–49.

"Definitions of Culture." *New Statesman* 61, no. 6 (June 2, 1961): 812.

"Society: The Idea and Its Sources". *Revue internationale de philosophie* 15, no. 55 (1961): 93–114. Reprinted in *Center and Periphery: Essays in Macrosociology* (1975), pp. 17–33.

"The Need for Disciplined Inquiry." *Universities Quarterly* 16, no. 1 (December 1961): 14–18.

"Professor Mills on the Calling of Sociology." Review of *The Sociological Imagination*, by C. Wright Mills (New York: Oxford University Press, 1959). *World Politics* 13, no. 4 (July 1961): 600–21.

"Metropolis and Province in the Intellectual Community." In *Changing India: Essays in Honour of Professor D. R. Gadgil*, ed. N. V. Sovani V. M. Dandekar (Bombay and London: Asia Publishing House, 1961), pp. 275–94. Reprinted in *The Intellectuals and the Powers and Other Essays* (1972), pp. 355–71.

"Mass Society and Its Culture." In *Culture for the Millions? Mass Media in Modern Society*, ed. Norman Jacobs (New York: D. Van Nostrand, 1961), pp. 1–27; also contributions to panel discussion on pp. 155–200. Paperback reprint, Boston: Beacon Press, 1964.

"Social Sciences and Law." In *The Great Ideas Today, 1961* (Chicago: William Benton, 1961).

"Organizational Goals and Primary Groups." In *Human Relations in Administration, with Readings and Cases*, ed. Robert Dubin (2nd ed., Englewood Cliffs, N.J.: Prentice-Hall, 1961), pp. 81–83.

(with Herbert Goldhamer) "Types of Power." In *Human Relations in Administration, with Readings and Cases*, ed. Robert Dubin (2nd ed., Englewood Cliffs, N.J.: Prentice-Hall, 1961), pp. 247–52

"Centre and Periphery." In *The Logic of Personal Knowledge: Essays Presented to Professor Michael Polanyi* (London: Routledge and Kegan Paul; New York: Free Press of Glencoe, 1961), pp. 117–30. Reprinted in *Selected Essays* (1970), pp. 1–14; *Center and Periphery: Essays in Macrosociology* (1975), pp. 3–16; *The Constitution of Society* (1982), pp. 93–109.

"Influence and Withdrawal: The Intellectuals in Indian Political Development." In *Political Decision Makers*, ed. Dwaine Marvick (New York: Free Press of Glencoe, 1961), pp. 29–56.

"Scientific Development in the New States." In *Science and the New Nations: The Proceedings of the International Conference on Science in the Advancement of New States at Rehovoth, Israel*, ed. Ruth Gruber (New York: Basic Books, 1961), pp. 217–26. Reprinted in *The Intellectuals and the Powers and Other Essays* (1972), pp. 457–66.

"The Calling of Sociology." In *Theories of Society: Foundations of Modern Sociological Theory*, ed. Edward Shils, Talcott Parsons, Kasper D. Naegele and Jesse R. Pitts (New York: Free Press of Glencoe, 1961), pp. 1405–48. Reprinted in

Selected Essays (1970), pp. 99–142; reprinted in expanded form in *The Calling of Sociology and Other Essays in the Pursuit of Learning* (1980), pp. 3–92.

"The Macrosociological Problem: Consensus and Dissensus in the Larger Society." In *Trends in Social Science*, ed. Donald P. Ray (New York: Philosophical Library, 1961), pp. 60–83.

"Class." In *Encyclopædia Britannica* (Chicago: Encyclopædia Britannica, 1961): 5:766–68. Reprinted in *Center and Periphery: Essays in Macrosociology* (1975), pp. 249–55.

1962

(ed.) *Minerva: A Review of Science, Learning and Policy* 1 (1962)-32 (1994).

Political Development in the New States. The Hague: Mouton, 1962. 91pp.

"The Theory of Mass Society." *Diogenes*, no. 39 (July-September 1962): 45–66. Reprinted in *Selected Essays* (1970), pp. 15–36; *Center and Periphery: Essays in Macrosociology* (1975), pp. 91–107; *The Constitution of Society* (1982), pp. 69–89.

"Politicians and Scientists." *Encounter* 18, no. 1 (January 1962): 103–6.

"Indian Students: Rather Sadhus Than Philistines." *Journal of Sociology* (Jabalpur, India) (1962): 33–52.

"Minerva" [editorial]. *Minerva* 1, no. 1 (Autumn 1962): 5–17.

"The Military in the Political Development of the New States." In *The Role of the Military in Underdeveloped Countries*, ed. John J. Johnson (Princeton, N.J.: Princeton University Press, 1962), pp. 7–67. Reprinted in *Center and Periphery: Essays in Macrosociology* (1975), pp. 483–516.

"The Autonomy of Science." In *The Sociology of Science*, ed. Bernard Barber and Walter Hirsch (New York: Free Press of Glencoe, 1962), pp. 610–22.

1963

"The Bookshop in America." *Daedalus* 92, no. 1 (Winter 1963): 92–104.

"Observations on the American University." *Universities Quarterly* 17, no. 2 (March 1963): pp. 182–93. Reprinted in *The Intellectuals and the Powers and Other Essays* (1972), pp. 298–306.

"The Theory of Mass Society." In *America as a Mass Society*, ed. Phillip Olson (New York: Free Press of Glencoe, 1963), pp. 30–47.

"The Bookshop in America." In *The American Reading Public: What It Reads, Why It Reads*, ed. Roger H. Smith (New York: R. R. Bowker, 1963), pp. 138–50.

"The Asian Intellectual." In *Asia: A Handbook*, ed. Guy Wint (New York: Frederick A. Praeger, 1963), pp. 596–607. Reprinted as "Asian Intellectuals" in *The Intellectuals and the Powers and Other Essays* (1972), pp. 372–85.

"Why the Failure." In *The Atomic Age: Scientists and World Affairs*, ed. Morton Grodzins and Eugene Rabinowitch (New York: Basic Books, 1963), pp. 76–91.

"America's Paper Curtain." In *The Atomic Age: Scientists and World Affairs*, ed. Morton Grodzins and Eugene Rabinowitch (New York: Basic Books, 1963), pp. 414–27.

"Demagogues and Cadres in the Political Development of the New States." In *Communications and Political Development*, ed. Lucian W. Pye (Princeton, N.J.: Princeton University Press, 1963), pp. 64–77. Reprinted in *The Intellectuals and the Powers and Other Essays* (1972), pp. 445–56.

"British Intellectuals." In *Encounters: An Anthology from the First Ten Years of Encounter Magazine*, editors: Stephen Spender, Irving Kristol, Melvin J. Lasky; selected by Melvin J. Lasky (London: Weidenfeld & Nicolson; New York: Basic Books, 1963), pp. 177–94.

"The Contemplation of Society in America." In *Paths of American Thought*, ed. Arthur M. Schlesinger, Jr., and Morton White (Boston: Houghton Mifflin, 1963), pp. 392–410. Reprinted in *The Calling of Sociology and Other Essays on the Pursuit of Learning* (1980), pp. 95–133.

1964

"Leo Szilard, A Memoir." *Encounter* 23, no. 6 (December 1964): 35–41.

"Know-Nothings and Eggheads." *Spectator* 212, no. 7077 (February 14, 1964): 217.

"The Charismatic Center." *Spectator* 213, no. 7115 (November 6, 1964): 608.

"The High Culture of the Age." In *The Arts and Society*, ed. Robert N. Wilson (Englewood Cliffs, N.J.: Prentice-Hall, 1964), pp. 315–62. Reprinted in *The Intellectuals and the Powers and Other Essays* (1972), pp. 97–134.

"The Military in the Political Development of the New States." In *Development and Society: The Dynamics of Economic Change*, ed. David E. Novak and Robert Lekachman (New York: St. Martin's Press, 1964), pp. 393–405.

"The Fortunes of Constitutional Government in the Political Development of the New States." In *Development: For What?*, ed. John J. Hallowell (Durham, N.C.: Published for the Lilly Endowment Research Program in Christianity and Politics by Duke University Press, 1964), pp. 103–43. Reprinted in *Center and Periphery: Essays in Macrosociology* (1975), pp. 456–82.

1965

"Charisma, Order and Status." *American Sociological Review* 30, no. 2 (April 1965): 199–213. Reprinted in *Center and Periphery: Essays in Macrosociology* (1975), pp. 256–75; *The Constitution of Society* (1982), pp. 119–42.

"Toward a Modern Intellectual Community in the New States." In *Education and Political Development*, ed. James S. Coleman (Princeton, N.J.: Princeton University Press, 1965), pp. 498–518. Reprinted in *The Intellectuals and the Powers and Other Essays* (1972), pp. 335–54.

1966

"Opposition in the New States of Asia and Africa." *Government and Opposition* 1, no. 2 (February 1966): 175–204.

"Privacy: Its Constitution and Vicissitudes." *Law and Contemporary Problems* 31, no. 2 (Spring 1966): 281–306. Reprinted in *Selected Essays* (1970), pp. 73–98.

"The African Intellectuals." In *Christianity and African Education: The Papers of a Conference at the University of Chicago*, ed. R. Pierce Beaver (Grand Rapids, Mich.: William B. Eardmans Publishing Co., 1966), pp. 123–38.

"Modernization and Higher Education." In *Modernization: The Dynamics of Growth*, ed. Myron Weiner (Washington, D.C.: Voice of America Forum Lectures, 1966), pp. 87–103; also published: (New York: Basic Books, 1966), pp. 81–97.

(with Morris Janowitz) "Cohesion and Disintegration in the Wehrmacht in World War II." In *Reader in Public Opinion*, ed. Bernard Berelson and Morris Janowitz (2nd ed., New York: Free Press, 1966), pp. 402–17.
"Mass Society and Its Culture." In *Reader in Public Opinion*, ed. Bernard Berelson and Morris Janowitz (2nd ed., New York: Free Press, 1966), pp. 505–28.
"Society." In *Chambers's Encyclopedia* (Oxford: Pergamon Press, 1966) 12:667–68.

1967

"The Intellectuals and the Future." *Bulletin of the Atomic Scientists* 23, no. 8 (October 1967): 7–14. Reprinted in *The Intellectuals and the Powers and Other Essays* (1972), pp. 213–28.
"Color, the Universal Intellectual Community, and the Afro-Asian Intellectual." *Daedalus* 96, no. 2 (Spring 1967), pp. 279–95. Reprinted in *The Intellectuals and the Powers and Other Essays* (1972), pp. 467–81.
"The Sanctity of Life." *Encounter* 28, no. 1 (January 1967), pp. 39–49. Reprinted in *Center and Periphery: Essays in Macrosociology* (1975), pp. 219–35.
"The Ways of Sociology." *Encounter* 28, no. 6 (June 1967): 85–91.
"Tendenza della Ricerca Sociologica." *Quaderni di Sociologia* 16, no. 1 (January-March 1967): 3–37.
"Privacy and Power." In *Contemporary Political Science: Toward Empirical Theory*, ed. Ithiel de Sola Pool (New York: McGraw-Hill, 1967). Reprinted in *Center and Periphery: Essays in Macrosociology* (1975), pp. 317–44.
"The Stratification System of Mass Society." In *Social and Economic Change: Essays in Honour of Prof. D. P. Mukerji*, ed. Balgit Singh and V. B. Singh (Bombay; New York: Allied Publishers, 1967), pp. 163–77. Reprinted in *Center and Periphery: Essays in Macrosociology* (1975), pp. 304–14.

1968

(ed.) *Criteria for Scientific Development: Public Policy and National Goals: A Selection of Articles from Minerva.* Cambridge, Mass.: M.I.T Press, 1968. 207pp.
(ed. with Talcott Parsons) *Hacia una teoría general de la acción* (translation of *Toward a General Theory of Action*). Buenos Aires: Editorial Kapelusz, 1968. 555pp.
"The Profession of Science." *Advancement of Science* 24, no. 122 (June 1968): 469–79.
"The Intellectual in Developing Nations." *Dialogue* 1, no. 2 (1968): 31–36.
"Consenso e Dissenso." *Rassegna Italiana de Sociologia* 9, no. 1 (January-March 1968): 23–48.
"The Implantation of Universities: Reflections on a Theme of Ashby." *Universities Quarterly* 22, no. 2 (March 1968): 142–66.
"Society and Societies: The Macro-Sociological View." In *American Sociology: Perspectives, Problems, Methods*, ed. Talcott Parsons (New York: Basic Books, 1968), pp. 287–303. Reprinted in *Center and Periphery: Essays in Macrosociology* (1975), pp. 34–47; *The Constitution of Society* (1982), pp. 53–68.
"Charisma." In *International Encyclopedia of the Social Sciences* (New York: Macmillan Co. & Free Press, 1968), 2:386–90. Reprinted in *Center and Periphery: Essays in Macrosociology* (1975), pp. 127–34; *The Constitution of Society*

(1982), pp. 110–18.

"The Concept of Consensus." In *International Encyclopedia of the Social Sciences* (New York: Macmillan Co. & Free Press, 1968), 3:260–66.

"The Concept and Function of Ideology." In *International Encyclopedia of the Social Sciences* (New York: Macmillan Co. & Free Press, 1968), 7:66–76. Reprinted as "Ideology" in *The Intellectuals and the Powers and Other Essays* (1972), pp. 23–41; *The Constitution of Society* (1982), pp. 202–223.

"Intellectuals." In *International Encyclopedia of the Social Sciences* (New York: Macmillan Co. & Free Press, 1968), 7:399–415.

"Karl Mannheim." In *International Encyclopedia of the Social Sciences* (New York: Macmillan Co. & Free Press, 1968), 9:557–62.

"The Sanctity of Life." In *Life or Death: Ethics and Options: Six Essays* (Portland, Ore.: Reed College, 1968), pp. 2–38. Reprinted, Seattle: University of Washington Press, 1970.

"Ritual and Crisis." In *The Religious Situation*, ed. Donald R. Cutler (Boston: Beacon Press, 1968), pp. 733–48. Reprinted in *Center and Periphery: Essays in Macrosociology* (1975), pp. 153–63.

"Deference." In *Social Stratification*, ed. John A. Jackson (Cambridge: Cambridge University Press, 1968), pp. 104–32. Reprinted in *Center and Periphery: Essays in Macrosociology* (1975), pp. 276–303; *The Constitution of Society* (1982), pp. 143–75.

1969

"Plenitude and Scarcity: The Anatomy of an International Cultural Crisis." *Encounter* 32, no. 5 (May 1969): 37–48. Reprinted in *The Intellectuals and the Powers and Other Essays* (1972), pp. 265–97.

"The Academic Profession in India." *Minerva* 7, no. 3 (Spring 1969): 345–72.

"The Intellectuals and the Powers: Some Perspectives for Comparative Analysis." In *On Intellectuals: Theoretical Studies, Case Studies*, ed. Philip Rieff (Garden City, N.Y.: Doubleday, 1969), pp. 25–48.

"Reflections on Deference." In *Politics, Personality, and Social Science in the Twentieth Century: Essays in Honor of Harold D. Lasswell*, ed. Arnold A. Rogow (Chicago: University of Chicago Press, 1969), pp. 297–345.

1970

Selected Essays. Chicago: Center for Social Organization Studies, Department of Sociology, University of Chicago, 1970. 142pp.

"Tradition, Ecology, and Institution in the History of Sociology." *Daedalus* 99, no. 4 (Autumn 1970): 760–825. Reprinted in *The Calling of Sociology and Other Essays on the Pursuit of Learning* (1980), pp. 165–256; *The Constitution of Society* (1982), pp. 275–383.

"Aspects of Sociology: The Tyranny of Tradition, Some Prefatory Remarks." *Encounter* 34, no. 3 (March 1970): 57–61.

"The Hole in the Centre: University Government in the United States" [editorial]. *Minerva* 8, no. 1 (January 1970): 1–7.

"How Many Scientists and Technologists?" [editorial]. *Minerva* 8, no. 2 (April 1970): 155–59.

"Are Academics Fit for Self-Government?" Review of *The American University: How It Runs, Where It Is Going*, by Jacques Barzun (London: Oxford University Press, 1969). *Minerva* 8, no. 2 (April 1970): 308–13.

"A Neglected Problem of Science Policy" [editorial]. *Minerva* 8, no. 3 (July 1970): 321–24.

Introduction to Reports and Documents: "Presidents and Professors in American University Government." *Minerva* 8, no. 3 (July 1970): 440.

"The Political University and Academic Freedom" [editorial]. *Minerva* 8, no. 4 (October 1970): 479–91.

"Student Participation: Consultation or Voting Power." Review of *The Rise of the Student Estate in Britain*, by Eric Ashby and Mary Anderson (London: Macmillan, 1970). *Minerva* 8, no. 4 (October 1970): 611–23.

"Report of the Committee on the Criteria of Academic Appointment." *University of Chicago Record* 4, no. 6 (December 17, 1970): 1–15.

1971

Génesis de la sociología contemporánea (translation of "Tradition, Ecology, and Institution in the History of Sociology"). Madrid: Seminarios y Ediciones, 1971. 169pp.

"Tradition." *Comparative Studies in Society and History* 13, no. 2 (April 1971): 122–59. Reprinted in *Center and Periphery: Essays in Macrosociology* (1975), pp. 182–218.

"The Disestablishment of Science." *Encounter* 37, no. 5 (November 1971): 88–93.

"Of Pride and Men of Little Faith" [editorial]. *Minerva* 9, no. 1 (January 1971): 1–6.

"Academic Appointment, University Autonomy and the Federal Government" [editorial]. *Minerva* 9, no. 2 (April 1971): 161–70.

"The Criteria of Academic Appointment" [report of the Committee on the Criteria of Academic Appointment, University of Chicago]. *Minerva* 9, no. 2 (April 1971): 272–90.

"No Salvation Outside Higher Education" [editorial]. *Minerva* 9, no. 3 (July 1971): 313–21.

Introduction to Reports and Documents: "Consultation or Voting Power," by Eric Ashby and Mary Anderson. *Minerva* 9, no. 3 (July 1971): 400.

"Anti-Science" [editorial]. *Minerva* 9, no. 4 (October 1971): 441–50.

"Deferencia." In *Estratificación social* (translation of *Social Stratification*), by John A. Jackson, Edward Shils, Mark Abrams and others (Barcelona: Ediciones Peninsula, 1971). pp. 125–59.

"From Periphery to Center: The Changing Place of Intellectuals in American Society." In *Stability and Social Change*, ed. Bernard Barber and Alex Inkels (Boston: Little, Brown, 1971): 211–43.

1972

The Intellectuals and the Powers and Other Essays. Selected Papers of Edward Shils 1. Chicago: University of Chicago Press, 1972. 481pp. Includes the following previously unpublished essay: "Intellectuals and the Center of Society in the United States."

"Lo sviluppo politico degli stati nuovi: la volontà di essere moderni." *Centro Sociale* 19 (December 1972): 49–78.

"Intellectuals, Tradition, and Traditions of Intellectuals: Some Preliminary Considerations." *Daedalus* 101, no. 2 (Spring 1972): 21–34.
"The Prospect of Civility." *Encounter* 39, no. 5 (November 1972): 32–37.
"*Minerva*: The Past Decade and the Next" [editorial]. *Minerva* 10, no. 1 (January 1972): 1–9.
Introduction to Reports and Documents: "The Obligations of Scientists as Counsellors." *Minerva* 10, no. 1 (January 1972): 107–10.
Introduction to Reports and Documents: "Universities in Danger: The United States Office for Civil Rights contra Columbia University." *Minerva* 10, no. 2 (April 1972): 319.
"Stanford and Berlin: The Spheres of Politics and Intellect" [editorial]. *Minerva* 10, no. 3 (July 1972): 351–61.
"The Invitation to Caesar" [editorial]. *Minerva* 10, no. 4 (October 1972): 513–18.

1973

"The American Private University." *Minerva* 11, no 1 (January 1973): 6–29.
"The Redemptive Power of Science" [editorial]. *Minerva* 11, no. 1 (January 1973): 1–5.
Introduction to Reports and Documents: "The Sociological and Psychological Study of Scientific Activity," by D. M. Gvishiani, S .R. Mikulinsky, and M. G. Yaroshevsky. *Minerva* 11, no. 1 (January 1973): 121.
"Trojan Horses" [editorial]. *Minerva* 11, no. 3 (July 1973): 285–89.
"Muting the Social Sciences at Berkeley" [editorial]. *Minerva* 11, no. 3 (July 1973): 290–95.
"The Freedom of Teaching and Research" [editorial]. *Minerva* 11, no. 4 (October 1973): 433–41.
(ed. and tr. with introductory note) "The Power of the State and the Dignity of the Academic Calling in Imperial Germany: The Writings of Max Weber on University Problems." *Minerva* 11, no. 4 (October 1973): 571–632.

1974

(ed. and tr. with introductory note) *Max Weber on Universities: The Power of the State and the Dignity of the Academic Calling in Imperial Germany*. Chicago: University of Chicago Press, 1974. 62pp.
"Twentieth-Century Classics Revisited: *Ideology and Utopia* by Karl Mannheim." *Daedalus* 103, no. 1 (Winter 1974): 83–89.
"Faith, Utility and the Legitimacy of Science." *Daedalus* 103, no. 3 (Summer 1974): 1–15.
"'Elitism'" [editorial]. *Minerva* 12, no. 1 (January 1974): 1–7.
Introduction to Reports and Documents: "The Reorganization of Higher Education in Sweden." *Minerva* 12, no. 1 (January 1974): 83–114.
"The Public Understanding of Science" [editorial]. *Minerva* 12, no. 2 (April 1974): 153–58.
Introduction to Reports and Documents: "Identity and Openness in Higher Education." *Minerva* 12, no. 2 (April 1974): 258.
"An Unresolved Dilemma" [editorial]. *Minerva* 12, no. 3 (July 1974): 295–302.

Introduction to Reports and Documents: "Social Science Policy in a New State: A Programme for the Stimulation of the Social Sciences in Indonesia," by Clifford Geertz. *Minerva* 12, no. 3 (July 1974): 365.

"The Enemies of Academic Freedom" [editorial]. *Minerva* 12, no. 4 (October 1974): 405–15.

"Sources of Charge in Character and Functions of Universities." *Universities Quarterly* 28, no. 3 (Summer 1974): 310–17.

"Memorial Tribute: Lloyd A. Fallers, 1925–1974." *University of Chicago Record* 8, no. 7 (November 1974): 214–17.

(sound recording with Hal Walker, moderator; Edward E. David, Jr.; and Herbert Goldhamer) *The Role of the Scientist in a Democracy.* Conversations from Wingspread; R-116. Racine, Wis.: Johnson Foundation, 1974. On 1 side of 1 sound cassette (28 min., 29 sec.). Copies in Michigan State University Library; University of Wisconsin, Parkside Library.

1975

Center and Periphery: Essays in Macrosociology. Selected Papers of Edward Shils 2. Chicago: University of Chicago Press, 1975. 516pp. Includes the following previously unpublished essays: "The Integration of Society," "Consensus," and "Opposition in the New States of Asia and Africa."

(with Talcott Parsons and Paul F. Lazarsfeld) *Soziologie, autobiographisch: Drei kritische Berichte zur Entwicklung einer Wissenschaft.* Stuttgart: Ferdinand Enke, 1975. 232pp.

"The Academic Ethos Under Strain." *Minerva* 13, no. 1 (Spring 1975): 1–37.

Introduction to Reports and Documents. "The Intellectual Situation in German Higher Education," by Walter Rüegg. *Minerva* 13, no. 1 (Spring 1975): 103.

"The Confidentiality and Anonymity of Assessment" [editorial]. *Minerva* 13, no. 2 (Summer 1975): 135–51.

Introduction to Reports and Documents: "The Right to Speak in American Universities: The University of Chicago; Yale University." *Minerva* 13, no. 2 (Summer 1975): 303, 305.

"Alternatives to Judgement by Peers" [editorial]. *Minerva* 13, no 3 (Autumn 1975): 341–48.

"Social Science as Centrality." *Society* 12, no. 5 (July-August 1975): 6–9.

"The Academic Ethos Under Strain." In *Universities in the Western World*, ed. Paul Seabury (New York: Free Press, 1975), pp. 16–46.

1976

Los intelectuales en los países en desarrollo (translation of *The Intellectuals and the Powers*). Buenos Aires: Ediciones Tres Tiempos, 1976. 214pp.

Los intelectuales en las sociedades modernas (translation of *The Intellectuals and the Powers*). Translated by Flora Setaro. México: DIMELISA, 1976. 327pp. Reprinted, Buenos Aires: Ediciones Tres Tiempos, 1981.

"Intellectuals and Their Discontents." *American Scholar* 45, no. 2 (Spring 1976): 181–203.

"What is a Liberal—Who is a Conservative? A Symposium" [contributor]. *Commentary* 62, no. 3 (September 1976): 95–97.

"A Great Citizen of the Republic of Science: Michael Polanyi, 1892–1976" [editorial]. *Minerva* 14, no. 1 (Spring 1976): 1–5.

Introduction to Reports and Documents: "The Criteria of Academic Appointment in American Universities and Colleges: Some Documents of Affirmative Action at Work." *Minerva* 14, no. 1 (Spring 1976): 97.

"The Criteria of Academic Appointment" [editorial]. *Minerva* 14, no. 4 (Winter 1976/77): 407–18.

Introduction to Reports and Documents: "Criteria of Academic Appointment: Switzerland: The University of Geneva: A Controversy About M. Jean Ziegler." *Minerva* 14, no. 4 (Winter 1976/77): 530.

"The Burden of 1917." *Survey* 22, no. 3–4 (Summer-Autumn 1976): 139–46.

"Legitimizing the Social Sciences: Meeting the Challenges to Objectivity and Integrity." In *Controversies and Decisions: The Social Sciences and Public Policy*, ed. Charles Frankel (New York: Russell Sage Foundation, 1976), pp. 273–90. Reprinted in expanded form as "The Pursuit of Knowledge and the Concern for the Common Good." in *The Calling of Sociology and Other Essays on the Pursuit of Learning* (1980), pp. 356–417.

1977

"A Profile of a Military Deserter." *Armed Forces and Society* 3, no. 3 (Spring 1977): 427–32.

Introduction to Reports and Documents: "The Soil and Air of Academic Life." *Minerva* 15, no. 2 (Summer 1977): 200–201.

"Social Science as Public Opinion" [editorial]. *Minerva* 15, no. 3–4 (Autumn-Winter 1977): 273–85. Reprinted in *The Calling of Sociology and Other Essays on the Pursuit of Learning* (1980), pp. 452–64.

Introduction to Reports and Documents: "The Military Potential of Civilian Nuclear Energy: Moving Towards Life in a Nuclear Armed Crowd?" by Albert Wohlstetter, Thomas A. Brown, Gregory Jones, David McGarvey, Henry Rowan, Vincent Taylor and Roberta Wohlstetter. *Minerva* 15, no. 3–4 (Autumn-Winter 1977): 387–88.

"Government and Universities." *Newsletter of the International Council on the Future of the University* 4, no. 1 (November 1977).

"The Academic Ethos." In *The Future of the University in Southern Africa*, ed. Hendrik W. van der Merwe and David Walsh (Cape Town: D. Philip, 1977; New York: St. Martin's Press, 1978), pp. 5–22.

1978

(ed. with Peter Davison and Rolf Meyersohn) *Literary Taste, Culture, and Mass Communication*. Cambridge: Chadwyck-Healey; Teaneck, N.J.: Somerset House, 1978–80. 14 vols.

"The Academic Ethos." *American Scholar* 47, no. 2 (Spring 1978): 165–90.

"The Order of Learning in the United States from 1865–1920: The Ascendancy of Universities." *Minerva* 16, no. 2 (Summer 1978): 159–95.

Introduction to Reports and Documents: "A Life-time in Soviet Science Reconsidered: The Adventure of Cybernetics in the Soviet Union," by Arnost Kolman. *Minerva* 16, no. 3 (Autumn 1978): 416.

Introduction to Reports and Documents: "The Study of Political Science in the Universities of Bangladesh," by W. H. Morris-Jones. *Minerva* 16, no. 3 (Autumn 1978): 425.

"Mass Society and Its Culture." In *Literary Taste, Culture, and Mass Communication*, vol. 1, *Culture and Mass Culture* (Cambridge: Chadwyck-Healey; Teaneck, N.J.: Somerset House, 1978), pp. 201–9.

"On the Eve." In *Literary Taste, Culture, and Mass Communication*, vol. 6, *The Sociology of Literature* (Cambridge: Chadwyck-Healey; Teaneck, N.J.: Somerset House, 1978), pp. 237–53.

"Daydreams & Nightmares: Reflections on the Criticism of Mass Culture." In *Literary Taste, Culture, and Mass Communication*, vol. 13, *The Cultural Debate*, pt. 1 (Cambridge: Chadwyck-Healey; Teaneck, N.J.: Somerset House, 1978), pp. 17–38.

"The Antinomies of Liberalism." In *The Relevance of Liberalism*, ed. Staff of the Research Institute on International Change, Columbia University (Boulder, Colo.: Westview Press, 1978), pp. 135–200.

"Government and Universities." In *The University and the State: What Role for Government in Higher Education?*, ed. Sidney Hook, Paul Kurtz and Miro Todorovich (Buffalo: Prometheus Books, 1978), pp. 177–204.

1979

"Who Reads Novels? A Symposium" [contributor]. *American Scholar* 48, no. 2 (Spring 1979): 187–90.

"Government and Universities in the United States: The Eighth Jefferson Lecture in the Humanities: 'Render unto Caesar . . .': Government, Society and the Universities in Their Reciprocal Rights and Duties." *Minerva* 17, no. 1 (Spring 1979): 129–77.

Introduction to Reports and Documents: "Governments, Foundations and the Bias of Research: Distortions of Economic Research," by Theodore W. Schultz. *Minerva* 17, no. 3 (Autumn 1979): 459.

"The Order of Learning in the United States: The Ascendancy of the University." In *The Organization of Knowledge in America, 1860–1920*, ed. Alexandra Oleson and John Voss (Baltimore: Johns Hopkins University Press, 1979), pp. 19–47.

(sound recording) "A New Declaration of Rights and Duties" (Eighth Jefferson Lecture in the Humanities; lecture no. 3 recorded at the University of Texas at Austin, 3 May 1979). Washington, D.C.: National Public Radio, 1979. 1 sound tape reel (59 min.). Copy in Brigham Young University Library.

1980

The Calling of Sociology and Other Essays on the Pursuit of Learning. Selected Papers of Edward Shils 3. Chicago: University of Chicago Press, 1980. 498pp. Includes the following previously unpublished essays: "The Confluence of Sociological Traditions," "Learning and Liberalism," and "The Legitimacy of Social Inquiry."

"Liberalism and the Jews: A Symposium" [contributor]. *Commentary* 69, no. 1 (January 1980): 66–69.

"Observations on Some Tribulations of Civility." *Government and Opposition* 15, no. 3–4 (Summer-Autumn 1980): 528–45.

Introduction to Reports and Documents: "The Zipfel Affair at the Free University of

Berlin: Autonomy, Publicity and the Disruption of Universities." *Minerva* 18, no. 1 (Spring 1980): 132–35.

Introduction to Reports and Documents: "Academic Freedom Then and Now: The Dismissal of Leo Arons from the University of Berlin." *Minerva* 18, no. 3 (Autumn 1980): 499–505.

"The Order of Science and Its Self-Understanding." Review of *A Guide to the Culture of Science, Technology, and Medicine*, ed. Paul T. Durbin (New York: Free Press, 1980). *Minerva* 18, no. 2 (Summer 1980): 354–60.

"Social Ownership and the Means of Production." *Survey* 25, no. 4 (Autumn 1980): 127–42.

1981

Tradition. Chicago: University of Chicago Press; London: Faber & Faber, 1981. 334pp.

"Some Academics, Mainly in Chicago." *American Scholar* 50, no. 2 (Spring 1981): 179–96.

Introduction to Reports and Documents: "The Education of Talented Students." *Minerva* 19, no. 3 (Autumn 1981): 480–81.

1982

The Constitution of Society. With a new introduction by the author. Heritage of Sociology series. Chicago: University of Chicago Press, 1982. 383pp. Essays reprinted from *The Intellectuals and the Powers and Other Essays* (1972), *Center and Periphery: Essays in Macrosociology* (1975), and *The Calling of Sociology and Other Essays on the Pursuit of Learning* (1980).

(ed. with Hans Daalder). *Universities, Politicians, and Bureaucrats: Europe and the United States*. Cambridge; New York: Cambridge University Press, 1982. 511pp.

"The University: A Backward Glance." *American Scholar* 51, no. 2 (Spring 1982): 163–79.

"Reflections on the Future of Our Learned Institutions." *Cambridge Review* 103 (January 29, 1982): 111–19.

"Knowledge and the Sociology of Knowledge." *Knowledge: Creation, Diffusion, Utilization* 4, no. 1 (September 1982): 7–32.

"The Academic Ethic." *Minerva* 20, no. 1–2 (Spring-Summer 1982): 105–208.

Introduction to Reports and Documents: "An Innovation in German Higher Education: The Private University." *Minerva* 20, no. 1–2 (Spring-Summer 1982): 213.

Introduction to Reports and Documents: "Academic Trade Unions and the Criteria of Academic Appointments at the University of Massachusetts." *Minerva* 20, no. 3–4 (Autumn-Winter 1982): 339–43.

"Great Britain and the United States: Legislators, Bureaucrats, and the Universities." In *Universities, Politicians, and Bureaucrats: Europe and the United States*, ed. Hans Daalder and Edward Shils (Cambridge; New York: Cambridge University Press, 1982), pp. 437–87.

1983

"Tradition and the Generations: On the Difficulties of Transmission." *American Scholar* 53, no. 1 (Winter 1983/84): 27–40.

360   The Order of Learning

Introduction to Reports and Documents: "An Achievement of Academic Citizenship: Professors, Government and the People of the Canton of Berne." *Minerva* 21, no. 1 (Spring 1983): 101–2.
Introduction to Reports and Documents: "The Constitution, Academic Self-Government and Academic Trade Unions in American State Universities and Colleges: A Decision of the United States Supreme Court." *Minerva* 21, no. 2–3 (Summer-Autumn, 1983): 296–97.
Introduction to Reports and Documents: "On the Criteria of Academic Appointment." *Minerva* 21, no. 4 (Winter 1983): 410–14.
"Lewis Mumford: On the Way to the New Jerusalem." *New Criterion* 1, no. 9 (May 1983): 38–44.
"The Academic Ethic." *Newsletter of the International Council on the Future of the University* (1983).
"Foreword: The Constitution of Nationality." In Dominique Schnapper, *Jewish Identities in France: An Analysis of Contemporary French Jewry*, translated by Arthur Goldhammer (Chicago: University of Chicago Press, 1983), pp. ix-xvi.
"Das Zentrum des Kosmos und das Zentrum der Gesellschaft." In *Sehnsucht nach dem Ursprung: zu Mircea Eliade*, ed. Hans Peter Duerr (Frankfurt am Main: Syndikat Autoren- und Verlagsgesellschaft, 1983), pp. 538–57.
"Academic Freedom and Academic Obligations." In *Sidney Hook: Philosopher of Democracy and Humanism*, ed. Paul Kurtz (Buffalo: Prometheus Books, 1983), pp. 113–38.

1984

The Academic Ethic: The Report of a Study Group of the International Council on the Future of the University. Chicago: University of Chicago Press, 1984. 104pp.
Introduction to Discussion: "The Condition of Humanistic Education in the United States: Malign Neglect," by Hugh Lloyd-Jones. *Minerva* 22, no. 3–4 (Autumn-Winter 1984): 404.
Introduction to Reports and Documents: "Secrecy and Freedom of Communication in American Science." *Minerva* 22, no. 3–4 (Autumn-Winter 1984): 421–23.
"The Governability of Modern Societies." *Notes et Documents: Institut International J. Maritain* 9, no. 7 (July-September 1984): 39–59.
"S. N. Eisenstadt: Some Personal Observations." In *Comparative Social Dynamics: Essays in Honor of S. N. Eisenstadt*, ed. Eric Cohen, Moshe Lissak and Uri Almagor (Boulder, Col.: Westview Press, 1984), pp. 1–8.

1985

"Raymond Aron." *American Scholar* 54, no. 2 (Spring 1985): pp. 161–78.
"En souvenir de Raymond Aron." *Commentaire* 8, no. 32 (Winter 1985/86): 1022–33.
"How Has the United States Met Its Major Challenges since 1945." *Commentary* 80, no. 5 (November 1985): 92–95.
Introduction to Reports and Documents: "Academic Freedom and Permanent Tenure in Academic Appointments." *Minerva* 23, no. 1 (Spring 1985): 96–100.
Introduction to Reports and Documents: "The Morality of Scientists." *Minerva* 23, no. 2 (Summer 1985): 272–75.
"On The Eve: A Prospect In Retrospect." In *The History of Empirical Sociology in*

Great Britain, ed. Martin Bulmer (Cambridge: Cambridge University Press, 1985), pp. 165–78.

"Raymond Aron, 1905–1983: A Memoir." In *History, Truth, Liberty: Selected Writings of Raymond Aron*, ed. Franciszek Draus (Chicago: University of Chicago Press, 1985), pp. 1–19.

"Sociology." In *The Social Science Encyclopedia*, ed. Adam Kuper and Jessica Kuper (London: Routledge and Kegan Paul, 1985), pp. 799–811.

1986

"The Universality of Science." In *Zeugen des Wissens*, ed. Heinz Maier-Leibnitz (Mainz: Hase and Koehler, 1986), pp. 819–36.

Introduction to Reports and Documents: "Some Reflections on the Universities after the Disturbances at the End of the 1960s." *Minerva* 24, no. 1 (Winter 1986): 98–99.

Introduction to Reports and Documents: "Universities in the New States of Africa and Asia: The Idea of the Developmental University," by James S. Coleman. *Minerva* 24, no. 4 (Winter 1986): 476.

"Wissenschaft und Wissenschaftler." *Der Monat*.

"Some Observations on the Place of Intellectuals in Max Weber's Sociology, with Special Reference to Hinduism." In *The Origins and Diversity of Axial Age Civilizations*, ed. S. N. Eisenstadt (New York: State University of New York Press, 1986), pp. 427–52.

1987

"Science and Scientists in the Public Arena." *American Scholar* 56, no. 2 (Spring 1987): 185–202.

"More at Home Than Out of Step." Review of *Out of Step: An Unquiet Life in the Twentieth Century*, by Sidney Hook (New York: Harper & Row, 1987). *American Scholar* 56, no. 4 (Autumn 1987): 577–86.

"Problematic Prophets." *Encounter* 69, no. 5 (December 1987): 20–22.

"Joseph Ben-David, 1920–1986" [foreword to commemorative issue]. *Minerva* 25, no. 1–2 (Spring-Summer 1987): 1–2.

"Joseph Ben-David: A Memoir." *Minerva* 25, no. 1–2 (Spring-Summer 1987): 201–5.

"Intellectuals." In *Encyclopedia of Religion*, ed. Mircea Eliade (New York: Macmillan, 1987): 7:259–63.

"Max Weber and the World since 1920." In *Max Weber and His Contemporaries*, ed. Wolfgang Mommsen and Jurgen Osterhammel (London: Allen and Unwin, 1987), pp. 547–73.

(with Morris Janowitz) "Cohesion and Disintegration in the Wehrmacht in World War II." In Morris Janowitz, *Social Research and Armed Forces* (Alexandria, Va.: United States Army Research Institute for the Behavioral and Social Sciences, 1987), pp. 1–48.

1988

"Arnaldo Momigliano, 5 September 1908–1 September 1987." *American Philosophical Society Year Book* (1988): 215–29.

"Citizen of the World: Nirad C. Chaudhuri." *American Scholar* 57, no. 4 (Autumn 1988): 549–73.

"The Unknown Indian." *Encounter* 71, no. 4 (November 1988): 64–67.

"The Community of Learning: Arnaldo Dante Momigliano, 1908–1987." *Encounter* 71, no. 5 (December 1988): 66–71.

Introduction to Reports and Documents: "The Hierarchy of Universities: The Ranking of Universities in the United States and Its Effects on Their Achievement," by Norman M. Bradburn. *Minerva* 26, no. 1 (Spring 1988): 89–90.

Introduction to Discussion: "The Academic Profession and Contemporary Politics." *Minerva* 26, no. 4 (Winter 1988): 575.

Introduction to Reports and Documents: "Affirmative Action Reaffirmed." *Minerva* 26, no. 4 (Winter 1988): 598.

"Totalitarians and Antinomians: Remembering the 30s and 60s." *New Criterion* 6, no. 9 (May 1988): 6–24.

"The Limits of Knowledge: An Ideal and Its Diffusion." In *Absolute Values and the Reassessment of the Contemporary World* (New York: Paragon Publishers, 1988), pp. 25–38.

"Center and Periphery: An Idea and Its Career, 1935–1987." In *Center: Ideas and Institutions*, ed. Liah Greenfeld and Michel Martin (Chicago: University of Chicago Press, 1988), pp. 250–82.

"Die Ausbreitung des europäischen organisierten Wissens." In *Europa und die Folgen: Castelgandolfo-Gespräche, 1987*, ed. Krzysztof Michalski (Stuttgart: Klett-Cotta, 1988), pp. 185–229.

"Max Weber und die Welt seit 1920." In *Max Weber und Seine Zeitgenossen*, ed. Wolfgang J. Mommsen and Wolfgang Schwentker (Gottingen; Zurich: Vandenhoek & Ruprecht, 1988), pp. 743–76.

"The University of Chicago and the City of Chicago." In *The University and the City: From Medieval Origins to the Present*, ed. Thomas Bender (New York: Oxford University Press, 1988), pp. 219–30.

"Values and Tradition." In *Values. A Symposium*, ed. Brenda Almond and Bryan Wilson (Atlantic Highlands, N.J.: Humanities Press International, 1988), pp. 47–55.

1989

(ed. with biographical note) *Arnaldo Dante Momigliano, 1908–1987*. Chicago: University of Chicago, [1989].

"Morris Janowitz, October 22, 1919–November 7, 1988." *American Philosophical Society Year Book* (1989): 201–7.

"Liberalism: Collectivism and Conservatism." *Chronicle of Culture* (Spring 1989): 12–15.

"The Limits on the Capacities of Government." *Government and Opposition* 24, no. 4 (Autumn 1989): 441–57.

Introduction to Reports and Documents: "The Discussion about Proposals to Change the Western Culture Program at Stanford University." *Minerva* 27, no. 2–3 (Summer-Autumn 1989): 223.

"The Modern University and Liberal Democracy." *Minerva* 27, no. 4 (Winter 1989): 425–60.

Introduction to Reports and Documents: "Reflections on the Obligations of Honesty in the University," by Sidney Hook. *Minerva* 27, no. 4 (Winter 1989): 505–6.

"Arnaldo Momigliano and Max Weber." *Storia della Storiografia*, no. 16 (1989): 54–64.

"The Sad State of Humanities in America." Review of *The Culture We Deserve*, by Jacques Barzun. *Wall Street Journal* (July 3, 1989), p. 5.

Memoir of Arnaldo Dante Momigliano. In *Arnaldo Dante Momigliano, 1908–1987* (Chicago: University of Chicago, [1989]), pp. 14–17.

1990

(ed. with Hans Daalder, with a postscript to the Japanese edition). *Daigaku Funsou no Shakaigaku* (translation of *Universities, Politicians, and Bureaucrats: Europe and the United States*). Translated by Fujisaki Chieko and others. Tokyo: Gendai Shokan, 1990.

"Robert Maynard Hutchins." *American Scholar* 59, no. 2 (Spring 1990): 211–35.

"Le buone maniere e il bene commune." *Biblioteca della Liberta* 25, no. 111 (October-December 1990): 1–36.

"Remembering the Congress for Cultural Freedom." *Encounter* 75, no. 2 (September 1990): 53–65.

"The Limits on the Capacities of Governments." *Government and Opposition* 24, no. 4 (Autumn 1989): 441–57.

Introduction to Reports and Documents: "Freedom of Expression and Disruptions at Meetings of Student Societies in University Buildings." *Minerva* 28, no. 1 (Spring 1990): 91.

Introduction to Reports and Documents: "The Progress of 'Affirmative Action': Yale Declares Itself." *Minerva* 28, no. 2 (Summer 1990): 217–20.

Introduction to Reports and Documents: "The University World Turned Upside Down: Does Confidentiality of Assessment by Peers Guarantee the Quality of Academic Appointment?" *Minerva* 28, no. 3 (Autumn 1990): 324–34.

"John Ulric Nef." In *John Ulric Nef, 1899–1988* (Washington, D.C., 1990), pp. 65–70.

1991

Lun Chuan Tung (translation of *Tradition*). Translated by Fu Keng. Shanghai: Shanghai Peoples Press, 1991. 448pp.

(ed. with Ernst W. Böckenförde, with an introduction) *Jews and Christians in a Pluralistic Society*. London: Weidenfeld & Nicolson in association with the Institute für Wissenschaften vom Menschen, Vienna, 1991.

(ed. with a foreword) *Remembering the University of Chicago: Teachers, Scientists, and Scholars*. Chicago: University of Chicago Press, 1991. 593pp.

"Robert E. Park, 1864–1944." *American Scholar* 60, no. 1 (Winter 1991): 120–27.

"The Virtue of Civil Society." *Government and Opposition* 26, no. 1 (Winter 1991): 3–20.

Introduction to Reports and Documents: "Academic Freedom at the University of Stockholm." *Minerva* 29, no. 3 (Autumn 1991): 321–30.

"Reflections on Tradition, Center and Periphery and the Universal Validity of Science: The Significance of the Life of S. Ramanujan." *Minerva* 29, no. 4 (Winter 1991): 393–419.

"Was ist eine *Civil Society*." In *Europa und die Civil Society: Castelgandolfo-*

364   The Order of Learning

Gespräche, 1989, ed. Krzysztof Michalski (Stuttgart: Klett-Cotta, 1991), pp. 13–51.
"Academic Freedom." In *International Higher Education: An Encyclopedia*, ed. Philip G. Altbach (New York: Garland Publishing, 1991) 1:1–22.
"Reflections on Religious Pluralism in Civil Societies." In *Jews and Christians in a Pluralistic Society*, ed. Edward Shils and Ernst W. Böckenförde (London: Weidenfeld & Nicolson in association with the Institute für Wissenschaften vom Menschen, Vienna, 1991), pp. 147–65.
"Intellectuals and Responsibility." In *The Political Responsibility of Intellectuals*, ed. Ian Maclean, Alan Montefiore and Peter Winch (Cambridge: Cambridge University Press, 1991), pp. 257–306.
"Ernest W. Burgess." In *Remembering the University of Chicago*, ed. Edward Shils (Chicago: University of Chicago Press, 1991), pp. 3–14.
"Robert Maynard Hutchins." In *Remembering the University of Chicago*, ed. Edward Shils (Chicago: University of Chicago Press, 1991), pp. 185–96.
"Harry G. Johnson." In *Remembering the University of Chicago*, ed. Edward Shils (Chicago: University of Chicago Press, 1991), pp. 197–209.
"Robert E. Park." In *Remembering the University of Chicago*, ed. Edward Shils (Chicago: University of Chicago Press, 1991), pp. 383–98.
"Concluding Remarks on Max Weber and East Asia." In *The Triad Chord: Confucian Ethics, Industrial East Asia and Max Weber*, ed. Tu Wei Ming (Singapore: Institute of East Asian Philosophies, 1991), pp. 414–26.
"Die doppelte Last der Universitäten." In *Die ungewisse Zukunft die Universität: Folgen und Auswege aus der Bildungskatastrophe*, ed. Hardy Bouillon and Gerard Radnitzky (Berlin: Duncker & Humblot, 1991), pp. 77–89.
"The Double Burden of the Universities as Institutions of Learning." In *Universities in the Service of Truth and Utility*, ed. Hardy Bouillon and Gerard Radnitzky (Frankfurt am Main; New York: Peter Lang, 1991), pp. 35–48.
"Henry Sumner Maine in the Tradition of the Analysis of Society." In *The Victorian Achievement of Sir Henry Maine*, ed. Alan Diamond (Cambridge: Cambridge University Press, 1991), pp. 143–78.
"A Link in the Apostolic Succession." In *Wie kommt Man auf einfaches Neues? Der Forscher, Lehrer, Wissenschaftspolitiker und Hobbyknoch Heinz Maier-Leibnitz*, ed. Paul Kienle (Zürich: Edition Interfrom, 1991), pp. 54–56.

1992

"Citoyen et sociologue: François Bourricaud, 1923–1991." *Commentaire* 15, no. 58 (Summer 1992): 434–36.
"The Universities, the Social Sciences and Liberal Democracy." *Interchange* (Toronto) 23, no. 1–2 (1992): 183–223.
Introduction to Reports and Documents: "Science in the Indian Universities." *Minerva* 30, no. 1 (Spring 1992): 51–52.
"The University of the Twenty-First Century: A Symposium to Celebrate the Centenary of the University of Chicago" [introductory note to issue containing papers from the symposium]. *Minerva* 30, no. 2 (Summer 1992): 129.
"The Service of Society and the Advancement of Learning in the Twenty-First Century." *Minerva* 30, no. 2 (Summer 1992): 242–68.
"The Situation of the Universities in the Twenty-First Century." *Minerva* 30, no. 2 (Summer 1992): 296–301.

"The Idea of the University: Obstacles and Opportunities in Contemporary Socíeties."
Minerva 30, no. 2 (Summer 1992): 301–13.
Introduction to Reports and Documents: "Old Strains and New Initiatives in the Universities of the Federal German Republic." *Minerva* 30, no. 3 (Autumn 1992): 422–23.
Introduction to Reports and Documents: "The Progress of Affirmative Action: Accreditation and Diversity." *Minerva* 30, no. 4 (Winter 1992): 531–34.
"Thirty Years of *Minerva*." *Minerva: Index to Volumes 1–30 (1962–1992)*, pp. iii-viii.
(with Roger Michener) "Series Editors' Foreword." In *Civility and Citizenship in Liberal Democratic Societies*, ed. Edward C. Banfield (New York: Paragon House, 1992), pp. vii-viii. The "Series Editors' Foreword" also appears in the six subsequent volumes published in the Liberal Democratic Societies series (1992–95).
"Civility and Civil Society." In *Civility and Citizenship in Liberal Democratic Societies*, ed. Edward C. Banfield (New York: Paragon House, 1992), pp. 1–15.
"The Propaganda of the Deed: An Old Device in a New Form and in New Circumstances." In *The Mass Media in Liberal Democratic Societies*, ed. Stanley Rothman (New York: Paragon House, 1992), pp. 19–35.
"Universities since 1900." In *Encyclopedia of Higher Education*, ed. Burton R. Clark and Guy R. Neave (Oxford: Pergamon Press, 1992) 2:1259–75.
"Le Società Liberaldemocratiche del 'Melting Pot': L'Immigrazione Giovanile nell Europa Contemporanea." In *I Giovani non Europe ed il Processo Díntegrazione: Per una Cultura della Tolleranza*, ed. Renzo Gubert (Trento: Reverdito Edizione, 1992), pp. 29–37.
"Liberal Democratic Societies and the Theory of the Melting Pot: European Immigrant Youth of Today." In *Non-European Youth and the Process of Integration: For a Tolerant Society*, ed. Luigi Tomasi (Trento: Reverdito Edizione, 1992), pp. 225–33.

1993

Etika Akademis (translation of *The Academic Ethic*). Translated by A. Nugroho. Jakarta: Yayasan Obor Indonesia, 1993.
"Do We Still Need Academic Freedom?" *American Scholar* 62, no. 2 (Spring 1993): 187–209.
"Nazionalismo, nazionalità e società civile." *Bibloteca della Libertà* 28, no. 123 (Oct.-Dec. 1993): 3–26.
Introduction to Reports and Documents: "The British Universities under Duress: Two Essays by Professor Elie Kedourie." *Minerva* 31, no. 1 (Spring 1993): 56.
"Reflections on the Teachers of Undergraduates." *Minerva* 31, no. 2 (Summer 1993): 211–27.
"Letter to Professor Walter Rüegg: On Being a European." In *Appreciation of Walter Rüegg: On the Occasion of His Seventy-fifth Birthday*, ed. Hinrich Seidel and Alison de Puymege-Browning (Geneva: Standing Conference of Rectors, Presidents and Vice-Chancellors of the European Universities [CRE], 1993), pp. 27–31.
"Die Beziehungen zwischen deutschen und amerikanischen Universitäten." In *Deutschland Weg in die Moderne: Politik, Gesellschaft und Kultur im 19. Jahrhundert. Gedenkschrift für Thomas Nipperdey*, ed. W. Hartwig and H. Brandl (München: C. H. Beck, 1993), pp. 185–200.

"La cultura delle comunitá locali." In *Le diversitá regionali in Europa: il ruolo delle loro culture nella costruzione dell Unione Europea* (Trento: Regione Trentino Alto-Adige, 1993), pp. 123–40.

"Nazionalismo, nazionalità e società civile." In *Le libertà dei contemporanei: conferenze "Fulvio Guerrini" 1884–1993*, ed. Piero Ostellino (Torino: Centro di Ricerca e Documentazione "Luigi Einaudi", 1993), pp. 223–51.

"Max Weber und der russische Liberalismus." In *Weltbürgerkrieg der Ideologien, Antworten an Ernst Nolte: Festschrift zum 70. Geburtstag*, ed. Thomas Nipperdey, Anselm Doering-Manteuffel and Hans-Ulrich Thamer (Berlin: Propyläen, 1993), pp. 73–83.

1994

"Leopold Labedz." *American Scholar* 63, no. 2 (Spring 1994): 239–57.

"Do We still Need Academic Freedom." *Minerva* 32, no. 1 (Spring 1994): 79–98.

Introduction to Discussion: "The Universities Between Their Internal and External Enemies: Thoughts on Professor Conrad Russell's *Academic Freedom*." *Minerva* 32, no. 2 (Summer 1994): 186–87.

"The British Universities in Tribulation." *Minerva* 32, no. 2 (Summer 1994): 200–19.

"The Career of Harold Laski." Review of *Harold Laski: A Life on the Left*, by Isaac Kramnick and Barry Sheerman (New York: Allen Lane The Penguin Press, 1993). *New Criterion* 12, no. 8 (April 1994): 24–30.

"Nationalisme, nationalité et société civile." *La Revue Politique Indépendante* (1994).

"The Sociology of Robert Park." In *Robert E. Park and the "Melting Pot" Theory*, ed. Renzo Gubert and Luigi Tomasi (Trento: Reverdito Edizione, 1994), pp. 15–34.

1995

"Karl Mannheim." *American Scholar* 64, no. 2 (Spring 1995): 221–35.

"Academic Freedom and Permanent Tenure." *Minerva* 33, no. 1 (Spring 1995): 5–17.

"Nationality, Nationalism and the Idea of Civil Society." *Nationality* 1, no. 1 (1995).

"On the Tradition of Intellectuals: Authority and Antinomianism According to Michael Polanyi." *Tradition and Discovery* 22, no. 2 (1995/96): 9–26.

"The Idea and Practice of Liberal Democracy and the Modern University, with Some Comments on the Modern Private University." In *The Balance of Freedom: Political Economy, Law, and Learning*, ed. Roger Michener (New York: Paragon House, 1995), pp. 107–82.

"La teoria della societá della Scoula sociologica di Chicago." In *Teoria sociologica ed investigazione empirca: La tradizione della Scuola sociologica di Chicago e le prospettive della sociologia contemporanea* (Milano: Franko Angeli, 1995), pp. 60–75.

"The Value of Community." In *Values and Post-Soviet Youth: The Problem of Transition*, ed. Luigi Tomasi (Milano: Franko Angeli, 1995), pp. 69–81.

1996

(ed. with Carmen Blacker, with an introduction) *Cambridge Women: Twelve Portraits*. Cambridge; New York: Cambridge University Press, 1996. 292pp.

"The Value of Local Community." In *The Local Community*, ed. Luigi Tomasi (Milano: Franko Angeli, 1996), pp. 3–28.

Forthcoming

Portraits: A Gallery of Intellectuals. Edited with an introduction by Joseph Epstein. Chicago: University of Chicago Press, 1997.
The Virtue of Civility: Selected Essays on Liberalism, Tradition, and Civil Society. With an introduction by Steven Grosby. Indianapolis, Ind.: Liberty Fund, 1997.
"The Main Themes of the History of European Universities, 1800 to 1945," "The Expansion of the European University Model, 1800 to 1945," and "A History of the Social Sciences in European Universities, 1800 to 1939." In *A History of the University in Europe* 3, ed. Walter Rüegg (Cambridge: Cambridge University Press, forthcoming).

Index

Academic Freedom, 72, 103–105, 157, 217–245, 247–260, 288, 299–300
  civil, 219, 221–222, 240, 251–252, 258, 333–335
  limits on, 261–282
  misuse of, 339
  to publish, 59, 227–228
Académie des sciences de Paris, 12
Academy of Sciences (Russia), 12
Accountability, 338
Adams Act of 1906, 33
Adams, Henry, 2
Adams, W., 211
Administration, 57, 64, 79, 121–123, 129–130, 258, 278–280, 333, 335–336, 338
Affirmative action, 76, 121, 126, 151, 179, 286, 336, 338
Africa, 56, 58, 143, 190, 193, 195
Agassiz, Louis, 30
Agricultural experimental stations, 6, 32–33
Althoff, Friedrich, 26
American Anthropological Society, 227
American Association for the Advancement of Science, 15, 16, 33
American Association of University Professors, 247, 334
American Civil Liberties Union, 334
American Legion, 276
American Museum of Natural History, 27
American National Endowment for the Humanities, 122

American Philosophical Society, 140
American Scholar, 338
Amis, Kingsley, 86
Andrews, E.B., 264
Angell, E., 267
Anti-intellectualism, 19, 103, 339
Anti-Semitism, 49, 100, 189–192
Army Specialist Training Program, 176
Arons, Leo, 232, 238
Ashby, Lord Eric, 134
Asia, 58, 193, 194
Assessment, concept of, 311–312, 319–321
Assessment, Faculty, 255–258, 291, 300
  anonymity in, 307–308, 320–321
  for publication, 305–308, 312, 317–318
Assessment, student, 309, 312–313
  confidentiality in, 313–318, 320–321
  federal regulation, 315–316
Athenaeum, 7
Atomes, 109
Atomic Energy Commission, 176
Atwater, Wilbur, 33
Australia, 39, 56
Austria, 39, 56
Autonomy, 42, 46, 72, 104–105, 144, 151–152, 157, 165, 172–173, 175, 223–226, 237, 241, 286, 288, 303–304
Ayers, Howard, 5

Babbitt, Irving, 36, 326, 339
Bancroft, George, 2
Barre, Raymond, 58
Beale, Howard K., 265
Beard, Charles, 22, 35, 238
Bell Telephone Company Laboratory, 2, 53
Bemis, E.W., 264
Berkeley. *See* California, University of
Berlin, University of, 232, 238
Bernal, J.D., 108
Bibliothèque Nationale, 7
Bloom, Allan, 82, 86
Boards, governing, 42, 145, 149–150, 157, 173, 258, 279–280, 285–286, 333–334
Boas, Frank, 21
Bocconi University (Milan), 137
Boyle, Robert, 3
British Academy of Sciences, 227
British Association for the Advancement of Science, 16
British Museum, 7
Brown University, 264
Brussels, University of, 210
Buckley, Senator James, 315
Bulletin of the American Association of University Professors, 334
Bureau of Ethnology, 2, 27
Burma, 190
Butler, Nicholas Murray, 156

Calcutta, University of, 152
California Institute of Technology, 7
California, University of , 22, 40, 115, 138, 139, 140, 146, 189, 208, 210, 229, 234, 302, 327, 333
    Lawrence Laboratory, 302
Cambridge University, 25, 39, 41, 50, 142, 144, 155, 172, 226, 236
Camelot du Roi, 190
Canada, 39, 50, 56, 108, 126
Carnegie Foundation for the Advancement of Teaching, 51
Carnegie Institution (Washington), 2, 4, 5, 31, 64
Cartter, Alan, 140, 330
Castro, Fidel, 192
Catholic University of the Sacred Heart (Milan), 143
Cattell, J. McKean, 35, 232, 238

Chamberlain, Owen, 302
Change, 109, 331
Chicago, University of, 5, 13–14, 20, 22–23, 25, 30, 37, 40, 86–87, 138–140, 146, 189, 264–265, 268, 276–277, 327–328, 330–331, 333
China, 40, 48, 52, 190, 193
Christianity, 17, 35, 145
Chronicle of Higher Education, 109, 331
Church of England, 142, 226
City College of New York, 189, 333
Clark University, 13, 14, 20, 30, 37
Coast Survey, 12
Cohn-Bendit, Daniel, 210, 211
Collège de France, 26, 102, 230, 233, 250
Columbia University, 8, 15, 21–22, 25, 35, 37, 138–139, 146, 152, 156, 210, 232, 238, 326–327, 333
Columbia University Press, 26
Columbia University Studies in Public Law and Political Science, 26
Common Market, 212
Commons, John R., 264
Communism, 49–50, 191, 237, 240
Communist International, 193, 205
Community colleges, 79
Conference Committee on National Preparedness, 276
Continuing education, 47, 76–77, 83
Cornell University Press, 26
Court of Arches, 230
Cracow, University of, 39
Crerar Library, 7
Curriculum, 16–17, 46, 72, 90–92, 132, 173–174, 225, 328–329
Czechoslovakia, 194

Dainton Report, 124
Dakar, University of, 210
Dalton, Hugh, 58
Dalton, John, 3
Darwin, Charles, 3, 231
Daughters of the American Revolution, 276
Davenport, Eugene, 33
Davy, Humphrey, 3
de Gaulle, General Charles, 195, 210, 212

Denmark, 56, 117
Departments, academic, 8, 16–18, 20–
    21, 23–24, 27, 29, 43–44, 57, 73,
    93–94, 96, 126, 157–158, 255–
    256, 292, 329, 335
    role of chair, 329–330
Dewey, John, 22, 35, 52, 267, 326, 334
Die Zeit, 109
Dilthey, Wilhelm, 29
Disciplines, academic. See depart-
    ments, academic
Discrimination, 226, 234, 293
Doehrn, Anton, 5
Dow Chemical Company, 211
Dutschke, Rudi, 210

Eastern Europe. See Europe
École normale supérieure, 61, 102
École pratique des hautes études, 26,
    102
Economics, 263–265
Egalitarianism, 20, 56, 309
Eisenhower, President Dwight, 210
Electives, 16
Elementary and Secondary Education
    Act of 1969, 315–317
Eliot, Charles William, 14, 18
Ellsberg, Daniel, 310
Ely, Richard, 35
Enzensberger, Hans Magnus, 205
Erhard, Ludwig, 58
Europe, 3–4, 39, 42–45, 49–50, 52– 53,
    63,71, 84, 101, 104, 127, 137,
    143, 174, 177–178, 185, 190–
    191, 194–195, 199, 207–208,
    226, 230, 240, 299, 309
Evolutionism, 231, 266–267
Eylesheimer, A.C., 5

Faculty, 42, 79, 123–124, 126, 129–
    130, 338–340
    appointment and promotion, 93,
        225, 259, 285–287, 289–296,
        301–302, 336
    career pattern, 25
    politicization of, 61, 77–78, 133,
        160, 288–290, 293, 332–333,
        340
    sanctions against, 230–233, 235–
        236, 238, 247–248, 250–251,
        253, 257, 260, 271–281

    unions, 127, 287
    See also assessment, faculty; tenure
Family Education Rights and Privacy
    Act of 1974, 315–317
Fanon, Frantz, 192
Fascism, 49, 100, 104, 191, 229, 240
Feldstein, Martin, 58
Field Museum, 5, 27
Finland, 56
Finley, Moses, 232, 236, 335
Flexner, Abraham, 109, 339
Florence, University of, 210
Fourah Bay College (Sierre Leone), 56,
    190
France, 3, 26, 39, 46, 48, 50–51, 61–
    63, 99–100, 103, 105–106, 109,
    116, 118, 121, 123–124, 126,
    128, 141, 143, 174, 190, 194–
    195, 199–200, 203–204, 207–
    208, 210, 212–213, 225, 236,
    289, 293, 295, 301
    Conseil nationale de la recherche
        scientifique, 51, 108, 122
France, Université de, 39, 141
Frankel, Charles, 334
Fraser, Leon, 232, 238
Free Church College (Aberdeen), 230,
    233
Freund, E., 22
Fundamentalism, religious, 19, 240,
    266–267, 276
Funding, 50–51, 56–57, 73, 75, 79–80,
    90, 124, 140–141, 148–149, 152,
    224, 280, 337–338

Gaitskell, Hugh, 58
General Electric Company Laboratory,
    2, 9, 53
Geneva, University of, 288, 289, 295,
    296
Geological Survey, 2, 12
Germany, 2 , 4–5, 9, 11, 13–16, 26, 29,
    31, 39, 42, 44, 46, 48–51, 54, 56,
    62– 64, 71–72, 93, 95, 100–101,
    103–104, 106, 108–109, 114,
    116, 118, 123–124, 126–128,
    133, 141–143, 146–147, 164,
    172, 174–175, 185, 189–190,
    194, 197–199, 203, 207–208,
    210, 212–213, 225–226, 230–
    231, 234–235, 237, 240, 244,
    287, 289, 293, 301

Fundamental Law (Grundgesetz), 237
Max-Planck-Gesellschaft, 108
Wissenschaftsrat, 175
Hochschulrahmengesetz, 175
Notgemeinschaft der deutschen Wissenchaft, 51
GI Bill of Rights, 55, 176
Gibbon, Edward, 3
Gilman, Daniel Coit, 14, 18, 23
Glass, David, 84
Goodman, Paul, 192
Göttingen Seven, 232
Göttingen, University of, 232
Governance, 143, 173, 225–226, 241
    by consensus, 300–302, 304
Gray, Asa, 30
Great Britain, 3, 16–17, 25– 26, 31, 39, 42–43, 47–48, 50– 52, 54, 56, 59– 62, 64, 71, 76, 82, 84, 99, 100–103, 105–107, 109, 114–116, 118, 121, 124–126, 128, 142–144, 164, 172, 174–175, 177–178, 187, 189, 194, 199, 203, 212, 225, 229, 293, 301, 308–309, 313
    Committee on Higher Education, 106
    University Grants Committee, 50, 142, 143, 175
    Council for Scientific and Industrial Research, 51
    Department of Education and Science, 175
    Medical Research Council, 51, 108
Greifswald, University of, 230, 232, 250
Grote, George, 3
Guardian, 109
Guevara, Ché, 192
Guggenheim Foundation, 4
Gumbel case (Heidelberg), 103
Gumbel, Emil, 232

Haldane, J.B.S., 300
Halle, University of, 250
Hall, G. Stanley, 18
Harper, William Rainey, 18, 23
Harvard Oriental Series, 26
Harvard University, 2, 8, 14–15, 22, 25, 37, 59, 138–139, 146, 152, 189, 268, 326, 327, 333

Harvard University Press, 26
Harvey, William, 3
Hatch Act of 1887, 32
Heidelberg, University of, 232
Henry, Joseph, 2, 30
Henry, William A., 33
Hersch, Jean, 289, 290
Hilgard, Eugene W., 33
Hobhouse, L.T., 79
Holland, see Netherlands
Holy See, 233
Huizinga, Johan, 202
Humanities, 77–78, 259, 339
Hume, David, 3
Hutchins, Robert Maynard, 327

Illinois Normal University, 2
Illinois Wesleyan University, 2
Illinois, University of, 22, 37, 40, 139
In loco parentis, 199, 204, 308–309
India, 16–17, 39–40, 48, 52, 56, 86, 95, 137, 143, 190, 193–195, 197–198, 210, 301
Indiana, University of, 37
Indonesia, 193, 195, 210
Industrial Workers of the World, 332
Institut Catholique (Paris), 143, 233
Institute of Defense Analysis, 211
Interdisciplinarity, 132
Iowa, University of, 40
Italy, 5, 49, 56, 61–62, 101, 103–104, 121, 123, 191, 195, 199, 208, 213, 225, 229, 237, 240, 301

James, E.J., 264
James, WIlliam, 29, 267
Japan, 40, 48, 53, 56, 86, 137, 195, 210, 301
Jena, University of, 5
Johns Hopkins Studies in History and Political Science, 26
Johns Hopkins University, 2, 13, 14, 20, 22, 25, 30, 32, 37, 40, 326
Johns Hopkins University Press, 26
Johnson, Samuel, 32
Jordan, David, 238
Journals, scholarly, 17, 109
Jowett, Benjamin, 230

Kaiser-Wilhelm Gesellschaft, 31
Kerr, Clark, 95

Keynes, John Maynard, 58
Key, Ellen, 201
Kimball, Roger, 82
King's College London, 230
Krippendorf, Ekkehard, 210
Kropotkin, Prince, 198
Küng, Hans, 233

Labour Party (UK), 194
Lafayette College, 266
Lancaster, University of, 309
Latin America, 58, 193, 195, 196
Laughlin, J.L., 264
Le Monde, 109
League for Industrial Democracy, 189
Learned societies, 2, 17, 27, 64, 226–227
Lea, Henry C., 2
Lessing case (Hanover), 103
Lessing, Theodor, 232
Levine, Louis (later, Lorwin), 35, 232, 264, 274
Liberal arts colleges, 7, 15
Libraries, 2, 6–7, 38, 73
Library of Congress, 6
Library of the Surgeon-General, 6, 7
Loi d'orientation of 1968, 141
London School of Economics, 80, 84, 189, 210
London, University of, 25, 48, 122
Louisy, Alfred, 233
Louvain, University of, 143
Lüthy, E., 290
Lyell, Charles, 230, 231

Macaulay, T.B., 3
Macdonald, Dwight, 205
Maine, Henry, 178
Manhatten Project, 176
Manpower training, 109
Mansfield amendment, 124
Mao Tsetung, 192
Marine Biological Laboratory at Wood's Hole, 4
Marxism, 61, 195, 198, 234, 258, 269, 295
Massachusetts Institute of Technology, 7, 59
McCarthyism, 229, 252, 331, 335
McCarthy, Senator Eugene, 152,192, 212, 336

Mecklin, J.M., 266, 267
Mencken, H.L., 36
Merriam, C. E.,22
Michelson, A., 22
Michigan, University of, 22, 37, 40, 115, 138, 139, 146, 151–152
Middle East, 190
Milan, University of, 210
Miller, H.A., 276
Mill, James, 3
Mill, John Stuart, 3
Minnesota, University of, 268, 276
Missoffe, M., 211
Missouri, University of, 266, 277
Momigliano, A.D., 236
Montana, University of, 35, 232, 264
Moore, H. L, 22
More, Paul Elmer, 36
Morrill Act, 176
Motley, J.L, 2

Nanterre, University of, 210
Nation, 327
National Academy of Sciences, 12, 13, 30, 227
National Bureau of Standards (Washington), 64
National Geographic Society, 5
National Institute of Mental Health, 122
National Institutes of Health, 124, 176
National Physical Laboratory, 31
National Physics Laboratory at Teddington (UK), 64
National Research Council, 13, 176
National Science Foundation, 122, 176
National University (China), 40
Nazism, 49–50, 100, 103–104, 106, 235, 240, 335
Nearing, Scott, 232
Netherlands, 56, 104, 117, 118, 226
New Deal, 61, 264, 333
New Republic, 327
New Scientist, 109
New York Museum of Natural History, 5
New York Public Library, 7
New York Times, 109
New York University, 147
New Zealand, 39, 56
Newbury Library, 7

Newcomb, Simon, 30
North Africa. *See* Africa
North London Polytechnic, 309
Norway, 56
NSDAP (Germany), 190
Numerus clausus, 204

Objectivity, 45, 62, 127, 288
    criticisms of, 332, 339
OECD, 77, 109
Office of Naval Research, 176
Ogburn, W., 327
Ohio State University, 276
Ohnesorg, Benno, 211
Open universities, 76
Oxford Union, 189
Oxford University, 25, 39, 41, 50, 61,
    122, 142, 144, 155, 172, 189,
    226, 230

Pakistan, 143
Paris, University of (Sorbonne), 26,
    102, 146, 155, 207, 211
Park, Robert, 22
Patten, Simon, 35
Patten, William, 5
Peking, University of, 52
Pell, Senator Claibourne, 315
Pennsylvania, University of, 22, 35,
    232, 264, 325, 327, 328, 330
Permanent Commission of the Naval
    Department, 12
Phelan, W.W., 266
Philanthropy, 51
Philippines, 137, 144
Physikalisch-technische Reichsanstalt
    (Berlin), 64
Piaget, Jean, 288
Piccioni, Oreste, 302
Pierce, Charles, 2
Pittsburgh, University of, 272, 276
Pluralism, 237, 288, 320, 336
Poland, 39, 50, 190, 194
Polanyi, Michael, 300
Political correctness, 82, 259
Pompidou, M., 212
Portugal, 103
Postgraduate training, 13–15, 28, 53,
    139, 207, 273, 281–282
Powell, J.W., 2, 11
Presidents, 10, 18–19, 23, 25–26, 157,
    337

Preussische Staatsbibliothek, 7
Priestly, Joseph, 3
Princeton University, 8, 15, 22, 139,
    140, 147, 326
    Institute of Advanced Study, 53
Professional schools, 7
Proudhon, H.,198
Provincialism, 334
Prussian Ministry of Religious Affairs,
    238
Public Safety Commission, 276
Pugh, Evan, 32

Racism, 265
Radiation Project, 176
Radicalism, 62, 67, 99, 116, 125, 127–
    129, 133, 151, 189–213, 238,
    260, 277, 287–289, 292–293,
    308–309, 336
    See also student movements
Rahmengesetz, 226
Reclus, Élisée, 198
Remedial instruction, 121
Renan, Ernest, 230, 233, 250
Rensselaer Polytechnic Institute, 7
Research, 8, 10–12, 14, 29, 33, 41, 43,
    58–60, 64, 72–75, 89, 95, 121–
    122, 291, 337
    industrial laboratories, 2, 9, 32, 38,
    53,
    institutes, 2, 4–6, 9, 30–31, 52, 64,
    95, 165,
    disputes over credit, 302–303
    and tenure, 253–254
    external sponsorship of, 51, 108,
    176, 331, 338
    grants, 281
    taboos, 267–269, 274–275
Ricardo, David, 3
Right to know, 310–311, 315–317,
    319–320
Right to privacy, 310–311, 315–317
Robbins report, 86
Robbins, Lord,106
Robinson, James Harvey, 22, 238
Rockefeller Foundation, 4, 176
Rockefeller General Education Board,
    51
Rockefeller Institute for Medical
    Research (NY), 2, 5, 31
Roman Catholic Church, 236

Rome, University of, 210
Roosevelt, F.D., 61
Ross, Edward A., 35, 232, 238, 264, 269
Rostovteff, M.I., 236, 326
Rothschild report, 124
Rothschild, Lord, 178
Roth, David, 301–302
Rousseau, Jean Jacques, 199
Route 128, 59
Rowe, Leo S., 264
Royal Institution, 31
Royal Society of London, 13
Russia, 12, 39, 48–50, 191, 231, 235, 240
Rutgers University, 232, 236

Sapir, E., 22
Sarte, Jean Paul, 192
Schaper, William, 276
Scholarship. *See* science; research
Scholars. *See* scientists; faculty
Science, 33–34, 59–60, 67–68
    freedom, 288, 299–300
    institutionalization w/in universities, 8
    promotion of, 107–108
    See also academic freedom
Scientists, 10, 58, 75, 95
    amateurs, 1–4, 6, 27–28
    self-centeredness of, 336–337
SDS, 211
Sedgwick, Ellery, 36
Segre, Emilio, 302
Seligman, E. R. A., 22
Shah of Iran, 208, 211
Shaw, G. B., 265
Silicon Valley, 59
Skye, Charles, 82
Smithsonian Institution, 5, 12, 30
Smith, W. Robertson, 230, 233, 250
Snow, C.P., 109
Social Democratic Party (Germany), 194
Social mobility, 55, 84
Social Science Research Council (UK), 122
Social sciences, 10, 22, 47, 60, 66–67, 74, 77–78, 94, 96, 125, 232, 259, 261–282, 293–294, 331–332, 339

Sociology, 264–265
Sons of the American Revolution, 276
South Africa, 56
Soviet Union. *See* Russia
Spain, 100, 103, 193, 199, 208, 209, 213
Specialization, 8, 21, 28–30, 32, 44, 65, 68, 92,
Springer concern, 208
Stanford University, 20, 25, 35, 37, 139, 232, 238, 264
Stanford, Mrs. Leland, 238
Stavisky scandal, 190
Stazione Zoologica (Naples), 5
Strong, D.S., 5
Student movements, 62, 125, 128, 189–213, 238, 308, 331, 336
Students, 44, 76–77, 308–309
    admissions, 75, 107, 224–225,
    financial aid, 338
    politicization of, 333
    rights, 315–316
    participation in decision-making, 285–286
    See also assessment, student
Suhrkamp, 116
Sukarno, President, 193, 210
Sweden, 103, 185
Switzerland, 104, 288, 289, 290, 295, 296
Syracuse University, 264

Tacit knowledge, 300, 313
Taylor, Frederick, 10
Teaching, 8, 41, 95, 106, 121, 255, 328
    and tenure, 253
Technische Hochsule (Hannover), 232
Tenure, 247–260
    devevelopent of, 328
    See also faculty, appointment and promotion
Thomas, W.I., 22, 265
Times of Higher Education Supplement, 109
Toulouse, University of, 26, 47
Touraine, A.,205
Tradition, academic, 45, 255, 308, 340
True, Alfred C., 33
Trustees. *See* boards, governing
Tübingen, University of, 233
Turner, R.E., 276

Tynan, K., 205

Un-American Activities Committee of
the United States House of
Representatives, 232
UNESCO, 77
United Kingdom. *See* Great Britain
United States Constitution, 237
Fifth Amendment, 232
United States Department of Agricul-
ture, 33, 34, 176
Office of Experimental Stations, 33
United States Department of Defense,
124, 152, 176
United States Department of Health,
Education, and Welfare, 156,
303, 315
United States Steel Company, 9
Universal access, 78–79
Université libre de Bruxelles, 137
Universities
and government, 50, 56, 58, 65, 75,
80, 87, 107, 125, 131, 133, 144,
151, 163–187, 224, 241, 277,
289–290, 300, 303, 315–316,
331, 337–338
and industry, 46–47, 58–59, 65
and the church, 42, 144–145, 171–
172, 224, 230–231, 233, 236,
240–241, 250, 286, 300
and the courts, 301–303
and the press, 268, 300, 330–332
competition among, 330
German influence on, 14–16, 19,
25, 35, 48
expansion of, 56, 121
hierarchy of, 167, 328
history of, 39–69, 137–160
politicization of, 61–64, 93, 96, 133,
175, 259, 296, 332–333, 339
prestige, 72
private, 81, 137–160
public, 13, 81, 139–143, 147, 149,
151, 158–160
reform and change, 99–134

See also open universities
University of California Press, 26
University of Chicago Press, 26
University presses, 26–27
University, idea of, 40, 44, 71–98, 217–
219
Utah, University of, 328
Utilitarianism, 34, 36, 339–340

Vanderbilt University, 140, 328
Veblen, Thorstein, 35, 108, 268, 276
Verein für Sozialpolitik, 16
Veteran's of Foreign Wars, 276
Vienna, University of, 39
Vogt, Carl, 5
von Humboldt, Wilhelm, 31, 44, 51,
58, 95, 113, 241, 338

Walgreen-Hearst Illinois Senate
investigation, 277
Warwick, University of, 309
Weber, Max, 2, 4, 15
Wellhausen, Julius, 230, 233, 250
Wells, H.G., 108
Wesleyan University, 33
Western Europe. *See* Europe
Wheeler, William M., 5
Whitehead, A. N., 326
White, Andrew, 18
Whitman, Charles Otis, 5
Wilson, Harold, 109
Wisconsin, University of, 22, 33, 37,
40, 138, 139, 146, 189, 211, 301,
333
Wood, Henry A., 276

Yale University, 8, 15, 22, 37, 138,
139, 326, 327
Yenching University, 52
Young Communist League (YCL), 189
Young People's Socialist League
(YPSL), 189

Zamansky, Dean Marc, 206
Ziegler, Dr. Jean, 289, 290, 295, 296